University of Michigan Museum of Anthropology
Technical Report 26

Early Settlement and Irrigation on the Deh Luran Plain

Village and Early State Societies in Southwestern Iran

by

James A. Neely
and
Henry T. Wright

Ann Arbor
1994

ISBN 978–0–915703–36–4 (paper)

ISBN 978–1–951538–22-4 (ebook)

The University of Michigan Museum of Anthropology currently publishes three monograph series: Anthropological Papers, Memoirs, and Technical Reports. We have over seventy titles in print. For a complete catalog, write to Museum of Anthropology Publications, 4009 Museums Building, Ann Arbor, MI 48109–1079 or call (313) 764–0485.

Contents

Figures

Tables

Foreword

Kent V. Flannery

THIRTY-THREE YEARS AGO this month, two young Americans had just crawled to the only patch of shade on the Deh Luran plain. That patch of shade was beneath a 1945 Jeep, and it was only cool because the radiator was leaking water. Outside in the 100° F heat sat a representative of the Iranian Antiquities Service, convinced that the two young Americans were crazy and that the Deh Luran Plain was the most desolate place he had ever seen.

Somehow Frank Hole and I survived the desolation and lured others, including James Neely and Henry Wright, to Deh Luran. Now their intensive survey, *Early Settlement and Irrigation on the Deh Luran Plain,* brings to fruition more than two decades of work in the area. Combined with earlier monographs on Ali Kosh, Tepe Sabz, Chagha Sefid, and Tepe Farukhabad, it makes the bleak and seemingly marginal little Deh Luran plain one of the most intensively studied areas of the Near East.

Because of its political instability, the Near East has had cycles of intense fieldwork followed by enforced moratoria. The 1930s were a kind of "golden age" for excavations in Iraq and Iran. When World War II shut fieldwork down, archaeologists were forced to start writing up their results. At the University of Chicago, Henri Frankfort saw the war as "a perfect time to synthesize the results of fieldwork," and he instituted a seminar for that purpose. The seminar produced such great syntheses as Ann L. Perkins' *The Comparative Archaeology of Early Mesopotamia* (1949) and Donald E. McCown's *The Comparative Stratigraphy of Early Iran* (1942).

The 1960s and early 1970s were another golden era for excavation and fieldwork. It was brought to a halt by a revolution in Iran and by a prolonged war between Iran and Iraq. The Deh Luran plain was right in the middle of the latter war, making further excavations impossible. Following Frankfort's lead, we might declare the 1990s "a perfect time to synthesize the results of fieldwork," and begin to write up the unpublished research of the 1960s and 70s. I hope that *Early Settlement and Irrigation on the Deh Luran Plain* will be the first of many such syntheses.

As I read through Neely and Wright's monograph, looking at the black-on-buff dancing men of the Mehmeh phase and the elegant beakers of the Bayat phase, it brought back the sights and sounds of an earlier and happier time. Kebabs broiling over a charcoal grill; a cold glass of dugh "Ab-i-Ali"; pomegranates and Persian melons; cool mast-i-khiar after a hot day in the field; sharing a bowl of saffroned rice and kebab-i-murgh while the strains of "Shirin Shirin" and "Qashgalai Shirazi" rose from our workmen's huts. Would I go back to that desolate little plain? Hey, I never really unpacked.

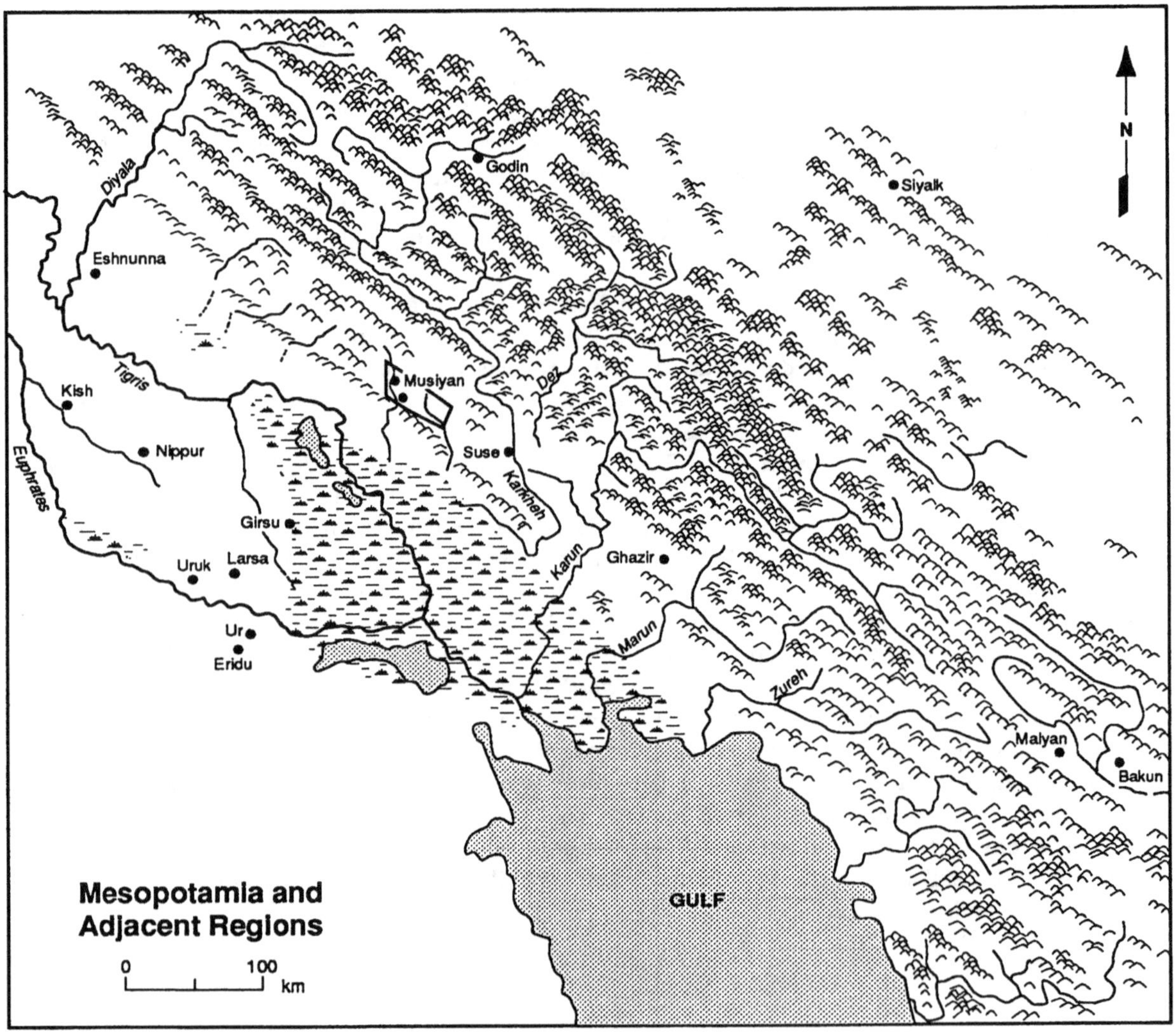

Figure I.1. Greater Mesopotamia and the Deh Luran Plain.

Chapter I

Introduction

The Deh Luran Plain is a small, seemingly insignificant element in the geographical panorama of Southwest Asia (Figure I.1). Separated from the Mesopotamian Plain only by the low ridge of the Jebel Hamrin, it has the limited rainfall and fierce summer heat of Mesopotamia. Nestled in the foothills of that portion of the Zagros front ranges known as "Pusht-i Kuh," it has only the erratic and seasonally saline water supply of several smaller Zagros streams. As a result, it can be viewed as a microcosm of Mesopotamia with some of its potential and many of its problems.

This plain is important for archaeologists because of the variety of past cultural processes which can be studied within its bounds. Close to the boundary between the desertic alluvial plains and the oak-forested Zagros mountains, it is an ideal place to evaluate hypotheses about the importance of these environments in the change from food collecting to food production and in the subsequent development of irrigation techniques. Located on a traditional transport route between Mesopotamia proper and other regions, it is an area in which one can collect data useful in the study of the relation between changes in inter-regional exchange and changes in social complexity. As a marginal province in successive transregional empires, Deh Luran's settlement patterns provide indices of the degree of imperial investment in agriculture and transport.

Archaeological survey has produced scattered evidence of Paleolithic foragers. Various small excavations on the plain provide an almost unbroken stratigraphic sequence covering the seven-thousand-year span of development from the establishment of early seasonal herding and collecting camps around 8000 B.C. up to the collapse of the early transregional empires around 1300 B.C. With the ceramic evidence from this sequence, we can date surface sites and define the settlement pattern of each period. With the evidence of subsistence, raw material extraction, crafts, and houses from this sequence, we can evaluate ideas about the development of settlement systems during this long period of time. This technical report presents a synthesis of archaeological survey data from the plain relevant to periods earlier than 2600 B.C., together with a reassessment of changing regional patterns. This is the first of three planned reports. The second will document the settlement history of the plain under the control of successive Mesopotamian, Elamite, and Persian dynasties up to about 300 B.C. The third will continue the story up to the end of the Early Islamic period with impact of the Mongol Invasion around A.D. 1250.

Geography of the Deh Luran Plain

The ridges and valleys of the Zagros front ranges formed during the last ten million years as the Arabian fragment of the African continental plate has slid beneath the Eurasian plate, compressing and folding the abyssal sediments of the ancient Tethys Sea. The synclinal depression in front of the folded and uplifted outer Zagros has filled with sediments deposited by the tributaries of the Euphrates, Tigris, and Karun rivers. In the past few millennia, the sea has risen to fill the lower, eastern end of this depression and create the Gulf. The northeast edge of the Tigris-Euphrates alluvium is marked by the low anticlinal fold of the Jebel Hamrin, which reaches a maximum elevation of only 400 m. The Deh Luran Plain is in a small synclinal trough between the Jebel Hamrin and the first great fold of the Pusht-i Kuh, the oak-covered Kuh-i Siah, a limestone anticlinal fold which rises to an elevation of nearly 1400 m. Northeast of this fold is an almost continuous scarp of soft Tertiary sandstone, siltstone, and gypsum, the upper surface of which is a plateau at about 1300 m. The plain itself (Figure I.2), including its alluvial fans, averages almost 20 km in width from the Jebel Hamrin on the southwest to the foot of the Kuh-i Siah on the northeast. It extends for almost 60 km from northwest to southeast below the mountain front. The valley floor, that is areas with slopes of 5% or less, covers approximately 940 square kilometers. The topography of the plain has been formed by the action of two small rivers. The Mehmeh cuts through the scarp and enters the north corner of the plain, flows southeast to the middle of the plain, then turns abruptly southwest, cuts across the Jebel Hamrin and disappears into the Tigris alluvium. The Dawairij River cuts through the scarp and enters the northeast edge of the plain near its midpoint, then turns southeastward and flows out the southeast end of the plain, ultimately turning west around the southeast end of the Jebel Hamrin and disappears into the Tigris alluvium.

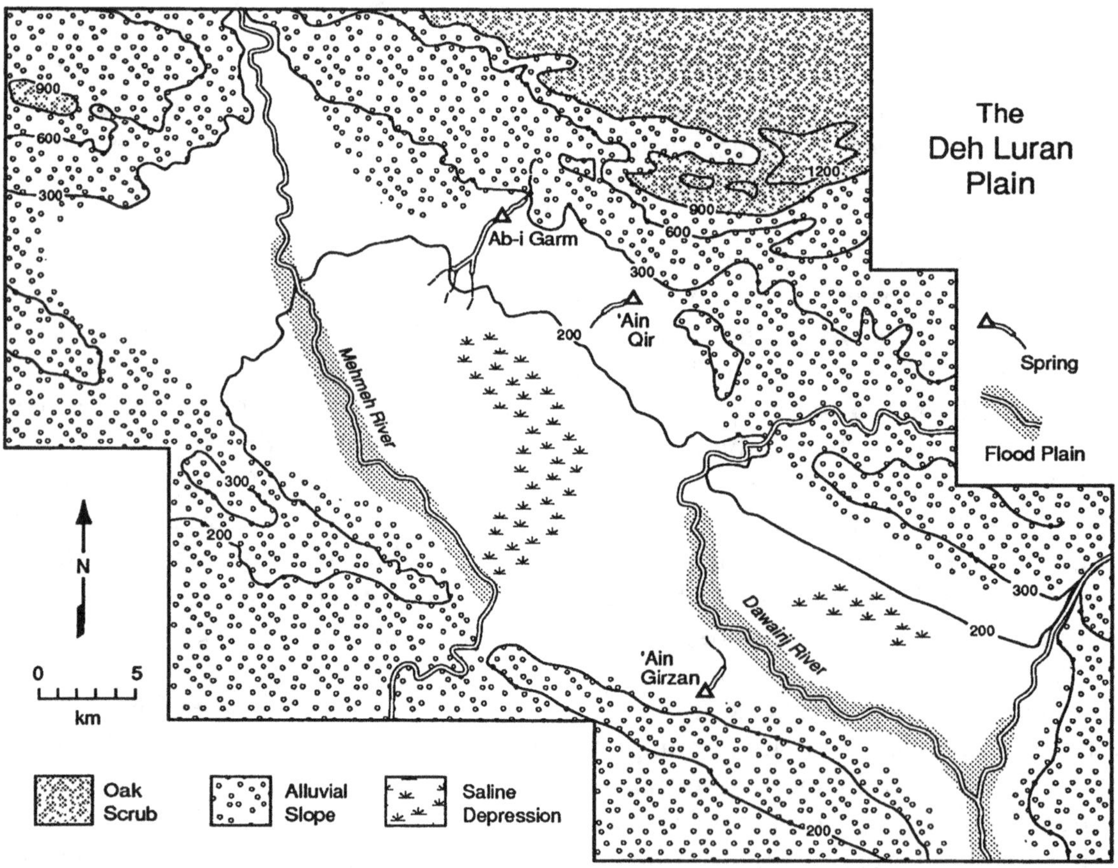

Figure I.2. Natural environments of the Deh Luran Plain

Michael Kirkby (1977) has reported an invaluable study of the soils, hydrology, and vegetation of the Deh Luran Plain, particularly useful in understanding land use on the plain since the rivers cut down into their fans around 2000 B.C. Kirkby found that as one moves from the steep margins of the plain toward its lowest point there is a strong positive correlation between decreasing angle of slope, decreasing depth of dissection by erosional gulleys, decreasing quantity of stones on the surface, and increasing salinity (ibid.: 254–263). The rivers, seasonal wadis, and springs watering the plain have varying levels of salinity, higher in the summer and lower in the winter, particularly after rainfall in the mountains brings sudden floods. Only 'Ain Girzan, 7 km south-southeast of Tepe Musiyan (DL-20), provides a regular supply of fresh water. The salts are dissolved out of the coarser sediments on the slopes of the valley margins, but accumulate in finer grained soils in and around the centrally located seasonal swamp, the drainage of which is blocked by the fans of the Mehmeh and Dawairij. Although these changes in soils and salinity are continuous, characteristic vegetation associations allow one to divide the plain into four distinct areas, each of which presents different opportunities to farmers and herders (Hole, Flannery and Neely 1969:16–19).

(1) The alluvial slopes have a dense grassy cover on Pleistocene gravels where rivers enter the plain, and a cover of sparse grass and *Zizyphus* or jujube trees elsewhere. These areas ordinarily do not retain enough moisture for rainfall agriculture, but various forms of hillslope terracing, the use of checkdams in wadis, and small-scale irrigation with the water of various springs have allowed some farming in the past. Traditionally, they have been used for grazing sheep and goats by Luri transhumant pastoralists who moved seasonally between higher montaine summer pastures and lower winter pastures on the Deh Luran Plain. Wild sheep and gazelle were common in such areas.

(2) The older alluvial plain formed by the fans of the two rivers, with denuded silty and sandy soils, has patches of such shrubs as *Prosopis*, a small legume, and *Alhaghi*, or camel thorn. These areas can retain moisture sufficient for dry-farming in one year out of two, especially in areas where the water table is higher or where floodwaters can be concentrated. Floods late in the growing season, however, can easily destroy crops in such areas. Gazelle are still seen in this area, and in the past the wild half-ass or onager must have grazed here.

(3) The present river floodplains, now incised four to six meters below the surface of the alluvial fans, are subject to frequent flooding, and consequently have irregular surfaces with gravel and sand banks as well as channel scars. Dense thickets of *Tamarix*, the salt-cedar, and *Glycyrhrhyza*, the wild licorice, thrive because of the high water table. Fallow deer and wild boar lived in these thickets until recently.

(4) The saline depressions within the older alluvial plain are flooded in the winter and become muddy salt-flats in the summer. A range of salt-loving shrubs live in this environment. Wild boar will hide in such areas during the day, and range in nearby fields at night.

Since this report focuses on the periods from around 5400 B.C. to 2600 B.C., it is important to ascertain what the plain was like prior to downcutting and before the deposits of alluvial sediments on the plain had reached their present depth. Kirkby (1977:285–287) argues for the existence of braided streams with shifting multiple channels, allowing irrigation with the simplest of diversion systems. Though the river flood plains would have been limited in area, the botanical samples from the excavated sites show that *Tamarix* was easily obtained, and we can presume that it was dispersed on the edges of fields, as it is today in a few areas below the village of Deh Luran. The faunal samples from the excavated sites indicate that aquatic resources were more heavily used before 5000 B.C. Although Kirkby does not believe that a permanent lake could have existed on the Deh Luran Plain (ibid.:286–287), it seems likely that water supplies were more regular and less saline. We will refine our understanding of water and land use in discussions of the settlement systems of each successive period in Chapter V.

A History of Archaeological Survey on the Deh Luran Plain

The plain was first surveyed in 1903 by J.-E. Gautier and G. Lampre of the Mission Archéologique en Perse. They followed the path of an earlier survey party led several years before by the director of the mission, Jacques de Morgan, westward through the Pusht-i Kuh region toward Kermanshah. Their task was to investigate the remains near the large mound of Tepe Musiyan, but they did visit a number of other sites on the central portion of the plain and provided a brief description and a map (Gautier and Lampre 1905:60–62, Fig. 94). The observations of Gautier and Lampre are cited under the site descriptions in Chapter IV.

Nearly sixty years later, the Director of the University of Chicago's Prehistoric Project, Robert J. Braidwood, and one of the project's geologists, Richard A. Watson, visited the plain to re-examine the site which Gautier and Lampre called "Tépé Mohammed Djafar." Braidwood thought this might be the site of an early village involved in the process of plant and animal domestication. In the following year, the Prehistoric Project supported a visit by Frank Hole and Kent Flannery to the Deh Luran Plain for several weeks of survey on the plain and of test excavations at this site, which is today called "Tepe Ali Kosh." Since Hole and Flannery did not have copies of Braidwood's survey notes, but assumed that he had recorded fewer than twenty sites, they gave the fourteen sites they visited on the central plain numbers ranging from DL-20 to DL-33 (Hole and Flannery 1962). In 1963, Hole instituted the Rice University Archaeological Project and returned with Flannery and James A. Neely to conduct major excavations at Tepe Ali Kosh (DL-21) and the later site of Tepe Sabz (DL-31), relevant to the beginnings of irrigation agriculture (Hole, Flannery and Neely 1969), with support from a U.S. National Science Foundation Grant (GS-724). Some sites were revisited, but no formal survey was done. The enthusiastic reports of Hole, Flannery and Neely about the potential of Tepe Fakrabad (Gautier and Lampre 1905: 84) or Farukhabad (DL-32) for resolving problems of the development of urban life led Henry T. Wright of the University of Michigan Museum of Anthropology to come to the plain at the beginning of 1968 for a season of excavation (Wright 1981). This excavation project was supported by National Science Foundation Grant GS-1938. A number of sites were visited by the Farukhabad team, but permanent site numbers were not given. Instead, most of these sites were re-visited in 1969 by Neely and Wright together, and these were entered into Neely's 1969 number series. All of the information acquired in 1960, 1961, 1963, and early 1968 has been incorporated without specific citation into the descriptions in Chapter IV. The recovered ceramics are at Yale University.

The survey project undertaken by Neely, then established at the University of Texas at Austin, in late 1968 and early 1969 was the first actually directed at the full recording of regional settlement patterns. Both Neely's survey and simultaneous excavations of Hole at Chagha Sefid (DL-23) (Hole 1977) were supported by a grant from the National Science Foundation (GS-2194). Hole's strong support throughout the project is gratefully acknowledged. The survey began on 1 November 1968 and concluded on 30 March 1969. At various times, Neely was joined in the field by Anne and Michael Kirkby from the University of Bristol, the project's geographical specialists, Lynn Berry Fredlund from the University of Colorado, Nathalie Berset-Desse, visiting from the Délégation Archéologique Française, and Henry Wright and Robert C. Gibbs from the University of Michigan. Barbara Hole provided special support for the laboratory work. Pierre de Miroschedji of the Délégation Archéologique

Française made a special contribution to the analysis of Uruk-related sites. Elizabeth Carter, then of the University of Chicago's Oriental Institute, analyzed all Elamite materials. John Hansman of the University of London gave invaluable advice on the dating of later ceramics.

The methods used during the survey are discussed in detail in Chapter II. Sites found during this season were given temporary field numbers followed by the letter '"x." Later, serial numbers were assigned in approximate geographic order from northwest to southeast. Since it had been learned that Braidwood had used only names, rather than numbers, for the sites he had visited, Neely began his renumbering with sites DL-1 to DL-19 in the northwest foothills and alluvial slopes of the plain near the town of Deh Luran, passed over the already assigned numbers DL-20 to DL-33, scattered around the central plain, and continued with DL-34 on the far southeast to DL-311 in the far northwest. Thus, for example, DL 81x became DL-292. The latter number series has been used in this report, though future researchers may find that some of the sherds and field notes have "x" numbers, and for this reason we also give these numbers in Chapter IV. Most sherds from the 1968–69 survey are at present curated at the Texas Archaeological Research Laboratory of the University of Texas at Balcones Research Center in Austin, Texas.

Portions of the survey data have been cited in several previous publications, and since we have modified our interpretation of the data over the years, some discussion of these earlier publications is warranted. The results of the original 1961 survey were used in the preliminary report on that season (Hole and Flannery 1962), several interpretive articles using data from the 1961 and 1963 seasons (Hole and Flannery 1968, Flannery 1969), and the final report on the 1963 season (Hole, Flannery and Neely 1969:342–366). In none of these publications were settlement pattern maps given for particular phases, and statements about numbers of settlements are always cautiously phrased in terms of the known minimum number of sites. Thus, the increases in the number of sites recorded by our more intensive surveys do not greatly affect these earlier statements. The results of the 1968–1969 survey were used in an article on later irrigation systems (Neely 1974b), an article on cultural relations at the beginning of the IVth millennium B.C. in southwestern Iran (Wright et al. 1975), an article using the evidence from the period of early state formation in southwestern Iran to evaluate hypotheses about the development of states (Wright and Johnson 1975:276), and in the final report on the excavations at Tepe Farukhabad (Wright 1981). The first is not relevant to the present report. The second includes a discussion and settlement pattern map for two phases. The third includes a table of site numbers and aggregate areas for phases of between 4500 and 2500 B.C., and the fourth includes discussions and settlement pattern maps for the same phases. Since these publications, we have made several reassessments of the chronology—most importantly the period termed "Late Jemdet Nasr" is now recognized as "Early Dynastic I–II"—and we have reassessed particular sherds and thus the dates of some sites with small samples.

Since 1969, several archaeologists have visited the Deh Luran Plain, but the only formal survey undertaken was that conducted in 1976 of the area between the Susiana and Deh Luran Plains by Pierre de Miroschedji of the Délégation Archéologique Française. Miroschedji (1981) focused on sites ruled by the Neo-Elamite, Achaemenid, and Seleucid dynasties during the Ist millennium B.C. This survey recorded a few early sites on the eastern end of the Deh Luran Plain, and assigned site numbers beginning with the designation "DK." The valuable information provided by Miroschedji is cited in the site descriptions in Chapter IV.

We have no knowledge of what has happened to archaeological sites on the Deh Luran Plain since 1976. It seems likely that many sites have been damaged or destroyed during the long hostilities. Given such dangers as mines and explosives, it seems unlikely that further research will be possible for many years.

Plan of the Present Work

Following this introduction, we present in Chapter III the research design for the survey and the methods used both to recover the data demanded by the research design and to analyze these data in the laboratory. In Chapter III, we undertake the task of describing those artifact categories of each phase, primarily ceramics, which were found on the surfaces of sites. A series of phase assemblages have been illustrated, and are presented in Figures III.1 to III.9. Counts of the occurrence of many of the categories of artifacts found in most sites are included in Appendix Tables A1 to A8. As the understanding of these materials improves, scholars may use these figures and counts to re-interpret the settlement data. In Chapter IV the details of each site are presented. Included are: (1) the numerical designations for the site and the site's name, if known; (2) a grid location in terms of a Transverse Mercator Grid used on the maps of the National Iranian Oil Company, the only modern maps available to us; (3) the site's dimensions; (4) a brief statement about the site's environmental context; (5) a discussion of any features such as surface irregularities, stone constructions, unusual concentrations of artifacts, and later post-occupational disturbances; (6) discussion of the cultural phases present; (7) any comments necessary on the interpretation of the site's size or characteristics in particular phases, and finally; (8) any published references. Maps of most of the sites, made by Neely with pace and compass unless otherwise noted, and detailed illustrations of many samples of sherds—with captions presenting category designations, detailed attribute observations, and references—are also included in this chapter. In Chapter V, the evidence is synthesized in terms of successive settlement patterns. In Chapter VI, some arguments about changing irrigation and population of the Deh Luran Plain are presented.

Chapter II

Research Design and Methods

Neely's segment of the 1968 proposal to the NSF focused solely on an investigation of the irrigation systems. Three specific tasks were proposed:

> 1) an intensive reconnaissance of the Deh Luran Plain to discover and record the presence of water control and irrigation features; 2) to conduct limited test excavations to help define the structure and function of these features as well as provide information for their dating; and 3) to relate these data to the information the Kirkbys obtain on physiographic features and land use practices today so that a reasonable reconstruction of prehistoric conditions may be made.

Within the first few weeks of fieldwork, however, Neely became aware of two major problems that were impeding the work proposed: 1) it was evidently not going to be possible to determine the chronological placement of the vast majority of the water control and irrigation features and systems solely through a study of the features and systems themselves, and 2) a reasonable reconstruction of the prehistoric conditions would apparently not fully explain the structure and function of the features and systems without some knowledge of the prehistoric and early historic communities as well as the settlement patterns and systems present during the long occupation of the Deh Luran Plain. In order that the water control and irrigation features and systems might be seen in their proper chronological and socio-cultural perspective, Neely augmented the three original tasks by initiating a site survey. He initially set out to record all of the sites on the central part of the Deh Luran Plain. The number, complexity, and preservation of these sites, however, soon led him to realize that only a portion of the plain's area could be surveyed in the time available, and that a sample of the sites present would have to suffice. In response to this situation, Neely devised the "band" and "zone" sampling methodology (see below) by means of which approximately 70% of the plain was surveyed. He also worked with relatively high altitude, low resolution aerial photographs to plot the locations of the visible sites, as well as canals and other water control features, with as much precision as possible.

In the beginning of his field notebook, Neely wrote that it was the intent of his survey to examine an area of about one thousand square kilometers of the central part of the plain in order "to find, describe, and relate every site on the Deh Luran Plain to the environment as well as to the society and culture of the prehistoric and historic inhabitants." This concise statement does not do justice to the varying experience and questions which those who participated in the surveys of the 1960s brought to this part of southwestern Iran.

—Hole and Flannery came to Deh Luran directly from Braidwood's Kermanshah project in the western Zagros, where they had witnessed and participated in a valley-wide survey focused on the evidences of the earliest village and pastoral camp sites. They had a specific interest in the association of sites with different aspects of the natural environment.

—Neely had been intimately involved in projects in the American Southwest (Neely 1974a, Neely and Olson 1977) and in the Tehuacan area of Mexico (Woodbury and Neely 1972) which were focused not only on settlement but on the direct evidences of canals, dams, and fields. He had a specific interest in the evolution of agricultural and water-control systems.

—Just before his season in Deh Luran, Wright had surveyed in the far south of Iraq on the southern margins of ancient Sumer (Wright 1981a) under the tutelage of Robert McC. Adams. This survey was directed at relations between agricultural systems, population changes, and changes in settlement organization. He had a specific interest in assessing past population and hierarchical relations between settlements.

In the preliminary report prepared in 1969 for the National Science Foundation (Hole 1969), Neely elaborated on these interests:

> the survey and test excavations were to accomplish the following objectives: 1) to discover and record the presence, temporal placement, structure, and function of prehistoric and early historic water control and irrigation systems; 2) to provide an overall picture of the relationship of such systems to the settlement patterns, cultivated fields, crop yields and population trends.

In the intellectual milieu of the late 1960s, there were five general questions—widely discussed, though not cited in the grant proposals which funded Neely's survey—which one could hope to resolve with the evidence of surveys and small excavations. Some may seem naive today, but they determined the kinds of observations which we made.

1. With the establishment of agriculture, was there a shift from high water table locations conducive to dry farming to alluvial fan locations conducive to the construction of irrigation canals?

2. Was the development of increasingly larger central settlements correlated with evidences of overall population growth throughout the plain?

3. With the development of increasingly complex technologies and increased demand for raw materials, was there evidence that the settlements at key nodes on the inter-regional trade routes crossing the plain grew differentially?

4. Did the larger centers show evidence of increased fortification?

5. Did the appearance of larger and more elaborate water-control systems correlate with the rise of the historical empires as Adams had suggested for both the Susiana Plain (Adams 1962) and Mesopotamia (Adams 1965)?

As a result of these interests, we approached the denuded landscape of the Deh Luran Plain with the intention of examining every square kilometer and mapping precisely all types of sites, occupational and otherwise, but we were limited by circumstances.

—We did not wish to survey only a sample of the area because we did not believe we could retrieve water control systems or patterns of emerging settlement hierarchies without full coverage. However, as the season progressed, it became evident that because of the large number of sites, it would not be possible to complete the survey in the time available. Therefore, some portions of the survey area termed "zones" were fully surveyed. Other portions of the area were surveyed in a set of parallel "bands" or transects crossing the area (Figure II.1). It was hoped that some of the areas surveyed by the "band" technique could be fully surveyed with the "zone" technique in subsequent seasons, but this was never possible.

—We did not attempt to undertake a complete walking survey, because the team was always small and because vehicle survey, giving the team the perspective of height, was usually possible. Only in certain areas, as noted below, did Neely attempt coverage on foot.

—We only rarely had a survey instrument which could be used to map each site precisely. Also, we did not have low-altitude, high-resolution air photographs that would have allowed detailed photogrammetric mapping. Usually, we were forced to use simpler techniques with Brunton pocket transit, tape, and pacing.

The field procedures on a typical day were as follows. The area selected for survey was visited early in the morning when the angle of the sunlight was low. The area was traversed by Landrover in parallel transects about 25 meters apart, looking for low mounds, stone footings, or sherd and lithic scatters. When a feature was found, it was located on a 1:50,000 aerial photograph in terms of nearby water-courses, roads, bushes, and larger mounds evident on the photos. Once a number of sites had been located or the angle of the light became higher, making it difficult to locate sites even at close range, the revisiting of sites was begun. At each, a pace and compass map was made and features were measured with a tape. The site was then divided into sectors, and diagnostic sherds and other artifacts were collected from each sector. In the evening, the locational information was copied onto base maps obtained from the National Iranian Oil Company. Sherds were washed and numbered during the next few days, and chronological assessments were made. Special circumstances required changes in this daily procedure. Survey of the rugged margins of the plain or areas with deep gulleys necessitated that the coverage be largely on foot. The study of large and topographically complex sites such as Tepe Musiyan (DL-20) required days of mapping and sectorial collecting in topographically defined areas. Large relatively featureless sites were divided into measured rectangular zones, conforming where possible to indications of the outcrop of strata. On such sites, special attention was paid to erosional cuts and old excavations in order to assess stratigraphic accumulation. Often, so many diagnostic rim, base, and decorated sherds were found in each sector of such sites that they were classified, counted, and left on the site, with only a small type sample being retained for further study. Possible earlier sherds from the surface of such sites, however, were retained for future study.

While the original 1961 survey was restricted to the central part of the plain between the Mehmeh and the Dawairij Rivers, Neely intended the 1968–69 survey to cover the entire plain, almost 1000 square kilometers. Though much more was examined than in 1961, it was not possible to cover the northwestern extremity of the plain, beyond a kilometer or so from the eastern bank of the Mehmeh. Also, coverage of the southeastern extremity, distant from the project base in the village of Deh Luran, was not as intensive as elsewhere. Fortunately, this is the area re-examined by Miroschedji (1981), so coverage is better than we had expected. All told about 70% of the plain was examined, and within that part, we believe that about 80% of all of the visible sites extant on the plain were recorded. However, coverage of those sites of the earlier periods which do rise above the early Holocene sediment cover—sites which are the particular focus of this report—is probably nearly complete within the part of the plain actually examined.

At the end of the season, through the generosity of the Iranian Archaeological Service, all of the sherds collected during the survey were sent to the University of Texas at Austin for analysis. The procedures used were those used in analyzing ceramics from the excavated sites: an initial division into "wares" with characteristic clay bodies, inclusions, and colors; a further division into "types" based on surface treatment; and a final division into variants based on the vessel shape and decorative motifs (Hole, Flannery and Neely 1969:109–111). Drawings of ceramics from a series of sites, at least one representing each cultural

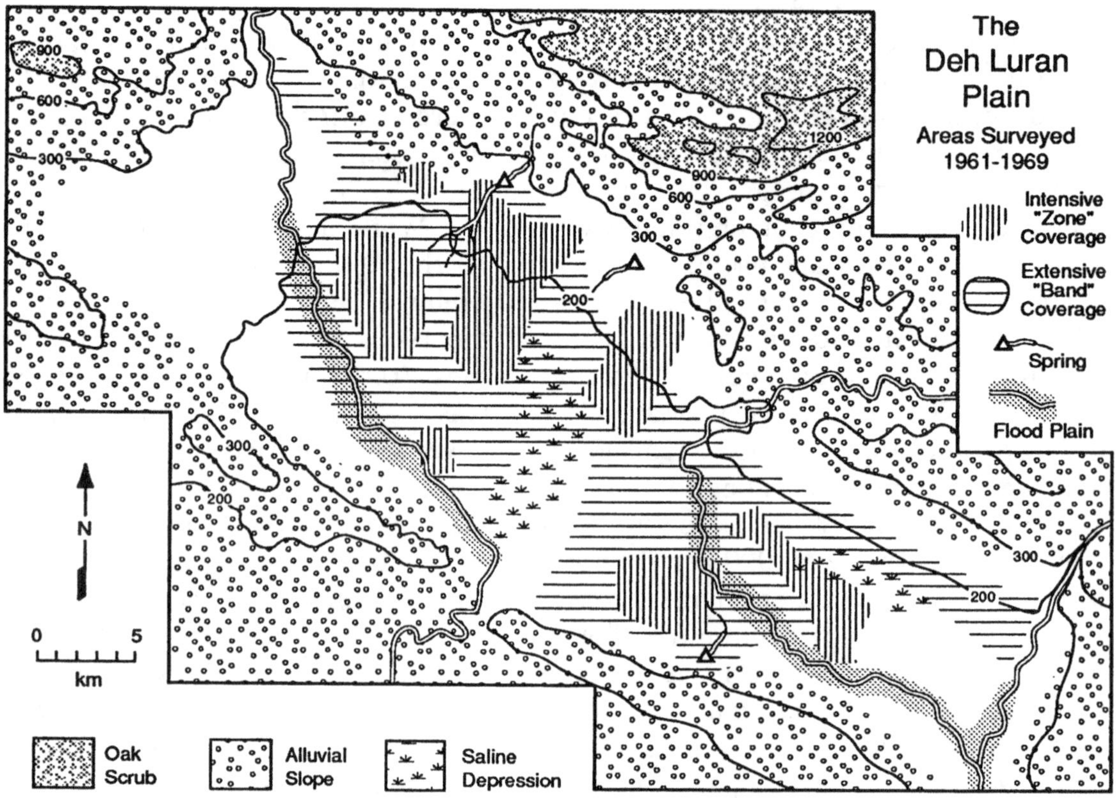

Figure II.1. Survey coverage of the Deh Luran Plain.

period, were drawn. The ceramic variants in the samples in Texas and some of the samples at Yale have been counted, and the counts are presented in the Appendix. It must be emphasized, however, that these counts are not directly comparable to those given for the screened excavated samples in the various Deh Luran excavation reports, since plain body sherds were not uniformly recovered and retained for analysis.

Chapter III

Ceramic Phase Indicators in Surface Assemblages

The excavations at Ali Kosh, Chagha Sefid, Tepe Sabz, Tepe Musiyan, and Tepe Farukhabad have resulted in the definition of a sequence divided into nineteen successive cultural phases dating between sometime in the VIIIth millennium B.C. and the middle of the IInd millennium B.C. The presence of any of these phases on a site can be recognized if only a few diagnostic stone tools or ceramics are present in a surface collection. Some earlier phases, however, have been recognized only in the excavations, and not identified in the survey samples. The following discussion considers only thirteen of these phases. In this chapter, the assemblages are illustrated by complete or reconstructable examples of types common on the surface. Examples illustrated in the corpora of surface ceramics in Chapter IV are also cited.

The Early Phases

(Figure III.1)

Diagnostic sherds of the earliest vegetal-tempered wares are common on the surface only at Tepe Ali Kosh and Chagha Sefid, and we have chosen not to deal with the surface assemblages of these well-known excavated sites in this study. The earliest ceramics which are definitely represented in our samples are a few bowl rims of the Chogha Mami Transitional phase (ES-RB-7; Figs. III.1 a, c; IV.24 a; IV.53 c) and the Sabz phase (ES-RB-10; Figs. III.1 d; IV.24 f; IV.53 a). The layers of these phases are apparently so deeply buried that only a few sherds were brought to the surface when later inhabitants dug pits and moved sediments for construction purposes. Although the ceramics of these phases are well defined from excavations, it is not possible to speak of surface assemblages from any of the sites found by our surveys.

The Khazineh Phase

(Figure III.1)

The earliest phase actually represented by ceramic assemblages on the surfaces of sites is the Khazineh phase, known from excavated contexts at Tepe Sabz (Hole, Flannery and Neely 1969: 138–49). Khazineh surface assemblages, as well as those of succeeding phases up to the Farukh phase, have sherds of the coarse, poorly fired, handmade "Khazineh Red" ware (ES-SJ-1; ibid.: 120–24; Fig. III.1 e), usually from spherical "hole-mouth" jars, but these relatively soft vegetal-tempered sherds do not often survive on the ground surface. Predominating in Khazineh assemblages is well-fired, handmade Susiana ware, usually thicker than later examples and with visible sand grains, but with a few fine bowls that are thinner and lack visible inclusions (ibid.:124–132). The painted Susiana Black-on-buff (ibid.:132–159) types have reddish to black paint colors, with the latter often matte and sometimes vitrified.

Among the painted Susiana vessel parts of Khazineh assemblages are the sherds of hemispherical bowls, some with wide painted bands (ES-RB-1; Fig. III.1 j; IV.53 j), and basins, some with triangles on the lip (ES-RB-18; Fig. IV.24 b), but these continue into the Mehmeh phase. Small incurved bowls with exterior motifs occur, and those with negative zig-zag motifs (ES-RB-15; Figs. III.1 i; IV.53 b; IV.24 g, h) seem to be exclusively Khazineh. Most common and chronologically useful are the sherds of carinated bowls with painted exterior bold zig-zags and elaborate interior designs (Figs. IV.53 c, f, g; IV.24 e-f, j), of which those with interior cross hatch (ES-RB-11; Fig. III.1 f; IV.53 g) and interior negative zig-zag elements (ES-RB-13; Fig. III.1 g, IV.24 c) on the inner wall seem to be exclusively Khazineh, but a range of interior (Fig. IV.24 d, e) and basal motifs occur. Jars of the Khazineh phase are poorly known (Fig. IV.53 e).

Also useful in recognizing earlier Susiana assemblages are painted star-shaped spindle whorls (ES-O-1; Fig. III.1 l; IV.53 h). These originate in the Chogha Mami Transitional phase, but continue into Sabz and even Mehmeh times (Hole, Flannery and Neely 1969: 206).

Figure III.1. Ceramic vessels of the Chogha Mami Transitional, Sabz, and Khazineh phases

[These representations are primarily of reconstructed complete forms known from the excavated sites. More detailed information will be found in the cited excavation report. Examples without citation are examples found during our surveys.]

[ES is an abbreviation for "Early Susiana."
RB indicates "Rim of Bowl."
RJ indicates "Rim of Jar."
SJ indicates "Rim of Straw-tempered Jar."
O indicates "Other Artifact."]

a.	ES-RB-7.	DL-23 (Chagha Sefid) Hole 1977, Figure 50 c, d.
b.		Same, ibid., Figure 51 a.
c.	ES-RB-7.	Same, ibid., Figure 50 a, b.
d.	ES-RB-10.	DL-31 (Tepe Sabz) Hole, Flannery and Neely 1969, Figure 50 f.
e.	ES-SJ-1.	DL-14.
f.	ES-RB-11	DL-31 (Tepe Sabz) Hole, Flannery and Neely 1969, Figure 50 f.
g.	ES-RB-13.	Same, ibid., Figure 56 g, 57 j.
h.		Same, ibid., Figure 56.
i.	ES-RB-15.	Same, ibid., Figure 52 b, d.
j.	ES-RB-1	Same, ibid., Figure 54 b.
k.	ES-RB-12.	Same, ibid., Figure 56 a.
l.	ES-O-1.	Same, ibid., Figure 88 e.

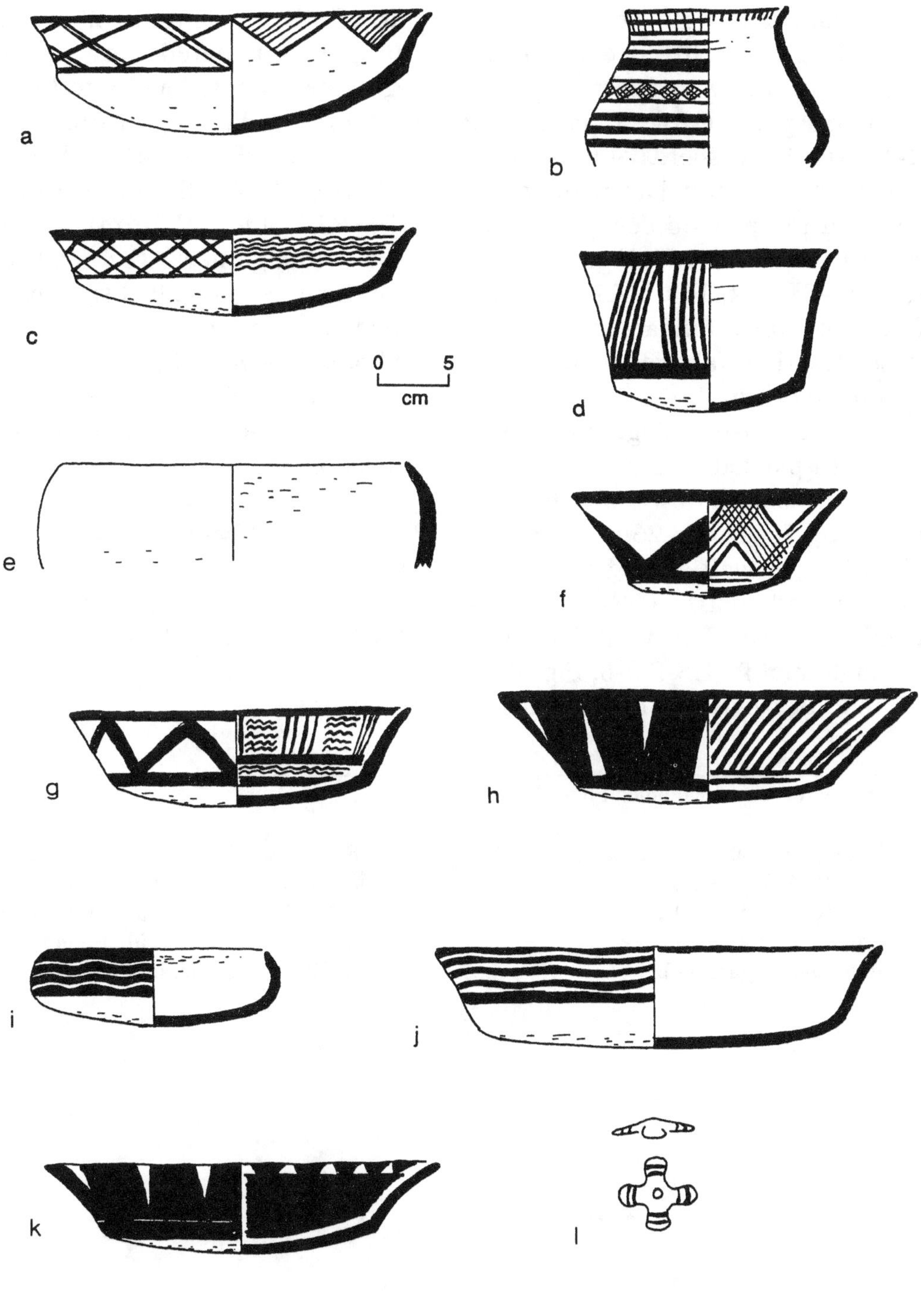

Figure III.1. Ceramic vessels of the Chogha Mami Transitional, Sabz, and Khazineh phases

The Mehmeh Phase
(Figure III.2)

Ceramics of the Mehmeh phase are known from excavated contexts at both Tepe Sabz and Tepe Musiyan. They are richly decorated, and several associations of design and form appear to be distinctive of this phase (Hole, Flannery and Neely 1969:149–50). A few sherds of the vegetal- and grit-tempered hole-mouth jars with red-to-brown surfaces and red painted designs, termed "Mehmeh Red-on-Red" (ibid.:159, Fig. 65), occur on the surface (ES-SJ-1, 2; Fig. IV.26 a). Most sherds are of Susiana wares, similar to those of the Khazineh phase described above. Fine fabrics, however, are more common.

A Mehmeh surface assemblage will have a range of bowls with painted exterior decoration, for example, fine bell-shaped bowls with horizontal chevrons (LS-RB-7; Fig. IV.26 c, e) or other motifs (Fig. IV.26 i), as well as larger examples with exterior diamond motifs (ES-RB-4; Fig. IV.26 d), ladder motifs (ES-RB-5; cf. Fig. IV.26 g), and right triangle motifs (ES-RB-6; Fig. IV.26 l). Basins with interior bands and lip triangles are common (ES-RB-18; Fig. IV.26 b), and goat motifs (ES-RB-19; Fig. IV.26 h) occur. Smaller and simpler carinated bowls, continuing from Khazineh times, have interiors with bands (ES-RB-14; Fig. IV.53 j) or fully painted (ES RB-12) and bases (ES-BB-4) with radial motifs (Fig. IV.26 k). Jars with low necks and interior ledges (ES-RJ-2; Fig. IV.26 m) become common, and jars with high necks (LS-RJ-1) occur. It is during the Mehmeh phase that star-shaped whorls are replaced by concavo-convex or "chariot wheel" whorls (ES-O-2; Fig. IV.26 j).

Several elements among those noted above seem to be good indicators of Mehmeh phase occupation:

ES-SJ-1, 2:	Mehmeh Red-on-red jar sherds,
ES-RB-6:	The Susiana Black-on-buff bowl with right triangles,
ES-RB-19:	The Susiana Black-on-buff bowl with goat motifs.

Figure III.2. Ceramic vessels of the Mehmeh Phase

a.	ES-RJ-2.	DL-31 (Tepe Sabz) Hole, Flannery, and Neely 1969, Figure 58 d.
b.	ES-RB-18.	Same, ibid., Figure 59 a.
c.	ES-SJ-2.	Same, ibid., Figure 65 b, i.
d.	ES-RB-19.	Same, ibid., Figure 59 b.
e.	ES-RB-12.	Same, ibid., Figure 53 h.
f.	ES-RB-4.	Same, ibid., Figure 53 j.
g.	ES-RB-19.	Same, ibid., Figure 62 d.
h.	ES-RB-6.	Same, ibid., Figure 62 c.
i.	ES-RB-5.	Same, ibid., Figure 61 f.

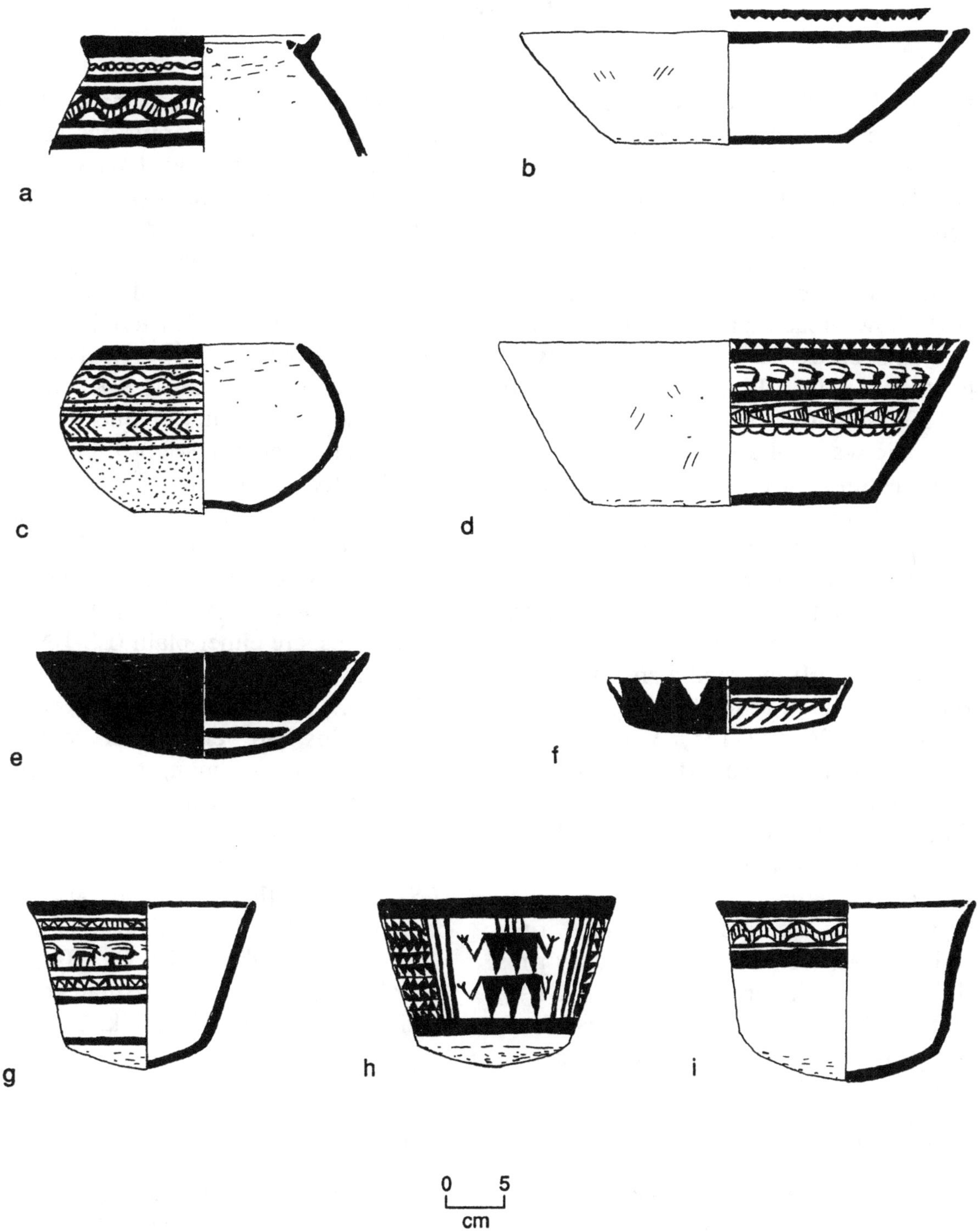

Figure III.2. Ceramic vessels of the Mehmeh Phase

The Bayat Phase
(Figure III.3)

Ceramics of the Bayat phase have the simplest design repertoire of any assemblage in the Susiana tradition. No motif is restricted to this phase alone. It is difficult to recognize a Bayat occupation on a site with other later Susiana ceramic assemblages. Fortunately, the evidence of stratified deposits from both Tepe Sabz and Tepe Farukhabad shows that there are minor design variants which seem to have been made only by Bayat potters (Hole, Flannery and Neely 1969:150–153; Wright 1981:57–59).

The ceramic wares of a Bayat surface assemblage usually include bowl rims (Fig. IV.27 a) and sherds of "Bayat Red" ware with a fine compact reddish clay and slip (Hole, Flannery and Neely 1969:164). The great majority of sherds in these surface assemblages, however, comprises Susiana buff wares with a compact fine or sandy clay body, well-controlled firing, and a smoothed surface, often with painted reddish-brown to black designs (ibid.:124–126, 132–135). Very thin, fine sherds are characteristic of Bayat and later Susiana assemblages. Recovery of only a few sherds of these variants indicates site use during the later Susiana phases, but one cannot argue for use during specific phases.

A Bayat surface assemblage will have fine, unpainted, bell-shaped bowls represented by rims (LS-RB-1) usually with narrow bases (LS-BB-2; Fig. III.3 d; IV.27 d, e). Painted examples occur, but are rare (Fig. IV.27 f-h). Similar but somewhat larger bowls have horizontal bands, either single (LS-RB-2) or multiple (LS-RB-3; Fig. IV.27 c), and some bowls have black paint covering the entire upper body (LS-RB-4; Fig. III.3 e). Other bowls have horizontal motifs such as curved or zig-zag lines (LS-RB-5; Fig. III.3 f; IV.27 g-i), multiple curved lines (LS-RB-6), and horizontal chevrons (LS-RB-7; Fig. III.3 h; Fig IV.27 c). Bowls with vertical designs include those with vertical lines (LS-RB-8; Fig. IV.27 o) and those with a curved line with two vertical lines on either side (LS-RB-9; Fig. III.3 c; IV.27 l, m). Finally, some bowls had diamond motifs painted solid (LS-RB-11) or cross-hatch (LS-RB-12) between horizontal curved lines. These small to medium-sized bowls have either wide (LS-BB-1) or ring bases (LS-BB-4). Basins, the largest open forms, are either plain (LS-BN-1; Fig. IV.27 b) or have a horizontal painted line on the rim (LS-BN-2; Fig. IV.49 a). It is likely that some of these basins had vertical curved line motifs, as discussed below. Among the restricted jar forms are sherds of high-necked jars, usually with complete exterior painting on the neck (LS-RJ-1; Fig. III.3 a; IV.27 p), though sometimes unpainted (LS-RJ-2). Both basins and jars had large flat bases (LS-B-1). During the Bayat phase, "chariot wheel" spindle whorls (ES-O-2; Fig. III.3 i; IV.27 k) are replaced by whorls that are lenticular in section (LS-O-1; Fig. III.3 j, k; IV.27 j).

Figure III.3. Ceramic vessels of the Bayat Phase [LS is an abbreviation for "Late Susiana."]

a.	LS-RJ-1.	DL-31 (Tepe Sabz). Hole, Flannery and Neely 1969, Figure 58 g.
b.	LS-RJ-4.	Same, ibid., Figure 58 q.
c.	LS-RB-9.	Same, ibid., Figure 60 i.
d.	LS-RB-1.	Same, ibid., Figure 48 h.
e.	LS-RB-4.	
f.	LS-RB-5.	DL-32 (Farukhabad). Wright 1981, Figure 16 b.
g.	LS-RB-9.	DL-31 (Tepe Sabz). Hole, Flannery and Neely 1969, Figure 60 j.
h.	LS-RB-7.	Same, ibid., Figure 62 l.
i.	ES-O-2.	Same, ibid., Figure 89 c.
j.	LS-O-1.	Same, ibid., Figure 90 a.
k.	LS-O-1.	Same, ibid., Figure 90 c.

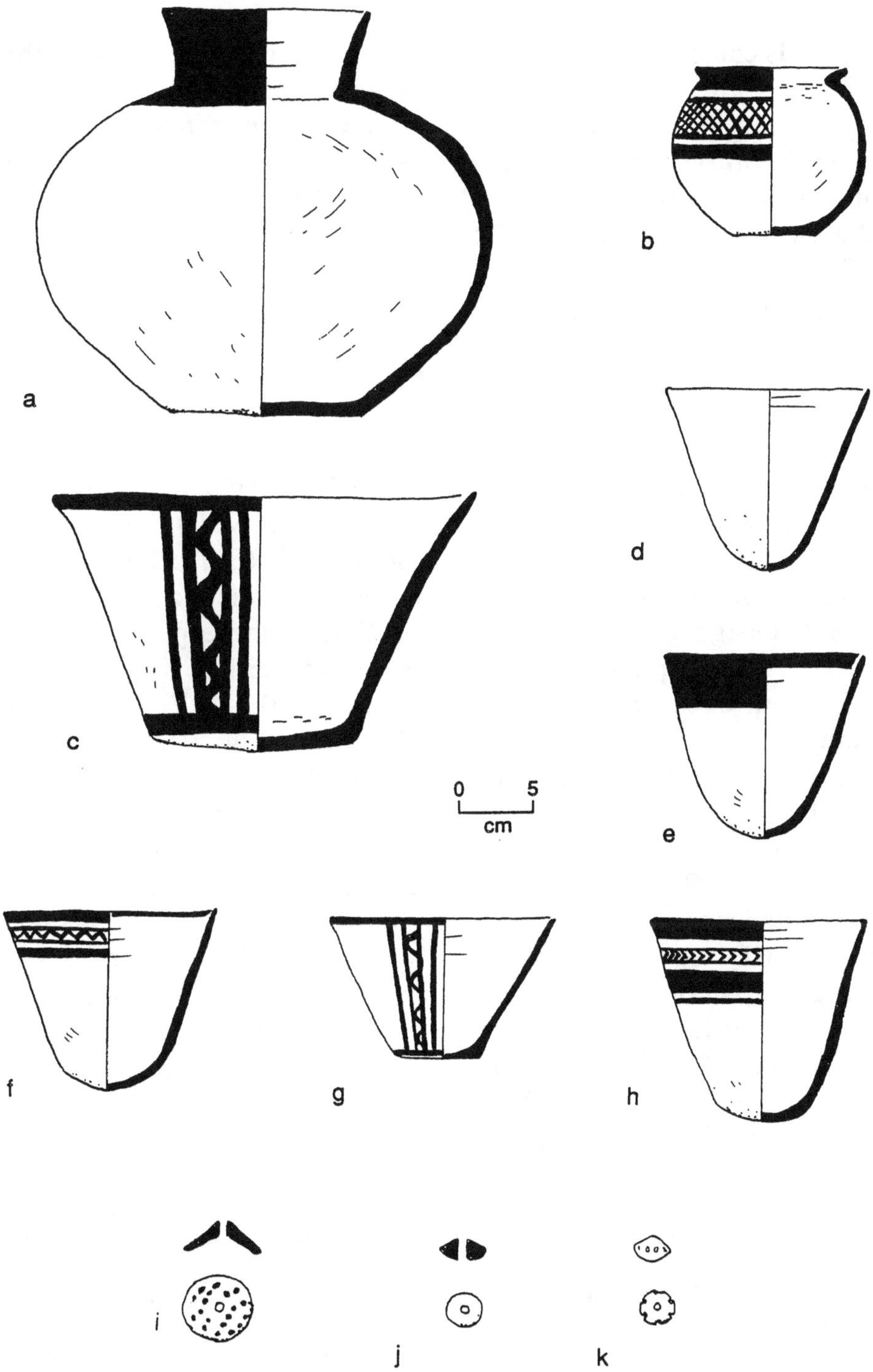

Figure III.3. Ceramic vessels of the Bayat Phase

Two variants of the elements noted above appear to be characteristic of Bayat assemblages and are very rare, if not completely absent, in earlier Mehmeh and later Farukh assemblages. Both are decorations found on the exteriors of open bowl forms.

—LS-RB-7 (Fig IV.26 c): At Tepe Sabz, the horizontal chevron motif by itself is known only in Bayat phase layers. However, it can be an element in more complex Mehmeh designs (Fig. IV.26 e; Hole, Flannery and Neely 1969: Fig. 61

e), so only large rim sherds can be confidently ascribed.

—LS-RB-9, Large variant (Fig. IV.27 l): The vertical curved line motif with vertical lines 0.40 cm or wider are known only from Bayat phase layers at Sabz and Farukhabad (Wright 1981:59; Fig. 30; Table C1:342).

A site with later Farukh phase diagnostics can be ascribed to the Bayat phase only if these variants are found. It is possible that on some sites with small ceramic samples, the Bayat occupation has not been recognized.

The Farukh Phase

(Figure III.4)

Assemblages of this phase, known from the excavations at Farukhabad, exhibit the same fabrics and paints as those of the Bayat phase. They have a wide range of decorated sherds, and a number of associations of design and form appear to be characteristic only of this phase (Wright 1981:57–59). Identification, even in small samples, is straightforward.

A Farukh phase surface assemblage has fine, unpainted, bell-shaped bowls represented by rims (LS-RB-1), narrow bases (LS-BB-2), and shaved bases (LS-BB-3; Figs. III.4 d; IV.13 j). Various out-leaned or vertical-sided bowls had exterior bands (LS-RB-2, 3; Fig. III.4 e, f; IV.49 b, c), horizontal curved lines (LS-RB-5, 6) (Wright 1981: Fig. 16 a-d), vertical lines (LS-RB-8; Fig. IV.7 i,) vertical curved lines (LS-RB-9) (ibid.: Fig. 16 f-h), fine dot motifs (LS-RB-10; Fig. III.4 h, i; IV.13 a, b) diamond motifs (LS-RB-11–13; Fig. III.4 k; IV.7 f, j,), sigma motifs (LS-RB-14; Fig. III.4 j; IV.7 j; IV.13 d, e, k; IV.49 e), step motifs (LS-RB-15; Fig. III.4 l; IV.13 c, f; IV.49 d), and rectilinear motifs (LS-RB-16; Fig. III.4 i). As before, these painted small to medium-sized bowls had either wide bases (LS-BB-1) or ring bases (LS-BB-4; Fig. III.4 l). Large basins, usually plain (Fig. III.4 c), but with some interior bands (Wright 1981: Fig. 23), are common. High-necked jars with plain (LS-RJ-1) (ibid.: Fig. 24 e) or fully painted (LS-RJ-3) (ibid.: Fig. 24 a, c, d, f, g) necks continue, and similar jars with painted bands on the neck (LS-RJ-2, 3; Fig. III.4 a) appear. The sherds of small low neck jars are rare in the surface collections (LS-RJ-4; Fig. III.4 b; cf. Fig. IV.49 j).

Several elements and variants among those listed above seem to be good indicators of Farukh phase occupation:

Figure III.4. Ceramic vessels of the Farukh Phase [BN indicates "Basin Rim"; BB indicates "Bowl Base."]

a. LS-RJ-3. DL-32 (Farukhabad). Wright 1981, Plate 8 c, Figure 24 b.
b. LS-RJ-4. Same, ibid., Figure 24 h.
c. LS-BN-1. Same, ibid., Figure 23 a-f.
d. LS-BB-3. Same, ibid., Figure 13 a, b; 14 a.
e. LS-RB-3. Same, ibid., Figure 15 c.
f. LS-RB-3. Same, ibid., Figure 12 a; 15 h.
g. LS-RB-8. DL-20 (Musiyan).
h. LS-RB-10. DL-32 (Farukhabad). Wright 1981, Figure 17 e-g.
i. LS-RB-10, 16. Same, ibid., Figure 17 b.
j. LS-RB-14. Same, ibid., Figure 18 a.
k. LS-RB-13. Same, ibid., Figure 20 b.
l. LS-RB-15. DL-20 (Musiyan). Gautier and Lampre 1905, Figure 151; cf. also (Wright 1981: Figure 19).

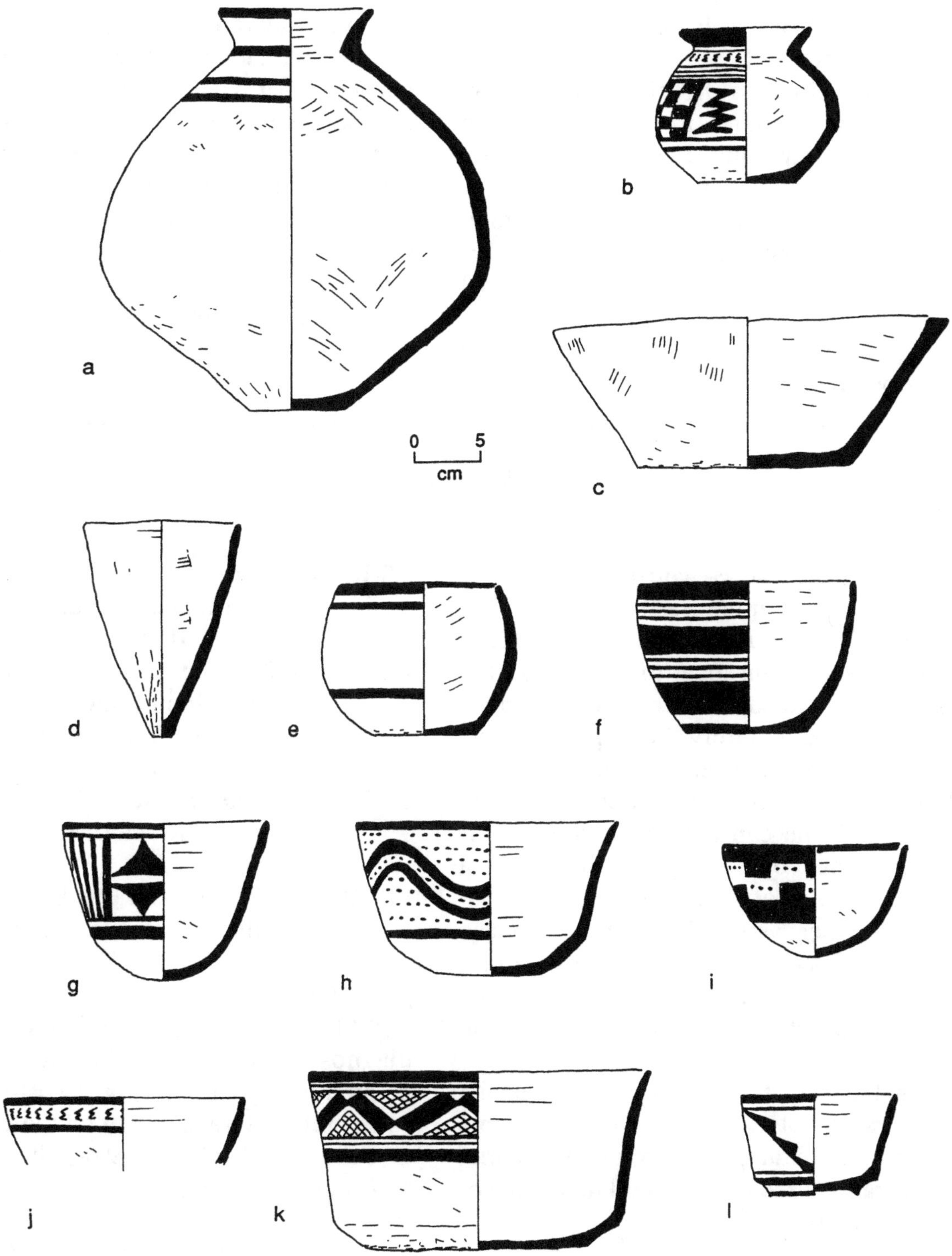

Figure III.4. Ceramic vessels of the Farukh Phase

LS-BB-3: The Susiana Buff shaved cup base.

LS-RB-10: The Susiana Black-on-buff bowl with fine dots.

LS-RB-13: The Susiana Black-on-buff bowl with diamond motifs filled with oblique parallel lines (Wright 1981: Fig. 20 c; 21 d, f).

LS-RB-15: The Susiana Black-on-buff bowl with step motifs.

LS-RB-16: The Susiana Black-on-buff bowl with rectilinear motifs.

LS-RJ-2, 3: The Susiana Black-on-buff jar necks with horizontal bands.

It is important to note, however, that diamond motifs are relatively early in the Farukh phase sequence at Farukhabad, dot motifs and step motifs are most common in the middle of the sequence, and by the end of this sequence step motifs and sigma motifs predominate (Wright 1981:57–58), with the latter continuing into the Suse phase. Confirmation of these suggestions with further stratigraphic work would allow a finer dating of our surface samples.

The Suse Phase

(Figure III.5)

Although this phase is well represented by excavated samples from the Susiana Plain to the east (Dollfus 1971, Le Brun 1971), no assemblage of the Suse phase variant local to the Deh Luran Plain has been excavated, and we have no surface collections from any purely Suse phase sites. Fortunately, certain characteristic painted motifs on the bowls are unknown in earlier Deh Luran assemblages and one can recognize with confidence the presence of Suse phase sherds in a sample. Two samples of these ceramics are illustrated here. Surface assemblages of this phase exhibit the same Bayat Red and Susiana Buff fabrics as those of the preceding Farukh phase, but vitrified glossy paints occur more frequently on the bowls.

Though the Bayat Red bowls and Susiana basins and jars do not seem to be distinguishable from Farukh phase examples, several characteristic bowl decorations seem to be good indicators of Suse phase occupation:

LS-RB-17: The Susiana Black-on-buff bowl with large vertical chevrons (Fig. III.5 c; IV.49 p).

LS-RB-18: The Susiana Black-on-buff bowl with checkerboard or grid motifs (Figs. III.5 g; IV.14 l ; IV.49 m, n).

LS-RB-19–21: The Susiana Black-on-buff bowl with branch motifs, both heavy (Figs. III.4 f; IV.14 q; IV.49 i, l) and light (Fig. IV.14 n).

LS-RB-22: The Susiana Black-on-buff bowl with "X" motif (Fig. III.5 e; IV.14 i, j).

LS-RB-23: The Susiana Black-on-buff bowl with line-dot motifs (Fig. IV.14 o, p).

Another possible Suse element is the fine line motif (Fig. IV.14 m, n). An interesting Suse phase diagnostic from Tepe Musiyan is a piece of a painted trumpet cone (Fig. IV.14 b), well-known as an architectural element on the central platform at Suse itself (Canal 1978, Stève and Gasche 1971) and from smaller sites on the Susiana Plain (Dollfus 1971).

We have little indication of the latest unpainted Suse Phase ceramics, the "Terminal Susa A Phase" (Johnson 1973:59–61) of the Susiana Plain, which would be termed earliest Uruk in Mesopotamia proper (Adams and Nissen 1972).

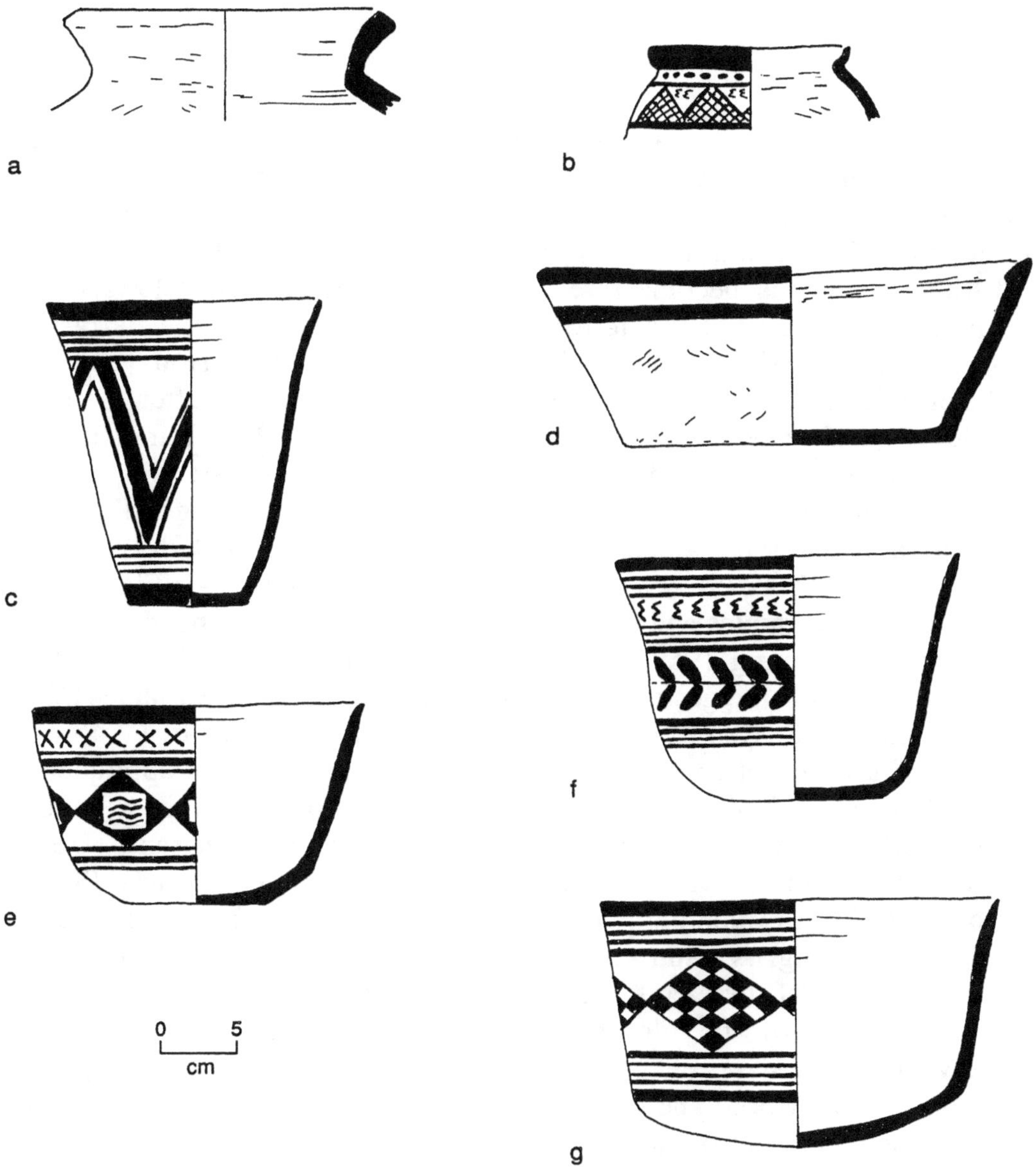

Figure III.5. Ceramic vessels of the Suse Phase

Figure III.5. Ceramic vessels of the Suse Phase

a. LS-RJ-2. DL 20 (Musiyan).
b. LS-RJ-14. DL 20 (Musiyan).
c. LS-RB-17. DL 247.
d. LS-BN-2. DL 20 (Musiyan).
e. LS-RB-22. DL 20 (Musiyan).
f. LS-RB-21. DL 247.
g. LS-RB-18. DL-247.

The Early Uruk Phase
(Figure III.6)

This phase marks a technical and stylistic break with the Susiana ceramic tradition which was practiced on the Deh Luran Plain for much of the VIth millennium B. C., and all of the Vth. Fabrics with sand inclusions become rare, and those with mixtures of crushed calcite and chopped grass, perhaps animal dung, predominate. A range of differentiated bowl and jar forms replace the simple range of vessel shapes characteristic of Susiana assemblages. Painted decoration is restricted to a few jar forms, and simply decorated appliqué is common. In an earlier article (Wright, Neely, Johnson, and Speth 1975), we noted the similarity between these ceramics and those from Godin Tepe Period VI (Young 1969) and other sites in central Luristan, and suggested that early in the IVth millennium B.C. Deh Luran communities were drawn into the network of highland Zagros potters. However, Godin VI cannot be earlier than the middle of the Uruk period, i.e. the mid-IVth millennium. In the absence of detailed publications on early IVth millennium ceramics from the northern Zagros and northern Mesopotamia, the affinity of these craft materials from Deh Luran cannot be determined. Fortunately, however, this issue is not particularly important for the present work. The earliest assemblages in this new ceramic tradition are not known from excavated contexts, but we do have surface samples from several sites which do not seem to have had lengthy occupation, and these are illustrated in detail in the following figures. Only the end of the Early Uruk phase is represented by stratified deposits excavated at Tepe Farukhabad (Wright 1981:168).

Ceramics of the Early Uruk phase with the distinctive inclusions noted above are termed "Sargarab ware" after a site of that name (DL-169) on the Deh Luran Plain. Among the open forms on this ware are "fine bowls" with tapered rims (US-RB-3; Figs. III.6 k, l; IV.3 a-b; IV.44 a-d) and a related slightly restricted form termed a "fine jar" (US-RJ-1; Figs. III.6 c; IV.4 d; IV.44 f-g). Heavier open bowls with conical form include round lip variants (US-RB-4; Figs. IV.3 c, IV.44 j) and beaded lip variants (US-RB-6; Figs. III.6 g; IV.3 d, e; IV.44 l-q; IV.45 e) often with various kinds of impressed appliqué strips. Heavier open bowls with incurved or hemispherical forms include round lip variants (US-RB-9; Fig. IV.44 i) and beaded lip variants (US-RB 10, 11, 12; IV.3 f, g; IV.45 c), frequently with impressed strips. Extremely large and heavy basins with similar rim variations, both open (US-RB-8; IV.3 i; Figs. IV.45 b) and incurved (US-RB-13; Figs. III.6 i, IV.3 j; IV.45 d; IV.56 d), also occur. Flat-bottomed, straight-sided trays (US-RB-15; Fig. IV.44 h) are present as well.

Figure III.6. Ceramic vessels of the Early Uruk Phase

a. US-RJ-2. DL-11. (Garmasi).
b. US-RJ-10. DL-292.
c. US-RJ-1. DL-32 (Farukhabad). Wright 1981, Figure 43 a.
d. US-RJ-3 variant. DL-169 (Sargarab).
e. UU-RJ-9. DL-169 (Sargarab).
f. US-RJ-6. DL-32 (Farukhabad). Wright 1981, Figure 42 b.
g. US-RB-6. DL-169 (Sargarab).
h. US-RB-7. DL-32 (Farukhabad). Wright 1981, Figure 41 a.
i. US-RB-13. DL-169 (Sargarab).
j. US-RB-1. DL-11. (Garmasi).
k. US-RB-3. DL-169 (Sargarab).
l. US-RB-3 variant. DL-169 (Sargarab).

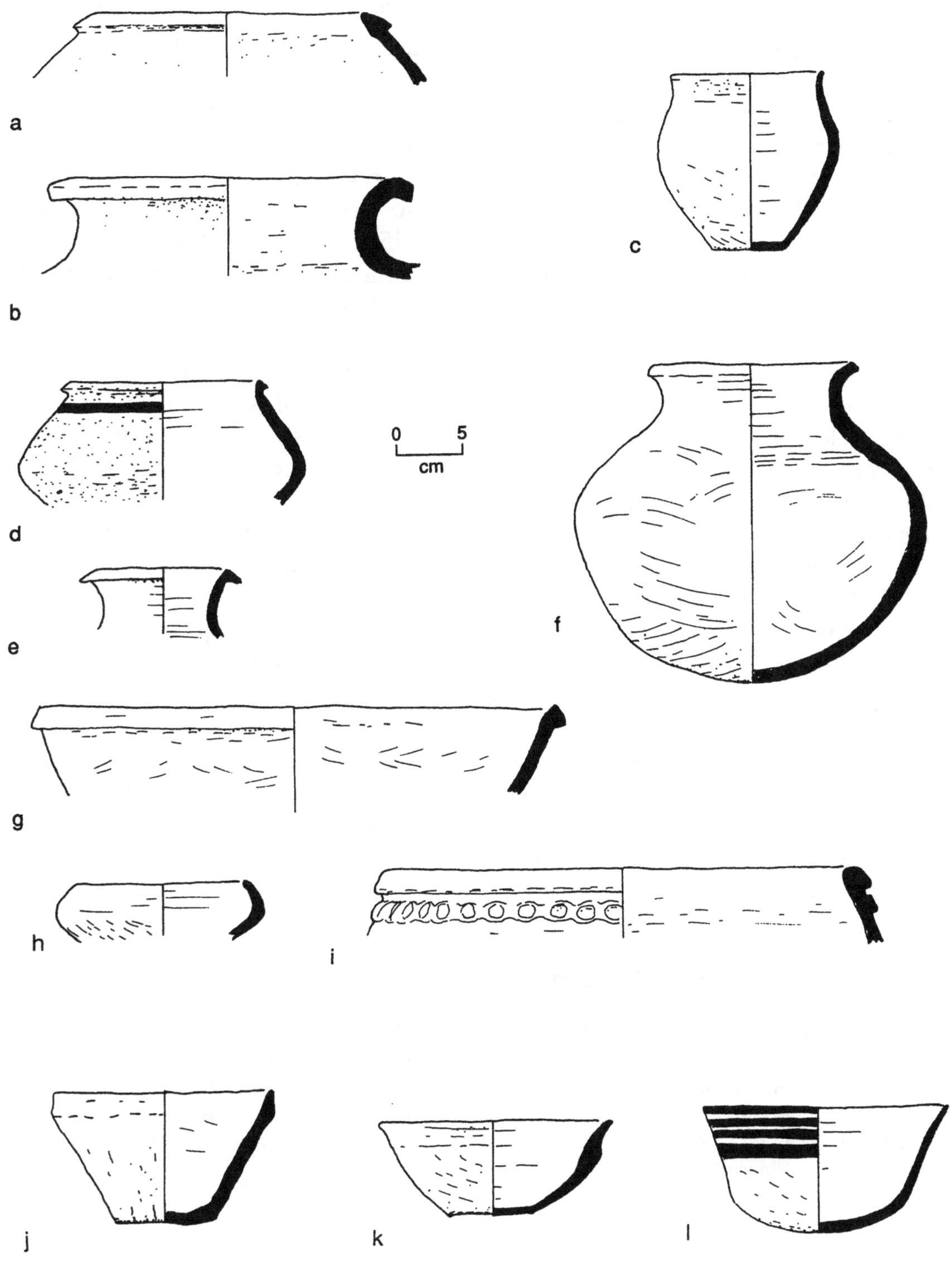

Figure III.6. Ceramic vessels of the Early Uruk Phase

Among the restricted forms in Early Uruk Sargarab ware, the simplest are the neckless ledge-rim jars (US-RJ-2; Figs. III.6 a, IV.4 a-c; IV.45 l-m; IV.56 j). These always have coarse, crushed calcite inclusions with little vegetal material, which may indicate that they came from a particular shop or were intended for a particular use. Perhaps related are low neck, beaded rim jars on Sargarab ware, some of which are painted with red slip and black bands (US-RJ-3; Fig. III.6 d). There are also straight neck jars with rounded (US-RJ-4; Figs. IV.45 i-k; IV.56 m) or flattened (US-RJ-5; IV.4 m; Fig. IV.45 h) lips. By far the most common restricted jars, however, are the flared neck jars, also with rounded lips (US-RJ-6; Figs. III.6 f; IV.4 f, i; IV.46 d-j; IV.56 n) and grooved lips (US-RJ-9; Figs. IV.45 m-n; IV.4 g, h, j), which occasionally have red slips and painted black bands. Very large and heavy jars with round lips (US-RJ-8; Figs. IV.4 l; IV.56 k, l) and the flat lip variant termed a "high expanded band rim jar" (US-RJ-10; Figs. III.6 b; IV.4 k; IV.56 q, r) are present as well.

Fragments of vessels of other wares occur with Sargarab ware on several sites. Clay with chopped grass inclusions, so-called "straw-tempered ware" (Wright 1981:126–130) was used to produce the beveled rim bowls with tapered lip, termed "proto-beveled rim bowls" (Caldwell 1968, Johnson 1973), but these occur at few sites (Fig. III.6 j). More interesting are the occurrences of ceramics with sand inclusions. From Sargarab (DL-169) are sherds of a large ledge-rim bowl (UU-RB-6; Fig. IV.45 f) and several ledge-rim jars (UU-RJ-9; Fig. III.6 e; IV.46 o) as well as a straight spout (UU-O-9; Fig. IV.46 q). Since such forms have Middle Uruk funerary associations at Farukhabad (ibid.:87–89: Figs. 20, 39 a), it is possible that their occurrence on the surface of Sargarab results from the disturbance of a burial. Also from Sargarab is the rim of a basin (Fig. IV.45 g) of a fabric and form characteristic of "Terminal Susa A" assemblages on the Susiana Plain (Johnson 1973; Wright, Neely, Johnson, and Speth 1975). We take this as an indication of the relatively early date of the site of Sargarab within the Early Uruk span. From Garmasi (DL-11) is a similar but slightly restricted basin (Fig. IV.3 l) and a carinated bowl rim (UU-RB-5; Fig. IV.3 k), both well known in early Uruk contexts.

If indeed Sargarab is relatively early in this period, then the occurrence of a majority of bowls with conical form and of a majority of flared neck jars with rounded lips is an indication of occupation earlier within the Early Uruk. If the excavated samples from Farukhabad are relatively late in this period, then a majority of the Sargarab ware bowls with the incurved form and the flared neck jars with the grooved lip is a local indication of occupation later within the Early Uruk span.

Figure III.7. Ceramic vessels of the Middle Uruk Phase

a.	US-RJ-9	DL-32 (Farukhabad). Wright 1981, Figure 40 a.
b.	US-RJ-9.	Same, ibid., Figure 40 b.
c.	US-RB-3.	Same, ibid., Figure 40 c.
d.	UU-O-8.	Same, ibid., Figure 57 d.
e.	US-RJ-5.	Same, ibid., Figure 44 l.
f.	UU-RJ-2.	Same, ibid., Figure 50 a.
g.	US-RB-6.	Same, ibid., Figure 41 m.
h.	UU-RB-5.	Same, ibid., Figure 47 a.
i.	US-RB-2.	Same, ibid., Plate 11 f.
j.	US-RB-8.	Same, ibid., Figure 42 m.

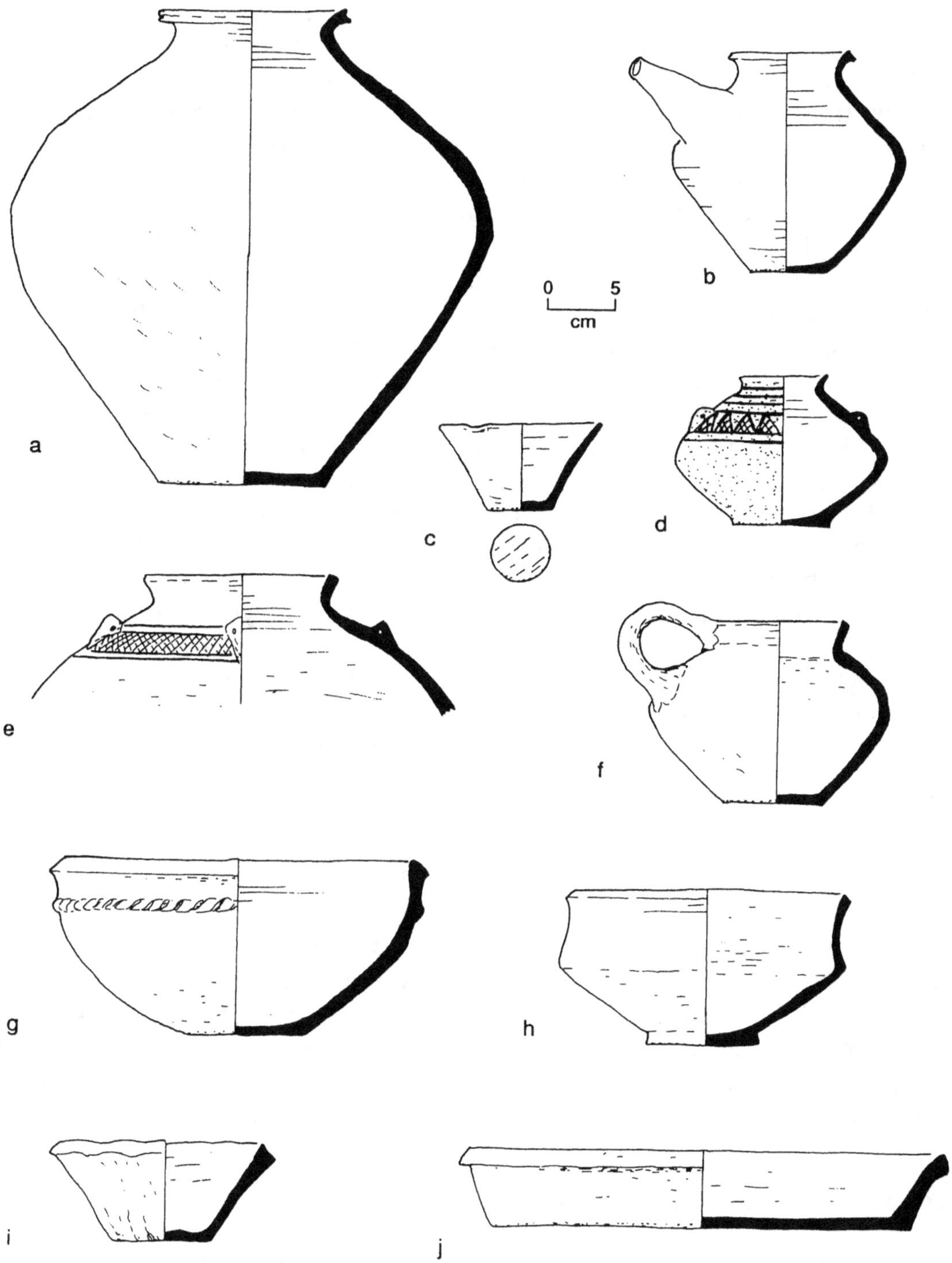

Figure III.7. Ceramic vessels of the Middle Uruk Phase

The Middle Uruk Phase
(Figure III.7)

The Middle Uruk ceramic assemblages excavated in stratigraphic context at Farukhabad (Wright 1981:169), have from 25% to 65% Uruk ware vessels with sandy inclusions. Surface assemblages from the small rural sites, however, do not have such high proportions of Uruk ware. These have the same range of Sargarab ware bowls and jars as the later Early Uruk assemblages, but design variations common on Uruk ware become evident on the Sargarab vessels. For example, cross-hatch incising appears on Sargarab jar shoulders (Fig. III.7 e) and biconical spouts replace long straight spouts (Fig. III.7 b). Among the widespread Middle Uruk ceramic variants are standard beveled rim bowls in 'straw tempered ware' (US-RB-2; Fig. III.7 i)), but these also characterize Late Uruk assemblages. Present, though uncommon, during both periods were Uruk ware plain hemispherical bowl forms with round (UU-RB-2) or flat (UU-RB-3) lips, incurved bowls with round lips (UU-RB-4; cf. Fig. IV.19 a), carinate bowls with beveled lip (UU-RB-5; Figs. III.7 h; IV.3 k), and ledge-rim bowls (UU-RB-6; Figs. III.7 g; IV.45 f). Uruk ware jar forms occur as heavy round lip jars (UU-RJ-3; Fig. IV.41 b), low expanded band rim jars (UU-RJ-6; Fig. IV.41 e), out-turned expanded rim jars (UU-RJ-7; Fig. IV.19 h), heavy expanded rim jars (UU-RJ-8; Fig. IV.41 d), and ledge-rim jars (UU-RJ-9; Fig. IV.41 a). Small globular straight neck jars (UU-RJ-1, 2) with grooved shoulders (UU-O-2; Fig. IV.19 d) have plain strap handles (UU-O-12; Fig. IV.41 j). Jar shoulders with such embellishments as reserve slip (UU-O-4; Fig. IV.41 a), cross-hatch incised bands (UU-O-5, Fig. 41 g) and nose lugs (Fig. IV.41 g) become common, but all continue to be made in Late Uruk times. Red slip jars with black painted designs (UU-O-8; Fig. IV.41 i) seem to be found only in Middle Uruk samples. Unfortunately, these do not preserve well on the surface. So, as in the case of Bayat layers overlain by Farukh layers, it may be difficult to recognize Middle Uruk layers overlain by Late Uruk layers. In practice, however, the occurrence of Sargarab ware variants usually indicates Middle Uruk occupation.

The Late Uruk Phase
(Figure III.8)

By this period, Sargarab ware was probably rarely made. The degree of abrasion on the few examples found in Late Uruk layers at Farukhabad suggest that they are earlier extrusive examples. Beveled rim bowls (ST-RB-2) are very common, but wheel-thrown conical cups (UU-RB-1) are present as well. Most of the Uruk ware variants discussed above continue, but there are a number of distinctive new additions to the ceramic repertoire (Wright 1981:169, 172). Small straight neck jars often have incised oblique lines across their shoulder grooves (UU-O-3; Figs. III.8

Figure III.8. Ceramic vessels of the Late Uruk Phase

a. UU-RJ-8, UU-O-6. DL-32 (Farukhabad). Wright 1981, Plate 11c.
b. UU-RJ-11, UU-O-11. Same, ibid., Figure 54a, 55h.
c. UU-RJ-6. Same, ibid., Figure 52a.
d. UU-RJ-1, UU-O-3, UU-O-14. Same, ibid., Figure 55g, l.
e. UU-RB-3, ED-RB-2. Same, ibid., Figure 47d.
f. UU-RJ-3. Same, ibid., Figure 48e.
g. US-RB-2. Same, ibid., Plate 11f.
h. UU-RB-1. Same, ibid., Figure 45a, b.

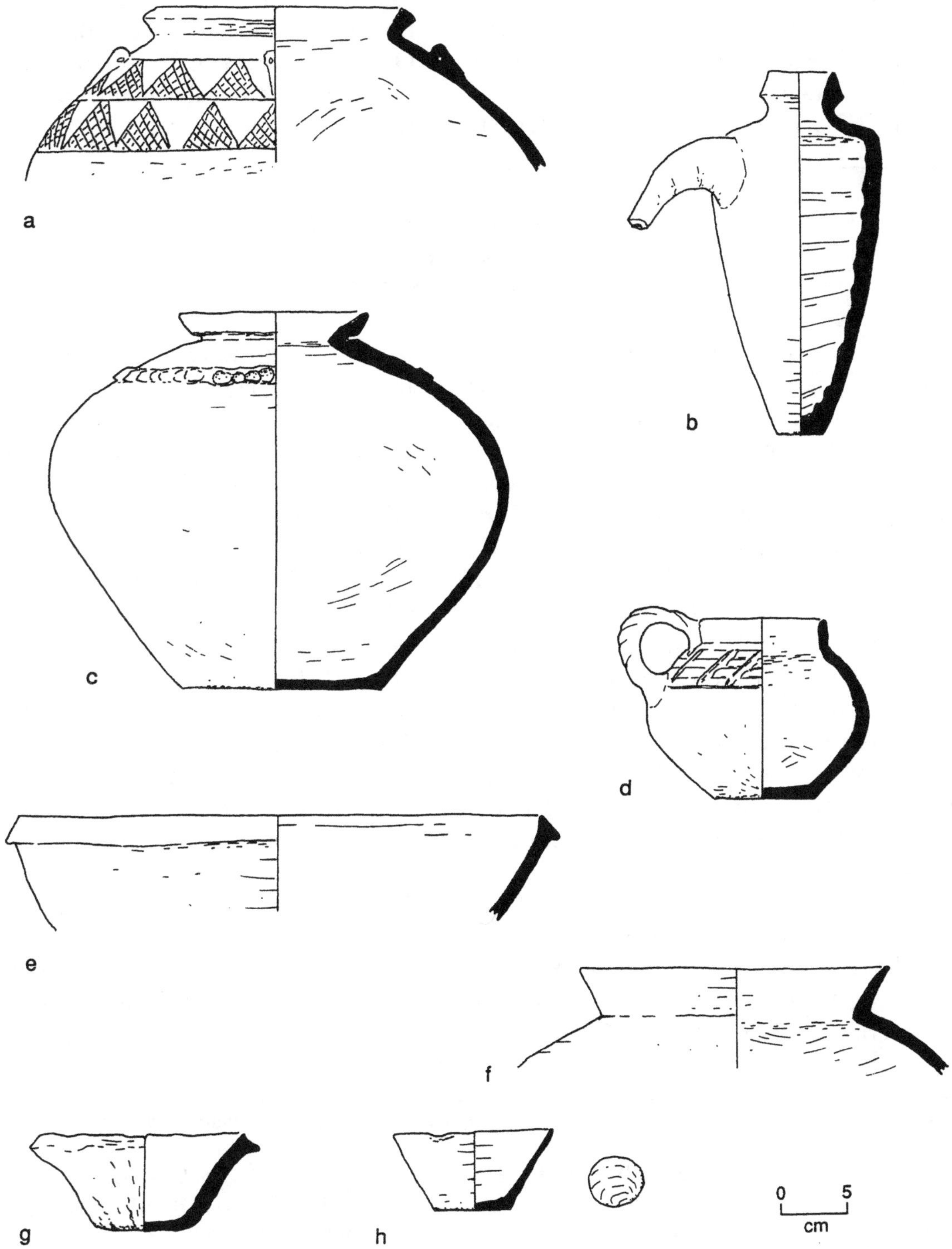

Figure III.8. Ceramic vessels of the Late Uruk Phase

d, IV.41 h; IV.19 m) and various kinds of twisted handles (UU-O-13, 14; Fig. III.8 d, IV.19 i-k). The four-lugged jars with incised shoulders now sometimes have triangles filled with cross-hatch incising (UU-O-6; Fig. III.8 a, IV.19 l). Low expanded band rim jars usually have very low necks, or none at all (UU-RJ-6; Fig. III.8 c, IV.19 f). Wheel-thrown bottles, with both ledge-rims (UU-RJ-10; Fig. IV.19 b) and band rims (UU-RJ-11; Fig. III.8 b, IV.41 f) become common. These bottles usually had markedly drooping spouts (UU-O-11; Fig. III.8 b, IV.19 c). With so many distinctive variants, the identification of Late Uruk sites is straightforward.

The Jemdet Nasr and Early Dynastic I–II Phases
(Figure III.9)

The transition from the Late Uruk phase to the Jemdet Nasr phase for the most part involves the loss of distinctive features. Even though a continuous stratigraphy is available from Farukhabad (Wright 1981:172–173), it is not easy to establish useful criteria for distinguishing Jemdet Nasr (termed "Early Jemdet Nasr" in the Farukhabad report) from Early Dynastic I–II ("Late Jemdet Nasr" in the Farukhabad report) surface assemblages. In the present discussion, we consider these two cultural phases together. During these periods, Uruk ware with sandy inclusions remains the predominate fabric. However, heavy cooking vessels are no longer made from a coarser Uruk ware, but are handbuilt from a clay with calcite inclusions and fired in a reducing atmosphere.

The characteristic surface assemblage of this time period has a preponderance of conical cup fragments. The rims of true conical cups (ED-RC-1; Figs. III.9 f, h; IV.42 e; IV.9 b; IV.33 c, d) and an incurved variant (ED-RC-2; Fig. III.9 g; IV.42 d) occur, but the roughly braced variant found in Jemdet Nasr layers at Farukhabad (Wright 1981: Fig. 63e) has not been noted in surface samples. The string-cut bases of conical cups include solid-footed (ED-BC-1; Figs. III.9 g; IV.42 b, c; IV.9 b; IV.33 b), narrow (ED-BC-2; Fig. III.9 f; IV.42 a), and wide (ED-BC-3; Figs. III.9 h; IV.9 a; IV.33 a) variants. Standardized round lip (ED-RB-1; Fig. IV.42 f), beveled lip (ED-RB-2; Figs. IV.9 d; IV.33 f, IV.42 h-k), and ledge-rim (ED-RB-3; Figs. IV.9 e; IV.33 g, h) bowls are relatively common. Jar rims occur in round lip forms (ED-RJ-1; Figs. IV.42 l; IV.9 f, g), and include a thinner high round lip variant (ED-RJ-2; Fig. IV.9 h), a flared neck, flattened lip form (ED-RJ-3; Fig. IV.9 i), a ledge-rim form (ED-RJ-4; Figs. III.9 b; IV.9 j-k; IV.42 n-o), and a band rim form (ED-RJ-5; Figs. IV.9 l, m; IV.42 p). Jar embellishments, largely produced as the jars were turned on a wheel, include the addition of plain (ED-O-1; Fig. IV.9 o) and hatched raised strips and the painting of a variety of monochrome motifs (ED-O-3; Fig.

Figure III.9 Ceramic vessels of the Jemdet Nasr and Early Dynastic phases [BC indicates "Base of Cup."]

a. ED-RJ-7, UU-O-6. DL-32 (Farukhabad). Wright 1981, Figure 65a, Plate 11a.
b. ED-RJ-4, ED-O-6, ED-B-3. Same, ibid., Figure 58g.
c. ED-RJ-2, ED-O-1. Same, ibid., Figure 49b.
d. Dentate stamped grayware jar. Same, ibid., Figure 63n, also DL-20 (Musiyan) Gautier and Lampre 1905 Figure 287.
e. ED-RJ-5, ED-O-6, ED-B-3. DL-32 (Farukhabad). Wright 1981, also DL-20 (Musiyan) Gautier and Lampre 1905, Plate VII.
f. ED-BC-2. DL-32 (Farukhabad) Wright 1981, Fig. 45e.
g. ED-BC-1. Same, ibid. Figure 45 f, also DL 20 (Musiyan) Gautier and Lampre 1905 Figure 287.
h. ED-BC-3. DL-32 (Farukhabad) Wright 1981, Figure 45i, j.

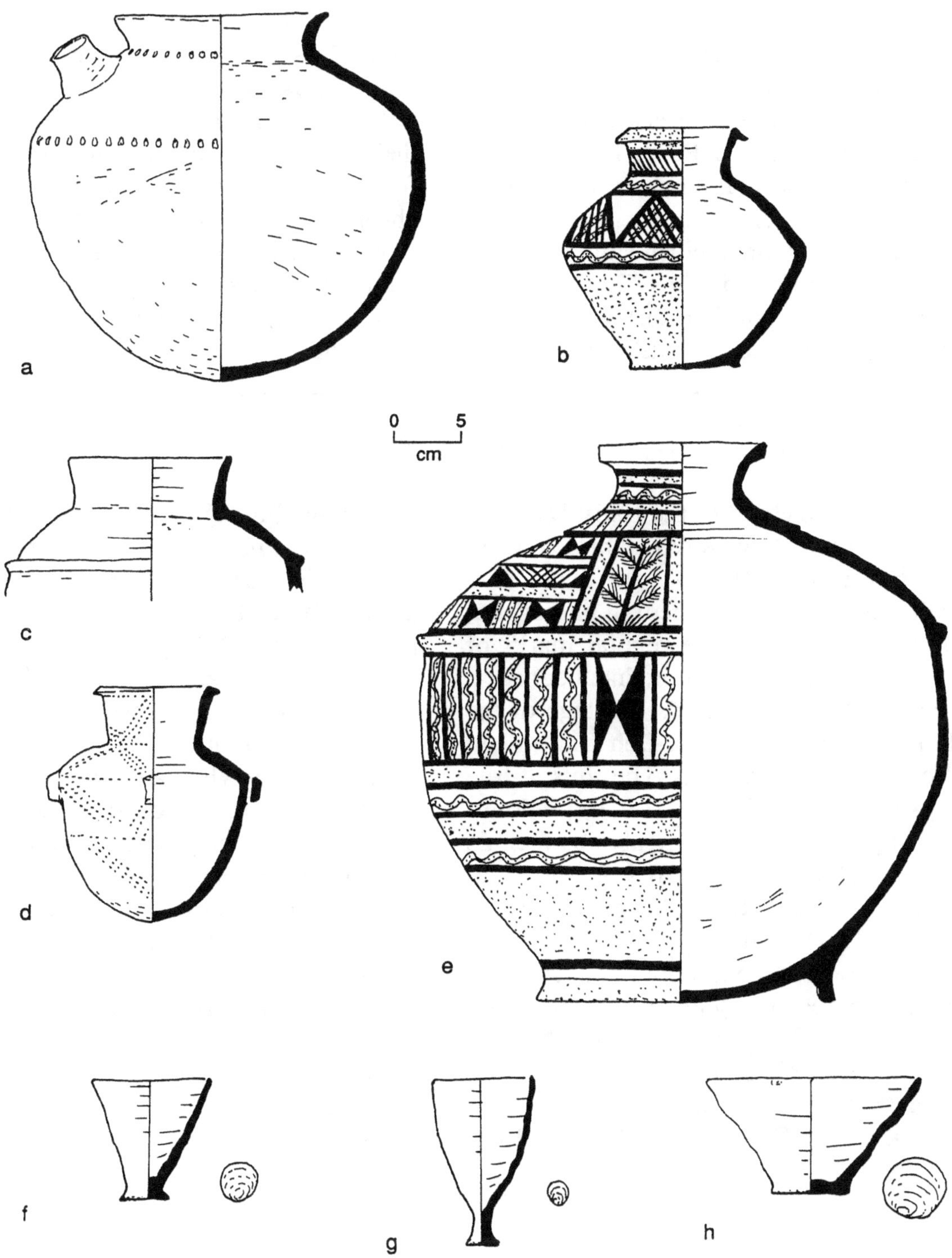

Figure III.9. Ceramic vessels of the Jemdet Nasr and Early Dynastic phases

IV.9 p), bichrome lines (ED-O-4), and various bichrome motifs (ED-O-5; Fig. IV.9 o). Jars and bowls may have flat bases (ED-B-2) or ring bases tooled on the wheel (ED-B-3; Fig. IV.9 s, t), including a high variant (ED-B-4; Fig. IV.9 v), and some jars have rough ring bases formed by pinching the soft clay of the base (ED-B-5; Fig. IV.9 u). The gray ware jars of these phases are uncommon in surface assemblages (ED-RJ-7; Figs. III.9 a; IV.9 n; IV.42 q). Also common are denticulate sickle blades (Fig. IV.9 r).

The excavated Jemdet Nasr samples from Farukhabad (those referred to as "Early Jemdet Nasr" in the original publication) were distinguished by the presence of diminishing quantities of later Uruk decorated variants and beveled rim bowls. Such characteristics, however, are difficult to distinguish if sherds of a preceding Uruk occupation are also present on a site. The earliest painted polychrome motifs, bold cross-hatch triangles in simple arrays (Figure III.9 b), could be a criterion as they are restricted to the end of the Late Uruk period and the Jemdet Nasr period, but their paint is fugitive, and no examples have been found in surface samples. In contrast, the polychrome motifs of the Early Dynastic I period (termed "Late Jemdet Nasr" in the Farukhabad publication) are often preserved on the surface (Fig. III.9 e) and allow a more precise dating of some sites.

The Early Dynastic III Phase

Ceramics from the end of the Early Dynastic period, known from excavated samples from Farukhabad (Wright 1981:173), are made of a fabric similar to that of the preceding phases, but the sherds are heavier and the regular marks of fast wheel throwing are much more in evidence.

The characteristic surface assemblage of the later Early Dynastic phase on the Deh Luran Plain has many conical cup fragments. The rims of true conical cups (ED-RC-1; Fig. IV.33 c, d) predominate. The string-cut bases of conical cups include mostly wide (ED-BC-3; Fig. III.9 h; IV.33 a) variants. Round lip (ED-RB-1), beveled lip (ED-RB-2; Fig. IV.33 f), and ledge-rim (ED-RB-3; Fig. IV.33 g, h) bowls remain common. A small carinated bowl or pot is added to the repertoire (ED-RB-4; Fig. IV.33 q, r). Jar rims occur in round lip forms (ED-RJ-1; Fig. IV.33 i), including both heavier (ED-RJ-1) and thinner, higher variants (ED-RJ-2; Fig. III.9 c), a ledge-rim form (ED-RJ-4; Fig. IV.33 o, p), and band rim forms (ED-RJ-5; Fig. IV.33 l, m). Jar embellishments include the addition of heavy raised strips, either plain (ED-O-1; Fig. III.9 c) or obliquely impressed (ED-O-2; Figs. IV.9 q; IV.33 e, p). A new small carinated jar or goblet form (ED-RJ-6; Fig. IV.33 s) was often painted in a variety of monochrome motifs (ED-O-3, 4, 5; Fig. IV.33 t, u). Jars and bowls may have flat bases (ED-B-2) or ring bases tooled on the wheel (ED-B-3; Fig. IV.9 s, t), including the high variant (ED-B-4; Fig. IV.9 v) noted before. The handmade gray ware jars of these phases, sometimes with crushed fresh-water shell inclusions, are uncommon in surface assemblages (ED-RJ-7; Figs. IV.42 q; IV.9 n). A wheel-thrown grayware with dentate impressions (Fig. III.9 d) apparently begins in this period. Denticulate sickle blades are still common on these sites.

Chapter IV

The Archaeological Sites and Their Interpretation

This chapter presents the recorded details of each site which produced artifacts dated earlier than 2300 B.C., the end of the Early Dynastic Period.

The text and maps provide evidence recorded in our notebooks, while the illustrations and tables give details not covered in the text or maps. The dating of the sites is based upon our present chronological understandings and utilizes the artifact samples conserved in collections at the Texas Archaeological Research Laboratory in Austin and Yale University in New Haven. Ceramics illustrated by Gautier and Lampre (1905) in their still useful report on the project of the Délégation en Perse in the Spring of 1903, and by Pierre de Miroschedji (1981) in his exemplary report regarding a survey under the auspices of the Délégation Archéologique Française en Iran in 1977 were also useful. There are many additional questions about these sites which we could answer if it had been possible for us to return to the Deh Luran Plain or to study additional collections in France and Iran. Unfortunately, only limited travel has been possible.

The following is a catalogue listing *only* the early sites having components dating prior to 2300 B.C. recorded on the Deh Luran Plain. The sites are presented in numerical order.

1a. **Number**: DL-7 (DL-53X)
1b. **Name**: Tepe Gendarmary (Police Mound)
2. **Grid**: 1711.0–1189.6
3. **Dimensions**:

Length:	42 m (NE-SW)
Width:	32 m (NW-SE)
Height:	1.75 m
Circumference:	175 m
Area:	0.24 ha

4. **Modern Environmental Context**: On a terrace northwest of the Ab-i Garm stream on the northern alluvial slopes of the plain, not far from the rich irrigated fields of the modern village of Deh Luran.

5. **Features**: This small site is composed of a single irregularly rectangular mound (Fig. IV.1). At least three relatively large multi-roomed structures are evident, apparently dating to the Uruk Period occupation of this site. These three structures and a possible fourth early construction have been disturbed through the relatively recent use of the site for what appears to be an early 20th century Gendarme post (now in ruins) and a small mid-20th century mud-brick structure, apparently abandoned and poorly preserved.

At the northeast end of the mound, the stone foundation or "footing" of a four-room structure is evident. It consists of a 17 m long by 3 m wide room block oriented NW-SE and divided into at least three rooms of unequal size. Extending from the northeast wall of this roomblock is the footing of a fourth large room measuring 4.5 m by 9.5 m. The stone exterior wall footings of the long, rectangular roomblock, as well as the wall footings of

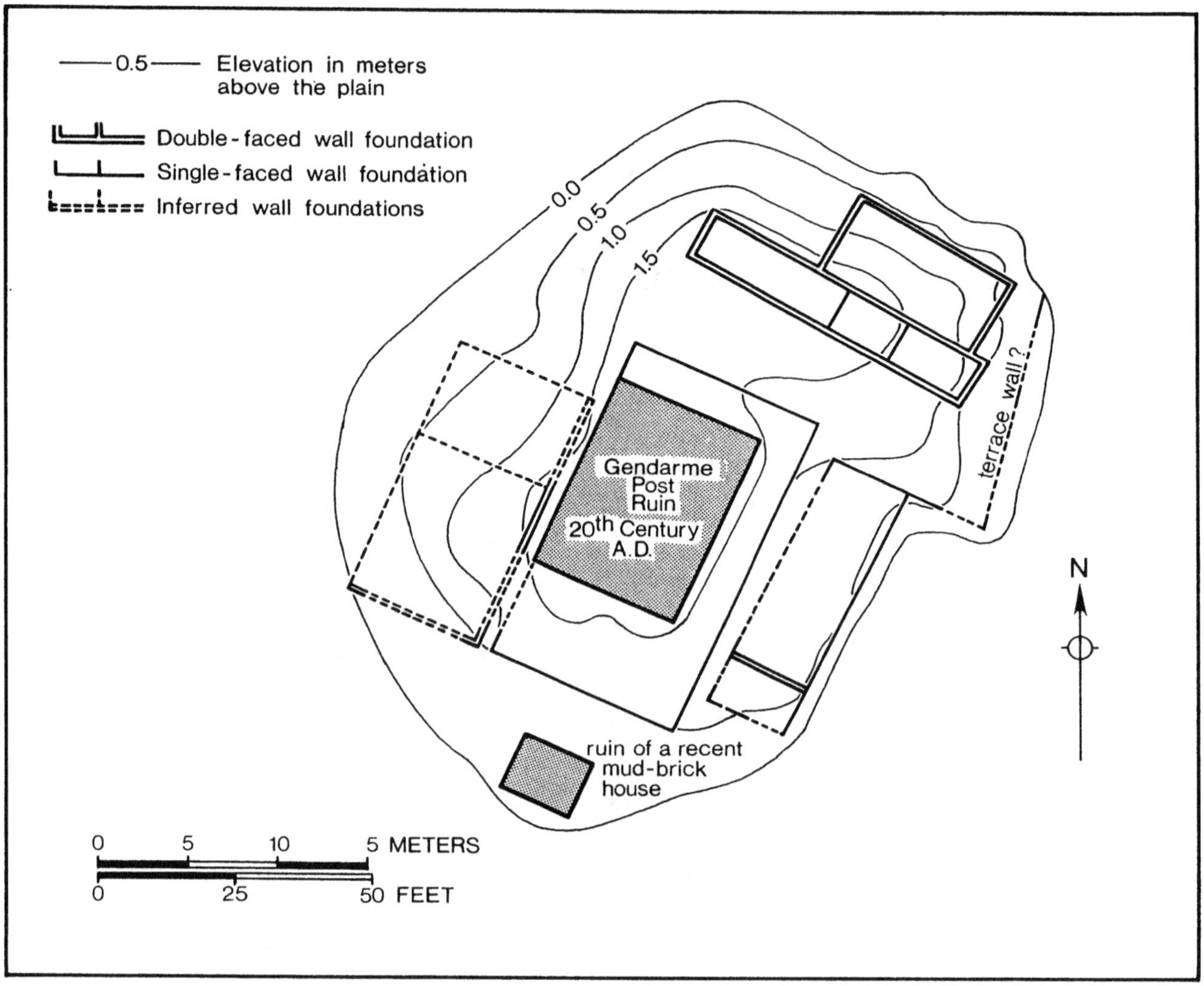

Figure IV.1. Map of Tepe Gendarmary (DL-7)

the large room added to its northeast side, are all of a pebble, cobble, and clay core construction with both the interior and exterior surfaces faced with larger stones. The two walls forming the three rooms within the long, rectangular structure are made of a single course of large stones.

A second long, rectangular structure oriented NE-SW, about 4.5 m by 16 m, was found near and generally paralleling the southeastern edge of the mound. The exterior wall footings of this structure consist of a single course of large stones. A single interior, room-divider wall was observed near the southwestern end of this structure. This was a narrow double-faced wall with a pebble and clay core. The northeastern wall of the long, rectangular structure extended farther to the southeast, and then made a sharp, acute-angle turn to extend northward. This single-course stone wall may have functioned as a terrace or retaining wall.

The third structure is not very clearly defined. It nearly parallels the long, rectangular structure just described, but it is located on the mound near its northwestern edge. It too is rectangular, about 7.5 m wide by 16 m long, but appears to be constructed using both single coursed and double-faced stone wall footings. A ridge, possibly representing a mud-brick or packed mud interior wall, apparently divides this structure into two large rooms.

The possible fourth structure underlies the ruined Gendarme post. The rectangular outline of this large structure, roughly 11 m by 19.75 m and oriented NE-SW, is indistinctly visible as a ridge. This may be an Uruk Period structure with mud-brick or packed mud walls, or it might be a badly decomposed compound wall dating to the period of the Gendarme post.

An old canal (DL-276A) that passes some 35 m east of this site also passes close to Chagha Sefid (DL-23) and one of its branches passes close to Chakali (DL-19). As all three sites have both Uruk and Sasanian/Early Islamic occupations, it seems likely the canal may date to one of these periods. Very few lithic artifacts were in evidence. Ceramics were in moderately great numbers, with the a majority dating to the Uruk Period scattered over the entire site. A very few sherds that appear to be Sasanian/Early Islamic were found on the northern half of the site.

6. **Phases**: The presence of Sargarab ware and absence of Uruk ware indicate an occupation during the Early Uruk phase. The occurrence of both open forms (US-RB-6) and incurved examples among the bowl rims (US-RB-9, 10) suggest occupation throughout the period of time covered by this phase, but the sample is small and lacks the chronologically useful impressed strips and other variants.

7. **Comment**: The footings resemble an Early Uruk house footing excavated at Farukhabad (Wright 1981:78, Fig. 36 a) in both construction and magnitude. Setting aside the fourth footing, which may be later, the three better preserved footings at DL-7 indicate an enclosed area of about 280 square meters. By comparison with recent houses of similar construction (Kramer 1980), as well as with worldwide samples of houses (LeBlanc 1971, Naroll 1962), the three architectural units would have housed about 28 people, with a density, if these were the only three contemporary houses belonging to this Early Uruk hamlet, of about 115 people per hectare. The map (Fig. IV.1) was drawn by Neely and Pierre de Miroschedji.

1a. **Number**: DL-11 (DL-10X)
1b. **Name**: Tepe Garmasi
2. **Grid**: 1705.3–1189.0
3. **Dimensions**:

Length:	210 m (NE-SW)
Width:	160 m (E-W)
Height:	2.0 m
Circumference:	544 m
Area:	2.35 ha

4. **Modern Environmental Context**: At the juncture of the northern alluvial slopes of the plain and the alluvial fan of the Mehmeh River, about two kilometers northeast of the present Mehmeh channel.

5. **Features**: The site is situated on a triangular terrace remnant located at the juncture of two intermittent drainages that form the terrace's southern boundary (Fig. IV.2). The site was comprised of three features that nearly covered the surface of the terrace.

First, along the southeast edge of the site paralleling the edge of the terrace and the stream channel were a series of cobble concentrations. These formed a single row of at least five distinctly separate, low (averaging about 0.1 m in height) piles of rock averaging about 0.5 m in diameter. No artifacts were found in association. The use of these concentrations of cobbles is not known, although they may have been used as buttresses for a brush-and-earth or packed-mud terrace wall. Or they could be quite recent features constructed by transhumant pastoralists to keep their belongings off of the ground.

Second, along the southwest edge of the terrace was a linear arrangement of what appeared to be house foundations of unmodified cobble and boulder-size stones. Portions of at least three distinct wall footings or foundations were seen being exposed by erosion. However, not enough of these foundations was exposed to determine the shape and dimensions of the structures represented. They appear to have been constructed generally to parallel the terrace edge and the stream channel. A few non-diagnostic sherds and flaked lithic fragments were associated.

Third, north of the cobble concentrations and the house foundations was an irregularly rectangular, slightly raised (about 0.30 m in height) area (perhaps a platform) that was about 140 m in diameter and 445 m in circumference. This raised area was characterized by a heavier concentration of sherds and lithics and supported a moderate-sized, centrally located, roughly circular, dome-shaped mound that was about 60 m in diameter, 200 m in circumference, and 2.0 m in height. Also atop the raised area, and generally surrounding the dome-shaped mound, were five smaller mounds. These smaller mounds averaged about 10 meters in diameter and 0.50 meters in height. There was an especially heavy concentration of ceramics and chipped stone artifacts and debitage covering the main mound of this site. This heavy artifact concentration may have been, at least in part, the result of eight small recent pits, approximately 1.0 m in diameter and 0.5 m deep, excavated into exposed walls made of very large, unmodified boulders of a white, chalky gypsum or limestone. Many sherds and chipped stone tool fragments were seen in the walls of these pits. The especially heavy concentration of chipped stone implements and chipping debris suggests that the site was a lithic tool production center.

The remnants of what appears to have been a dam were found extending into both sides of the stream channel bordering the east side of the terrace on which the site is located. These masonry remnants consisted of a double-faced wall made of cobbles and boulders, with a rubble core between the facing stones. The walls were about 1.0 m in width/thickness, but the height and length of the walls could not be determined. No mortar was visible. Just above this dam, a remnant of what may have been an ancient canal joins the wadi from the east.

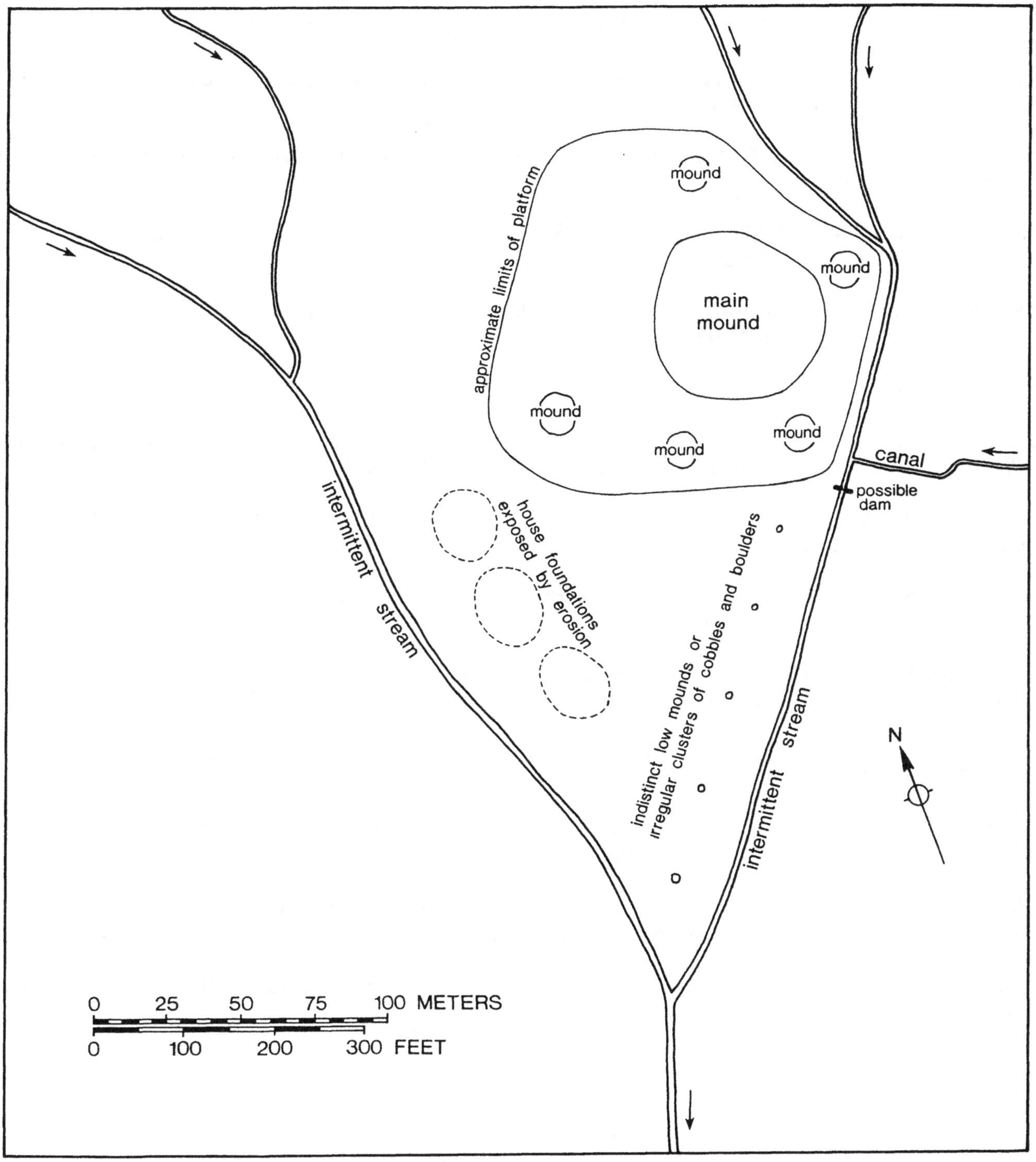

Figure IV.2. Map of Garmasi (DL-11)

Figure IV.3. Early Uruk bowl parts from Garmasi (DL-11)

a. Fine Bowl (US-RB-3) (53) Vegetal and calcite inclusions, Body orange (5Y 7/7), Diam 17 cm, Surface pale orange-yellow (10YR 8/3) (cf. Wright 1981: Fig. 40e).

b. Same (26) Vegetal inclusions, Body light brown (5YR 6/6), Diam ca. 14 cm, Surface yellowish gray (10YR 8/2) (cf. Wright 1981: Fig. 43b-c).

c. Round Lip Bowl (US-RB-4) (52) Vegetal and calcite inclusions, Body light brown (5YR 6/6), Diam 28 cm, Surface pale orange-yellow (10YR 8/3) (cf. same).

d. Open Beaded Rim Bowl (US-RB-6) (41) Vegetal and calcite inclusions, Body yellowish white (7.5Y 9/2), Diam ca. 39 cm, Surface yellowish gray (2.5Y 8/3) (cf. Wright 1981: Fig. 41g, l).

e. Same (31) Same inclusions, Body yellowish pink (5YR 7/4), Diam ca. 36 cm, Surface eroded (cf. same).

f. Incurved Beaded Rim Bowl with Impressed Strip (US-RB-12) (1) Vegetal and calcite inclusions, Body yellowish gray (5Y 8/2), Diam ca. 50 cm, Surface yellowish white (7.5Y 9/2) (cf. Wright 1981: Fig. 41c, k).

g. Incurved Beaded Rim Bowl (US-RB-10) (45) Same inclusions, Body yellowish gray (2.5Y 7/2), Diam 26 cm, Surface yellowish gray (5Y 8/2). (cf. 41 l, m).

h. Beaded Rim Bowl (US-RB-6) (47) Vegetal and calcite inclusions, Body yellowish gray (7.5Y 8/2), Diam ?, Surface eroded (cf. Wright 1981: Fig. 41b, m).

i. Heavy Open Beaded Rim Bowl (US-RB-8) with Impressed Strip (Type ??) (35) Vegetal and calcite inclusions, Body yellowish gray (7.5Y 7/2), Diam ca. 46 cm, Surface eroded.

j. Heavy Incurved Beaded Rim Basin (US-RB-13) (40) Vegetal inclusions, Body yellowish green (10Y 8/2), Diam ca. 55 cm, Surface grayish yellow (5Y 8/3).

k. Carinated Bowl with Flattened Lip (UU-RB-5) Fine sand inclusions, Body yellowish gray (7.5Y 8/2), Diam 26 cm, Surface grayish yellow (5Y 8/3) (cf. Wright 1981: Fig. 47 a, r).

l. Flattened Lip Bowl with Impressed Strip (UU-RB-3). Fine sand and vegetal inclusions, Body pale orange- yellow (10YR 8/4), Diam ca. 24 cm, Surface pale orange-yellow(10YR 8/2) (cf. Wright 1981: Fig. 41 o-p).

m. Strainer (US-O-6) (8) Calcite and vegetal inclusions, Body light yellowish brown (10YR 7/4), Diam ca. 21 cm, Surface grayish yellow (5Y 8/3).

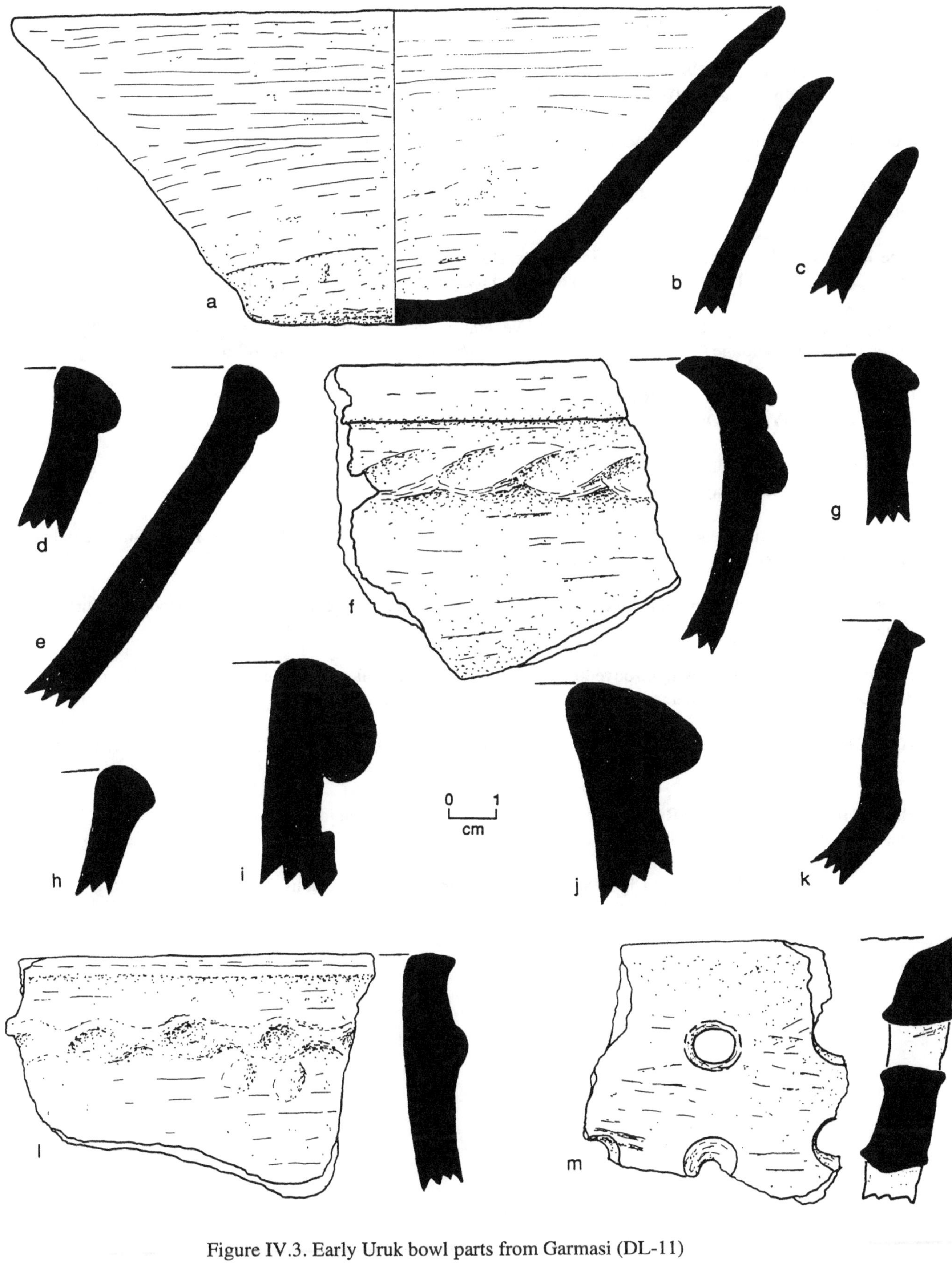

Figure IV.3. Early Uruk bowl parts from Garmasi (DL-11)

Figure IV.4. Early Uruk jar parts from Garmasi (DL-11)

a. Neckless Ledge Rim Jar (US-R J-2) (1) Coarse crushed calcite inclusions, Body brownish gray (7.5YR 3/1), Diam 22 cm, Surface yellowish gray (10YR 7/2) (cf. Johnson 1973: Pl. III 1).

b. Same (3) Coarse crushed calcite inclusions, Body orange (2.5YR 6/8), Diam 24 cm, Surface eroded (cf. same).

c. Same (2) Coarse crushed calcite inclusions, Body brown (5YR 3/4), Diam 16 cm, Surface yellowish gray (5Y 8/2) (cf. same).

d. Fine Jar (US-RJ-1) Vegetal and calcite inclusions, Body yellowish gray (5Y 8/2), Diam 14 cm, Surface yellowish gray (5Y 8/2) (cf. Wright 1981: Fig. 43a-c). Note vertical use scratches at point of maximum diam.

e. Heavy Thickened Round Lip Jar (5) Calcite and vegetal inclusions, Body brownish orange (2.5YR 5/8), Diam 20 cm, Surface brownish orange (2.5YR 5/8), Red slip (7.5R 4/5) (cf. Wright 1981: Fig. 42 b, c, e).

f. Flared Expanded Neck Jar with Round Lip (US-RJ-6) and Black-on-red Paint (US-O-3) Vegetal inclusions, Body yellowish gray (7.5Y 8/1), Diam 20 cm, Red slip (7.5R 4/5) (cf. Wright 1981: Fig. 40a, 44b-j, especially h, i).

g. Flared Expanded Neck Jar with Grooved Lip (US-RJ-9) (36) Vegetal and calcite inclusions, Body pale yellow (5Y 8/3), Diam 19 cm, Surface grayish yellow (2.5Y 7/4) (cf. same, especially 44e).

h. Same (20) Calcite and vegetal inclusions, Body light reddish brown (2.5YR 6/5), Diam 19 cm, Surface pale orange-yellow (10YR 8/4), Red slip (10R 4/6) (cf. same, especially Fig. 44h, i).

i. Flared Expanded Neck Jar with Round Lip (US-RJ-6) (37) Vegetal and calcite inclusions, Body and surface yellowish white (7.5Y 9/2), Diam 30 cm, Red slip (7.5R 4/6) (cf. same, especially Fig. 44f, g).

j. Flared Expanded Neck Jar with Grooved Lip (US-RJ-9) (32) Vegetal and calcite inclusions, Body yellowish gray (5Y 8/2), Diam 22 cm, Surface pale yellow (5Y 8/3) (cf. same, especially Fig. 44b).

k. High Expanded Band Rim Jar (US-RJ-10) (46) Vegetal and calcite inclusions, Body light olive gray (5Y 5/2), Diam ca. 27 cm, Surface yellowish gray (5Y 7/2), Overfired vessel (cf. Wright 1981: Fig. 44a).

l. Heavy High Expanded Band Rim Jar (cf. US-RJ-8) Vegetal and calcite inclusions, Body pale yellow (5Y 8/3), Diam 30 cm, Surface pale yellow (5Y 8/3).

m. Straight Neck Jar with Flattened Lip (US-RJ-5) Vegetal and calcite inclusions, Body pale yellow (5Y 8/3), Diam 25 cm, Surface yellowish gray (2.5Y 8/2).

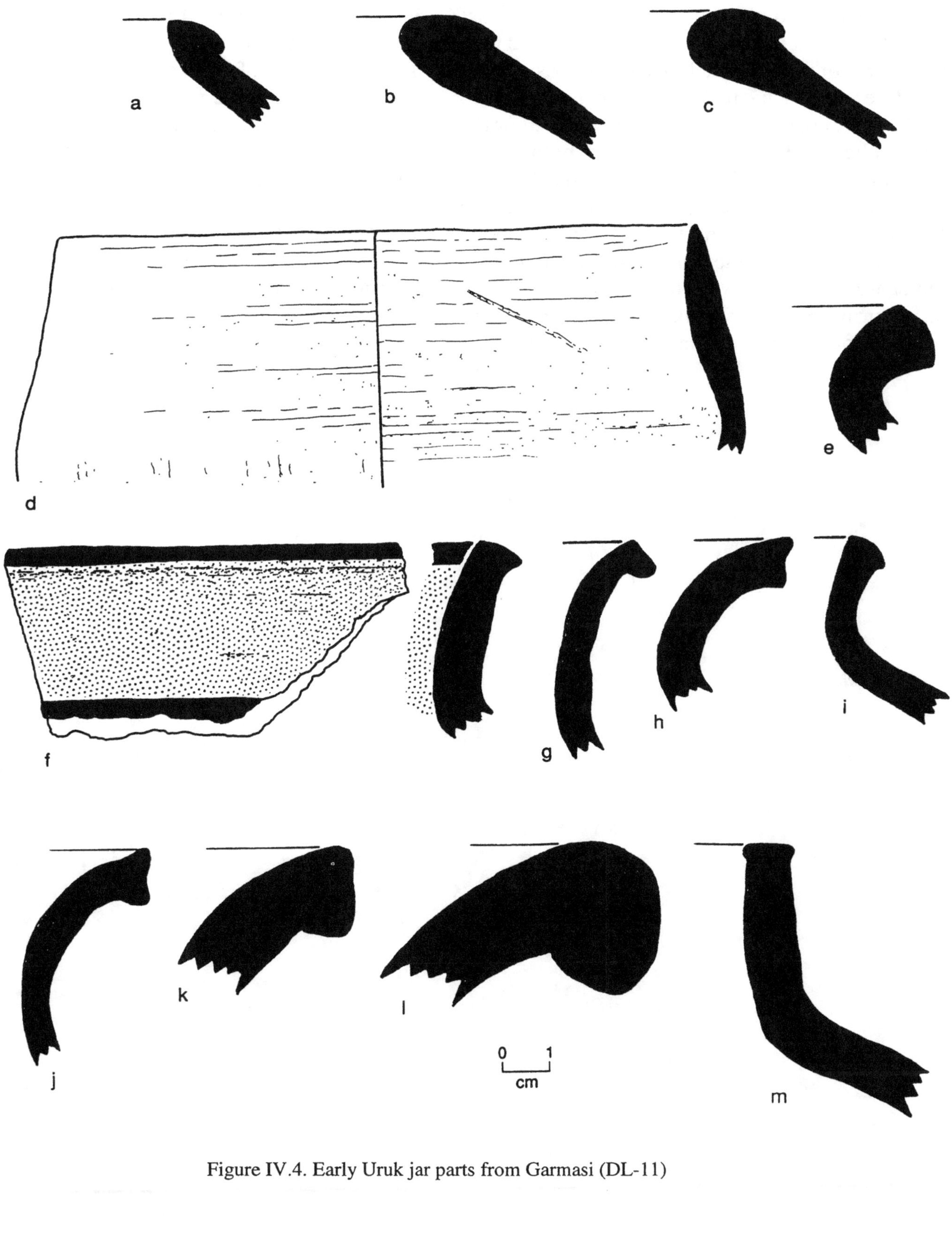

Figure IV.4. Early Uruk jar parts from Garmasi (DL-11)

6. **Phases**: Among the Susiana ceramics, there is a carinated bowl variant with interior cross-hatch (ES-RB-11) characteristic of the Khazineh phase and other carinated bowls and basins that could be either Khazineh or Mehmeh (ES-RB-2, 12, 18), but none diagnostic of the Mehmeh or the Bayat phases. There are, however, both bowls with dot motifs and hatched diamonds (LS-RB-10, 13) and a banded jar neck fragment (LS-RJ-3) diagnostic of the Farukh phase. Among the post-Susiana ceramics, predominance of Sargarab ware and scarcity of Uruk ware indicate an occupation early during the Early Uruk phase. The predominance of open forms among the bowl rims (US-RB-6; Fig. IV.3 d, e, h, i) and neckless ledge-rim jars (US-RJ-2; Fig. IV.4 a-c) suggests occupation relatively early in the time covered by this phase. The occurrence of beveled rim bowls (ST-RB-2) and a few Uruk ware vessels (e.g. UU-RB-5; Fig. IV.3 k) could indicate exchange with communities elsewhere or use of the site later in the period and perhaps even into Middle Uruk times.

7. **Comment**: We assign the 0.28 ha area of the dome-shaped mound to the Khazineh phase, and the full 1.54 ha area of the possible platform to the Farukh and Early Uruk phases.

1a. **Number**: DL-14 (DL-13X)
1b. **Name**:
2. **Grid**: 1704.0–1188.4
3. **Dimensions**:
Diameter: Mound 58 m; Site: 121 m
Height: 1.0 m
Circumference: Mound 183 m; Site: 380 m
Area: Mound: 0.27 ha; Site: 1.15 ha

4. **Modern Environmental Context**: On the alluvial fan of the Mehmeh River, about half a kilometer northeast of the present channel.

5. **Features**: DL-14 is situated atop an extensive natural terrace paralleling an intermittent stream bed. The primary feature of the site is a moderately large, low, roughly circular mound. In addition, the remnants of about ten boulder and cobble foundations were found eroding out of the foot of the mound and the surface of the alluvium surrounding the mound. These foundations were exposed enough to discern the definite rock alignments, but not to determine the size and shape of the structures. A moderate number of sherds were found on the alluvial plain's surface surrounding the mound as well as on the mound itself. The total size of the site, as defined by the foundations and the artifact scatter, was about 380 meters in circumference. In addition to the sherds, a small number of chipped stone tools, as well as a few perforated stones, either door pivot sockets (Hole, Flannery and Neely 1969:196–198) or loomweights (Wright 1981:49, 147–149, Plate 13), and saddle-shaped grinding slabs (Hole, Flannery and Neely 1969:171, Figs. 71–73; Wright 1981:141–146) comprised the artifacts on the surface. To the east of the intermittent stream bed that runs past the site are numerous agricultural terraces of stone cobbles and boulders. It is likely that these terraces date to the later, probably Sasanian, reoccupation of DL-14.

6. **Phases**: The collection from this small site is large, but weathered. Nonetheless, it can be confidently ascribed to a phase. There are a large number of Khazineh Red sherds including jar (ES-SJ-1; Fig. IV.5 a) and basin (Fig. IV.5 b) rims. Fragments of hemispherical bowls with bands (ES-RB-1), exterior chevrons (ES-RB-2), diamonds (ES-RB-4), full painting (ES-RB-9), and vertical lines (cf. Hole, Flannery and Neely 1969: Fig. 55 a), all of which are Khazineh phase or later, are present. In addition, there are four fragments of carinated bowls, one with interior crosshatch (ES-RB-11; Fig. IV.5 d) and one with wavy elements (ES-RB-13), both characteristically Khazineh, as well as five with fully painted interiors (ES-RB-12; Fig. IV.5 c), either Late Khazineh or Mehmeh, and two nondescript basal sherds (ES-BB-4). A fully painted jar neck fragment (cf. LS-RJ-1), a jar shoulder with bands (ES-SJ-3), and a plain basin rim (ES-RB-16), all of which have long time spans, were also found. An unusual bowl (Fig. IV.5 b) cannot be dated. Diagnostic motifs of the Mehmeh phase, and later very fine clay bodies and motifs, are absent. The most conservative interpretation is that this mound was occupied during the Khazineh phase.

7. **Comment**: We assign the full 1.15 ha area of the debris scatter to the Khazineh phase.

Figure IV.5. Khazineh ceramics from DL-14

a. Khazineh Red Jar Rim. (ES-SJ-1) Medium Sand Inclusions, Body pink (5YR 7/4), Diam 27 cm, Reddish yellow slip (5YR 7/5) (Hole, Flannery and Neely 1969: Fig 46 a-b).

b. Khazineh Red Basin Rim, Coarse Vegetal Inclusions, Body pink (5YR 7/4), Diam warped, Trace of red slip, (cf. Hole, Flannery and Neely 1969: Fig 45 o).

c. Hemispherical Bowl with Exterior Zig-Zag, Interior Wavy Elements. Trace of Fine Sand Body white (2.5Y 8/2), Diam 15 cm, Paint dark gray (10YR 4/1) (cf. Hole, Flannery and Neely 1969: Fig 52).

d. Carinated Bowl Rim with Variant of Fully Painted Interior (ES-RB-12) Trace of Fine Sand, Body white (2.5Y 8/2), Diam ca. 34 cm, Paint dark gray (10YR 4/1) (Hole, Flannery and Neely 1969: Fig 57 n).

e. Carinated Bowl Sherd with Interior Cross-hatch (ES-RB-11) Trace of Fine Sand, Body very pale brown (10YR 8/3), Diam ?, Paint dark gray (10YR 4/1). (Hole, Flannery and Neely 1969: Fig 56 d, e).

f. Bowl Sherd with Exterior Diamond Motif? Trace of Fine Sand, Body very pale brown (10YR 8/3), Diam ?, Paint Gray (N5).

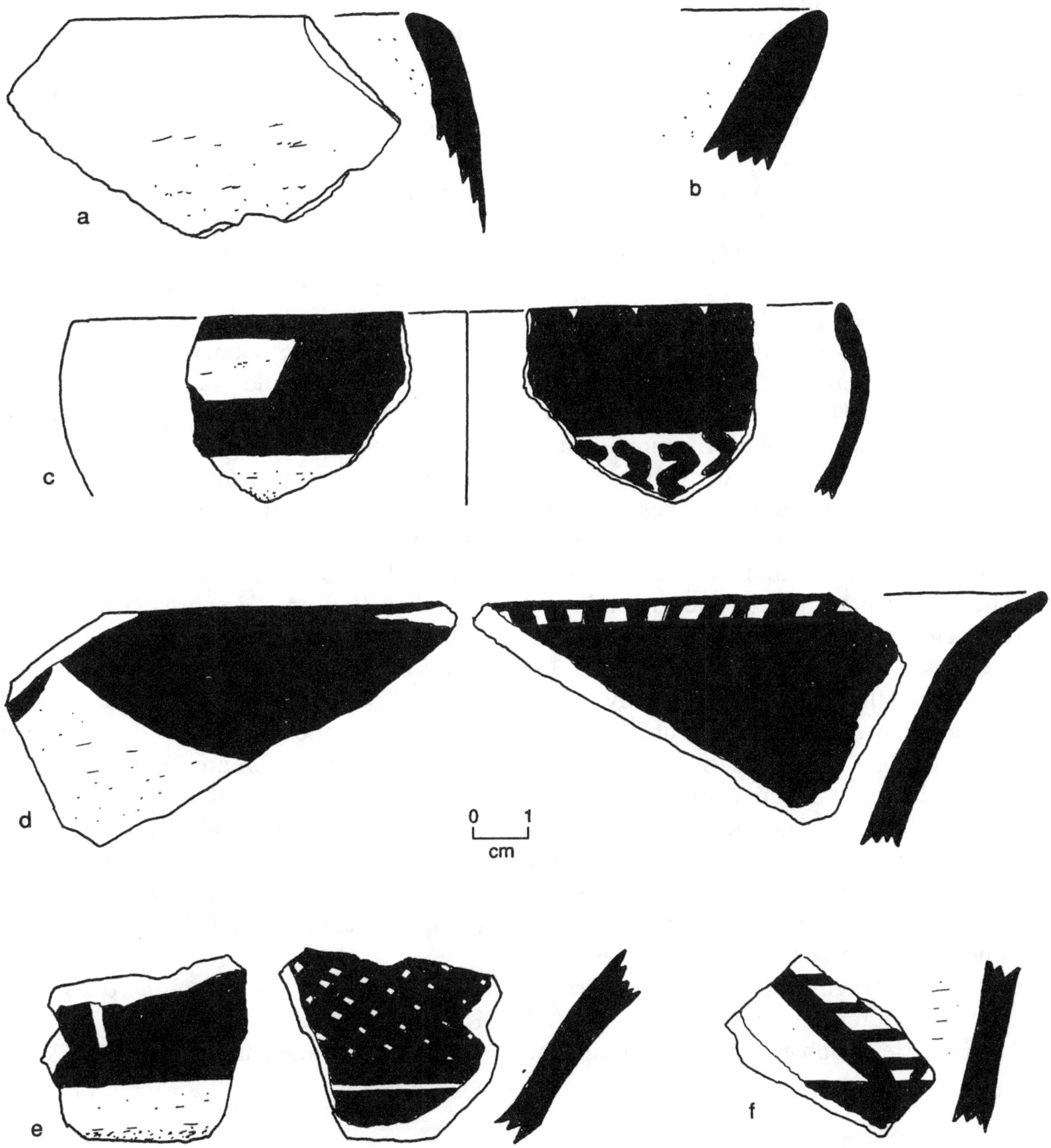

Figure IV.5. Khazineh ceramics from DL-14

1a. **Number**: DL-15 (DL-5X)
(DL-30 of the 1961 survey)
1b. **Name**:
2. **Grid**: 1704.6–1186.6
3. **Dimensions**:

Length:	80 m (N-S)
Width:	65 m (E-W)
Height:	3.0 m
Circumference:	290 m
Area:	0.67 ha

4. **Modern Environmental Context:** On the alluvial fan of the Mehmeh River, a few hundred meters northeast of the present Mehmeh channel.

5. **Features**: The elliptically shaped platform mound located at the northwest corner of this large site (Fig. IV.6) represents the earliest evidence of occupation. The dimensions given above pertain specifically to this platform mound. It is characterized by three fairly distinct lobes or smaller mounds atop its summit. These smaller mounds are generally circular in form, range from about 12 to 20 meters in diameter, and vary in height. The northeastern-most lobe or mound rises about 1.5 meters above the general level of the platform, and is the highest point on the site at 3.0 meters above the alluvial plain. The southwestern mound is slightly lower, rising to about 2.7 meters above the plain. The northwestern mound is the lowest, being about 2.2 meters above the plain. A much smaller elliptical mound lies 32 meters south of the large platform mound. This small mound measures 20 meters (NW-SE) by 8 meters (NE-SW) and is 0.60 meters in maximum height. This mound is bordered on the west and south by a terrace wall, averaging about 0.20 meters in height and 0.40 meters in width, constructed of dry-laid unmodified cobbles and small boulders. Both early and late (i.e. Sasanian or Early Islamic) ceramics were found on and around this small mound. It is not possible to determine without excavation whether this portion of the site was actually occupied in both periods, or whether early sherds were transported by later peoples with construction fill taken from the platform mound. No stone or clay wall footings or other architectural features were visible at this site. The vast majority of this site, not discussed here, evidently dates to the Sasanian or Early Islamic Period. The late portions of this site and the adjacent site (DL-251) lie to the south and east of the early tri-lobed platform mound described above. See Chapter VI for a discussion of the canals associated with this site.

6. **Phases**: The second lobe of DL-15 has a carinated bowl side fragment with the interior painted wavy elements, typical of the Khazineh phase (ES-RB-13; Fig. IV.7 b). However, important in the ceramics from all parts of the site are those of the Mehmeh phase, with hemispherical bowl fragments with right triangle motifs (ES-RB-6), ladder motifs (ES-RB-5; Fig. IV.7 e), and Mehmeh Red-on-red sherds (ES-SJ-2) being diagnostic. Solidly painted jar necks (LS-RJ-1) and fine bowls with Horizontal Chevron motifs (LS-RB-7; Fig. IV.7 d) suggest a Bayat occupation, but none of the diagnostic Bayat variants were noted. Also common are Farukh phase ceramics, including jar necks with painted bands (LS-RJ-2) as well as bowl rims with vertical line motifs (LS-RB-8; Fig. IV.7 i), dot motifs (LS-RB-10), diamonds with oblique lines (LS-RB-13; Fig. IV.7 f, j), and sigma motifs (LS-RB-14; Fig. IV.7 j).

7. **Comment**: We assign 0.25 ha to the Khazineh phase and the full 0.67 ha area of the site to the Mehmeh and Farukh phases.

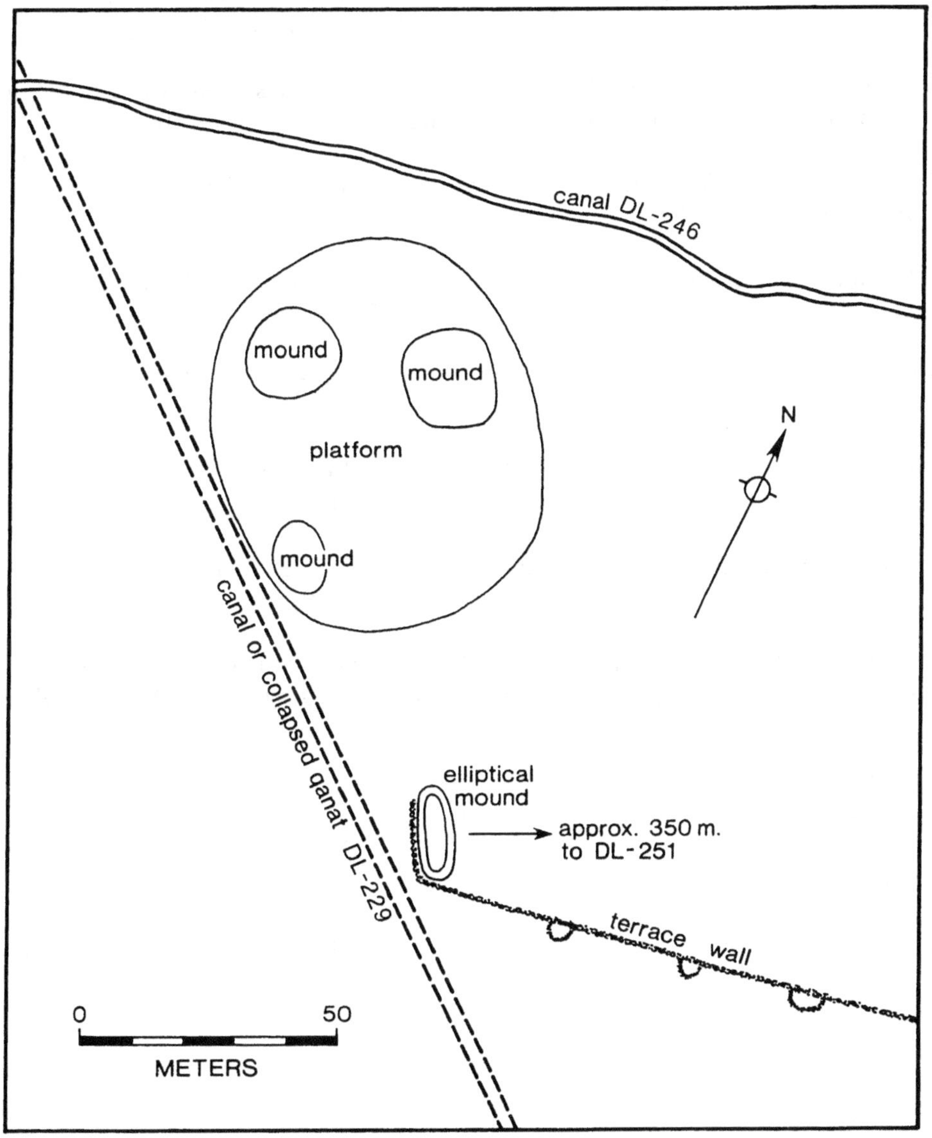

Figure IV.6. Map of DL-15

Figure IV.7. Mehmeh and Farukh ceramics from DL-15

a. Khazineh Red Jar Rim (ES-SJ-1) Vegetal and calcite inclusions, Body reddish yellow (5YR 7/5), Diam ?, Surface light red (2.5YR 6/6) (Hole Flannery and Neely 1969: Fig. 45 a-d, Wright 1981: Fig 10 f, g).

b. Bowl Sherd with Interior Wavy Elements (cf. ES-RB-13) Trace fine sand, Body pale yellow (2.5YR 7/4), Diam ?, Paint very dark gray (2.5Y 3/1), (Hole Flannery and Neely 1969: Fig. 56 g, 57 i, j).

c. Carinated Bowl Sherd with Fully Painted Interior (cf. ES-RB-12) Fine sand inclusions, Body pale yellow (10YR 7/2), Diam ?, Paint very dark gray (2.5YR 3/1), (Hole Flannery and Neely 1969: Fig. 57 n, o).

d. Bowl Sherd with Horizontal Curved Line (LS-RB-5) No visible inclusions, Body white (2.5Y 8/2), Diam ?, Paint very dark gray (10YR 3/1), (Hole Flannery and Neely 1969: Fig 62 e, Wright 1981: Fig 16 b).

e. Bowl Rim with Ladder Motif (ES-RB-5) Medium sand inclusions, Body white (10YR 8/2), Diam ca. 28 cm, Paint eroded, (Hole Flannery and Neely 1969: Figs 55 j, 61 l).

f. Bowl Rim With Oblique Hatch Diamonds (LS-RB-13) No visible inclusions, Body pale yellow (2.5Y 4/1), Diam ca. 25, Paint dark gray (2.5Y 4/1) (Hole Flannery and Neely 1969: Fig 62 i, Wright 1981: Figs. 20c, 21d, f,).

g. Bowl Rim with Exterior Wavy Motif, No visible inclusions, Body white (2.5Y 8/2), Diam ?, Paint dark grayish brown (2.5Y 4/2),

h. Incurved Bowl Rim with Triangle Motifs, No visible inclusions, Body reddish yellow (5YR 7/5), Diam 14 cm, Paint very dark gray (5YR 3/1) (cf. Hole Flannery and Neely 1969: Fig 52)

i. Small Bowl Rim with Vertical Lines (LS-RB-8) No visible inclusions, Body pink (7.5YR 8/3), Diam 9 cm, Paint dark gray (7.5YR 3/1) (Wright 1981: Fig 22 b).

j. Bowl sherd with Oblique Hatch Diamonds (cf. LS-RB-13) and Sigma Motifs (cf. LS-RB-14). No visible inclusions, Body very pale brown (10YR 7/4), Body Diam 17 cm, Paint very dark gray (2.5YR 3/1), (Wright 1981: Fig. 21d).

Figure IV.7. Mehmeh and Farukh ceramics from DL-15

1a. **Number**: DL-18 (DL-X)
1b. **Name**: Sohz (Sabz East)
2. **Grid**: 1708.2–1182.6
3. **Dimensions**:

Length:	375 m
Width:	West: 90 m; East: 138 m
Height:	5.0 m
Circumference:	ca. 620 m
Area:	3.1 ha

4. **Modern Environmental Context**: Where the alluvial fan of the Mehmeh River meets the saline depression, about one and a half kilometers northeast of the present Mehmeh channel.

5. **Features**: DL-18 is a large complex of six mounds divided into three distinct groupings (Fig. IV.8). The largest cluster of four mounds was constructed on a large irregular platform, roughly in the shape of the letter "J," that averages about 1.5 meters in height above the surrounding alluvial plain.

A canal (DL-329) runs from north to south along the east and south edges of the platform, cutting into the lower edge of the platform at its southern and southwestern extremes. This canal, which generally conforms to the shape of the platform's eastern and southern edges, may well be a modern re-excavation of an ancient irrigation feature. As with many such features we have observed during the this survey of the Deh Luran Plain, such canals very likely served the dual purpose of supplying water to the site's occupants as well as to the agricultural fields along its course.

At the western end of the J-shaped platform, there is a small elliptical mound (Fig. IV.8 a), measuring 65 meters (N-S) by 25 meters (E-W) and with a maximum height of 1.0 meter above the platform. The second largest of the four mounds on the platform lies approximately 30 meters to the southeast (Fig. IV.8 b). Its maximum dimensions were 100 meters in length by 65 meters in width. Its slightly rounded summit rose to a maximum height of 3.5 meters above the platform. It is approximately 370 meters in circumference. In plan, this mound appears to have two parts or lobes, a result either of the erosion of the two sides of the mound or of the presence of two originally discrete architectural complexes which blended together into a single mound as they weathered. On the northwest edge of this bi-lobed mound is a cobble foundation about three meters square. It probably represents a modern transhumant pastoralists' tent footing.

A few meters east of the large mound just described were the remnants of what appeared to be excavated tombs. An area of about 45 meters (NE-SW) by 20 meters (NW-SE) had been badly disturbed, evidently as a result of looting. There were a series of pits, excavated to a depth of about 1.5 meters, with adjacent piles of debris thrown out of them. At the bottom of these pits one could see enough stonework to generally reconstruct what appeared to be the lower portion of the tombs—a large rectangular area of stone slabs laid flat to form the floor and additional slabs set on edge to form the lower walls. This construction appears to have been about 22 by 12 meters, but there may well be more than one tomb represented. Many large sherds were found on the piles of debris. Parts of a polychrome "scarlet ware" jar with goat and branch motifs were recovered.

On the extreme northern end of the platform was an irregularly rectangular mound measuring 125 meters (NE-SW) by 60 meters (NW-SE) and about 264 meters in circumference (Fig. IV.8 c). The southwestern edge of this mound is separated from the large bi-lobed mound described above by a 9 meter-long saddle-shaped portion of the platform, which rises about 1.25 meters above the alluvial plain. The approximate center of the northwest face of the mound is distinctly "notched." It was not clear if this "notched" area was part of the mounds original configuration or if it was a result of efforts to locate and loot tombs. This mound rises to a height of 5.0 meters above the plain and about 3.26 meters above the platform. The entire northwestern edge of this mound has been

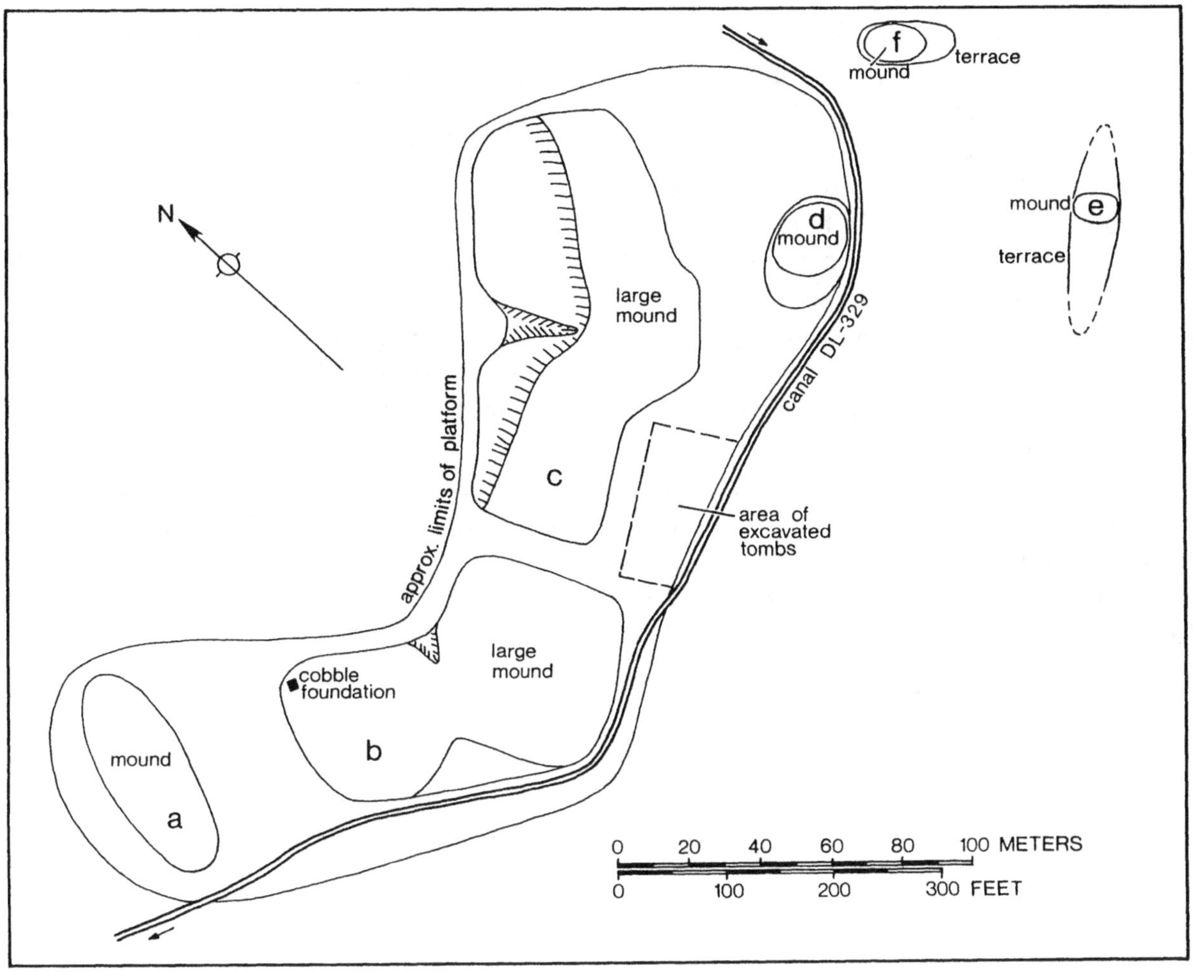

Figure IV.8. Map of Tepe Sabz East (DL-18)

subjected to severe erosion. The reason why this large area has been so affected while adjacent areas remain relatively intact is not clear.

About 20 meters to the east, a smaller mound was located on the platform near its northeastern edge (Fig. IV.8 d). At its base, this mound was generally elliptical and measured 35 meters (NE-SW) by 21 meters (NW-SE) and rose about 3.25 meters above the platform. On the northeastern portion of this mound was a smaller, irregularly circular mound, 20 meters in diameter, 110 meters in circumference, rising about 1.5 meters above the lower mound and about 4.75 meters above the platform.

Sixty-three meters southeast of the above described small mound, and of the northeastern edge of the J-shaped platform, lies another small elliptical mound (Fig. IV.8 e). It is 13 meters (NW-SE) by 8 meters (NE-SW) and about 1.0 meters in maximum elevation above the surrounding plain. A 21 meter long terrace-like feature extended from the northeastern side of this mound. At the point where this terrace joined the main mound, it was about 0.50 meter in elevation above the plain. To the northeast, this terrace narrows to a point and drops in elevation to blend imperceptibly into the alluvium. A similar terrace feature extends from the southwestern side of this mound. This one, however, is lower, reaching only 0.25 meter above the plain at its juncture with the mound, and longer, approximately 33 meters in length.

The sixth and final mound comprising DL-18 is located between and a little to the north of the large J-shaped platform and the mound with opposing terraces just described (Fig. IV.8 f). It was irregularly elliptical, measuring 18 meters (NW-SE) by 11 meters (NE-SW), 51 meters in circumference and about 0.50 meters in height above the plain. A low terrace, 0.30 to 0.50 meters in elevation, extends from the southeast side of this small mound for a distance of eight meters.

6. **Phases**: Ceramics were common on the central J-shaped complex and rare on the other mounds. There is no evidence of different ceramics on different parts of the site. The fine variant of the ledge-rim jar (ED-RJ-4; Fig. IV.9 k) and a small wall cone (cf. Wright 1981:154, Fig. 76 c) could indicate either Late Uruk or Jemdet Nasr occupation, but none of the other Late Uruk elements or characteristic Jemdet Nasr painted motifs which might confirm those phases were noted. Characteristic of the Early Dynastic I–II phase are conical cup rims (ED-RC-1; Fig. IV.9 c) and bases (ED-BC-3, 1; Fig. IV.9 a-b) including the solid-footed variant most common in this phase, the finer variant of the round lip jar (ED-RJ-2; Fig. IV.9 h), the finer variants of hatched strips (ED-O-2; Fig. IV.9 q), as well as the characteristic polychrome (ED-O-5, Fig. IV.9 o) and monochrome (ED-O-3, Fig. IV.9 p) jar shoulders.

7. **Comment**: We assign the full 3.1 ha area of the platform to the Early Dynastic I–II phase.

8. **References**: Wright 1981:191.

Figure IV.9. Early Dynastic ceramics from DL-18

a. Wide Conical Cup Base (ED-BC-3) (Area 2) Fine sand inclusions, Body yellowish pink (5YR 7/4), Base diam 4.5 cm, Surface pale orange-yellow (10YR 8/3) (cf. Wright 1981: Fig. 45c-d).

b. Solid-footed Cup Base (ED-BC-1) (Area 3) Fine sand inclusions, Body pale yellowish pink (2.5YR 8/3), Base diam 2.7 cm, Surface pale yellowish pink (2.5YR 8/3) (cf. Wright 1981: Fig. 45f-g).

c. Conical Cup Rim (ED-RC-1) (Area 3) Fine sand inclusions, Body grayish red-orange (10R 6/6), Diam 8 cm, Surface pale orange-yellow (10YR 8/4) (cf. Wright 1981: Fig. 45h-j).

d. Beveled Lip Bowl (ED-RB-2) (Area 3) Fine sand inclusions, Body light yellowish brown (10YR 7/4), Diam ca. 30 cm, Surface light grayish yellow brown (10YR 7/3) (cf. Wright 1981: Fig. 47h).

e. Ledge Rim Bowl (ED-RB-3) (Area 6) Medium sand inclusions, Body yellowish pink (5YR 7/4), Diam ?, Surface light yellowish brown (10YR 7/3) (cf. Wright 1981: Fig. 47e-f).

f. Round Lip Jar (ED-RJ-1) (Area 3) Fine sand inclusions, Body yellowish white (10YR 9/2), Diam 14 cm, Surface yellowish white (2.5Y 9/2) (cf. Wright 1981: 49a, c-f).

g. Round Lip Jar (ED-RJ-1) (Area 3) Fine sand inclusions, Body light olive brown (2.5Y 6/2), Diam 11 cm, Surface yellowish gray (2.5Y 8/2) (cf. Wright 1981: Fig. 49b, h-j).

h. Fine Round Lip Jar (ED-RJ-2) (Area 2) Fine sand inclusions, Body pale yellow (5Y 8/3), Diam 10 cm, Surface pale yellow (2.5Y 8/4) (cf. Wright 1981: Fig. 49b, h-j).

i. Flared, Expanded Rim Jar (ED-RJ-3) with Impressed Strip (ED-O-2) (Area 2) Fine sand inclusions, Body yellowish white (5Y 9/2), Diam 13 cm, Surface yellowish white (7.5Y 9/2) (cf. Wright 1981: Fig. 51 l-o).

j. Ledge Rim Jar (ED-RJ-4) (Area 2) Medium sand inclusions, Body light brown (5YR 6/5), Diam 12 cm, Surface yellowish white (7.5Y 9/2) (cf. Wright 1981: Fig. 53c, g).

k. Same (ED-RJ-4) Fine sand inclusions, Body grayish yellow (2.5Y 7/3), Diam 15 cm, Surface yellowish gray (10YR 8/1), Trace of red slip (7.5YR 6/5) (cf. Wright 1981: Fig. 53f, h-j).

l. Band Rim Jar (ED-RJ-5) (Area 2) Fine sand inclusions, Body pale orange-yellow (10YR 8/3), Diam 14 cm, Surface yellowish white (2.5Y 9/1) (cf. Wright 1981: Fig. 54e-g).

m. Same, heavy variant (cf. ED-RJ-5) Same inclusions, Body pale orange yellow (10YR 8/3), Diam 20 cm, Surface yellowish gray (2.5Y 8/1).

n. Gray Ware Round Lip Jar (ED-RJ-7) (Area 6) Crushed calcite inclusions, Body light grayish yellow-brown (10YR 6/2), Diam 14 cm, Surface pale orange-yellow(10YR 8/3) (cf. Wright 1981: Fig. 66f-i).

o. Polychrome Jar Shoulder (ED-O-6) (Area 2) Fine sand inclusions, Body grayish yellow (2.5Y 7/3), Shoulder diam 21 cm, Surface yellowish gray (5Y 8/1), Grayish red paint (7.5R 4/6) (cf. Wright 1981: Fig. 58f).

p. Monochrome Jar Shoulder (ED-O-3) (Area 3) Fine sand inclusions, Body grayish yellow (2.5Y 7/3), Surface yellowish white (10YR 9/1), Refired reddish brown paint (10R 4/3) (cf. Wright 1981: Fig. 58j).

q. Impressed Strip (ED-O-2) (Area 3) Fine sand inclusions, Body grayish yellow (7.5Y 8/3), Shoulder diam ca. 32 cm, Surface yellowish gray (7.5Y 8/2).

Figure IV.9. Early Dynastic ceramics from DL-18, continued

r. Denticulate Sickle Blade (Area 4) Medium gray chert.

s. Turned Ring Base (ED-B-3) (Area 3) Fine sand inclusions, Body brownish pink (7.5YR 7/3), Base diam 13 cm, Surface light yellowish brown (10YR 7/ 3) (cf. Wright 1981: Fig. 56b, d-e).

t. Same (ED-B-3) (Area 2) Fine sand inclusions, Body orange (5YR 7/6), Base diam 9 cm, Surface brownish pink (7.5YR 7/ 3) (cf. same).

u. Pinched Ring Base (ED-B-5) (Area 2) Fine sand inclusions, Body yellowish gray (5Y 7/2), Base diam 13 cm, Surface yellowish gray (5Y 8/2) (cf. Wright 1981: Fig. 56f-i).

v. High Turned Ring Base (ED-B-4) (Area 6) Medium sand inclusions, Body pale orange-yellow (10YR 8/3), Base diam ca. 18 cm, Surface yellowish white (10YR 9/1) (cf. Wright 1981: Fig. 56c).

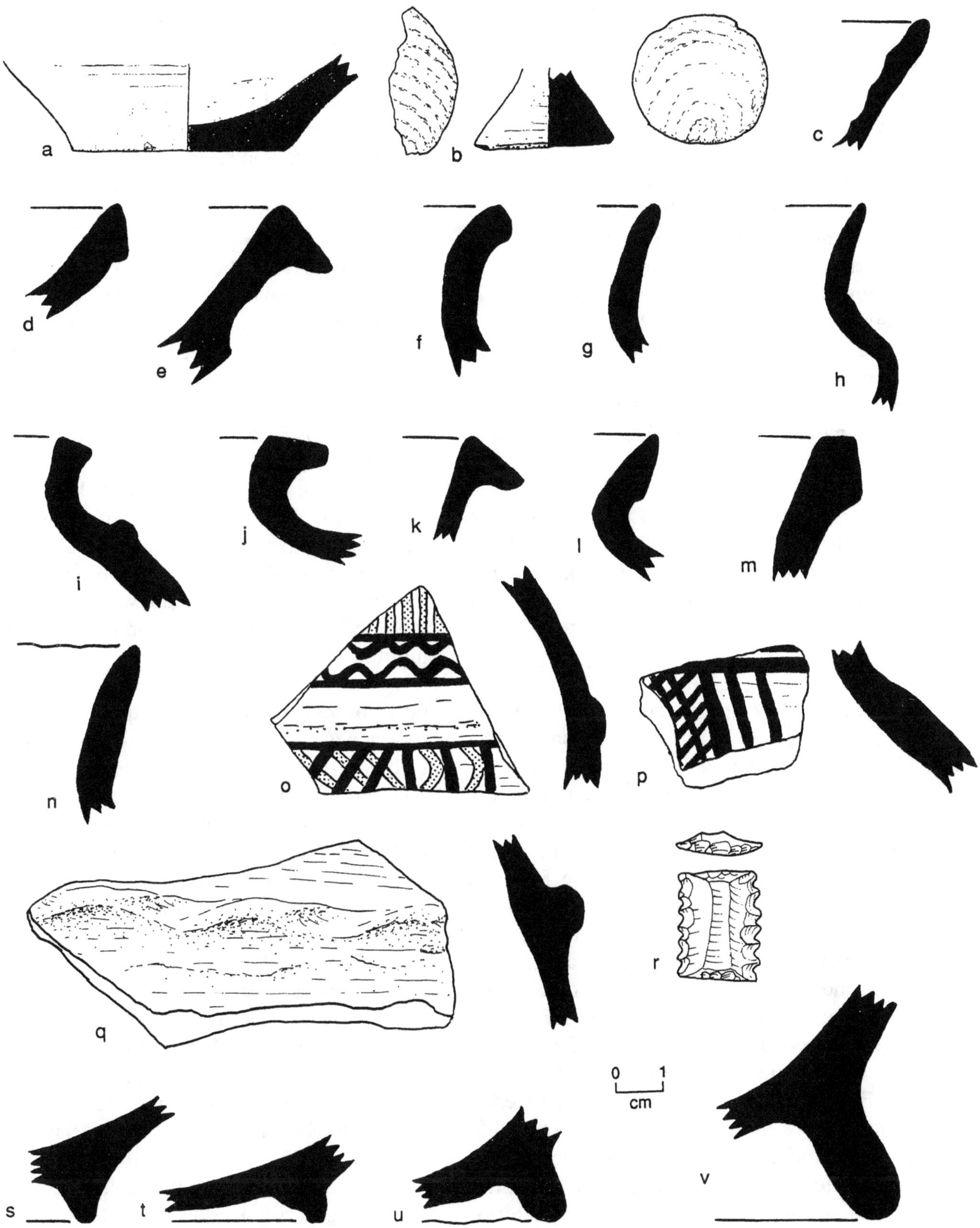

Figure IV.9. Early Dynastic ceramics from DL-18

1a. **Number**: DL-19 (DL-54X)
1b. **Name**: Tepe Chakali (The Jackal)
2. **Grid**: 1711.0–1188.5
3. **Dimensions:**

Length: Entire Site:	252 m (NW-SE)
Northwest mound:	62 m (N-S)
Southeast mound:	195 m (NW-SE)
Width: Entire Site:	168 m (NE-SW)
Northwest mound:	62 m (E-W)
Southeast mound:	168 m (NE-SW)
Height: Northwest mound:	2.6 m
Southeast mound:	3.9 m
Circumference:	615 m
Area: Entire Site:	2.59 ha
NW mound:	0.26 ha
SE mound:	2.31 ha

4. **Modern Environmental Context**: At the juncture of the alluvial fan of the Dawairij River and the saline depression, about four kilometers west of the present Dawairij channel and seven kilometers east of the present Mehmeh River channel.

5. **Features**: This site is comprised of two mounds joined by a low, but distinct "saddle" of earth. The northwest mound is smaller and irregularly square in form, while the southeast mound is much the larger and is irregularly oval in shape (Fig. IV.10). Several wall footings were found eroding from these two mounds. These footings were only found on the western half of the smaller mound, but appeared more widely distributed on the larger, main mound. The footings are similar to those found at DL-7 and probably date to the earlier occupations of this site, as they are generally larger and do not appear to be of the same masonry techniques seen at the later (i.e., Sasanian/Early Islamic) sites. Most of the exterior walls evident have footings consisting of a rubble (i.e., pebbles and clay) fill faced on both sides with unmodified cobbles and boulders. The interior, room-dividing, walls as well as a few exterior walls were constructed of a single course of large, boulder-size stones. Some remnants of clay-brick and packed-clay walls were present, but they were indistinct and difficult to interpret. A few dome- or loaf-shaped, lightly fired(?), reddish clay brick fragments were found on the smaller northwestern mound. There appeared to be fewer artifacts and less densely clustered groupings of artifacts on the western half of both mounds. Ceramic types similar to those of Sargarab (DL-169), indicating occupation early in the Early Uruk phase, are seldom found above the one meter contour line on either mound. The small canals excavated on and around the site were nearly filled in with earth at the time of our survey, but very probably were constructed after the site was abandoned. However, they do branch from a channel (DL-276B) that we do believe serviced fields around this site. The design and relationship of the more recent canals to the contours of the site and the surrounding terrain indicate that they had been excavated to collect precipitation run-off from the higher areas and channel the water to fields on the lower edges of the site and on the surrounding alluvium.

6. **Phases**: A very large quantity of ceramic sherds was collected systematically from this site. Lithic artifacts and debitage were present in lesser numbers, but they were in large quantities relative to other sites in the area. Only a small sub-sample of the Chakali ceramics is available for restudy. Fortunately, we have a detailed unpublished description and distributional study prepared by Neely and Miroschedji. A few Susiana sherds were found on the smaller northwest mound. The only diagnostic sherd is a carinated bowl rim with interior painted multiple zig-zag motif (cf. Hole, Flannery and Neely 1969: Fig. 57 q), probably of the Khazineh phase. The major occupation of this site dates to the Uruk period. The fine jars (US-RJ-1) and bowls (US-RB-3) of Sargarab ware tempered with crushed calcite and plant matter, sometimes painted with monochrome bands, various straight rim jars (US-RJ-4, 5) and various flared neck jars (US-RJ-6, 7, 9) of Sargarab ware as well as the black-on-red jar shoulder decoration

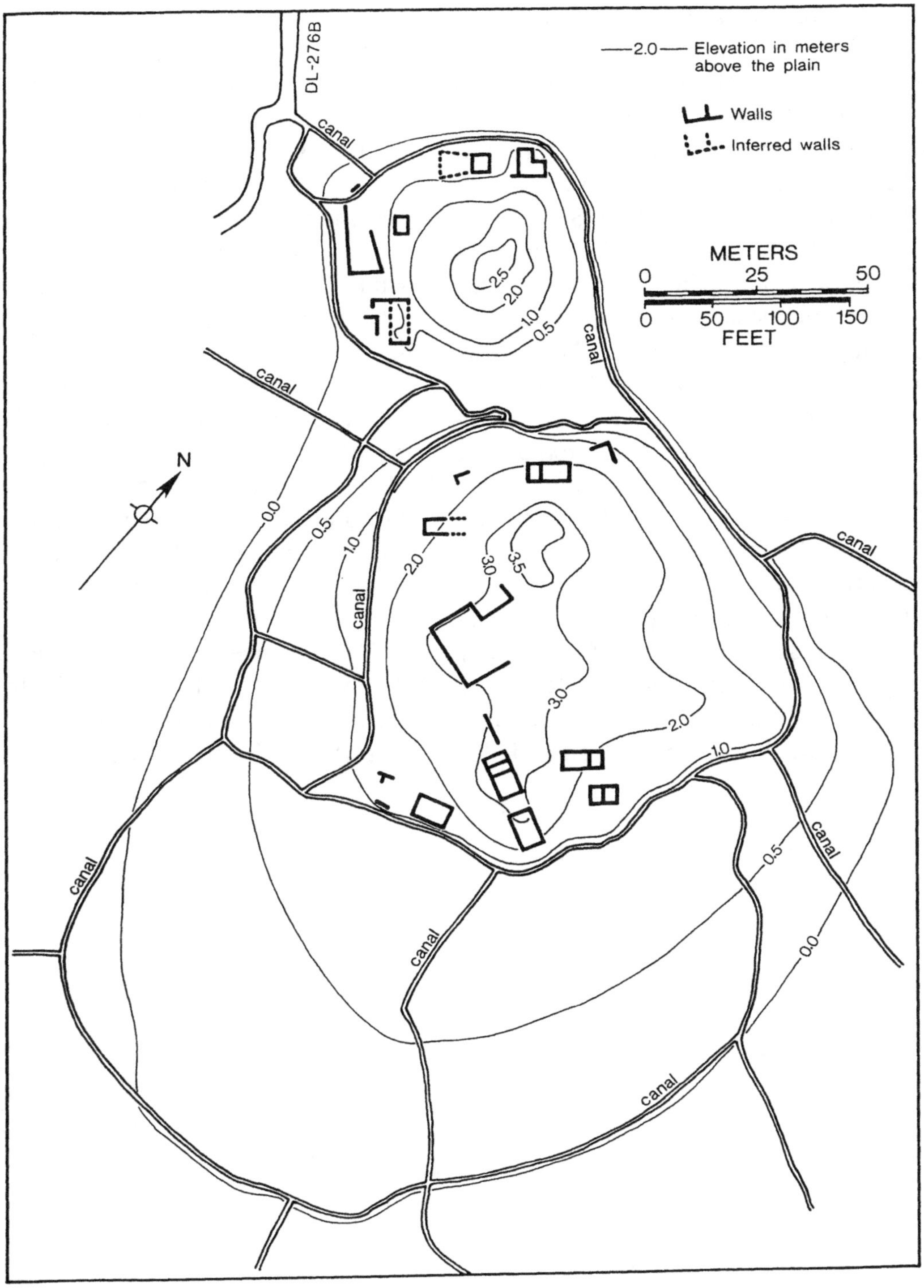

Figure IV.10. Map of Chakali (DL-19)

(UU-O-8) of sand tempered Uruk ware could be either Early or Middle Uruk. Early Uruk occupation is indicated by the occurrence of tapered-rim beveled rim bowls (US-RB-1), open bowls with round (US-RB-4) or beaded (US-RB-6) lips, incurved beaded rim bowls with thumb-impressed strips (US-RB-11), high expanded band rim jars (US-RJ-10) and long straight spouts (US-O-5), all of Sargarab ware. These variants tend to occur on the larger southeast mound. Middle Uruk occupation is indicated by the occurrence of quantities of standard beveled rim bowls (US-RB-2) and incurved beaded rim bowls (US-RB-11), particularly those with obliquely hatched strips (US-RB-12). In addition, there are various flared expanded neck jars (UU-RJ-3, 4, 6), jar shoulders with cross-hatched bands (US-O-2), thumb impressed strips (US-O-4), and rocker stamped (UU-O-7) shoulder decoration, some of Uruk ware. These indicators of Middle Uruk occupation are scattered on both mounds. Droop spouts (UU-O-11) and a low expanded band rim jar (UU-RJ-6) of Uruk ware are the only indications of Late Uruk occupation. However, the absence of any of the other common and very characteristic Late Uruk types suggests a limited and/or specialized use. Other interesting items in the collection are baked clay wall cones, a typical form of architectural decoration used on special buildings of the Late Uruk (Wright 1981:154, Fig. 76 c) and Jemdet Nasr periods. These and the few late Uruk sherds are concentrated around the high point at the north end of the larger southeast mound. There is a small Late Sasanian/Early Islamic period occupation, to be discussed in a subsequent volume.

7. **Comment**: We assign the 0.26 ha area of the northwest mound to the Khazineh phase, the 2.31 ha of the southeast mound to the Early Uruk phase, and the full 2.59 ha area of the site to the Middle Uruk phase. There may have been a Late Uruk shrine or administrative building on the north end of the main mound.

8. **References**: Wright, Neely, Johnson, and Speth 1975:134. In this article, the height and the area of the mound are over-estimated. The site map (Fig. IV.10) is by Miroschedji and Neely.

1a. **Number**: DL-20
1b. **Name**: Tepe Musiyan
(Mussian, Moussian)
2. **Grid**: 1711.0–1174.2 (center)
3. **Dimensions**:

Diameter:	535 m (N-S)
Width:	320 m (E-W)
Height:	17.5 m
Circumference:	1475 m
Area:	17.31 ha

4. **Modern Environmental Context**: On the alluvial fan of the Dawairij River, about one kilometer west of the present Dawairij channel.

5. **Features**: Tepe Musiyan is by far the largest single mound on the Deh Luran Plain (Fig. IV.11). Many of its surface details must result from major IInd millennium B.C. and later construction on the site, but its basic configuration probably results from architectural accumulation during and before the IIIrd millennium B.C. Though we will discuss the details of the mound's surface in a subsequent volume, a general discussion is warranted here. We have used the topographic map of Gautier and Lampre (1905: Fig. 95), even though their contour lines do not agree precisely with their elevation points, to determine the dimensions of the site and to augment our description. Their plan actually differs only slightly from their written description of length and width (ibid.:62). However, the indication that the site had a circumference of almost 1500 meters differs from a measurement made with the odometer of our vehicle, in which we found the outer edge of the talus to be a little less than 2000 meters in circumference. It seems likely that in the 65 years since the work of Gautier and Lampre, the site's circumference had increased as a result of depositional processes as the sides of the mound and the debris of their excavations were eroded and washed downward around the mound. Although the edges of the mound are quite irregular, the overall configuration in plan is rectangular. The southern half of the site is oriented North-South, while the northern half is slightly angled to about 15° East-of-North. The French expedition of 1903 worked for three months with a crew of 140 men, excavating five large excavations (labeled A to E on fig. IV.11) and several smaller test units.

A thorough, albeit rapid, surface investigation of this site required six full days of fieldwork. This study, augmented by a study of the profile of Gautier and Lampre's "Excavation E" in 1963 (Hole, Flannery and Neely 1969:65–72) and Joseph Caldwell's profiling of the large erosional cut in the northwestern portion of the site, has indicated occupation of Tepe Musiyan from at least the Mohammed Jaffar phase (ca. 7000 B.C.) into at least the Early Islamic period (ca. A.D. 1250)

Because of the complexities of this huge site, we will discuss its early occupational history in necessarily general terms. In the succeeding section, the extent of each phase will be detailed in chronological order. Phases from Mohammed Jaffar until the Suse phase constitute the lowest 8 to 10 meters of the site's exposed slopes. The uppermost 7.5 to 9.5 meters of accumulation are of the Jemdet Nasr and later phases.

Many cobble wall foundations or footings can be seen eroding from the site. Some of those visible in the southeast quadrant of the site are similar to those found at Ashrafabad (DL-29) and Sabz (DL-31), which were attributed to the Mehmeh phase (Hole, Flannery and Neely 1969: 58–60, 73, Fig. 17). However, Mehmeh phase walls cleaned in the southwest quadrant were entirely of mud-brick (ibid.:65–68). Other wall footings noted in the northeastern quadrant of Musiyan were more massive in both the stone material used and the overall size of the structures. One measured structure was 15 by 4 meters. We do not know the date of these footings. We also made observations on the large mud-brick building partially exposed in Unit A in the north-central part of the site by Gautier and Lampre (1905:67–68, Fig. 97), but it is probably of the IInd millennium and will be dealt with in a later survey report. Similarly, the various baked bricks which we found and measured were probably from phases after the Early Dynastic Period, and will not be dealt with here.

The configuration of the mound suggests that at some point, probably late in its history, it was surrounded by a large wall with entryways. Whether such a wall dates to the last time the site was a major settlement, the Sukkalmahhu Elamite phase of the early IInd millennium B.C., or earlier, to the Early Dynastic period or before, can only be resolved by excavation.

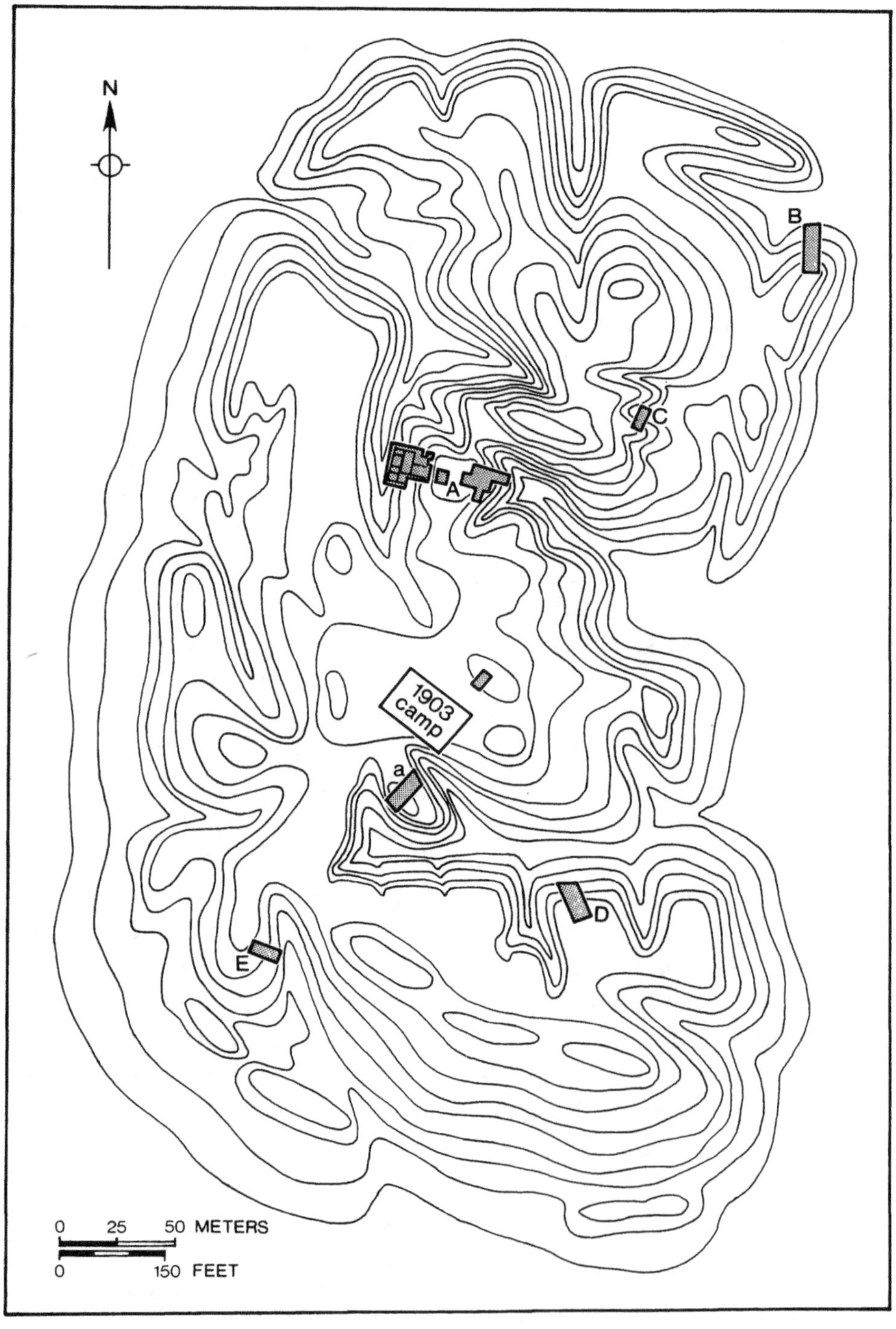

Figure IV.11. Map of Musiyan (DL-20)

6. **Phases**: The earliest occupations of Musiyan are indicated by the occurrence of small microlithic, "bullet-shaped" blade cores concentrated in the southwest quadrant. Somewhere, no doubt deeply covered, must be a smaller mound of the Mohammed Jaffar phase, if not earlier, but we can say nothing more about it. A Chogha Mami Transitional bowl with painted interior pendant triangles was found in the southeast quadrant of the mound, and Gautier and Lampre (1905: Fig. 165) report another possible example. Similarly, a Sabz phase sherd was found in the southwest quadrant of the mound, and Gautier and Lampre (1905: Fig. 167) report a possible Sabz "sauce boat" fragment. All we can infer from these occurrences is that there are small occupational sites of these phases buried somewhere deeply in Musiyan.

Khazineh phase diagnostics are somewhat more common on the surface. Three carinated bowl fragments, including one with interior crosshatch (ES-RB-11; Fig. IV.12 a), fully painted interior (ES-RB-12), and one with closely spaced interior multiple bands (ES-RB-14), were found in the southern third of the mound. Another carinated bowl fragment with interior wavy elements was found in the same area (ES-RB-13; Fig. IV.12 b) and another is illustrated by Gautier and Lampre (1905: Fig. 143). An isolated carinated bowl base fragment was found in the center of the site in an area with otherwise predominantly later material. It may have been transported there in early fill used in later construction. Mehmeh phase diagnostics are widely distributed on the surface with basins with goat motifs (ES-RB-19) and bowl fragments with right triangle motifs (ES-RB-6; Fig. IV.12 d) in the southern and central parts of the site (Fig. IV.15). Gautier and Lampre illustrate many more Mehmeh phase goat motifs (ibid.:Figs. 211–213, 215, 217–19, 221–223, 230–31) and right triangle motifs (ibid.:Figs. 160–163, 194, 264), as well as many other probable Mehmeh sherds, but we have no way of knowing exactly where they were found on the mound. We do know that Mehmeh architecture has been observed at points in the southwest and southeast quadrants, about 150 meters apart. Assessment of the Bayat phase distribution is difficult because there is only one common diagnostic, the heavy vertical curved line motif (LS-RB-9; Fig. IV.12 i), recognizable in a situation where Farukh overlays Bayat, certainly the case at Musiyan. This motif is distributed throughout the southern and central parts of the site (Fig. IV.15), in a pattern similar to that of the Mehmeh diagnostics. In summary, there is probably a small Khazineh phase site covering no more than two hectares somewhere under the southern end of Musiyan. The site probably grew to cover at least four hectares during the Mehmeh phase and remained about the same size during Bayat times.

Farukh phase indicators are common on all areas of the mound (Fig. IV.15). Shaved base cups (LS-BB-3; Fig. IV.13 j), bowl fragments with dot motifs (LS-RB-10; Fig. IV.13 a, b), sigma motifs (LS-RB-14; Fig. IV.13 d, e), step motifs (LS-RB-15; Fig. IV.13 c, f), and concentric circle motifs (LS-RB-20), as well as fragments of jars with painted neck bands (LS-RJ-3), are common in the north and south ends of the site, and are found in lesser numbers everywhere. Few of these were illustrated by Gautier and Lampre, who were interested in the more varied and geometric Mehmeh and Suse phase ceramics. Accounting for the movement of fill outward as a result of the building of the later walls and leveling of the site, we suggest that the Farukh phase settlement extended 500 meters from north to south and 250 meters from east to west, with an area of at least 9 ha.

In contrast, Suse phase diagnostics such as fragments of bowls with large vertical chevrons (LS-RB-17), grid motifs (LS-RB-18; Fig. IV.14 L), "X" motifs (LS-RB-21; Fig. IV.14 i-j), branch motifs (Fig. IV.14 n, q), line dot motifs (Fig. IV.14 o, p), and fine line motifs (Fig. IV.14 m, n) are found primarily in the far north and northwestern parts of Musiyan (Fig. IV.15). Also found here was a piece of a Suse phase painted wall cone, termed a "clou" at Susa, where they decorated the façade of the Acropole (Canal 1978,

Figure IV.12. Khazineh, Mehmeh and Bayat ceramics from Musiyan (DL-20)

a. Carinated Bowl Fragment with Interior Cross-hatch (ES-RB-11) (3-1) Fine Sand Inclusions, Body white (10YR 8/2), Paint very dark gray (7.5YR 3/1), (Hole, Flannery and Neely 1969: Fig. 56 d, e).

b. Carinated Bowl Fragment with Interior Wavy Elements (ES-RB-13) (3-1) Trace Fine Sand, Body very pale brown (10YR 8/3), Paint very dark gray (10YR 3/1) (Hole, Flannery and Neely 1969: Figs 56 g, 57i, j).

c. Carinated Bowl Fragment with Interior Vertical Elements (2-2) Fine Sand Inclusions, Body white (10YR 8/2), Paint very dark gray (10YR 3/1) (Hole, Flannery and Neely 1969: Figs 57i, j).

d. Bowl Sherd with Right Triangle Motif (cf. ES-RB-6) (6w-1) No visible inclusions, Body very pale brown (10YR 8/4), Paint very dark gray (7/5YR 3/1) (Hole, Flannery and Neely 1969: Figs 62c).

e. Bowl Rim with Variant of Horizontal Chevron (LS-RB-7) (3-3) No visible inclusions, Body light gray (5Y 7/2), Diam 20 cm, Paint gray (2.5Y 5/1) (Hole, Flannery and Neely 1969: Figs 56 g, 57i, j).(cf. Hole, Flannery and Neely 1969: Figs 61 l, Wright 1981: 16e).

f. Fine Plain Bowl Rim (LS-RB-1) (3-3) No visible inclusions, Body white (2.5Y 8/1), Diam 17 cm, (Hole, Flannery and Neely 1969: Fig. 48g-h).

g. Same (4-1) No visible inclusions, Body white (5Y 8/1) , Diam ?, (cf. same).

h. Bowl Sherd with Vertical Curved Lines (cf. LS-RB-9) (3-3) No visible inclusions. Body very pale brown (10YR 8/3), Body diam 25, Paint dark gray (10YR 4/1), (cf. Hole, Flannery and Neely 1969: Figs 60i, j, Wright 1981: Fig 16e-h).

i. Bowl Sherd with Heavy Vertical Curved Lines (cf. LS-RB-9) (4-2), Medium sand inclusions, Body pale yellow (5Y 8/3), Base Diam ca. 21, Paint (10YR dark gray 3/1) (cf. Hole, Flannery and Neely 1969: Figs 60i).

j. Sherd of "Sabz Pot" Variant (1) Medium sand inclusions, Body pale yellow (2.5Y 8/3), Paint very dark gray 7.5YR 3/1) (Hole, Flannery and Neely 1969: Fig 49 c).

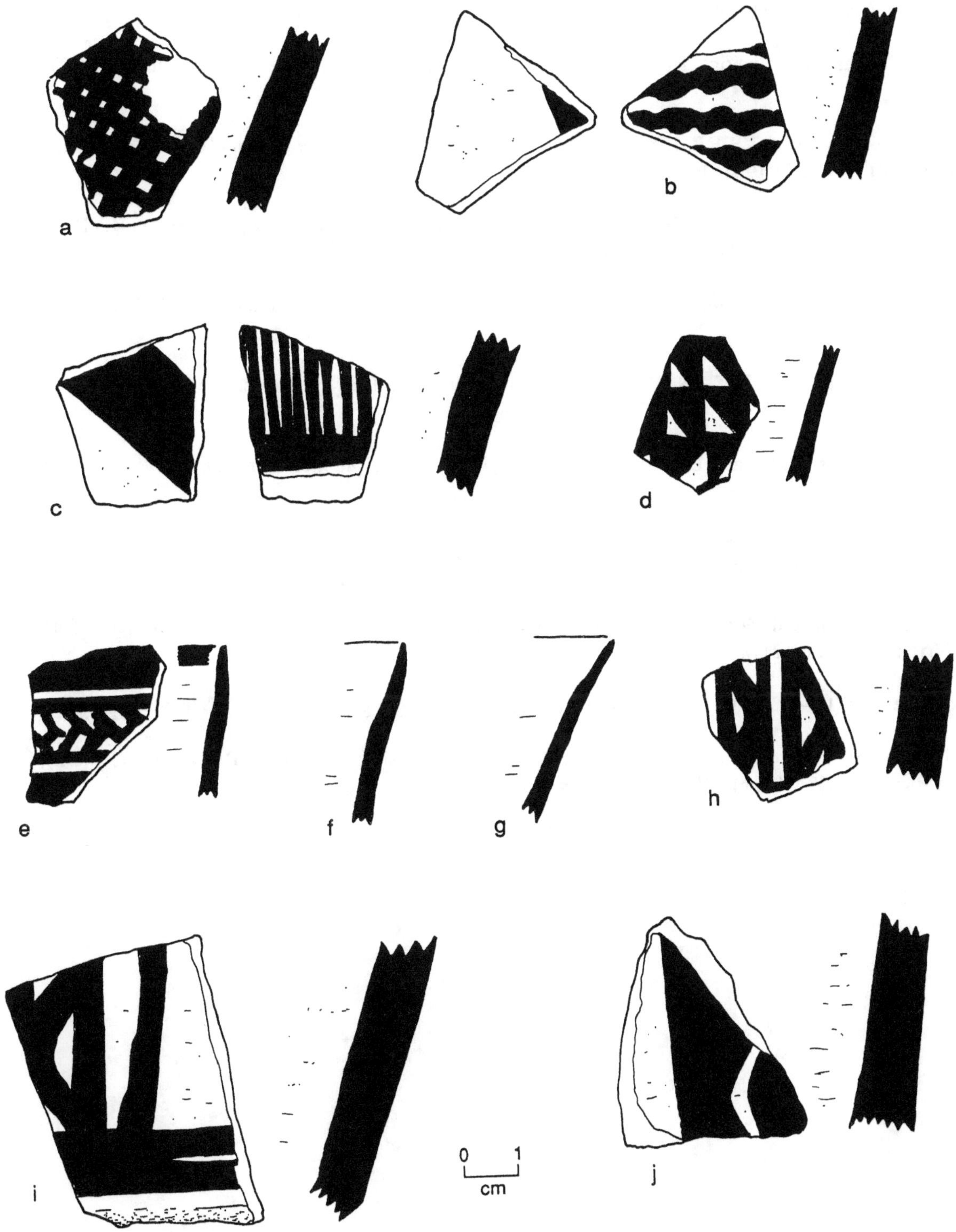

Figure IV.12. Khazineh, Mehmeh and Bayat ceramics from Musiyan (DL-20)

Figure IV.13. Farukh Phase ceramics from Musiyan (DL-20)

a. Bowl Rim with Dot Motifs (LS-RB -10) (4-2) No visible inclusions, Body white (2.5Y 8/2), Diam ca. 28 cm, Paint very dark gray (5YR 3/1) (cf. Wright 1981: Fig. 17).

b. Same, (5-1) No visible inclusions, Body white (7.5Y 8/2), Diam ?, Paint dark reddish brown (5YR 4/2) (cf. Wright 1981: Fig. 17e).

c. Bowl rim with Step Motif (LS-RB-15) (4-1) Trace fine sand, Body very pale brown (10YR 8/3), Diam ca. 16 cm, Paint gray (10YR 5/1) (Wright 1981: Fig. 19).

d. Bowl Rim with Sigma Motifs (LS-RB-14) (6-4) No visible Inclusions, Body very pale brown (10YR 7/4), Diam ca. 18 cm, Paint dark gray (5YR 4/1) (Wright 1981 :Fig. 18 a-d).

e. Same, (2-2) No visible Inclusions, Body pale yellow (2.5Y 8/4), Diam ?, Paint dark gray (7.5YR 4/1) (Wright 1981: Fig. 18 a-d).

f. Bowl Sherd with Step Motif (cf. LS-RB-15) (6-2E) Trace fine sand Body yellowish white (2.5Y 8/2), Body diam ca. 10 cm, Paint grayish brown (10YR 4/1) (Wright 1981: Fig. 19).

g. Bowl Rim with Cross Hatch and Diamonds (LS-RB-12) (4-1) No visible inclusions, Diam 18, Colors not recorded. (cf. Wright 1981: Fig. 20b).

h. Bowl Rim with Vertical Line Motif (LS-RB-8) (4-1) No visible Inclusions, Body white (2.5Y 8/2), Diam 15 cm, Paint dark gray (7.5YR 4/1) (Wright 1981: cf. Fig. 20 e).

i. Bowl Sherd with Unusual Motif (6-c2) No visible inclusions, Body pinkish gray (7.5YR 7/3), Paint dark gray (7.5YR 4/1) (Wright 1981: Fig. 21j).

j. Shaved Base Cup (LS-BB-3) (3-3) No visible inclusions. Body light gray (2.5Y 7/2) (Wright 1981: Fig. 13a, b, 14a).

k. Bowl Sherd with Variant Sigma Motif (cf. LS-RB-15) (5-1) No visible Inclusions, Body white (5Y 8/2), Diam ca. 14 cm, Paint dark gray (2.5Y 4/1) (cf. Wright 1981: Fig. 18 c).

Figure IV.13. Farukh Phase ceramics from Musiyan (DL-20)

Figure IV.14. Suse Ceramics from the north end of Musiyan (DL-20)

a. Plain Basin Rim (LS-BN-1), No visible inclusions, Body yellowish gray (7.5Y 8/1), Diam ca. 52 cm, Surface yellowish gray (2.5Y 8/1) (cf. Dollfus 1971: Fig. 10:6-11; Wright 1981: Fig. 23a-f).

b. Possible Wall decoration, Trace of vegetal inclusions, Body yellowish gray (5Y 8/1), Diam 12 cm, Surface yellowish gray (2.5Y 8/1), Paint grayish brown (Dollfus 1971: Fig. 20:23).

c. Plain High Neck Jar Rim (LS-RJ-3), Medium sand inclusions, Body yellowish gray (5Y 8/1), Diam 22 cm, Surface pale orangish yellow (10YR 8/3).

d. Bayat Redware Bowl Rim , Trace fine calcite inclusions, Body grayish reddish orange (10R 6/6), Diam 44 cm, Slip light reddish brown (10R 5/7) (Dollfus 1971: Fig. 19:14; Wright 1981: Fig. 10l-m)

e. Basin Rim with Interior Painted Bands (LS-BN-2), Fine sand inclusions, Body light yellowish brown (7.5YR 7/5), Diam ca. 30 cm, Surface yellowish gray (5Y 8/1), Paint grayish brown (7.5YR 3/2) (Wright 1981: Fig. 23g)

f. Low Neck Jar with Dots, Triangles, Sigmas (LS-RJ-4), No visible inclusions, Body yellowish gray (5Y 8/1), Diam 14 cm, Surface yellowish gray (5Y 8/1), Paint grayish brown (7.5YR 4/2) (cf. Dollfus 1971: Fig. 16:6-21; Wright 1981: Fig. 24h-j).

g. Bowl with Chevron "W"s , Trace of fine sand inclusions, Body yellowish gray (5Y 8 /2), Diam 14 cm, Surface pale yellow (5Y 8/3), Paint grayish yellow-brown (10YR 4/2) (cf. Dollfus 1971: Fig. 13:10,11)

h. Bowl with Rectangle, No visible inclusions, Body yellowish gray (5Y 8/2), Diam ca. 18 cm, Surface yellowish gray (2.5Y 8/1), Paint brownish gray (10YR 3/ 1).

i. Same, Trace of fine calcite inclusions, Body white (7.5Y 9/1), Diam 21 cm, Surface white (7.5Y 9/1), Paint dark yellowish brown (10YR 3/2) (Dollfus 1971: Fig. 13:1)

j. Same, Fine sand inclusions, Body yellowish gray (5Y 8/1), Diam 22 cm, Surface yellowish gray (2.5Y 8/1), Paint brown (7.5YR 4/3).

k. Bowl sherd with Unusual Diamond Motif, No visible inclusions, Body white (7.5Y 9/1), Diam ca. 25 cm, Surface white (5Y 9/1), Paint brownish gray (10YR 4/1).

l. Body sherd with Grid Motif (cf. LS-RB-18), No visible inclusions, Body yellowish gray (7.5Y 8/1), Diam ca. 20 cm, Surface yellowish gray (7.5Y 8/1), Paint brownish gray (10YR 3/1).

m. Bowl sherd with Fine-line Chevron, No visible inclusions, Body yellowish gray (5Y 8/2), Surface yellowish gray (2.5Y 8/3), Overfired paint light olive brown (2.5Y 5/2).

n. Bowl sherd with Fine-line Branch Motif (LS-RB-19), No visible inclusions, Body light yellowish brown (10YR 7/3), Surface yellowish gray (2.5Y 8/3), Paint grayish brown (7.5YR 4/2) (Dollfus 1971: Fig. 12:15).

o. Bowl sherd with Line-Dot Motif, No visible inclusions, Body yellowish gray (5Y 8/2), Surface yellowish gray (2.5Y 8/2), Paint brownish gray (10YR 5/2).

p. Same, Fine sand inclusions, Body yellowish gray (5Y 8/1), Surface yellowish gray (2.5Y 8/2), Paint dark yellowish brown (10YR 3/3).

q. Bowl sherd with Heavy Branch Motif, No visible inclusions, Body yellowish gray (2.5Y 8/2), Surface pale orangish yellow (10YR 8/3), Paint yellowish brown (10YR 4/3).

Figure IV.14. Suse Ceramics from the north end of Musiyan (DL-20)

Stève and Gasche 1971). We suggest that the Suse phase occupation covered the northern half of Musiyan, probably an area of 5 ha, but that in some areas it is sealed by meters of later Early Dynastic and Elamite debris.

Though Uruk pottery is durable and the Musiyan samples are large, we have not found any Uruk material, and we can only infer that the site was abandoned during most of the IVth millennium B.C.

Early Dynastic ceramics, particularly those typical of the Early Dynastic I–II phase such as the solid-footed conical cups (ED-CB-1), high, thin, round lip jars (ED-RJ-2), finer ledge rim jars, often painted (ED-RJ-4) with characteristic polychrome jar shoulder decoration (ED-O-6), and handmade jars of calcite tempered gray ware (ED-GR-1) are found everywhere (Fig. IV.15). We believe the site covered about 15 ha, and would not be surprised to find that it was walled at this time. Among the many sherds in our samples, there is not one definite Jemdet Nasr piece. However, Jemdet Nasr diagnostics are rare and do not preserve well. There must have been some occupation in the area, since there are tombs of the Jemdet Nasr period at nearby Aliabad (DL-71) (Gautier and Lampre 1905: Fig. 282). Jemdet Nasr ceramics may be masked by Early Dynastic I–II material at Musiyan. Early Dynastic III seems similarly widespread, but further study of our massive Musiyan samples is required to sort it from ceramics of Carter's (1971) Awan phase, which existed during the Agade Dynasty, and later Elamite Dynasties.

7. **Comment**: The phase identifications and areas assigned to each phase above are tentative because of the problem of the transport of construction fill from place to place on the site.

8. **References**: Carter 1971, Gautier and Lampre 1905: 62–72; Hole, Flannery and Neely 1969.

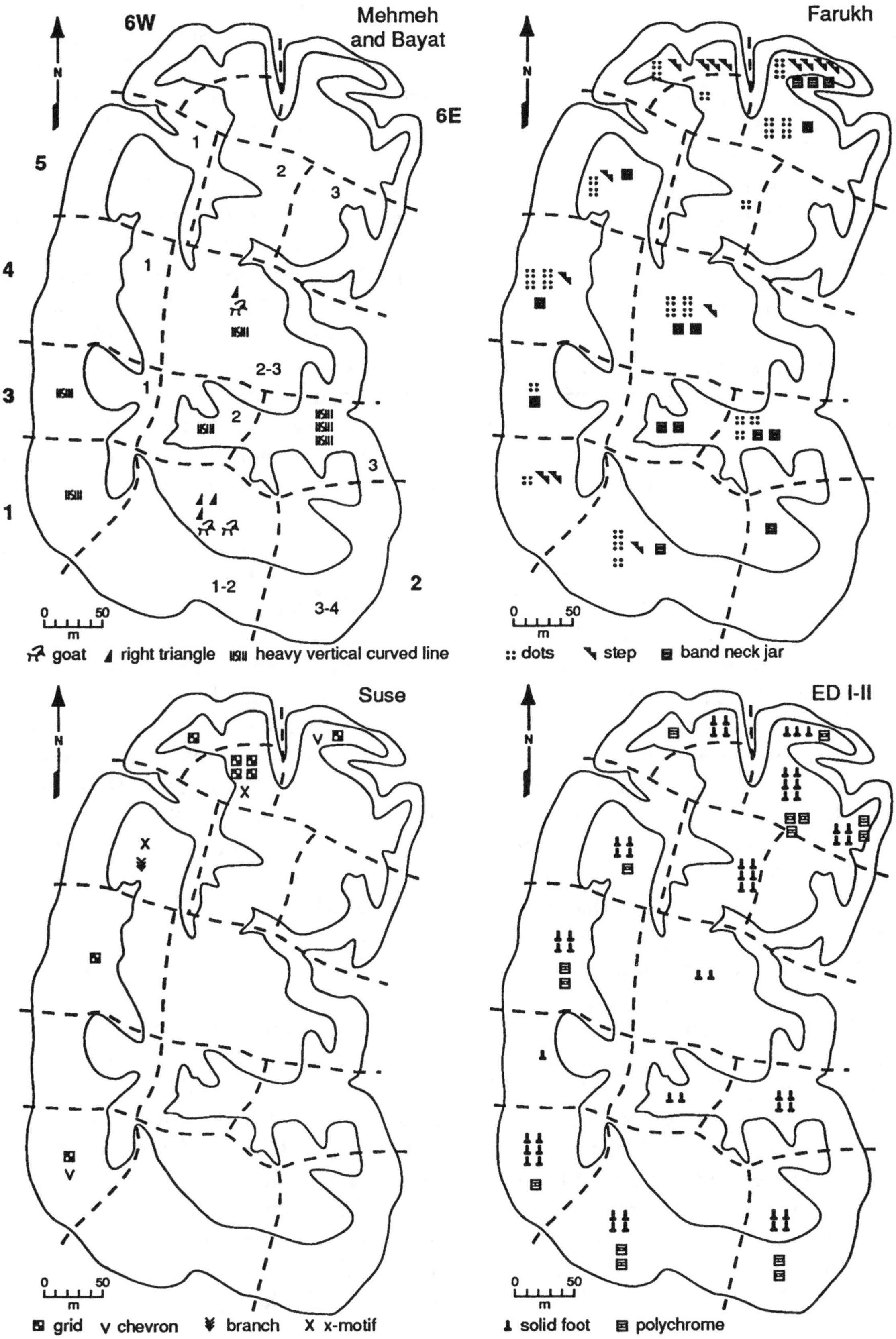

Figure IV.15. The distribution of early ceramics on Musiyan (DL-20)

1a. **Number**: DL-21
1b. **Name**: Ali Kosh (Tepe Mohamed-Djaffar; Tepe Bus Mordeh)
2. **Grid**: 1717.9–1174.6
3. **Dimensions**:

Length:	141 m (E-W)
Width:	129 m (N-S)
Height:	4.0 m
Circumference:	424 m
Area:	1.43 ha

4. **Modern Environmental Context**: At the juncture of the alluvial fan of the Dawairij River and the saline depression, about four kilometers west of the present Dawairij channel and seven kilometers east of the present Mehmeh River channel.

5. **Features**: Ali Kosh is a large mound, roughly circular in plan. It has a nearly level summit, and its lower slopes blend almost imperceptibly into the surrounding alluvial plain (Fig. IV.16). As with all of the sites on the Deh Luran Plain, continuous erosion, here most evident and advanced on the south side of the mound, is reducing the height of the site and leaving behind a fairly dense scatter of small boulder- to pebble-sized stones from wall and pavement constructions, as well as many fragments of flaked stone and ceramic sherds. Ali Kosh has the distinction of having the most archaeological testing of any site on the Deh Luran Plain. The French archaeological mission of 1903 (Gautier and Lampre 1905:81–83) investigated this site, which they named Tepe Mohamed-Djaffar. It seems likely that an old, eroded pit (approximately 7 by 7 meters in size) found just below the summit on the northeast side of the site (Hole, Flannery and Neely 1969:29, Fig. 4) represents a test excavation by the French, though it is not mentioned in their report.

Apparently, DL-21 received no further archaeological attention until it was visited and surface collected by Richard Watson and Robert J. Braidwood in 1960. Subsequent test excavations were undertaken in 1961 (Hole and Flannery 1962) and 1963 (Hole, Flannery and Neely 1969). The 1963 intensive surface collection of artifacts and test excavations suggest that Ali Kosh may originally have been a "double" or bi-lobed mound site. The earlier preceramic artifacts cluster on the east and southeast parts of the site, while the later, predominantly ceramic artifacts are more prevalent on the west and northwest slopes of the mound. The 1963 excavations also showed that the alluvial plain had built up some 3 meters around the lower slopes of the site; thus, the total height or thickness of the cultural deposits was 7 meters. The reader is referred to the report on the 1963 excavations (Hole, Flannery and Neely 1969) to obtain details regarding the rich array of architectural features and artifacts from which were reconstructed three phases of cultural development.

6. **Phases**: We will not recapitulate the evidence of the excavations, detailed elsewhere. The 1963 excavations indicate that Ali Kosh was a developing village community during the Bus Mordeh, Ali Kosh, and Muhammed Jaffar phases (Hole, Flannery and Neely 1969:342–354). Some ceramics excavated from the uppermost 0.70 meters of deposit in the 1961 test excavation were of the Chogha Mami Transitional phase (Hole and Flannery 1962: Plate VII, 1, [ES-RB-7; cf. Hole 1977: Fig. 50 d, Plate 35 a-c] and perhaps VII 3 and VII 7). Other ceramics from this "Upper Mixed Zone" and from the surface, particularly in a 50 by 35 meter concentration in the northeast quadrant of the sites (ibid.: Fig. 2) represent the Khazineh phase (Hole and Flannery 1962: Plate VII 9, [ES-RB-13, cf. Hole, Flannery and Neely 1969: Figs. 56 b, g; 57 i, j, l]) and the Mehmeh phase (Hole and Flannery 1962: Plate VII 2, 4, [cf. Hole, Flannery and Neely 1969: Plate 27 c] and VII 5 [ES-RJ-2; cf. Hole, Flannery and Neely 1969: Fig. 58 a-d)].

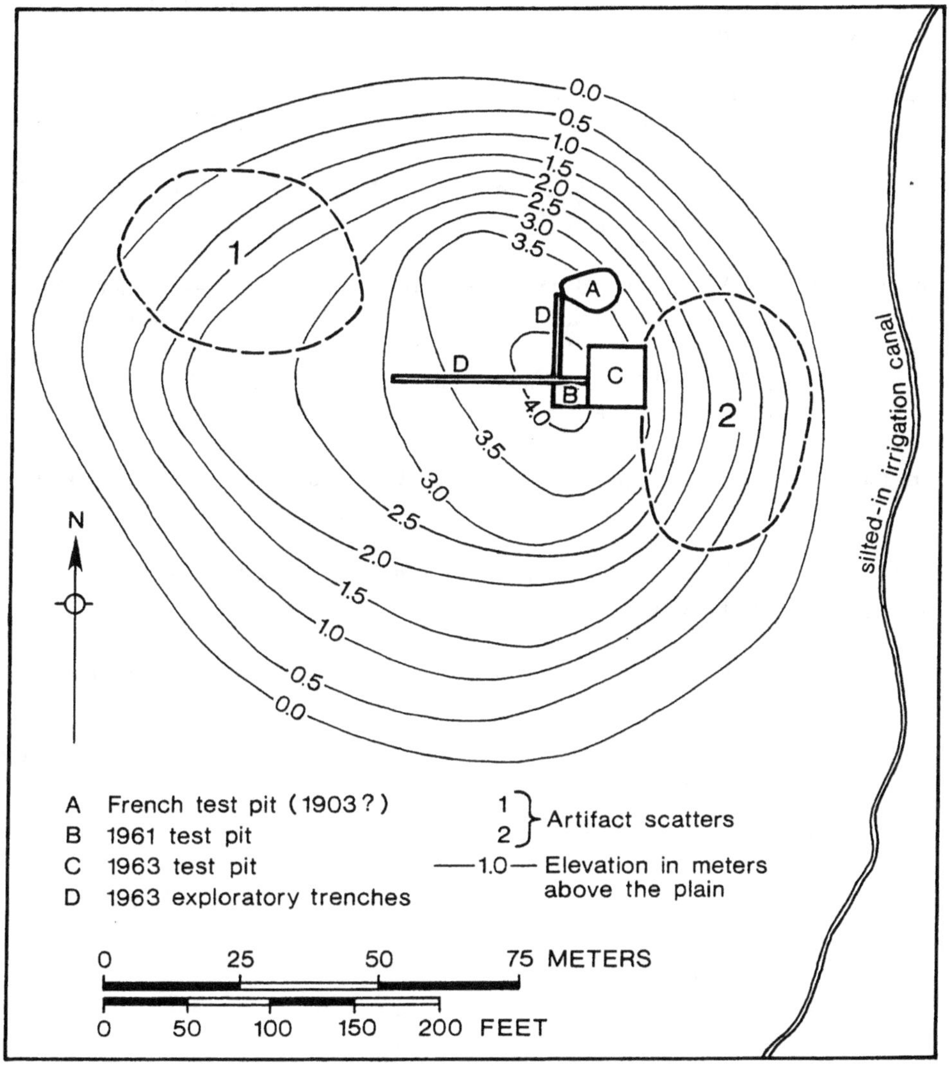

Figure IV.16. Map of Ali Kosh (DL-21)

7. **Comment**: We assign a 0.40 ha area on the west side of the mound to the Chogha Mami Transitional phase and the 0.15 ha area of the sherd scatter in the northwest quarter to the Khazineh and Mehmeh phases.

8. **References**: Gautier and Lampre 1905; Hole 1962, 1977; Hole and Flannery 1962; Hole, Flannery and Neely 1965, 1969.

Figure IV.17. Khazineh, Mehmeh, and Early Dynastic ceramics from Tepe Sefid (DL-22)

a. Large Bowl sherd with Exterior Cross-hatch, Medium sand inclusions, Body white (2.5Y 8/2, Body Diam ca. 24, Paint very dark gray (10YR 3/1) (cf. Hole, Flannery and Neely 1969: Fig. 50h).

b. Carinated Bowl Sherd with Wavy Elements (cf. ES-RB-13), Fine sand inclusions, Body pale yellow (2.5Y 8/3), Paint dark gray (10YR 3/1) (Hole, Flannery and Neely 1969: Fig. 56b, 57m).

c. Carinated Bowl Sherd with Parallel Lines (cf. ES-RB-14) and Cross-hatch, Medium sand inclusions, Body white (2.5Y 8/3), Paint dark gray (10YR 4/1) (cf. Hole, Flannery and Neely 1969: Fig. 53h, i, 57o).

d. Carinated Bowl Sherd with Exterior Wavy Zig-zag (cf. ES-RB-15), Medium sand inclusions, Body light brown (10YR 6/3), Paint gray (10YR 4/1) (Hole, Flannery and Neely 1969: Fig. 54 a, b).

e. Bowl Sherd with Right Triangle Motif (ES-RB-6) and Anthropomorph, Medium sand and calcite inclusions, Body light gray (2.5Y 7/2), Body diam ca. 30 cm, Paint gray (2.5Y 4/1) (Hole, Flannery and Neely 1969: Fig. 62 c).

f. Bowl Rim with Vertical Lines, Trace of fine sand inclusions, Body white (2.5Y 8/2), Diam ca. 28 cm, Paint dark brown (2.5Y 4/1) (Hole, Flannery and Neely 1969: Fig. 54 d-f).

g. Bowl Rim with Exterior Bands, Medium sand inclusions, Body pinkish gray (7.5YR 7/3), Diam ?, Paint brown (7.5YR 4/2).

h. Jar Sherd with Polychrome Motifs (ED-O-6), Medium sand inclusions, Body very pale brown (10YR 7/3), Body diam ca. 50 cm, Paints gray (10YR 5/1) and red (10R 4/3), (Wright 1981: Plate 1).

i. Bowl Rim with Interior Motif, Medium sand inclusions, Body overfired gray (10YR 4/1), Diam 14 cm, Paint dark gray (2.5Y 3/1).

Figure IV.17. Khazineh, Mehmeh, and Early Dynastic ceramics from Tepe Sefid (DL-22)

1a. **Number**: DL-22
1b. **Name**: Tepe Sefid
2. **Grid**: 1718.3–1178.6 (approximate).
3. **Dimensions**:

Length:	70 m
Width:	30 m
Height:	2.0 m
Area:	0.15 ha

4. **Modern Environmental Context**: At the edge of the northeastern alluvial slope of the plain, adjacent to the east edge of the saline depression.

5. **Features**: A moderate density of sherds were scattered over this roughly elliptical mound. The Mehmeh phase sherds were concentrated on the northeast side.

6. **Phases**: The Khazineh phase is indicated by carinated bowl fragments with interior wavy elements (ES-RB-13; Fig IV.17 b), cross-hatched designs (ES-RB-11; Fig IV.17 c), and with an exterior negative wavy or zig-zag motif usually seen on incurved bowls (cf. ES-RB-15; Fig IV.17 d). The Mehmeh phase is indicated by a large bowl sherd with a right triangle field (ES-RB-6; Fig IV.17 e) associated with the hand of an anthropomorphic figure (cf. Hole, Flannery and Neely 1969: Fig. 62 c, Plate 25 a, b) and by basins with goat motifs (ES-RB-19). There is nothing definitively later than the Mehmeh phase except for a number of sherds of Early Dynastic I–II polychrome jars (ED-O-6; Fig IV.17 h). The limited range of Early Dynastic pottery shapes suggests use of the site as a cemetery.

8. **Comment**: Our observations and collections were made during the 1961 survey. Repeated efforts to relocate Tepe Sefid during the 1968–1969 survey were unsuccessful. It is possible that the site was destroyed to provide fill for the new road to Deh Luran built about 1966. We assign the full 0.15 ha area of the site to the Khazineh phase, and a 0.10 ha area to the Mehmeh phase.

1a. **Number**: DL-23
1b. **Name**: Chagha Sefid (Tepe Chakal Sefid)
2. **Grid**: 1710.7–1189.1
3. **Dimensions**:

Length:	165 m (NE-SW)
Width:	120 m (NW-SE)
Height:	16 m
Area:	1.98 ha

4. **Modern Environmental Context**: On a terrace northwest of the Ab-i Garm stream on the northeast alluvial slopes of the plain, almost surrounded by the rich irrigated fields of the modern village of Deh Luran.

5. **Features**: Chagha Sefid is irregularly oval in plan (Fig. IV.18). Its east, south, and west sides are relatively steep, but the north side of the mound is much steeper. This steeper aspect is due to the presence of the intermittent stream channel (DL-276A) that passes close by the base of the site at its northern side and then curves around the western side of the mound before coursing southward. This stream is presently cutting through cultural deposits, which are clearly visible in the cut-banks. The site was therefore originally somewhat larger and of a different shape than what is presently discernible. A now-ruined fort was constructed in 1908 (Lorimer 1908:17) by a local leader, the Wali of Pusht-i-Kuh, atop the summit of the mound. Hole's (1977: Fig. 2) excavations indicated that the base of the site is 3.5 to 5 meters below the modern ground surface.

Although recorded as Tepe Chakal Sefid on the 1903 French expedition's map of the Deh Luran Plain (Gautier and Lampre 1905: Fig. 94), no further mention is made of the site in their report. Evidently the next archaeological investigation of Chagha Sefid occurred with Hole and Flannery's 1961 survey (Hole 1962; Hole and Flannery 1962). The site was again briefly visited and studied during our 1963 field season (Hole, Flannery and Neely 1969). Our intensive survey of 1968–1969, and Hole's (1977) excavations during those same years, comprise the most recent archaeological research at Chagha Sefid.

An initial intensive surface survey was undertaken that covered all but the extremely steep northern slopes of the site. This was done not only to determine the overall artifact distributions, but also to determine the most likely locations where test excavations would encounter cultural deposits spanning an archaeological discontinuity that was recognized in previous work on the Deh Luran Plain (Hole, Flannery and Neely 1969:358). The intensive survey suggested that the eroded western slope of Chagha Sefid (Hole 1977: Figs. 1, 2; Plates 1b, 2) was the most likely location to reveal deposits spanning the period from the Mohammed Jaffar through the Sabz phases (ca. 6400–5000 B.C.). As reported by Hole (1977), the predictive accuracy of our survey was gratifying. The survey recorded numerous indications of architecture eroding from the mound as well as the nature of the ceramic and lithic artifacts observed.

6. **Phases**: Frank Hole's (1977) excavations indicate that Chagha Sefid evidently had a continuous occupation from the Ali Kosh phase through the Sabz phase. Systematically collected surface samples, not fully studied, indicate continued occupation during the Khazineh and Mehmeh phases. Bayat phase ceramics, including diagnostic heavy bowl fragments with vertical curved line motifs (LS-RB-9), but also characteristic very fine bowls, either plain (LS-RB-1) or with solid exterior paint (LS-RB-4) or horizontal chevrons (LS-RB-7), and high jar necks with solid paint (LS-RJ-1) are common on all slopes of the mound. Limited Farukh phase occupation is indicated by two bowl sherds with dot motifs (LS-RB-10) found on the southeast slope. The site was then evidently abandoned for several centuries, until its reoccupation during Early Uruk times as indicated by the occurrence of beveled rim bowls with tapered rims (so-called "proto-beveled rim bowls") (US-RB-1), fine bowls (US-RB-3), various larger bowls with thumb impressed strips (US-RB-7, 11), and neckless, ledge rim jars (US-RJ-2), all

but the first on Sargarab ware. Occupation during Middle Uruk times is indicated by the occurrence of a cross-hatch incised band (US-O-2) on Sargarab ware. Significant Late Uruk occupation is indicated by band rim and ledge-rim (UU-RJ-10; Fig. IV.19 b) bottles and droop spouts (UU-O-11; Fig. IV.19 c), expanded band rim jars with very low necks (UU-RJ-6; Fig. IV.19 f) and shoulders with cross-hatch incised triangles (UU-O-6; Fig IV.19 l) typical of such jars, twist handles of various types (UU-O-13, 14; Fig. IV.19 i-k), and groove-and-oblique shoulder decoration (UU-O-3; Fig. IV.19 m) from small jars. At the end of the Late Uruk phase, Chagha Sefid was again abandoned, and evidently remained so until a possible small Sasanian/Early Islamic period occupation occurred.

7. **Comment**: The excavations revealed Chogha Mami Transitional phase layers from 102.3 to 104.5 meters elevation on the southwest slope, and somewhat higher on the northeast slope indicating a surface area of at least 0.42 ha. Sabz phase layers were immediately above at 104.5 to 105.5 meters, indicating an area of at least 0.33 ha. Surface distributions indicate that Khazineh and Mehmeh phase layers may have been planed off and dumped over the edges of the mound, but they may have covered about 0.31 ha. Bayat phase layers outcrop at an elevation of about 106 meters and cover at least 0.26 ha. Farukh phase debris is of limited extent and has been assigned an area of 0.12 ha. Early and Middle Uruk debris outcrops at about 108 meters and covers an area of about 0.31 and 0.17 ha, respectively. Late Uruk debris occurs under the early 20th century fort, outcropping at about 110 meters and covering at least 0.09 ha. Because of the steepness of the mound, it is likely there has been some lateral erosion, and the original surface areas have probably been somewhat reduced. See Chapter VI for a discussion of the drainage (DL-276A) passing just north of this site.

8. **References**: Gautier and Lampre 1905: Fig. 94; Hole 1962; Hole and Flannery 1962; Hole, Flannery and Neely 1969; Lorimer 1908:17).

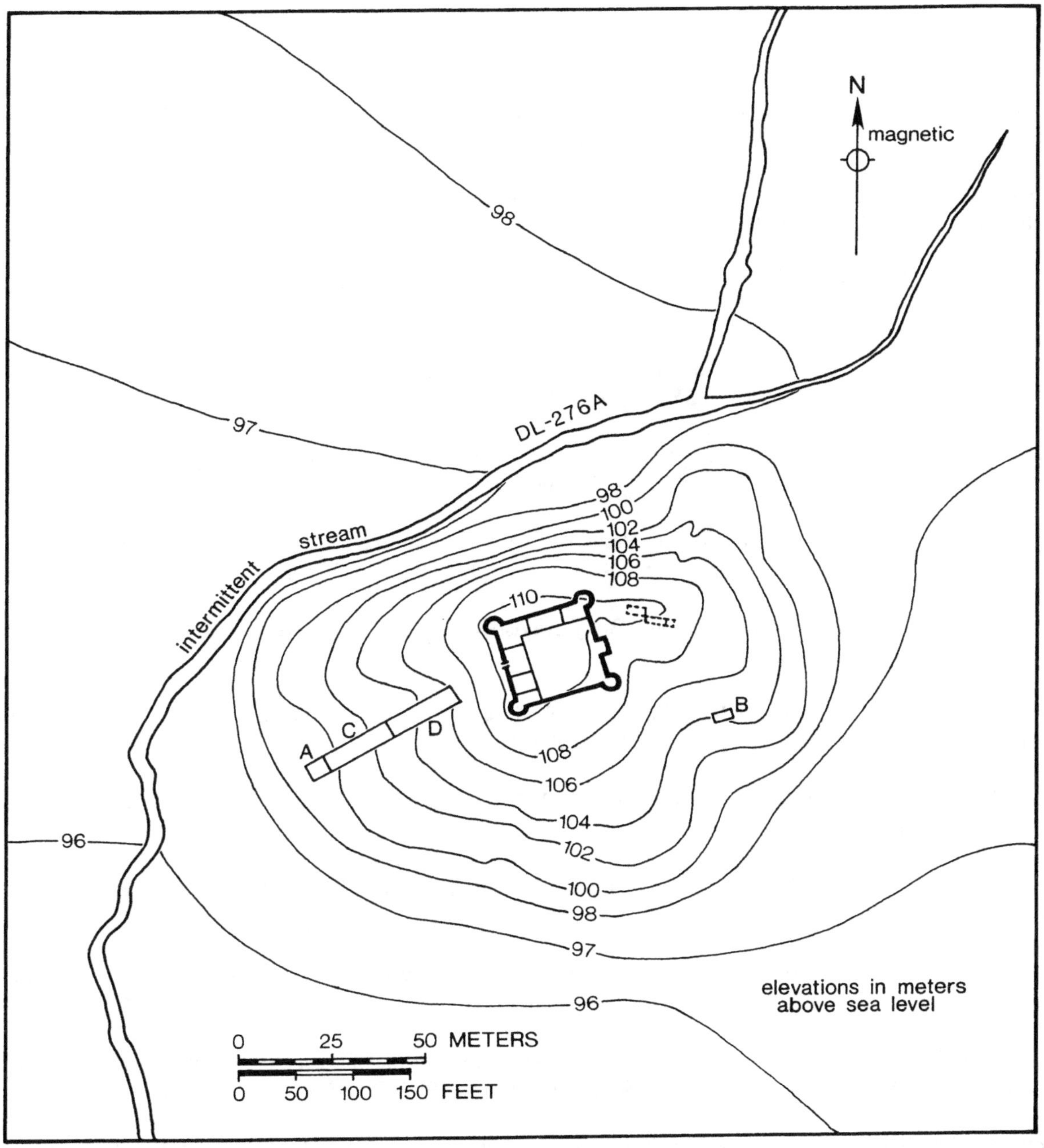

Figure IV.18. Map of Chagha Sefid (DL-23)

Figure IV.19. Late Uruk ceramics from Chagha Sefid (DL-23)

a. Incurved Bowl with Band Rim and Impressed Strip (cf. UU-RB-4) Fine sand inclusions, Body light brown (2.5YR 6/6), Diam ca. 21 cm, Surface yellowish white (2.5YR 9/2).

b. Ledge Rim Bottle (UU-RJ-10) Fine sand and vegetal inclusions, Body yellowish gray (7.5Y 8/2), Diam 4.5 cm, Surface pale yellow (5Y 8/3) (cf. Wright 1981: Fig. 54b).

c. Droop Spout (UU-O-11) Fine sand inclusions, Body pale yellow (5Y 8/3), Surface pale yellow (2.5Y 9/2) (cf. Wright 1981: Fig. 55n).

d. Small Round Rim Jar (UU-RJ-1) with Grooved Shoulder (UU-O-2) Fine sand inclusions, Body yellowish gray (2.5Y 8/2), Diam 7 cm, Surface pale yellow (2.5Y 8/3) (cf. Wright 1981: Fig. 48g-h, 55j, l).

e. Round Rim Jar (UU-RJ-2) with Grooved Shoulder (UU-O-2) Fine sand inclusions, Body grayish yellow (2.5Y 7/3), Diam 10 cm, Surface grayish yellow (2.5Y 7/2) (cf. same).

f. Low Expanded Band Rim Jar (UU-RJ-6) with Punctates. Fine sand and vegetal inclusions, Body yellowish gray (10YR 8/2), Diam 14 cm, Surface yellowish gray (2.5Y 8/2) (cf. Wright 1981: Fig. 52a-g).

g. Small Expanded Rim Jar. Fine sand inclusions, Body grayish yellow (5Y 7/4), Diam 11 cm, Surface pale yellow (5Y 8/3) (cf. Wright 1981: Fig. 50a- e).

h. Out-turned Expanded Rim Jar (UU-RJ-7) Fine sand inclusions, Body light yellowish brown (7.5YR 7/5), Diam ca. 14 cm, Surface pale yellow (2.5Y 8/3) (cf. Wright 1981: Fig. 50 l-p).

i. Flat Twist Handle (UU-O-13) Fine sand inclusions, Body light yellowish brown (10YR 7/4), Surface yellowish white (10YR 9/1) (cf. Johnson 1973: Pl. VII e).

j. Double Full Twist Handle (cf. UU-O-14) Fine sand and calcite inclusions, Body light brown (5YR 5/5), Surface pale orange-yellow (10YR 8/3).

k. Full Twist Handle (UU-O-14) Fine sand inclusions, Body light yellowish brown (10YR 7/3), Surface pale yellow (2.5Y 8/3) (cf. Wright 1981: Fig. 55 l; Johnson 1973: Pl. VIII a).

l. Jar Shoulder with Incised Cross Hatch Triangles (UU-O-6) Fine sand inclusions, Body pale yellow (7.5Y 8/3), Surface yellowish white (7.5YR 9/2) (cf. Wright 1981: Fig. 55e; Johnson 1973: Pl. IV b).

m. Jar Shoulder with Grooves and Oblique Incisions (UU-O-3) Fine sand and calcite inclusions, Body light yellowish brown (7.5YR 6/5), Surface yellowish pink (5YR 7/4) (cf. Wright 1981: Fig. 55f-g).

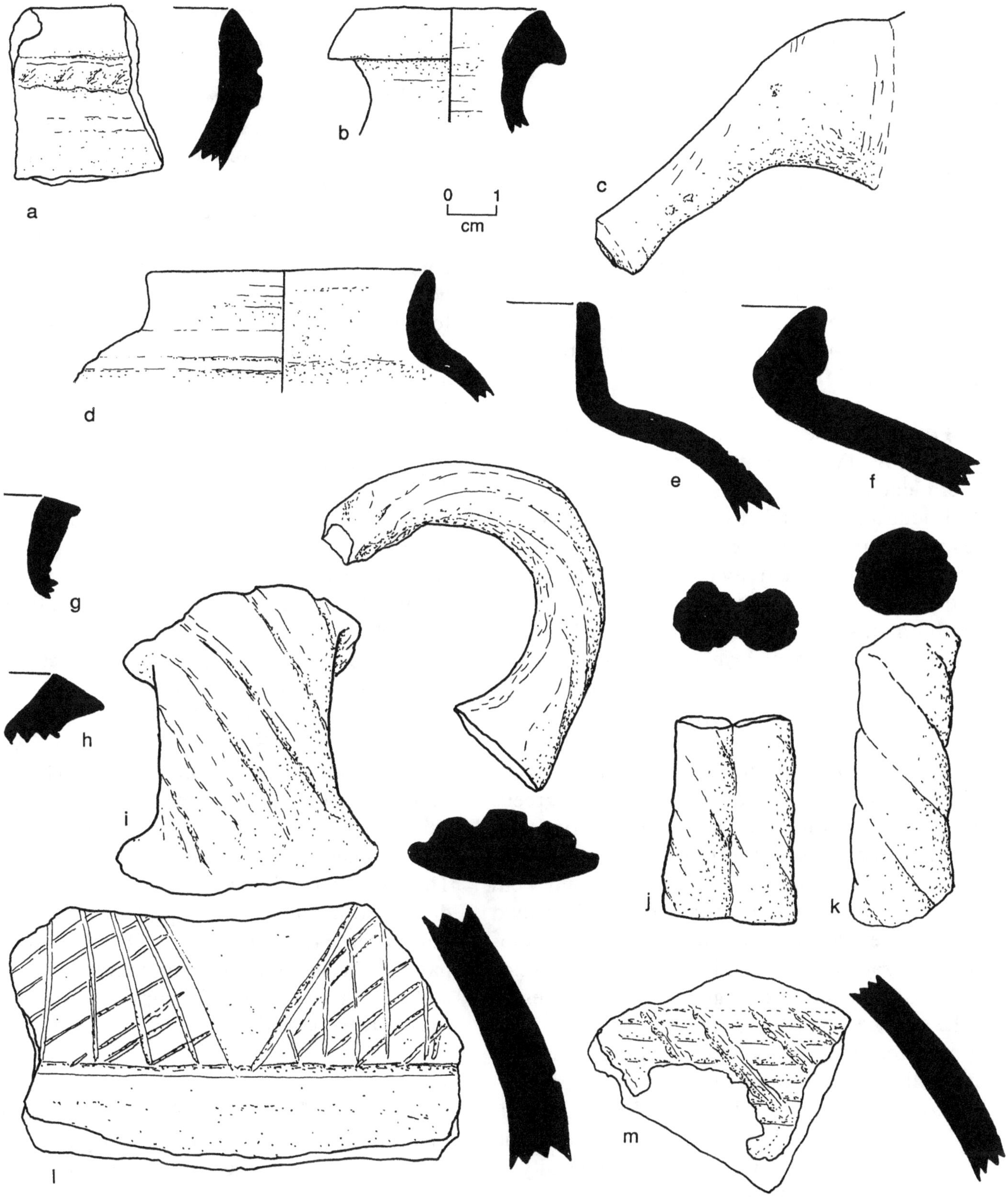

Figure IV.19. Late Uruk ceramics from Chagha Sefid (DL-23)

1a. **Number**: DL-24
1b. **Name**: Baulah
2. **Grid**: 1704.6–1182.6
3. **Dimensions**:

Diameter:	230 m
Height:	5.0 m
Circumference:	725 m
Area:	4.18 ha

4. **Modern Environmental Context**: On a terrace northeast of the Ab-i Garm stream where it leaves the northern alluvial slopes of the plain and spreads out into the saline depression, today an area of irrigated fields.

5. **Features**: The overall form of this site is elliptical (Fig. IV.20), with its outer limits being rather clearly defined by a small recent canal and the agricultural fields that surround it. This mound rises in four rather well-defined levels or terraces. Either some special activity occurred on the site or some of the later construction phases of this site were burned, since gray ash and fire-cracked rock are dense in the upper layers of the site and are being exposed in erosional cuts. A number of burials were found eroding from the northern portion of the second and third levels/terraces above the alluvial plain. Boulder wall footings were visible, scattered over the site's surface. A greenish-buff baked brick was found on the first terrace/level above the plain in the northwest quadrant of the site. It measured 20 by 22 cm and 5 cm in thickness, and had rather irregular surfaces and edges, and evidence of a good deal of chaff tempering. A rather large number of grinding stones and slabs, complete and fragmentary, were present on the surface. Many of these had apparently been exposed through the recent excavation of numerous shallow pits into the summit and upper levels/terraces of the site. A large number of denticulated sickle blades (Fig. IV.21 d-f) were found scattered over the site. The number and density of the blades, as well as the number of apparently unused blades present on the southwest quadrant of the site, indicates an activity area where blade tools were made and sickles were repaired.

6. **Phases**: A moderate quantity of ceramics was found, with the greatest amount appearing in the southwest quadrant of the site and the least in the northeast. There are Elamite and Sasanian/Early Islamic occupations, but the major occupations are those of the IIIrd and IInd millennia. Clay wall cones (Fig. IV.21 c) and a stone bowl fragment, which could be either Uruk or Jemdet Nasr, were found on the south half of the site. Also found here was a string-cut bottle base (Fig. IV.21 p) and a hatched strip on a jar shoulder carination. These items, in the absence of any of the common and distinctive Late Uruk diagnostic ceramics, suggest occupation during the Jemdet Nasr phase. Early Dynastic I–II sherds were found over the entire site, with the greatest numbers and density occurring on the northern half of the site. Diagnostic sherds include solid-footed conical cup fragments (ED-BC-1; Fig. IV.21 b) and fragments of jar shoulders with polychrome motifs (ED-O-5; Fig. IV.21 n, o). Many plain appliqué strips (ED-O-1) and some oblique hatched examples (ED-O-2), and various jar rims (ED-RJ-1 to 5; Fig. IV.21 h-m) and bases (ED-B-1 to 4) of broadly Early Dynastic date are common. Rims (ED-RJ-6), monochrome decorated shoulders (ED-O-6) and bases (ED-B-5) of the small carinated pots of the Early Dynastic III phase are also widely scattered. The Akkadian, Elamite, and later ceramics will be discussed in subsequent reports. Suffice it to say that at least the south half of Baulah appears to have been occupied during Jemdet Nasr times, and the entire site was occupied throughout the Early Dynastic period.

7. **Comment**: We have assigned an area of 2.09 ha to the possible Jemdet Nasr occupation and the full site area of 4.18 ha to the Early Dynastic occupations. See Chapter VI for a discussion of associated channel DL-276B.

8. **References**: Carter 1971.

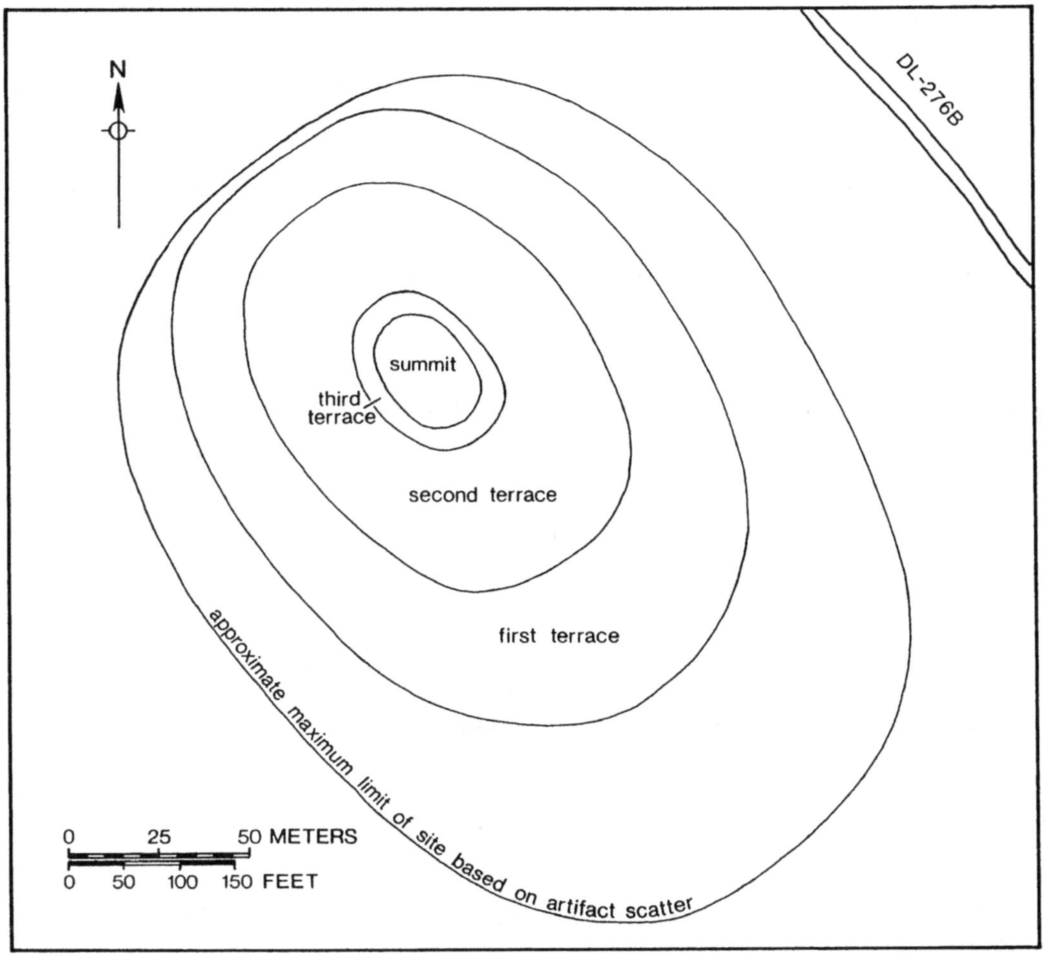

Figure IV.20. Map of Baulah (DL-24)

Figure IV.21. Jemdet Nasr and Early Dynastic ceramics from Baulah (DL-24)

a. Wide Cup Base (ED-BC-3) (Area 2) Fine sand inclusions, Body pink (7.5Y 8/3), Base diam 5.5 cm (Wright 1981: Fig 45c).

b. Narrow Cup Base (ED-BC-1) (Area 2) Trace of fine sand, Body white (5Y 8/2), Base diam 2.10 cm, (Wright 1981: Fig 45f, g).

c. Ceramic Cone (Area 2) Traces of fine sand and vegetal inclusions, Body pale yellow (5Y 8/3) (Wright 1981: Fig 76c).

d. Utilized Blade (Area 2) Fine Brown chert.

e. Single Denticulate Sickle Blade (Area 2), Fine translucent tan chert.

f. Double Denticulate Sickle Blade (Area 2) Medium gray chert.

g. Disc bead (Area 2) Oolitic marble, Note off-center double drilling, (cf. Wright 1981:158).

h. Round Lip Jar (ED-RJ-1) (Area 3) Fine sand inclusions, Body white (2.5Y 8/2), Diam 12 cm, (Wright 1981: Fig 49).

i. Same (Area 4) Fine sand inclusions, Body white (5Y 8/2), Diam 10 cm (cf. Same).

j. Flared Expanded Jar (ED-RJ-3) (Area 4) Fine sand inclusions, Body pale yellow (5Y 8/3), Diam 12.5 cm, (Wright 1981: Fig 51 l).

k. Band Rim Jar (ED-RJ-5) (Area 3) Fine sand inclusions, Body very pale brown (2.5Y 8/2), Diam ca 16 cm, (Wright 1981: Fig 54f).

l. Flared Expanded Jar (ED-RJ-3) (Area 3) Fine sand and calcite inclusions, Body white (5Y 8/2), Diam ca. 21 cm (Wright 1981: Fig 52h-j).

m. Ledge Rim Jar (ED-RJ-4) (Area 2) Fine sand and calcite inclusions, Body white (2.5Y 8/2), Diam 20.5 cm (Wright 1981: Fig 53m, p-q).

n. Jar Shoulder with Polychrome Motif (ED-O-6) Area 4) Fine sand, calcite, and vegetal inclusions, Body pinkish gray (7.5YR 7/3), Paints red (10R 4/4) and black (10R 3/1) (Wright 1981: Fig 61d, e).

o. Same (Area 4) Fine sand and calcite inclusions, Body pinkish gray (7.5YR 7/3), Paints red (10R 5/5) and black (10R 3/1) (cf. Same).

p. Bottle Base (cf. UU-RJ-10,11) (Area 2) Fine sand inclusions, Body pale yellow (5Y 8/3), Base Diam 3.08 cm .

q. Possible Foot Fragment of a "Flower Stand" (Area not recorded) Fine sand and calcite inclusions, Body pale red (2.5YR 7/3).

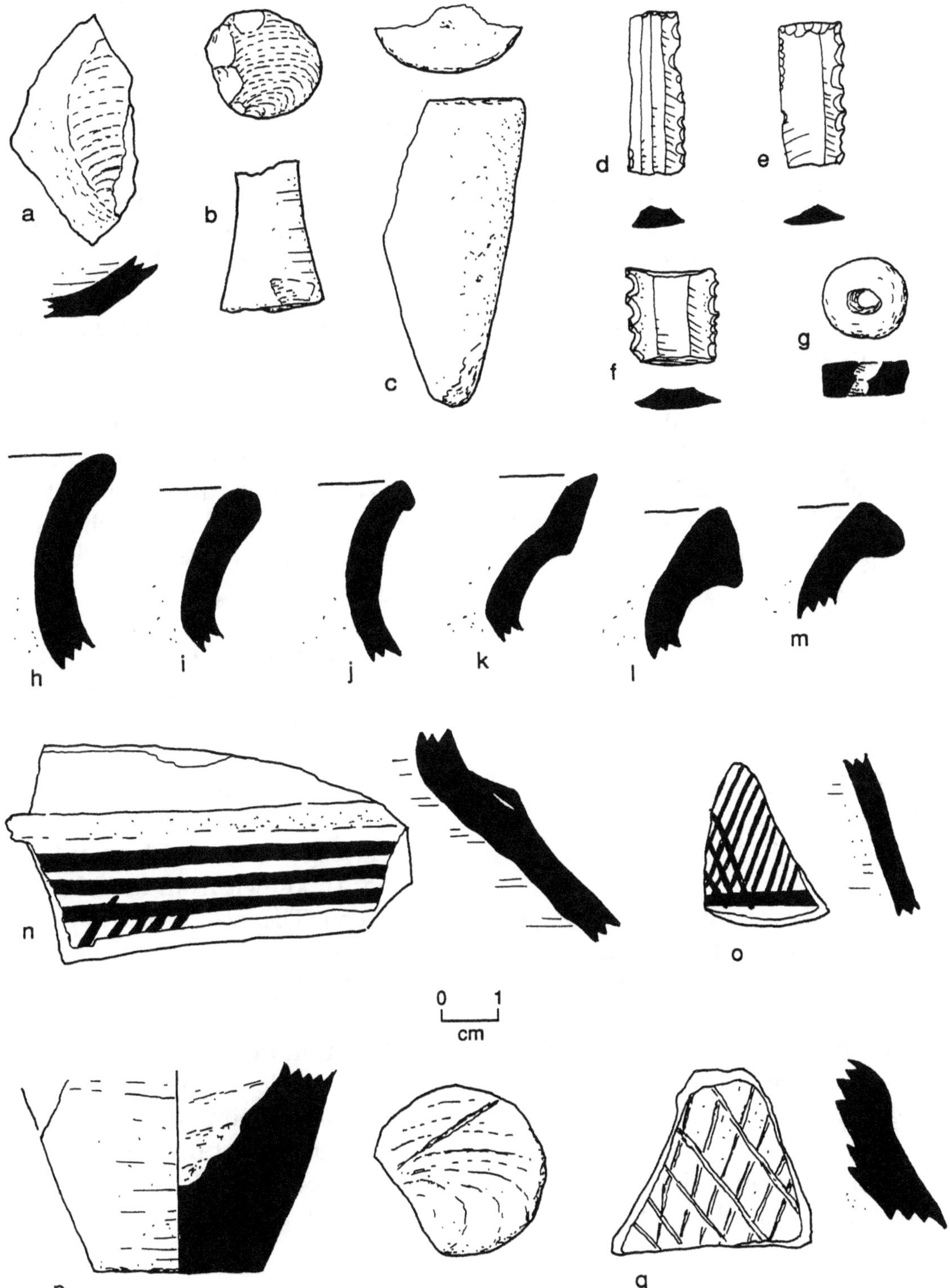

Figure IV.21. Jemdet Nasr and Early Dynastic ceramics from Baulah (DL-24)

1a. **Number**: DL-25
1b. **Name**:
2. **Grid**: 1704.5–1182.6
3. **Dimensions**:

Diameter:	25 m
Height:	ca. 2 m
Area:	0.05 ha

4. **Modern Environmental Context**: On the Mehmeh River alluvial fan, about 100 meters southwest of the present channel of the river.

5. **Features**: This small mound has a dense scatter of sherds and flaked stone.

6. **Phases**: The small available ceramic sample includes an inner rim embellishment commonly found on "Sabz pots" (ES-RB-10; cf. Hole, Flannery and Neely 1969: Figs. 50 a, 53 a) and a star-shaped spindle whorl (ES-O-1), found in both Chogha Mami Transitional and Sabz assemblages. There are four fragments of carinated bowls with interior cross-hatch (ES-RB-11) that are characteristically Khazineh. Also present are two jar shoulders with painted bands and sigma and X-motifs, a basin rim with painted band and triangles on the lip (ES-RB-18), and an incurved bowl with alternated opposed triangles and vertical lines (cf. Hole, Flannery and Neely 1969: Figs. 52 g, 54 e), all of which are common in the Khazineh and Mehmeh phases. The most conservative interpretation is that this mound was occupied during the Sabz and Khazineh phases.

8. **Comment**: The reported observations and collections were made during the 1961 survey. DL-25 was beyond the limits of the 1968 survey. We assign the full area of this small site to both the Sabz and Khazineh phases. See Chapter VI for a discussion of associated canals DL-319 and 320.

1a. **Number**: DL-26
1b. **Name**:
2. **Grid**: 1704.4–1182.6
3. **Dimensions**:

Diameter:	25 m
Height:	ca. 2 m
Area:	0.05 ha

4. **Modern Environmental Context**: On the Mehmeh River alluvial fan, about 100 meters southwest of the present channel of the river.

5. **Features**: A small mound only 25 meters east of DL-25 with densely scattered sherds, flaked stone, and ground stone over the surface.

6. **Phases**: In the small collection from this site, there is a Khazineh Red Ware rim (ES-SJ-1) and a fragment of a carinated bowl with interior cross-hatch (ES-RB-11), both of which are characteristically Khazineh. In addition, there is a basin rim with painted band and triangles on the lip (ES-RB-18), which may be either Khazineh or Mehmeh phase. Finally, a bowl rim with vertical zig-zag (cf. Hole, Flannery and Neely 1969: Fig. 55 q), known from the Mehmeh phase, was also found. The most conservative interpretation is that this mound was occupied during the Khazineh and Mehmeh phases.

8. **Comment**: Our observations and collections were made during the 1961 survey. DL-26 was beyond the limits of the 1968 survey. We assign the full area of this small site to both phases. See Chapter VI for a discussion of associated canals DL-319 and 320.

1a. **Number**: DL-27
1b. **Name**: Tenel Ramon
2. **Grid**: 1704.6–1182.8
3. **Dimensions**:

Length:	170 m (E-W)
Width:	150 m (N-S)
Height:	West: 8.0 m; East 7.0 m
Circumference:	ca. 600 m
Area:	2.49 ha

4. **Modern Environmental Context**: On the Mehmeh River alluvial fan, about 300 meters southwest of the present channel of the river.

5. **Features**: The site consists of a large oval mound having two distinct parts or "lobes" separated by a lower "saddle" (Fig. IV.22). The larger western lobe of the mound measures about 90 meters east-west by 110 meters north-south at the present level of the alluvial plain. The sides of the western lobe rise in an unbroken steep slope to a relatively broad, slightly mounded summit about 8 meters above the present level of the alluvial fan. This summit measures 38 meters east-west by 21 meters north south. The smaller eastern lobe measures some 72 meters east-west and 60 meters north-south at its base. The slightly convex summit rises about 7 meters above the plain, and measures 25 meters east-west by 12 meters north-south. A terraced area, about 5.5 meters above the plain, extends from the steeply sloping sides of the summit toward the east. The summits of both lobes have been rather badly disturbed by modern burials and what appear to be looter's holes.

Two distinct architectural terraces extend in a step-like fashion from the north side of the bi-lobed mound. The uppermost of the two stepped terraces to the north is about 2.5 meters above the

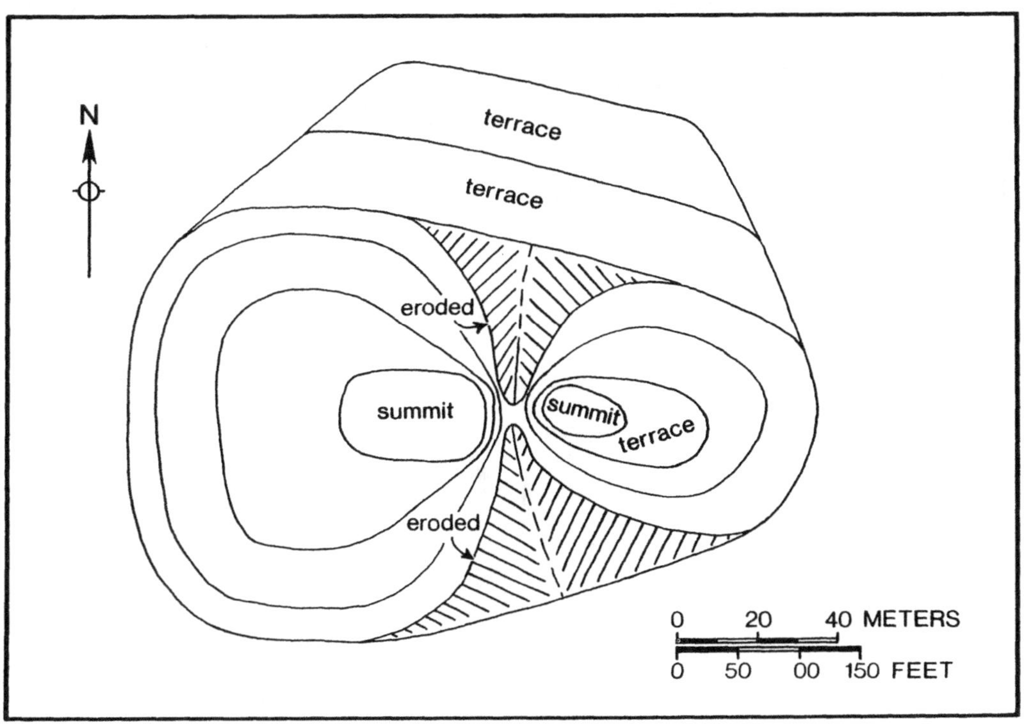

Figure IV.22. Map of Tenel Ramon (DL-27)

plain at its juncture with the bi-lobed mound. The lower terrace is about 1.5 meters above the plain at its juncture with the upper terrace. The northern end of the lower terrace blends into the surrounding alluvium.

A large number of cobble and boulder wall footings are being exposed by erosional processes on the summits and all slopes of the site. Several of the footings on the summits may be recent, but others are undoubtedly contemporaneous with the site's ancient occupations. Erosion has also exposed small portions of ceramic coffins on the southwest slope of the western lobe, at levels between three and four meters below its summit. Unfortunately not enough of these coffins were exposed to permit an assessment of their age.

6. **Phases**: A moderate to heavy sherd concentration was scattered over the surface of the site. Khazineh carinated bowls (ES-RB-11, 12, 14) as well as Mehmeh bowls with ladder motifs (ES-RB-5) and interior ledge rim jars (ES-RJ-2) occurred on the southwest slope of the western lobe up to 4 meters above the alluvial plain, that is, just below the level of the coffins. It is interesting to note that sherds of these phases did not extend this high on any other portion of the site. Similar Khazineh and Mehmeh sherds occurred on the east slope only up to two meters above the plain. Bayat bowls with vertical curved lines (LS-RB-9) and Farukh bowls with fine dot motifs (LS-RB-10) and step motifs (LS-RB-15) were widely scattered. The Early Uruk open bowl with thumb-impressed strip (US-RB-7), flared expanded jar (US-RJ- 9), and high expanded band rim jar (US-RJ-10) fragments, all of Sargarab ware, were also scattered over the site. Early Dynastic I–II occupation is indicated by a solid-footed conical cup base (ED-CB-1), thin round lip jars (ED-RJ-2), and jar shoulders with polychrome motifs (ED-O-5) scattered on and around the mound. Much Elamite pottery, as well as some later materials, will be reported in a subsequent study.

7. **Comment**: We assign the southwest portion of this site, covering about 0.50 ha, to the Khazineh and Mehmeh phases. As we are unable to assess the affects of disturbance by the lengthy later occupations, we arbitrarily assign areas of 1.00 ha. to the Bayat and Farukh phase occupations as well as to the Early Uruk reoccupation, and 2.0 ha to the Early Dynastic I–II occupation. See Chapter VI for a discussion of associated canals DL-319 and 320.

8. **References**: Carter 1971.

1a. **Number:** DL-28
1b. **Name**: Tepe Khazineh
2. **Grid**: 1722.1–1172.0
3. **Dimensions**:
Length: Originally ca. 90 m; modified to ca. 65 to 71 m.
Width: Originally ca. 62 m, modified to ca. 55 m
Height: ca. 5 m
Circumference: 255 m
Area: 0.52 ha

4. **Modern Environmental Context**: On the alluvial fan of the Dawairij River about one kilometer from the present Dawairij channel.

5. **Features**: DL-28 consists of a single mound, irregularly elliptical in plan-view (Fig. IV.23). About 10 meters of the northeastern end of the mound, and approximately 15 meters of its southeastern end, have been cut away perhaps for use as fill for the road joining the modern villages of Musiyan and Ain Girzan, which passes just east of the mound. The original length of the mound was determined by noting variations in the color and texture of the soils visible at present ground level. During the study of the southern end of the mound, while attempting to determine how much of it had been removed, a fragmentary small Early Dynastic polychrome decorated jar and some associated sherds of the same date were found eroding from the "floor" of the road fill cut. It is possible that these were part of a complex of artifacts from a grave, but without excavation (which our survey permit did not allow) this is not certain. It was not possible to discern the original southwestern extremity of the mound. Evidently the 1903 excavations and recent fill removal have

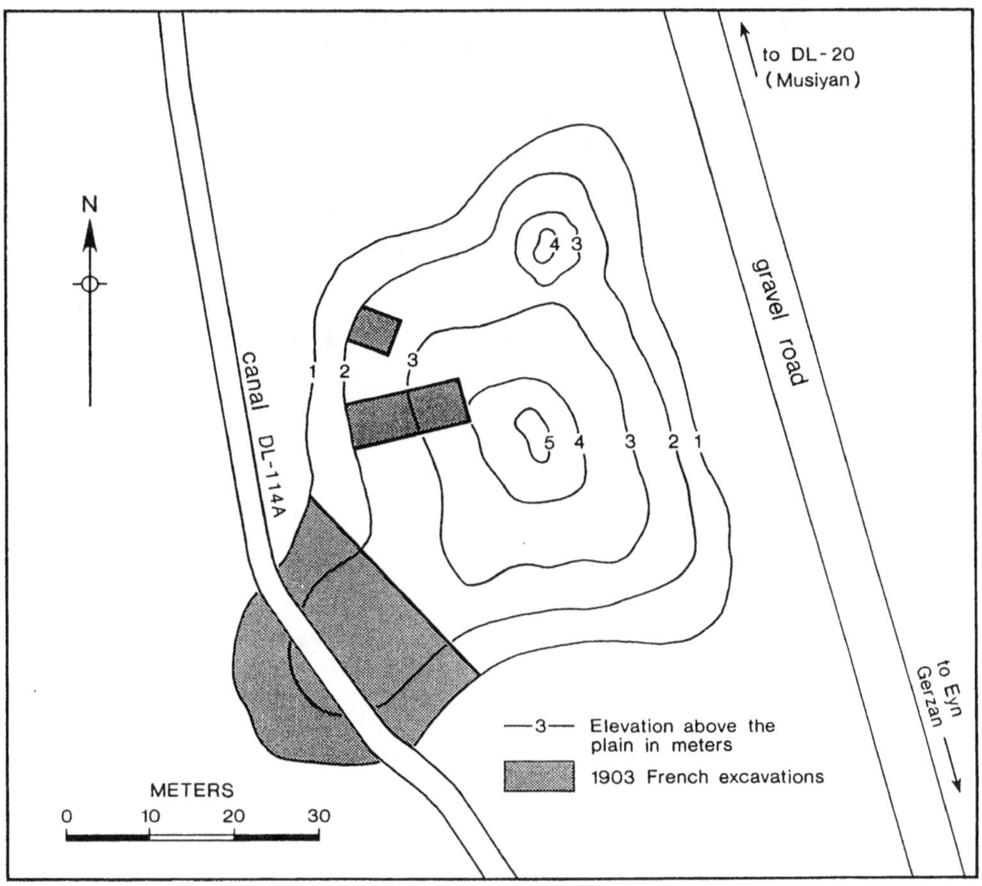

Figure IV.23. Map of Tepe Khazineh (DL-28)

Figure IV.24. Chogha Mami Transitional, Khazineh, and Mehmeh ceramics from Tepe Khazineh (DL-28)

a. Bowl Rim with Interior Pendant Triangles (ES-RB-7), Medium sand inclusions. Body white 5Y 8/2), Diam ca. 35 cm, Surface pale yellow (5Y 8/2) Paint dark grayish brown (10YR 4/2). (cf. Hole 1977: Fig. 50c-d).

b. Basin Rim with Rim Bands, Lip Triangles (ES-RB-18), Fine sand inclusions, Body pale yellow (5Y 8/2), Diam ?, Surface white (2.5Y 8/2), Paint very dark gray (10YR 4/1) (cf. Hole, Flannery and Neely 1969: Fig. 59a).

c. Carinated Bowl with Interior Negative Zig-Zags (cf. ES-RB-13), Fine sand inclusions, Body white (2.5Y 8/2), Diam ca. 24 cm, Surface pale yellow (2.5Y 9/3), Paint very dark gray (10YR 3/1) (cf. Hole, Flannery and Neely 1969: Fig. 56a, 57r).

d. Carinated Bowl Rim with Interior Vertical Lines etc., Fine sand inclusions, Body light red (2.5YR 6/5), Diam ?, Surface white (2.5Y 8/2), Paint very dark brown (10YR 2/2) (Hole, Flannery and Neely 1969: Fig. 57i-j).

e. Carinated Bowl Sherd with same, Fine sand inclusions, Body light olive gray (5Y 6/2), Surface pale olive (2.5Y 6/3), Paint dark gray (2.5Y 4/1) (Hole, Flannery and Neely 1969: Fig. 57 i-j).

f. Bowl Rim with Exterior Interlocking Diamonds (ES-RB-10), Fine sand inclusions, Body pale yellow (5Y 8/3), Diam ca. 35 cm, Surface white (5Y 8/2), Paint dark gray (10YR 4/1).

g. Incurved Bowl Sherd with Exterior Negative Zig-Zag (ES-RB-15), Fine sand inclusions, Body light yellowish brown (10YR 6/4), Surface white (2.5Y 8/2), Paint dark gray (10YR 4/1) (cf. Hole, Flannery and Neely 1969: Fig. 52).

h. Sherd with Exterior Negative Zig-Zag (ES-RB-15), No visible inclusions, Body white (5Y 8/2), Surface white (5Y 8/2), Paint dark gray (2.5Y 4/1) (Hole, Flannery and Neely 1969: Fig. 52b; Hole 1977: Fig. 50h).

i. Bowl Base with Interior Radial and Comb Motifs, Fine sand inclusions, Body white (2.5Y 9/2), Surface white (2.5Y 8/2), Paint very dark gray (10YR 3/1) (Hole, Flannery and Neely 1969:63o).

j. Bowl Sherd with Interior Zig-Zags, No visible inclusions, Body very pale brown (10YR 8/3), Surface very pale brown (10YR 8/3), Paint very dark grayish brown (10YR 3/2). (Hole, Flannery and Neely 1969: Fig. 56b, f).

k. Bowl Sherd with Exterior Right Triangle Motifs (ES-RB-6), No visible inclusions, Body very pale brown (10YR 8/3), Surface white (2.5Y 8/2), Paint very dark gray (10YR 3/1) (Hole, Flannery and Neely 1969: Fig. 62c).

l. Bowl sherd with Exterior Grid Motif, Fine sand and calcite inclusions, Body pale yellow (2.5Y 9/3), Surface pale yellow (5Y 9/3), Paint grayish brown (10YR 5/2).

Figure IV.24. Chogha Mami Transitional, Khazineh, and Mehmeh ceramics from Tepe Khazineh (DL-28)

erased all evidence of this part of the site. No indications of architecture were visible on the surface of the mound or on the surrounding alluvial plain. However, what appeared to be the truncated stubs of a few stone foundations with unfired mud brick walls were seen in the profiles of the cuts at both ends of the mound. The 1903 excavations by Gautier and Lampre (1905: Fig. 94, 72–73, Fig. 98) were not recognizable at the time of our visit to this site.

6. **Phases**: The earliest phase identified at Tepe Khazineh is the Chogha Mami Transitional phase, indicated by a bowl rim with pendant triangles (ES-RB-7; Fig. IV.24 a). There is a possible large variant of a Sabz phase "pot" (ES-RB-10, Fig. IV.24 f). A Khazineh phase occupation is definitely indicated by the presence of carinated bowls with wavy elements on the interior (ES-RB-13; Fig. IV.24 d, e; cf. Gautier and Lampre 1905: Figs. 172, 174) and by the presence of incurved bowls with negative zig-zags (ES-RB-15; Fig IV.24 g, h). Mehmeh phase occupation is definitely indicated by the presence of basin rims with goats (ES-RB-19; cf. Gautier and Lampre 1905: Figs. 200, 220, 225, 229), bowl fragments with a field of right triangle motifs (ES-RB-6; Fig. IV.24 k), and ladder motifs (ES-RB-5; cf. Gautier and Lampre 1905: Figs. 171, 220). The only later sherds from this site are of jars with polychrome motifs (ED-O-5; Gautier and Lampre 1905: Figs. 191, 192, 197, 250, 251) and of plain jars (Gautier and Lampre 1905: Figs. 269, 272) of the Early Dynastic I–II phase, probably from burials intrusive into the early site.

7. **Comment**: Gautier and Lampre recorded a width of 62 meters, which may have been the actual width of the tell before erosion of their own excavation on the southwest extension, as well as successive widenings of the canal (DL-114A) and the modifications made during construction of the nearby road. While the margins of this site have been modified by modern human activities, the summit of the mound has no evidence of recent disturbance. We have adapted Gautier and Lampre's (1905: Fig. 98) site map for our Figure IV.23 because it evidently more closely approximates the original form of the mound. It is likely that the contours shown on the otherwise exemplary French map were mistakenly numbered as 2 meters apart instead of 1 meter apart. We cannot assign a size to the deeply buried Chogha Mami Transitional and Sabz phase occupations of this site. We assign the full site area of 0.52 ha of this small high mound to the Khazineh and Mehmeh phases. See Chapter VI for a discussion of associated canals DL-114A.

8. **References**: Gautier and Lampre 1905: 72–73.

1a. **Number**: DL- 29
1b. **Name**: Tepe Ashrafabad
2. **Grid**: 1705.7–1186.9
3. **Dimensions**:
   Length: 100 m (N-S)
   Width: 90 m (E-W)
   Height: 3.0 m
   Circumference of main mound: 285 m
   Circumference of artifact scatter and footings: 400 m
   Area: 1.27 ha

4. **Modern Environmental Context**: At the juncture of the northern alluvial slopes of the plain, and the alluvial fan of the Mehmeh River, about one kilometer northeast of the present Mehmeh River channel.

5. **Features**: This single mound has relatively steep sides to the north and east, but to the west and south the slopes gently blend into the alluvial plain (Fig. IV.25). The mound is difficult to see unless the sun light is at a low angle due to its relatively low, flat form. A number of stone wall footings or foundations were found eroding

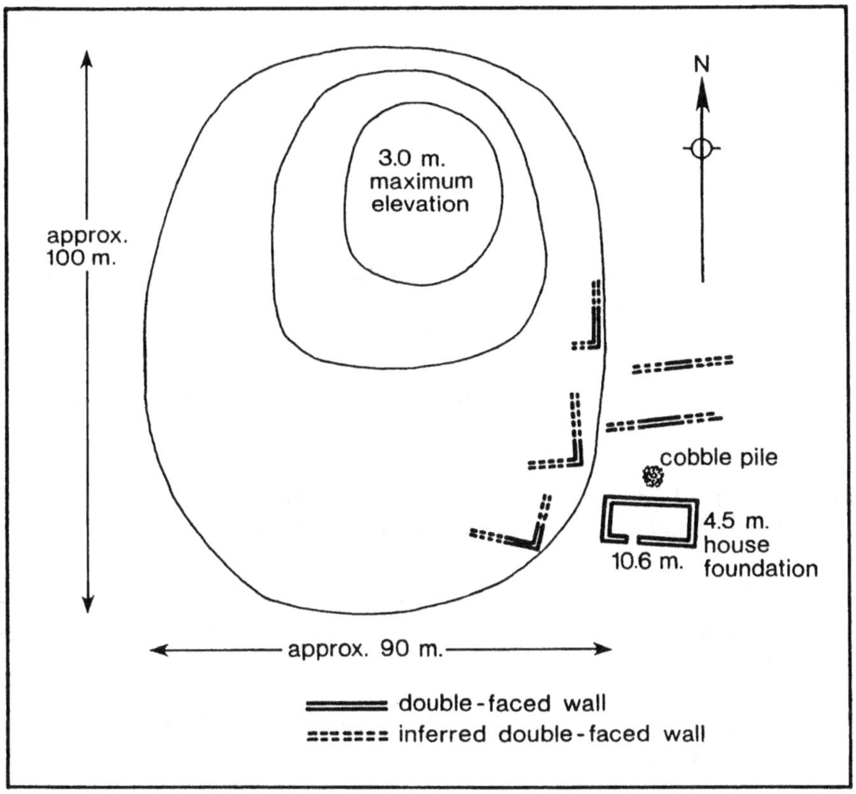

Figure IV.25. Map of Tepe Ashrafabad (DL-29)

from this site, with the greatest number located on the southeastern slope and extending out onto the plain. At first glance these appear to be late (Sasanian/Early Islamic), but closer observation of the construction, size, and associated artifacts indicates they are early (i.e., Mehmeh phase) structures. The most complete of these footings, outlining an east-west oriented, rectangular (approx. 10.6 m long, by 4.5 m wide) structure with well-defined internal features, as well as a southern doorway with a "doughnut-shaped" door pivot stone (see Hole, Flannery and Neely 1969:58–60, 73, Fig. 17, Plate 18 a), remained little changed in the some five years since Neely and Flannery originally mapped it. However, in that time evidences of several more similar structures have become apparent on the southeast slope of the site in close proximity to the footing described above.

6. **Phases**: Large ceramic collections from both the 1961 and 1968 surveys are available. Khazineh indicators include rims sherds of carinated bowls with interior cross-hatch designs (ES-RB-11) and wavy elements (ES-RB-13). Indicative of Mehmeh phase occupation are Mehmeh Red-on-red hole-mouth jar rims (ES-SJ-2; Fig. IV.26 a), bowls with ladder motifs (ES-RB-5; Fig. IV.26 e) and right triangle motifs (ES-RB-6; Fig. IV.26 l), and basins with goat

Figure IV.26 Mehmeh ceramics from Tepe Ashrafabad (DL-29)

a. Mehmeh Red-on-red Hole Mouth Jar Rim (ES-SJ-1), Chopped grass, limestone and hematite inclusions, Body light brown (7.5YR 6/5), Diam warped, Surface reddish-yellow (7.5YR 7/5), Paint reddish-brown (2.5YR 4/4) (Hole, Flannery and Neely 1969: Fig. 65i-j).

b. Basin Rim with Bands and Triangles on Lip (ES-RB-18), Fine sand inclusions, Body pale yellow (5Y 8/3), Diam warped, Surface white (2.5Y 8/2), Paint dark gray (7.5YR 4/1) (Hole, Flannery and Neely 1969: Fig. 59a).

c. Bowl Rim with Horizontal Chevrons (LS-RB-7), Fine sand inclusions, Diam ca. 28 cm, Body and Surface white (2.5Y 8/2), Paint gray (5Y 5/1) (Hole, Flannery and Neely 1969: Fig. 61 l).

d. Bowl Rim with Diamond Motifs (ES-RB-4), Fine sand inclusions. Body white (5Y 8/2), Diam ?, Surface light gray (2.5Y 7/2), Paint dark grayish brown (10YR 4/2).

e. Bowl Rim with Horizontal Chevron (LS-RB-7) and Horizontal Ladder Motifs (ES-RB-5) No visible inclusions, Body white (5Y 8/2), Diam ca. 22 cm, Surface white (2.5Y 8/2), Paint grayish brown (10YR 5/2) (Hole, Flannery and Neely 1969: Fig. 61e).

f. Rim with Negative Zig-Zag. No visible inclusions, Body pale yellow (5Y 7/3), Diam 10 cm, Surface pale yellow (5Y 7/3), Paint dark gray (7.5YR 4/1).

g. Bowl Rim with Possible Horizontal Ladder Motif (ES-RB-5), No visible inclusions, Body white (2.5Y 8/2), Diam 20 cm, Surface pale yellow (5Y8/3), Paint dark gray (10YR 4/1). (Hole, Flannery and Neely 1969: Fig. 61f).

h. Basin Rim with Interior Goat Motifs (ES-RB-19), Fine sand inclusions, Body white (2.5Y 8/2), Diam ca. 36 cm, Surface white 2.5Y 8/2), Paint reddish gray (5YR 5/2) (Hole, Flannery and Neely 1969: Fig. 59b-j, especially 59c, perhaps by the same painter; Wright 1981: Fig. 11e).

i. Bowl Rim with Various Motifs, Fine sand inclusions, Diam ?, Surface white (5Y 8/2), Paint dark gray (5YR 4/1). (Hole, Flannery and Neely 1969: Figs. 55i, 62h).

j. "Chariot Wheel" Spindle Whorl with Dot Motifs (ES-O-2), No visible inclusions, Body white (5Y 8/1), Surface light gray (2.5Y 7/2), Paint eroded, Weight 10.3 gm (Estimated ca. 20 gm when complete) (Hole, Flannery and Neely 1969: Fig. 89).

k. Basal Sherd of a Carinated Bowl with Radial Motif (ES-BB-4), Fine sand inclusions, Body pale yellow (5Y 9/3), Surface white (2.5Y 8/2), Paint gray (10R 5/1) (Hole Flannery and Neely 1969: Fig. 56b).

l. Sherd of Large Bowl with Right Triangle Motifs (ES-RB-6), No visible inclusions, Body white (5Y 9/2), Body Diameter ca. 28 cm, Surface very pale brown (10YR 7/3), Paint eroded (Hole, Flannery and Neely 1969: Figs. 61a, 62c; Wright 1981: Fig. 11c).

m. Jar Rim with Interior Ledge (ES-RJ-2), "X" Motifs on Shoulder, Fine sand inclusions, Body white (5Y 8/2), Diam 18 cm, Surface white (2.5Y 8/2), Paint reddish-gray (5YR 5/2) (Hole, Flannery and Neely 1969: Fig. 58a).

Figure IV.26 Mehmeh ceramics from Tepe Ashrafabad (DL-29)

Figure IV.27. Bayat Phase ceramics from Tepe Ashrafabad (DL-29)

a. Bayat Red Bowl Rim, No visible inclusions, Body red (2.5YR 5/6), Diam ca. 36 cm, Surface light red (2.5YR 6/5) (Hole, Flannery and Neely 1969: 67a; Wright 1981: Fig. 10 l, m).

b. Basin Rim with Grooved Lip (LS-BN-1), Coarse to medium sand inclusions, Body very pale brown (10YR 7/3), Diam 32 cm, Surface reddish yellow (7.5YR 7/5) (Hole, Flannery and Neely 1969: Fig 60e-f; Wright 1981: Fig. 23 d, f).

c. Large Bowl Rim with Multiple Bands (LS-RB-3), Medium sand inclusions, Body pale green (7.5Y 9/3), Diam warped, Surface pale yellow (7.5Y 7/3), Paint olive gray (5Y 4/2) (Wright 1981: Fig. 15f-g).

d. Small Plain Bowl Rim (LS-RB-1), Fine calcite inclusions indicated by fractures, Body white (2.5Y 8/2), Diam 13 cm, Surface pale yellow (2.5Y 8/3) (Note ridging indicating throwing of rim) (Hole, Flannery and Neely 1969: Fig. 48 g, h).

e. Same, No visible inclusions, Body very pale brown (10YR 8/3) Diam ca. 14 cm, Surface pale yellow (2.5Y 8/2) (Hole, Flannery and Neely 1969 Fig. 48 g, h; Wright 1981: Fig 13a-b).

f. Small Bowl with Oblique Element, No visible inclusions, Body light red (2.5YR 6/6), Diam ca. 21 cm, Surface white (10YR 9/3), Paint eroded (Hole, Flannery and Neely 1969: Fig. 68c).

g. Small Bowl with Horizontal Curved Line Motif (LS-RB-5), No visible inclusions, Body Pale yellow (5Y 9/3), Diam ?, Surface white (5Y 8/2), Paint reddish brown (5YR 4/3) (Hole, Flannery and Neely 1969: Fig. 61i; Wright 1981: Fig. 16a-c).

h. Same, Same inclusions, Body pale yellow (5Y 8/4), Diam ca. 16 cm, Surface pale yellow (5Y 8/4), Paint gray (5YR 5/1).

i. Same, Fine sand inclusions, Body pale yellow (5YR 8/4), Diam ?, Surface pale yellow (2.5Y 8/3), Paint dark brown (7.5YR 4/2)

j. Ovoid Spindle Whorl with Notches (LS-O-1), Fine sand inclusions, Body white (7.5Y 9/2), Diam 2.8 cms, Weight 7.7 gm, Surface pale yellow (5Y 7/3), Eroded paint splash on one side (Hole, Flannery and Neely 1969: Fig. 90d, 1981: Fig. 29i-j).

k. "Chariot Wheel" Spindle Whorl with "Comb" Motifs (ES-O-2), Fine calcite inclusions, Weight 14.6 gm (Estimated 19 gms complete), Body white (7.5Y 9/2), Surface pale yellow (5Y 7/3), Paint dark olive gray (5Y 3/2) (Hole Flannery and Neely 1969: Fig. 89b).

l. Sherd of Large Bowl with Vertical Curved Line Motifs (cf. LS-RB-9), Fine sand inclusions, Body reddish-brown (5YR 5/4), Diam ?, Surface white (5Y 8/2), Paint dark reddish gray (5YR 4/2) (Hole, Flannery and Neely 1969: Fig. 60i).

m. Small Bowl Base with Vertical Curved Line Motif (cf. LS-RB-9), No visible inclusions, Body white (7.5Y 9/3), Base diam 6.0 cm, Surface pale green (7.5Y 7/2), Paint eroded (Hole, Flannery and Neely Fig.: 60j; Wright 1981: Fig 16f-h).

n. Small Bowl Sherd with Concentric Circle Motifs, No visible inclusions, Body pale yellow (5Y 9/3), Body diam 11 cm, Surface light gray (7.5YR 7/2), Paint dark grayish brown (2.5Y 4/2) (cf. Hole, Flannery and Neely 1969: Fig. 62g; cf. Wright 1981: Fig. 22e).

o. Large Bowl Rim with Vertical Element (LS-RB-8) Medium sand inclusions, Body white (5Y 9/1), Diam 31 cm, Surface white (5Y 8/2), Paint dark grayish brown (10YR 4/2).

p. High Neck Jar Rim with Complete Exterior Neck and Shoulder Paint (LS-RJ-1) Fine sand inclusions, Body white (2.5Y 9/1), Diam ca. 19 cm, Surface white (2.5Y 8/1), Paint dark gray (10YR 4/1) (Hole Flannery, Neely 1969: Fig. 58f-g; Wright 1981: Fig. 24a).

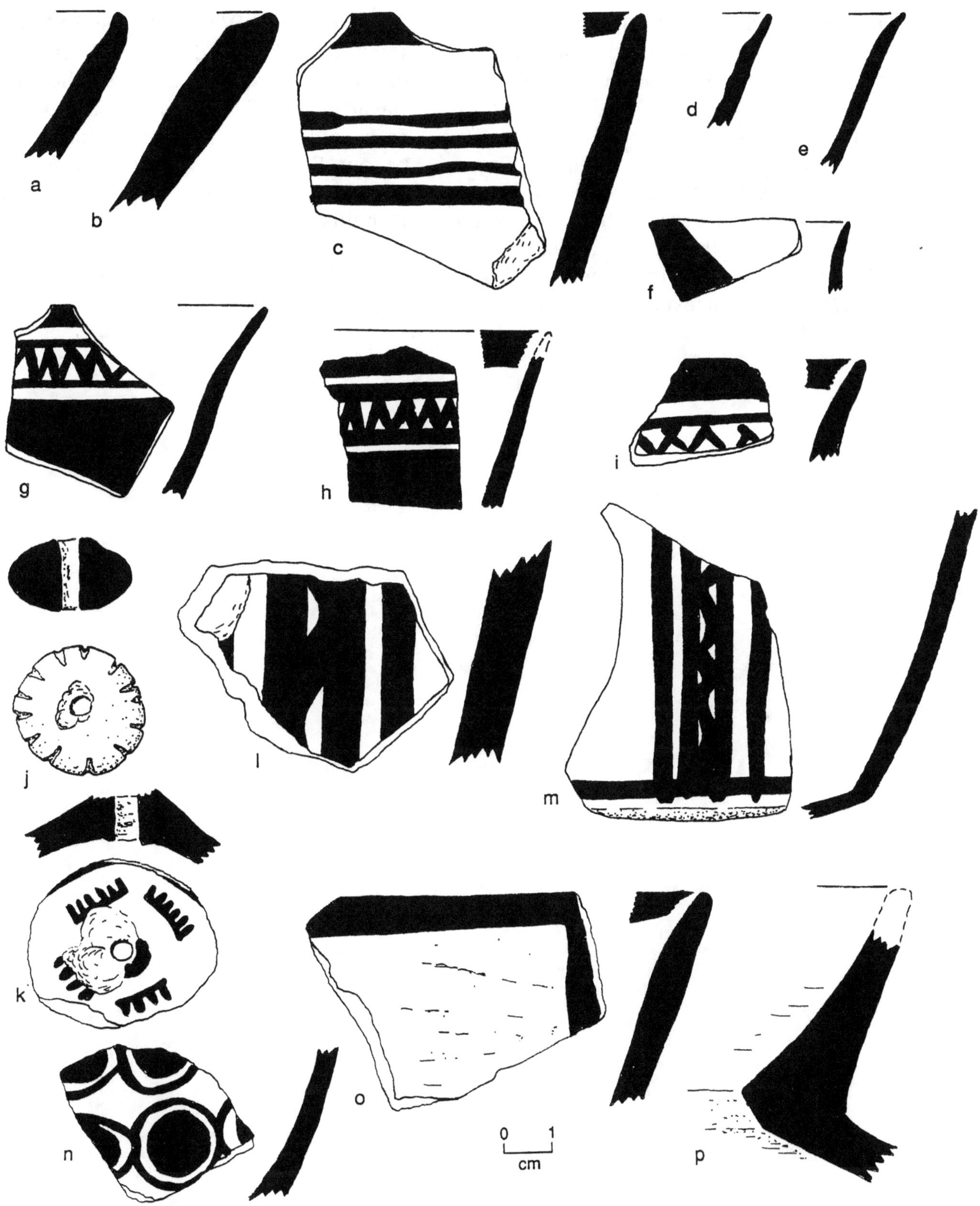

Figure IV.27. Bayat Phase ceramics from Tepe Ashrafabad (DL-29)

motifs (ES-RB-19; Fig. IV.26 h). Ceramics confirming a Bayat phase occupation are a bowl fragment with a heavy vertical curved line motif (LS-RB-9; Fig. IV.27 l), fine bowls with a horizontal curved line motifs alone (LS-RB-5; Fig. IV.27 g, h), and a predominance of high neck jars with completely painted necks (LS-RJ-1; Fig. IV.27 p). Suggestive of Farukh phase occupation are bowl fragments with solidly painted oblique diamonds (LS-BR-13) and sigma motifs (LS-BR-14), as well as high necked jars with painted bands (LS-RJ-3).

7. **Comment**: We ascribe the 0.54 ha area of the small central mound to the Khazineh phase and the full site area of 1.27 ha to the Mehmeh and Bayat phases. The Farukh phase occupation appears to be minor, and we arbitrarily ascribe 0.40 ha to it. See Chapter VI for a discussion of canals DL-13 and 246, which may have been associated with this site.

8. **References**: Hole, Flannery and Neely 1969:58–60, 73.

1a. **Number**: DL-31
1b. **Name**: Tepe Sabz (also Haft Chagha; Tepe Sa'za; Tepe Su'za)
2. **Grid**: 1708.1–1183.6
3. **Dimensions**:

Length:	140 m
Width:	120 m
Height:	7.0 m
Circumference:	435 m
Area:	1.51 ha

4. **Modern Environmental Context**: At the juncture of the alluvial fan of the Mehmeh River and the saline depression, about two and a half kilometers northeast of the present Mehmeh channel.

5. **Features**: Tepe Sabz, as seen from the east, is a large, low mound, the lower slopes of which blend almost imperceptibly into the flat, barren alluvial plain (Hole, Flannery and Neely 1969: Plate 14a). The mound was originally nearly square in plan-view, but approximately a third of the southwest portion of the site has been eroded away by the seasonal inundation of the adjacent alluvium when a channel (DL-276A) just west of the site overflows (Hole, Flannery and Neely 1969, Plate 14 b; see Fig. IV.28).

Test excavations revealed that the alluvial plain had covered the lower 3.5 meters of the site, so that the relatively small, level summit of the mound would have risen 10.5 meters above the original ground surface upon which the site was founded. Apparently the first archaeological study of Tepe Sabz was during the 1961 survey of the Deh Luran Plain (Hole 1962, Hole and Flannery 1962). Subsequent excavations were carried out by Neely in 1963 (Hole, Flannery and Neely 1969).

6. **Phases**: The report of the 1963 excavations (Hole, Flannery and Neely 1969) provides detailed information regarding the architectural features and artifacts representing the four local phases—Sabz, Khazineh, Mehmeh, and Bayat—that correspond with all the earlier periods of the Susiana Sequence (Alizadeh 1992: 19–26; Dollfus 1978; Le Breton 1947, 1957) that span some 1800 years (ca. 6200 B.C. to 4400 B.C.). Examination of the surface collection revealed sherds of all of these phases except the first, and no sherds of Farukh or later phases.

7. **Comment**: Unfortunately, resources for the planned extensive excavation of Tepe Sabz were never made available, and we also lack a sector-by-sector surface collection. We are forced to assume that it grew steadily from its modest beginning in the Sabz phase, as indicated by the single excavation. We arbitrarily assign areas of about 0.50 ha to the Sabz phase, 1.0 ha to the Khazineh phase, and the full 1.51 ha to the Mehmeh and Bayat phases. See Chapter VI for a discussion of channel DL-276A.

8. **References**: Hole 1961, 1966; Hole and Flannery 1962; Hole, Flannery and Neely 1965, 1969.

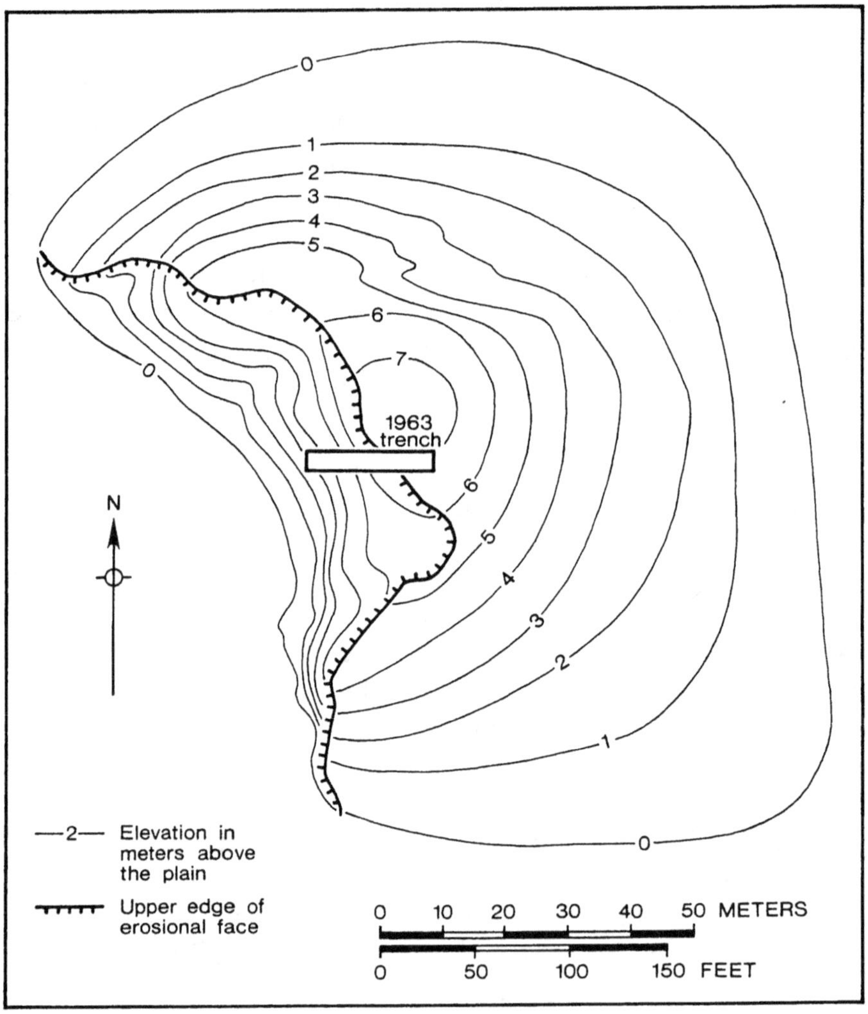

Figure IV.28. Map of Tepe Sabz (DL-31)

1a. **Number**: DL-32
1b. **Name**: Tepe Farukhabad
(Tepe Fakhrabad)
2. **Grid**: 1708.5–1177.9
3. **Dimensions**:
Length: Entire Site is now 207 m (NW-SE); Central Mound now 145 m (NW-SE), formerly about 200 m.
Width: Entire Site is now 140 m (NE-SW); Central mound now 90 m (NE-SW), formerly about 200 m.
Height: 25 m above level of the old alluvium.
Circumference: Entire Site now 620 m. Central Mound now 395 m, formerly about 520 m.
Area: Entire Site now 2.40 ha; Central Mound now 0.96 ha, formerly about 3.0 ha.

4. **Modern Environmental Context**: On the Mehmeh River alluvial fan, directly adjacent to the present channel of the river.

5. **Features**: DL-32 is one of most impressive sites on the Deh Luran Plain. Today, the highest part of Farukhabad appears as a steep-sided mound forming the western part of the site (Fig. IV.29). About half way down the eastern and southeastern slopes, a broad apron-like extension of the site drops northeastward to blend into the alluvial plain (Wright 1981: Fig. 3, Plate 2A). The very steep southwestern face of the mound (ibid.: Plate 2B; Hole, Flannery and Neely 1969:ii, frontispiece) is a result of long-term erosion and undercutting by the Mehmeh River. Wright (1981:4) estimates that originally the large, steep mound was about 200 meters in diameter, and that perhaps as much as 60 percent of it has been eroded away. Wright also observes that the erosion of the Mehmeh River has been downward as well as lateral in nature. He notes that while the present summit of the great mound rises about 30 meters above the current floodplain of the Mehmeh, the ancient floodplain of the river was approximately 5 meters higher. Wright's 1968 excavations did not attempt to reach the sterile ground surface on which the site was founded. However, the face cut by the river showed the original ground surface to be about 5 meters above the ancient flood plain Thus, the maximum cultural accumulation was about 20 meters, and the ancient floodplain of the Mehmeh River was about 5 meters below the former ground surface and the bottom of the mound.

6. **Phases**: Wright's (1981) extensive report on the 1968 excavations at Tepe Farukhabad provides detailed information pertaining to the architectural features and artifacts disclosed, which need not be recapitulated here. The fieldwork and analysis revealed evidence that the site had been discontinuously occupied during fifteen cultural phases. The earliest ceramics recovered (Wright 1981: Fig. 11) can be ascribed to the Chogha Mami Transitional phase (Hole 1977:35–36) as well as the Khazineh and Mehmeh phases (Hole, Flannery and Neely 1969:359–363). The earliest layers sampled in the excavation were of the Bayat phase (ibid.:363–364) and the immediately succeeding Farukh phase, the latter defined on the basis of work at Farukhabad (Wright 1981:55–70).

Afterwards, Farukhabad seems to have been abandoned for a period of several centuries. It was again occupied during the Early Uruk phase and remained in use until sometime during the Early Dynastic III phase (ibid.:164–194). Again, Farukhabad was evidently abandoned until the beginning of an Elamite occupation during the Shimashki phase, about 2100 B.C. Elamite occupation of the site continued through most of the following Sukkalmahhu phase (Carter in Wright 1981:200–223). An apparent brief abandonment of the site near the end of the previous phase ended with the beginning of the Elamite Transitional phase occupation at about 1600 B.C. This phase ended at about 1500 B.C. The latest

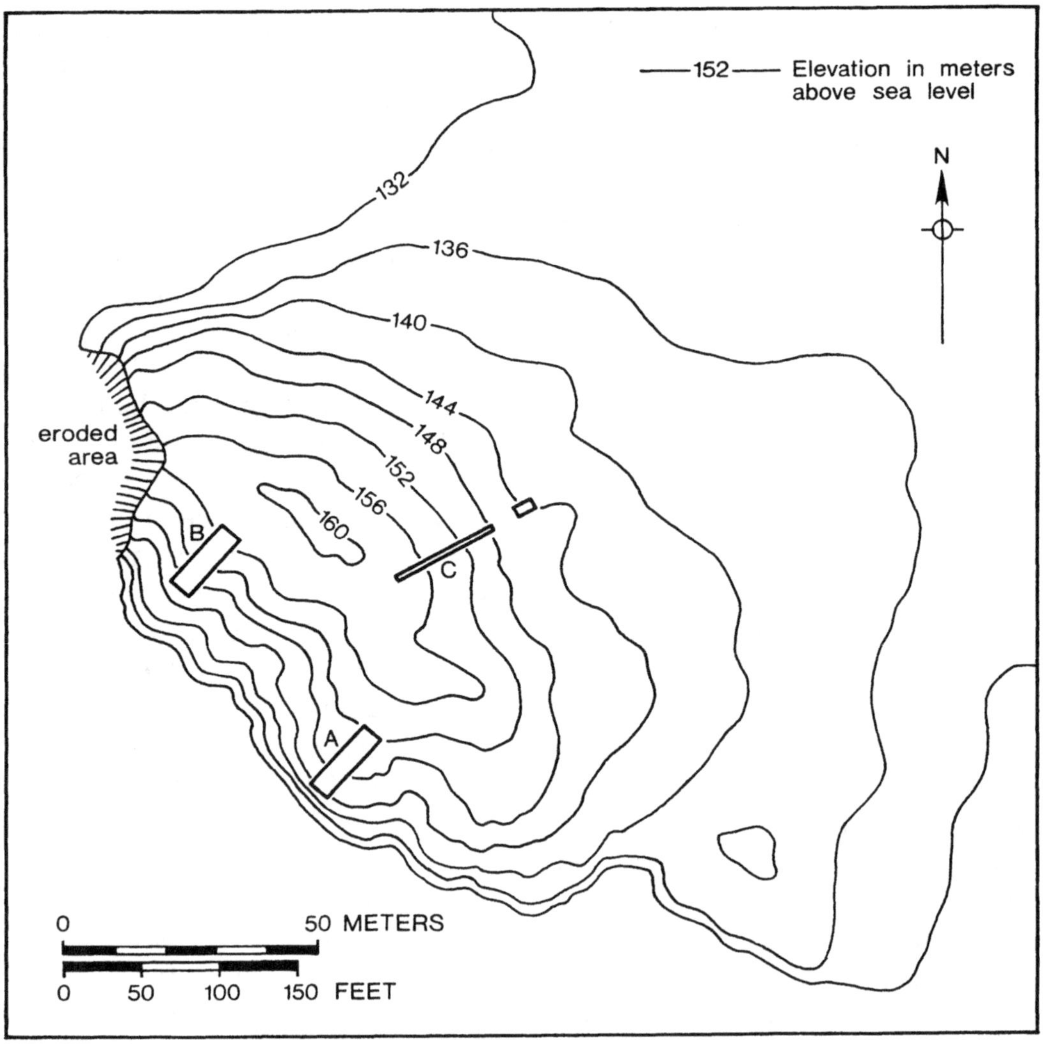

Figure IV.29. Map of Tepe Farukhabad (DL-32)

occupation at Farukhabad disclosed by Wright's excavations dated to the Late Parthian and Early Sasanian Periods (ca. 200 B.C. to A.D. 200). This last use of Farukhabad appears to center on the lower, broad, apron-like terrace forming the eastern and southeastern portions of the site (ibid.:224–226). It is interesting to note that it is this lower terraced area that pastoralists presently use for their occasional, short-term camp sites. The Elamite and later occupations will be discussed in a subsequent report.

7. **Comment**: We cannot assess the size of the deeply buried occupation of the Chogha Mami Transitional phase, but we arbitrarily assign areas of about 1.50 ha to the Khazineh and Mehmeh phases at Farukhabad. On the basis of excavated exposures, we ascribe 2.0 ha to the Bayat phase

and the full area of mound summit (before the river cut into its side) of 2.5 ha to the Farukh phase. The limited Early Uruk occupation could have covered about 1.0 ha. Middle Uruk expanded to cover the full central mound again, and Late Uruk buildings spread down its northeast side to cover about 3.0 ha. We presume that Jemdet Nasr and Early Dynastic I–II occupations covered about the same area, and that the brief later Early Dynastic occupation was somewhat smaller, since it does not seem to have fully covered even the summit of the mound.

8. **References**: Gautier and Lampre 1905: 84; Wright 1981.

1a. **Number**: DL-33
1b. **Name**:
2. **Grid**: 1709.9–1178.0
3. **Dimensions**:

Length:	200 m
Width:	125 m
Height:	1.5 m
Area:	1.75 ha

4. **Modern Environmental Context**: On the Mehmeh River alluvial fan, about a kilometer northeast of the present channel of the river, and not far from the saline depression.

5. **Features**: This site is located 1.4 kilometers east of Tepe Farukhabad (DL-32). It is generally elliptical in plan-view and consists of two, irregularly circular mounds separated by about 50 meters. The mounds are approximately the same size (about 25 meters in diameter and 1.5 meters high). The artifact scatter extends some 50 meters in all directions out from these visible raised elevations above the alluvial plain. The dimensions given above are the maximum dimensions of the artifact scatter. No evidence of architecture was found eroding from the mounds or the surrounding alluvial plain.

6. **Phases**: There is a moderately dense artifact scatter across the entire surface of the site. Ceramic sherds, flaked stone (including a flaked stone "hoe") and debitage, as well as ground stone (including a boulder mortar—see Hole, Flannery and Neely 1969: Fig. 76) were present. However, the ceramics and flaked stone were in roughly equal quantities and far outnumbered the ground stone artifacts. The few diagnostic sherds in the collections at Yale include a basin rim with painted pendant semi-circles (Fig. IV.30 d; cf. Hole, Flannery and Neely 1969: Fig. 60) which begins in the Khazineh phase but reaches its maximum frequency in the Mehmeh phase. There are also sherds from two small carinated bowls with bands and vertical lines on the exterior (Fig. IV.30 a-c; ibid.:143–144, Fig. 54 d-f) and five carinated bowl sherds with fully painted interiors (ES-RB-12; Fig. IV.30 c). Both of the latter types are typically Khazineh, but extend into the early Mehmeh phase as well. Since Mehmeh diagnostics are lacking, this small site is likely to have been occupied sometime in late Khazineh times.

7. **Comment**: For some reason, this site seems to have been more severely damaged by erosion than most, and the large size noted above probably results from this. Assuming that debris has been transported outward 25 meters in all directions, we suggest a total area of 0.78 ha is perhaps more reasonable for this late Khazineh phase occupation.

Figure IV.30. Khazineh ceramics from DL-33 and DL-84

a. Carinated Bowl Rim with Vertical Lines, Fine sand and calcite inclusions, Body light gray (2.5Y 7/2), Diam 20 cm, Paint dark gray (10YR 3/1) (Hole Flannery, and Neely 1969: Fig 54d, e).

b. Carinated Bowl Rim with Vertical Lines, Medium sand inclusions, Body light gray (2.5Y 7/2), Diam 20 cm, Paint reddish gray (5YR 4/2) (cf. same).

c. Carinated Bowl Sherd with Fully Painted Interior (cf. ES-RB-12) Fine sand inclusions, Body white (2.5Y 8/2), Paint dark gray (5YR 4/1) (cf. Hole Flannery, and Neely 1969: Fig. 53h, i, 57k, n).

d. Basin Rim with Pendant Semi-circle (ES-RB-16), Fine sand inclusions, Body light gray (2.5Y 7/2), Diam ?, Paint dark gray (10R 4/1) (Hole Flannery, and Neely 1969: fig. 60a, b).

e. Bowl Rim with Exterior Vertical Elements, Fine sand inclusions, Body light olive brown (2.5Y 5/3), Diam ?, Paint dark gray (5Y 4/1).

f. Carinated Bowl Rim with Exterior Zig-zag, Interior Pendant Triangles,(ES-RB-8) Fine sand inclusions, Body pinkish gray (7.5YR 7/3), Diam ca. 25 cm, Paint dark gray (10YR 4/1) (Hole 1977: Fig. 50c, d).

g. Sherd of Incurved Bowl (ES-RB-15), Fine sand and calcite inclusions, Body pale yellow (5Y 7/3), Paint very dark gray (10YR 3/1) (cf. Hole Flannery, and Neely 1969: Fig 52b).

h. Incurved Bowl Rim with Triangle Motifs, Fine sand inclusions, Body pale yellow (2.5Y 8/3), Diam 21 cm, Paint dark gray (7.5YR 4/1)

i. Perforator, Chert not identified.

j. Heavy Flared Jar Rim, Medium Sand inclusions, Body pale brown (10YR 6/3), Diam 23 cm,

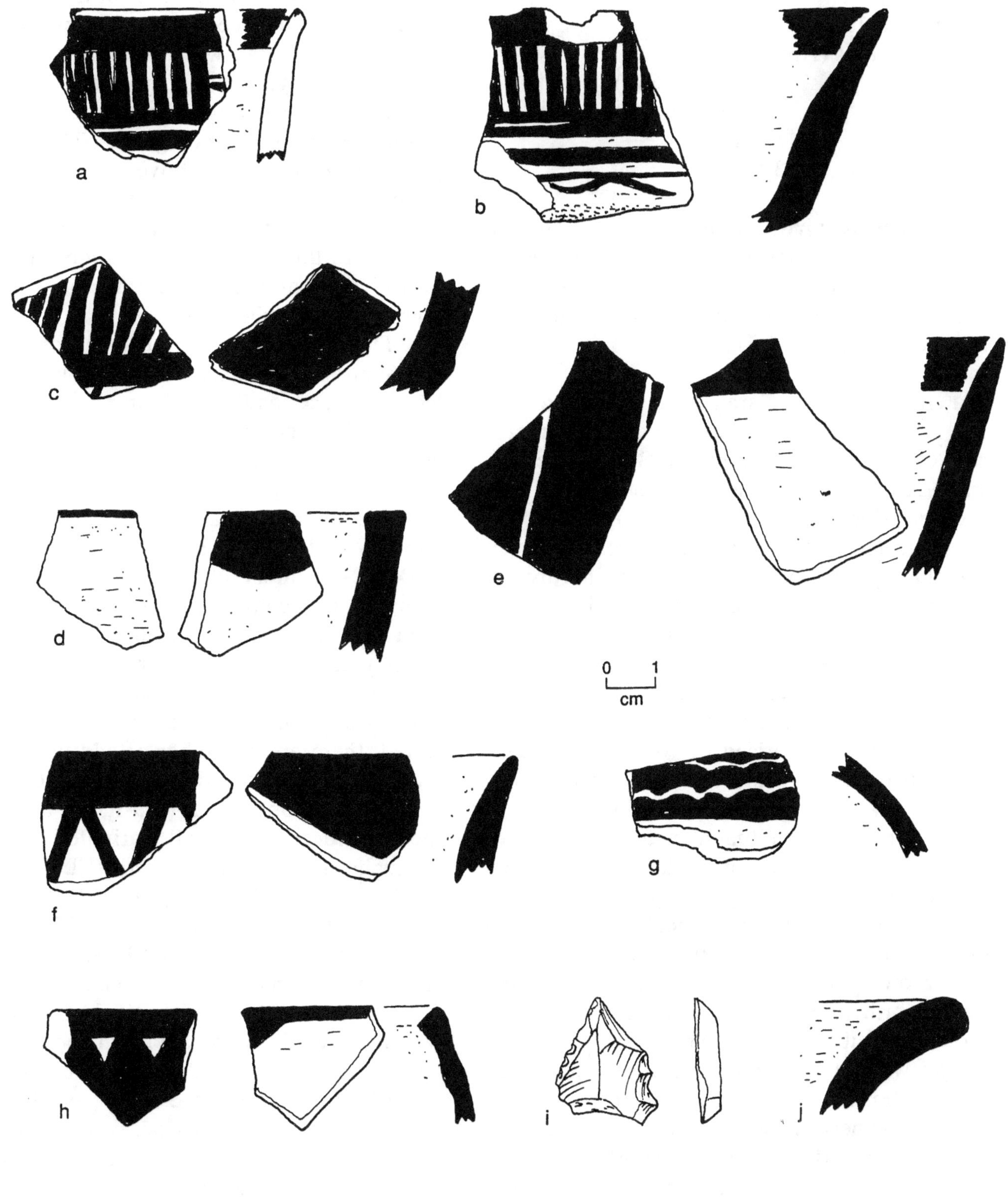

Figure IV.30. Khazineh ceramics from DL-33 and DL-84

1a. **Number**: DL-34
1b. **Name**: Tepe Garan (also Guran, Goughan)
2. **Grid**: 1719.1–1177.4
3. **Dimensions** (Area 6 only):

Length:	260 m (NE-SW)
Width:	180 m (NW-SE)
Height:	5.0 m
Area:	3.6 ha

4. **Modern Environmental Context**: On the alluvial fan of the Dawairij River, near the juncture with the northeastern alluvial slopes of the plain, about three kilometers northwest of the present Dawairij channel.

5. **Features**: Tepe Garan is a very large site (Fig. IV.31), evidently representing the major center of the later Ist millennium B.C. on the Deh Luran Plain. To provide some scale to the following description, the odometer reading of our vehicle indicated that the circumference of the site, not including the small mounds to the northwest, was approximately 2.5 kilometers, giving a total site area of about 40 hectares. It is estimated that the height of the large, conical-shaped mound, which is the tallest architectural feature of the site, was approximately 25 meters.

The site is comprised of five large, irregularly-shaped, platform-like structures that lie east, north, and west of the large, very high, conical-shaped construction situated near the southern boundary of the site. An irregularly-shaped open area, perhaps representing a large plaza or *meydan*, lies north of the high conical-shaped mound and separates it by a substantial distance from the northern-most large platform construction situated near the northern edge of the site. Several mounds are clearly visible atop the large platforms to the east and west of the large conical mound. Three small mounds lie south of the conical mound, and form the southern-most constructions of the site. About eight small mounds lie a short distance to the northwest of the Tepe Garan complex of platforms and mounds. As a lack of time did not permit us to examine these mounds, it is not known if they are part of this site complex.

Because of the magnitude of this site, and the time constraints placed on this survey, an accurate map of Tepe Garan was not drafted in the field. The accompanying plan map of this site has been drafted from the field sketch, which has been augmented by aerial photographs. The dimensions provided in item "3." above, are specific to the large platform and its associated mounds (DL-34, Area 6), that falls within the chronological purview of this report. Area 6 is located northeast of the conical mound and forms the eastern boundary of the site.

The majority of the surface configurations and features we mapped, and from which we collected surface materials, during our survey represent the later periods of site use, and will be discussed in a subsequent volume.

6. **Phases**: During a brief visit in the Spring of 1968, Wright found solid footed conical cups (ED-BC-1), most characteristic of the Early Dynastic I–II phase, eroding from the slope of a road cut into the northeastern part of Area 6. Subsequently, in November of that year, Neely and his team did an extensive surface study. Amidst the many more recent ceramics they collected, there are a number of additional finds of the Early Dynastic period from Area 6, including a high, thin round lip jar (ED-RJ-2), a sherd from the shoulder of a small carinated pot with a monochrome cross-hatch motif (ED-O-5), a typical form of the Early Dynastic III phase, a jar shoulder with a plain raised strip (ED-O-1), and a pinched ring jar base (ED-B-5). On the south slope of the large, conical mound, termed “Area 1,” another solid footed conical cup (ED-BC-1) was discovered, and on the north part of the lower terrace termed "Area 5," a wide conical cup base, made from the end of the Uruk period to the end of the Early Dynastic period, was found. The last two items, however, were much battered, and may have been transported in fill.

7. **Comment**: The most conservative interpretation of the evidence of IIIrd millennium occupation at Tepe Garan is that somewhere under the northern end of Area 6, is a site of the Early Dynastic period. It could be no larger than 2.0. ha, and we arbitrarily ascribe an area of 1.5 ha. Only careful surface study and test excavation will allow a more precise evaluation. See Chapter VI for a discussion of associated canal DL-121.

8. **References**: Gautier and Lampre 1905: 61.

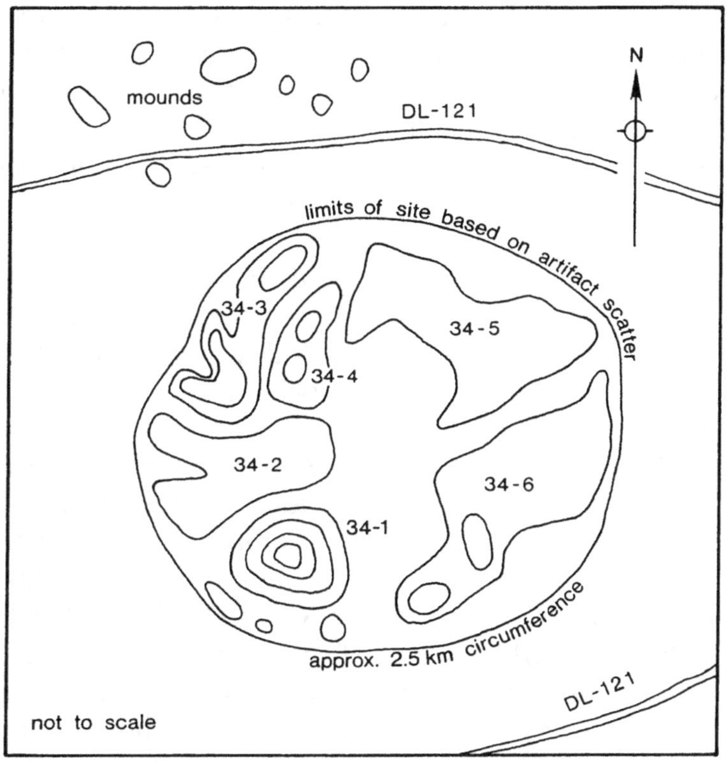

Figure IV.31. Map of Tepe Garan (DL-34).

1a. **Number**: DL-41 (Miroschedji DK-25)
1b. **Name**:
2. **Grid**: 1729.2–1170.0
3. **Dimensions**:

Length:	500 m (N-S)
Width:	400 m (E-W)
Height:	6 m
Area:	ca. 20 ha

4. **Modern Environmental Context**: On the Dawairij River alluvial fan, about two kilometers northeast of the present channel of the river, near the northern alluvial slopes of the plain.

5. **Features**: This is a rectangular site defined by traces of mud brick walls surviving as alignments of small elongated mounds. The degree of erosion of the walls and the fact that all areas of the site have IIIrd millennium occupation, while only one mound has Parthian occupation, suggest that these walls are early features. The larger mound within the space enclosed by the walls measure 200 meters (E-W) by 150 meters (N-S)

and 2.0 meters high. The smaller higher mound with Parthian debris measures 200 meters (N-S) by 80 m (E-W) and is about 6.0 meters high.

6. **Phases**: The 1968 survey team made only a preliminary visit to this site, and was unable to return to conduct a more careful examination. They recovered two hatched raised strips (ED-O-2) and two round lip jar rims (ED-RJ-1) of Early Dynastic affinity, as well as several Parthian sherds. Fortunately Miroschedji recovered a diagnostic solid footed conical cup fragment (ED-BC-1; Miroschedji 1981: Fig 61:3) and rims of small carinated jars (ED-RJ-6) with monochrome decorations (ED-O-6; ibid.: Fig 61:2, 5). The former suggests occupation during the Early Dynastic I–II phase; the other ceramics clearly indicate Early Dynastic III occupation.

7. **Comment**: The recognition of the importance of this site is entirely due to Pierre de Miroschedji, and the measurements and description of the site are based on his observations. It appears that as Musiyan (DL-20) was being abandoned, DL-41 was becoming the largest center on the plain. See Chapter VI for a discussion of canal DL-317.

8. **References**: Miroschedji 1981: 175, Fig. 61.

1a. **Number**: DL-43
1b. **Name**:
2. **Grid**: 1728.2–1170.1
3. **Dimensions**:

Length:	57 m (N-S)
Width:	46 m (E-W)
Height:	0.75 m
Area:	0.18 ha

4. **Modern Environmental Context**: On the Dawairij River alluvial fan, about two kilometers northeast of the present channel of the river, near the northern alluvial slopes of the plain.

5. **Features**: This site consists of a single, low mound that is generally elliptical in plan. The mound is surrounded by a small modern irrigation canal and formerly cultivated fields. It seems likely that the site was somewhat larger, but due to the disturbed nature of the alluvial plain surrounding the mound it is difficult to estimate its original area. No evidence of architecture was visible on the surface of the site.

6. **Phases**: A moderately dense scatter of ceramic sherds and flaked stone, as well as a few artifacts of ground stone, were found covering this site. These materials extended out beyond the small irrigation canal into the once cultivated fields in an irregular pattern, rapidly diminishing in numbers within a few meters. The collection includes one bowl rim with a ladder motif (ES-RB-5) and one fragment of a jar neck with an interior ledge (ES-RJ-2), which probably indicate Mehmeh phase occupation. A Bayat phase occupation is definitely indicated by vertical curved line motifs, one of the heavy variant (LS-RB-9), and high neck jars exclusively with solid painting (LSD-RJ-1). The other Susiana sherds tabulated from the site are all known from excavated Bayat phase contexts. Early Uruk occupation is indicated by open bowls with beaded lips (US-RB-6), a neckless ledge-rim jar (US-RJ-2), a flared round lip jar (US-RJ-6) with an inner neck groove, and a high expanded band rim jar (US-RJ-10), all of Sargarab ware. A droop spout (UU-O-11) of Uruk ware is likely to be of Late Uruk date, as are the standard beveled rim bowls (US-RB-2). Clay sickle fragments could be of either the Mehmeh or Late Uruk phases.

7. **Comment**: We ascribe the full area of this small site to the Mehmeh, Bayat, and Early Uruk phases. The Late Uruk items are limited and may indicate ephemeral occupation, for example as a field hut or a transhumant camp. See Chapter VI for a discussion of canal DL-317A and C.

1a. **Number**: DL-54 (Miroschedji DK-5)
1b. **Name**: Tepe Soza (Suzah)
2. **Grid**: 1726.0–1172.4
3. **Dimensions**:

Length:	244 m (NE-SW)
Width:	175 m (NW-SE)
Height:	4 m
Area:	3.22 ha

4. **Modern Environmental Context**: At the juncture of the northern alluvial slopes of the plain and the alluvial fan of the Dawairij River, about a kilometer and a half northeast of the present Dawairij channel.

5. **Features**: This is an interesting and rather complex site, apparently having a long history of occupation. The dimensions given above are our

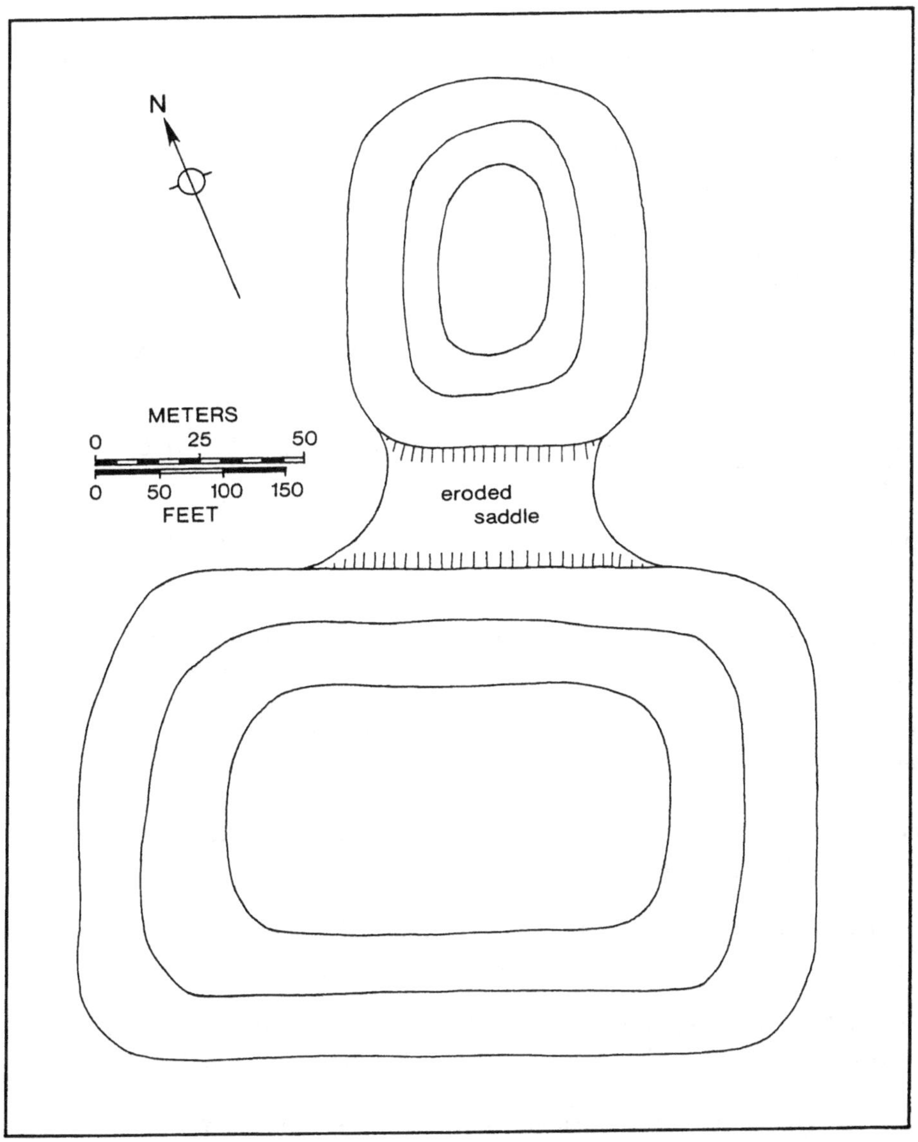

Figure IV.32. Map of Tepe Soza (DL-54)

Figure IV.33. Early Dynastic ceramics from Tepe Soza (DL-54)

a. Wide Conical Cup Base (ED-BC-3) Medium sand inclusions, Body light brown (7.5YR 6/5), Base diam 4.0 cm, Surface yellowish gray (5Y 8/2) (cf. Wright 1981: Fig. 45c).

b. Solid Footed Conical Cup Base (ED-BC-1) Fine sand inclusions, Body light yellowish brown (10YR 7/3), Base diam 2.5 cm, Surface light yellowish brown (7.5YR 7/3) (Wright 1981: Fig. 45f).

c. Conical Cup Rim (ED-RC-1) Fine sand inclusions, Body light yellowish brown (7.5YR 7/5), Diam 14 cm, Surface grayish yellow (2.5Y 8/3) (Wright 1981: Fig. 45k).

d. Conical Cup Rim (ED-RC-1) Trace fine sand inclusion, body grayish yellow (2.5Y 8/3), Diam ca. 15 cm, Surface grayish yellow (2.5Y 8/2) (Wright 1981: Fig. 45i).

e. Large Bowl with Impressed Strip (ED-O-2) Medium sand inclusions, Body light yellowish brown (10YR 7/4), Diam 43 cm, Surface yellowish gray (5Y 8/2) (Carter 1978: Fig. 43:3, 4).

f. Beveled Lip Bowl (ED-RB-2) Medium sand inclusions, Body light brown (7.5YR 6/5), Diam warped, Surface pale orangish yellow (10YR 8/3) (Wright 1981: Fig. 47 l).

g. Ledge Rim Bowl (ED-RB-3) Fine sand inclusions, Body grayish yellow (5Y 8/3), Diam ca. 26 cm, Surface yellowish white (5Y 9/2) (Wright 1981: Fig. 47f).

h. Ledge Rim Bowl (ED-RB-3) Medium sand inclusions, Body pale orange-yellow (10Y 8/4), Diam ?, Surface light yellowish brown (7.5YR 7/4) (Wright 1981: Fig. 47g).

i. Round Lip Jar (ED-RJ-1) Medium sand inclusions, Body yellowish gray (5Y 8/2), Diam 15 cm, Surface yellowish gray (5Y 8/2) (Wright 1981: Fig. 49a).

j. Same (ED-RJ-1) Medium sand inclusions, Body light yellowish brown (7.5YR 7/4), Diam 12 cm, Surface yellowish gray (2.5Y 8/2) (Wright 1981: Fig. 49 l).

k. Heavy Round Lip Jar (cf. ED-RJ-1) Coarse sand inclusions, Body grayish yellow (5Y 8/3), Diam 22 cm, Surface yellowish white (7.5Y 9/2).

l. Band Rim Jar (ED-RJ-5), Fine sand and calcite inclusions, Body yellowish pink (5YR 8/3), Diam 17 cm, Surface light brown (5YR 5/5), Slip grayish red-orange (2.5YR 6/6) (cf. Wright 1981: Fig. 52j).

m. Band Rim Jar (ED-RJ-5) Fine sand inclusions, Body light brown (5YR 6/4), Diam ca. 12 cm, Surface yellowish gray (10YR 8/1) (Wright 1981: Fig. 52j).

n. Expanded Rim Jar (cf. ED-RJ-3) Medium sand inclusions, Body orange (2.5YR 6/7), Diam 19 cm, Surface grayish yellow (2.5Y 8/3) (Wright 1981: Fig. 52h).

o. Ledge Rim Jar (ED-RJ-4) Fine sand and trace of calcite inclusions, Body orange (5YR 7/6), Diam 16 cm, Surface pale orangish yellow (10YR 8/3) (Wright 1981: Fig. 53b, d, g).

p. Ledge Rim Jar (ED-RJ-4) with Impressed Strip (Type ??) Fine sand inclusions, Body orange (5YR 6/6), Diam 25 cm, Surface light yellowish brown (7.5YR 8/3) (Wright 1981: Fig. 53m; Carter 1978: Fig. 43:8).

q. Carinated Bowl (ED-RB-4) Medium sand inclusions, Body grayish yellow (2.5Y 8/3), Diam 14 cm, Surface light yellowish brown (7.5YR 7/5) (Carter 1978: Fig. 43:2).

(continued p. 108)

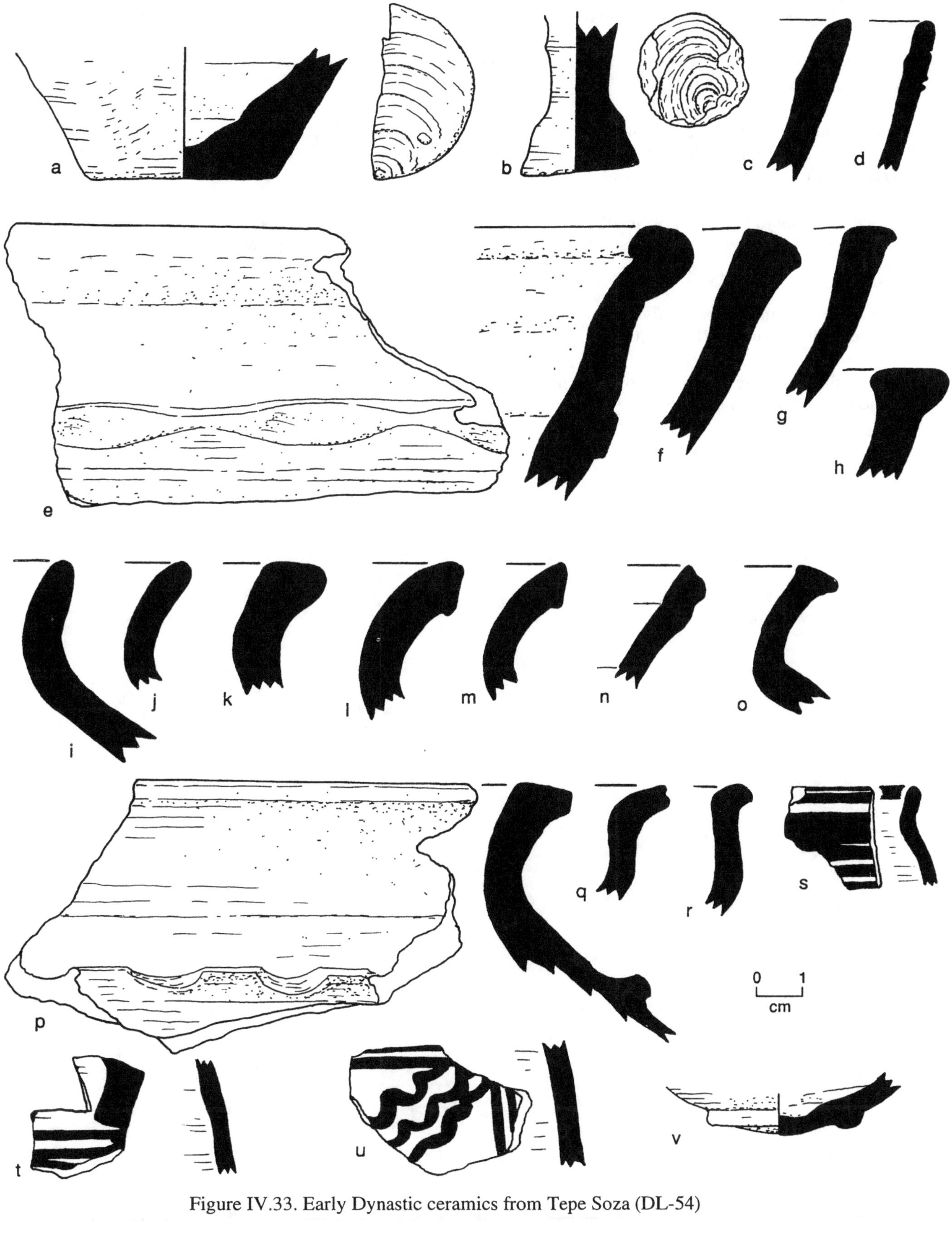

Figure IV.33. Early Dynastic ceramics from Tepe Soza (DL-54)

Figure IV.33. Early Dynastic ceramics from Tepe Soza (DL-54), continued from p. 106

r. Carinated Bowl (ED-RB-4) Fine sand inclusions, Body yellowish gray (5Y 8/1), Diam ca. 15 cm, Surface yellowish gray (5Y 8/1). (Carter 1978: Fig. 42:3).

s. Small Carinated Pot (ED-RJ-6) with Painted Bands (ED-O-3), Fine sand inclusions, Body grayish yellow (2.5Y 8/2), Diam 9 cm, Surface grayish yellow (2.5Y 8/2), Paint light grayish brown (7.5R 5/2) (Wright 1981: Fig. 56m; Carter 1978: Fig. 44:5).

t. Painted Body sherd (ED-O-5) of Small Carinated Pot (ED-RJ-6), Fine sand inclusions, Body light yellowish brown (10YR 7/3), Diam ca. 12 cm, Surface grayish yellow (2.5Y 8/3), Paint reddish brown (2.5YR 4/2) (Carter 1978: Fig. 44:9).

u. Same, Fine sand inclusions, Body yellowish gray (7.5Y 8/ 1), Body diam ca. 18 cm, Surface grayish yellow (2.5Y 8/3), Paint reddish brown (2.5YR 4/3) (Carter 1978: Fig. 44:10).

v. Fine Small Ring Base (ED-B-6) Coarse to medium sand inclusions, Body yellowish gray (7.5Y 8/1), Base diam 3.6 cm, Surface grayish yellow (2.5Y 8/3).

best estimates for the site size during the occupation phases covered by this report.

The site is composed of two relatively large mounds joined by a low, saddle-shaped land-form, as well as several smaller mounds and platforms located to the south and northeast (Fig. IV.32). It appears that these smaller mounds and platforms represent late reoccupations of the site, and, therefore, have not been included in the dimensions above or the site descriptions that follow.

The larger of the two mounds is roughly rectangular, measuring approximately 175 meters NW-SE, 120 meters NE-SW, and 4 meters in height. It is joined to a smaller mound by the low, saddle-shaped land-form that extends from the northeast side of the large mound, slopes downward for about 15 meters, then levels off for a few meters, only to rise again to join the southwest side of the smaller mound. This joining land-form is about 30 meters in length between the two mounds, 50 meters in width, and 2.5 meters high at its center point. The smaller mound to the northeast is generally elliptical in plan and measures about 90 meters NE-SW, 70 meters NW-SE, and is approximately 3 meters high. No definite evidence of architecture was found on this mound complex. However, a great deal of pebble-sized gravel was found on the site. This could represent the presence of some form of construction or pavements. The larger of the two mounds has been used in modern times as a cemetery by the residents of the village of Patak.

6. **Phases**: While there were relatively few ceramic sherds to be found on the mound complex, there was a rather dense accumulation of flaked stone tools and debitage. No ground stone tools were observed. Diagnostic ceramics perhaps representing an Early Dynastic I–II occupation, specifically solid-footed conical cup bases (ED-BC-1; Fig. IV.33 b) and a finer ledge-rim jar (ED-RJ-4; Fig. IV.33 o), were found on and around the low, saddle-shaped landform that joins the two mounds. A later Early Dynastic III phase occupation is indicated by the ceramics. For example, various heavier round lip (ED-RJ-1; Fig. IV.33 i-k) and band rim (ED-RJ-5; Fig. IV.33 l-m) jars with hatched strip decoration (ED-O-2; Fig. IV.33 p), carinated bowls (ED-RB-4; Fig. IV.33 q, r) and small carinated jars (ED-RJ-6; Fig. IV.33 s) with monochrome designs (ED-O-3 and 5; Fig. IV.33 s-u) were found on the surfaces of the two mounds and were noted to extend outward onto the alluvial plain a few meters. Ceramics indicating a yet later IIIrd millennium occupation were noted on the summit and just below the summit on the west side of the larger mound, as will be discussed in a subsequent survey monograph.

7. **Comment**: The deeply buried Early Dynastic I–II occupation can be assigned an arbitrary area of 1.0 ha. The full site area of 3.22 ha is ascribed to the Early Dynastic III occupation. Miroschedji (1981:173, 175) gives the overall dimensions at 200 meters by 100 meters and 3 meters in height, probably because he did not include the surrounding sherd scatter. See Chapter VI for a discussion of associated canal DL-317C.

8. **References**: Miroschedji (1981:173–175).

1a. **Number**: DL-61
1b. **Name**:
2. **Grid**: 1720.0–1174.7
3. **Dimensions**:

Length:	100 m (NW-SE)
Width:	75 m (NE-SW)
Height:	5.0 m
Circumference:	293 m
Area:	0.68 ha

4. **Modern Environmental Context**: On the alluvial fan of the Dawairij River, about two kilometers west of the present river channel.

5. **Features**: DL-61 appears to have had two major periods of occupation, a long-lived early habitation and a later, much shorter period of use. The dimensions noted above and the site description that follows pertain only to the earlier use of this site.

The earlier occupation of the site is apparently represented by a relatively large, low, and generally level earth platform with three mounds (Fig. IV.34). The platform is located about 250 meters north-northwest of Tepe Musiyan (DL-20). It is irregularly rectangular in plan, and constitutes the maximum length, width, and circumference dimensions given above. It is nearly level. However, its level nature is belied by the fact that it appears as a clearly defined feature 0.50 meters in height above the alluvial plain at its south-central edge (near the juncture of the canal [a branch of canal DL-115A] that flows north to south through the platform with the east-west coursing canal [a branch of canal DL-115B] that passes just south of the platform) while it blends almost imperceptibly into the alluvial plain along its north, northeast, and northwest extremes. The blending of the platform with the alluvial plain is evidently a result of the natural deposition of alluvium against the northern side of the platform. It was not possible for us to determine for certain if this platform dated to one of the earlier occupations of the site, or was in fact built around the base of the earlier mounds.

The largest of the three mounds is situated with its eastern edge about 10 meters west of the center of the platform. This mound is elliptical in plan and measures approximately 50 meters (NE-SW) by 20 meters (NW-SE), and rises about 4.5 meters above the platform and 5 meters above the

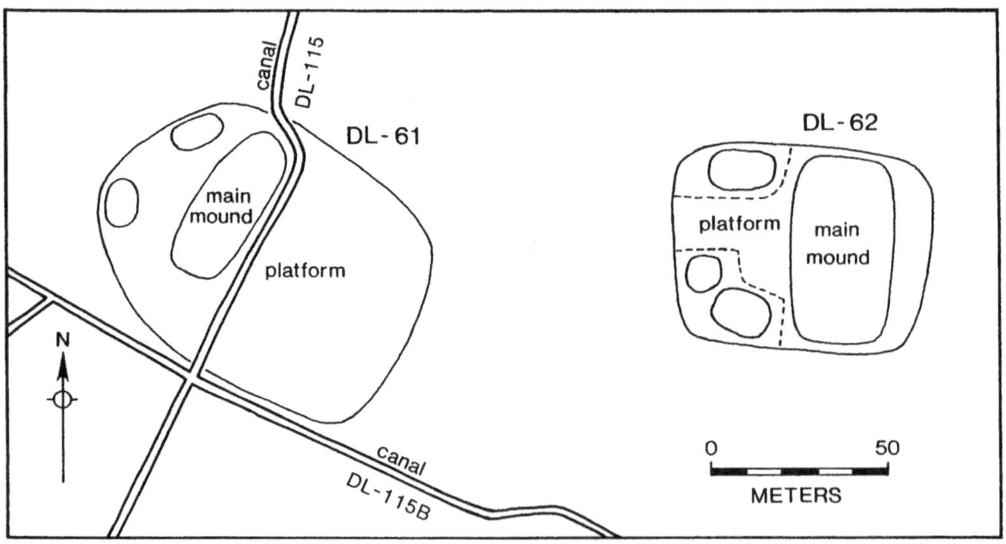

Figure IV.34. Map of DL-61 and DL-62

alluvial plain. The ceramics found atop and eroding from the sides of this mound date to the early occupation of the site.

The other two mounds are considerably smaller. Both are irregularly elliptical in plan, measure about 15 meters (N-S) by 10 meters (E-W), and rise about 0.50 meters above the level of the platform (approximately 1.0 meter above the level of the alluvial plain). Both of these smaller mounds appear to have been incorporated or partially built-into the western edge of the platform. The southern-most of these mounds is clearly visible, while the northern-most is difficult to discern as it has been severely disturbed by a modern Luri black-tent encampment which overlies and cuts into the small mound and butts up against the lower edge of the large mound's northwest face. It was not possible to determine if these smaller mounds dated to the early occupation of the site. It appears that the inhabitants of the black-tent camp collected all of the surface materials from these mounds, as well as from the western edge of the platform and the large mound, to construct low sleeping and activity platforms in their encampment.

Although we found small amounts of what appeared to be building stone on the surface of the site, no other evidence of architecture was seen, perhaps as a direct result of recent activities.

6. **Phases**: A moderately dense scatter of ceramics and flaked stone was observed. The ceramics represent most phases from the Mehmeh phase through the Early Dynastic I–II Phase (ca. 5700 B.C. to 3000 B.C.). The small sample of Susiana Black-on-buff sherds includes a bowl body with interior vertical lines which could be Khazineh phase (cf. Hole, Flannery and Neely 1969: Fig. 57 i, j). Mehmeh phase ceramics include a painted basin rim with interior pendant arcs and a bowl sherd with a right triangle motif (ES-RB-6). There is no definite indication of Bayat phase ceramics. Farukh phase diagnostics include bowl fragments with fine dot motifs and curvilinear elements (LS-RB-10r), as well as high jar necks with painted bands (LS-RJ-3). Probable Suse phase diagnostics include a bowl sherd with a branch motif (LS-RB-19). Sherds attributable to the Uruk phases are much more common. A neckless ledge-rim jar (US-RJ-2; Fig. IV.35 d), open beaded rim bowls (US-RB-6; Fig. IV.35 a, b) of Sargarab ware, and the flared neck jar (US-RJ-7; Fig. IV.35 e) indicate Early Uruk occupation. The incurved bowl of Sargarab ware with hatched appliqué strip and red slip is most likely to be Middle Uruk (US-RB-12; Fig. IV.35 c; cf. Wright 1981: Fig. 41 b, m), as are the jar shoulders with black-on-red decoration (UU-O-8; Fig. IV.35 g) of Uruk ware. Definite Late Uruk indicators include shoulder fragments with groove-and-oblique decoration (UU-O-3), twist handles (UU-O-13; Fig. IV.35 i), both from small jars of Uruk ware, and droop spouts (UU-O-11). The other Uruk ware sherds and the standard beveled rim bowls (US-RB-2) could be of either the Middle or the Late Uruk phase. Indicative of Early Dynastic I–II occupation are the solid-footed (ED-BC-1; Fig. IV.35 l) conical cup fragments. Handmade gray ware body sherds with shell temper are locally diagnostic of the Early Dynastic III phase (Bohr in Wright 1981:130).

7. **Comment**: Given that the large abandoned Susiana settlement of Tepe Musiyan was only a few hundred meters from DL-61, it is possible that the Uruk occupants used the ruin as a source of salt-free mud for their bricks, and inadvertently carried the Susiana sherds we have recorded to DL-61. The fact that Bayat phase ceramics, which did not occur at the nearby north end of Musiyan, are not represented in the DL-61 sample, strengthens this possibility. It is likely that, as is the case at Aliabad (DL-71) and Khazineh (DL-28), the few Early Dynastic sherds were introduced by intrusive graves. Only excavation at DL-61 can resolve these issues. We assign the platform area of 0.68 ha to the Uruk phases. See Chapter VI for a discussion of associated canal DL-115.

1a. **Number**: DL-62
1b. **Name**:
2. **Grid**: 1720.6–1174.7
3. **Dimensions**:

Length:	70 m (E-W)
Width:	60 m (N-S)
Height:	2 m
Area:	0.42 ha

4. **Modern Environmental Context:** On the alluvial fan of the Dawairij River, about two kilometers west of the present channel.

5. **Features**: DL-62 is a moderately large site located about 250 meters north of the north end of Tepe Musiyan and 110 meters east of the main mound of DL-61 (Fig. IV.34). DL-62, like DL-61, exhibits traces of several early phases as well as a shorter, very late period of use. Also, as at DL-61, a substantial portion of the site was constructed during the later occupation. In fact, it seems quite possible that the later components of DL-61 and DL-62 formed one large site that may have been related in some way with the late occupations at Tepe Musiyan (DL-20). The dimensions above and the following site description pertain only to the early occupations of DL-62.

The early occupations on this site appear to be localized on a fairly large, low, flat-topped mound or platform. This large main platform is surrounded on all but the west side by smaller mounds and other features—all of which date to the later occupation of the site. Atop the large, flat-topped platform are situated four small mounds. The largest of these is irregularly rectangular in plan. It is 0.50 meters high and 55 meters (N-S) by 28 meters (E-W). It is situated so that its western edge parallels the north-south centerline of the flat-topped platform mound on which it sits. Immediately east and west of this mound are open, flat, plaza-like surfaces.

The flat surface to the east, perhaps a terraced area, is about 10 meters (E-W) wide by 60 meters (N-S) long, and stands about 0.75 meters above the alluvial plain.

The other three small mounds are clustered at the western end of the platform mound. The largest is elliptical in plan and is situated on the northwest corner of the platform mound. It measures 20 meters (E-W), 12 meters (N-S), and is 0.50 meters high. The eastern edge of this mound appears to blend smoothly into the northwestern edge of the larger mound, only 5 meters away, described in the preceding paragraph. It is possible that these two mounds were originally joined. The remaining two small mounds are situated on the southwest corner of the platform. The larger of these two is irregularly oval in plan, and measures 18 meters (E-W) by 12 meters (N-S), and is 0.25 meters high. The smallest mound is circular in plan, 10 meters in diameter and 0.25 meters high, and is situated only a few centimeters north of the northwest corner of the larger mound previously described. Our survey data are not conclusive as to the dating of these three small mounds. It is possible that they are late additions atop the platform. In fact, it is conceivable that the western half of what we have called the platform mound was modified by the late occupants of the site so as to produce the flat, plaza-like areas upon which these three small mounds presently sit.

6. **Phases**: While there are moderate numbers of sherds and lithics scattered over the surface of DL-62, the majority are diagnostic of the late occupations. The relatively few early sherds were found on the large platform mound and around the small mounds adjacent to the platform mound. There are a few later Susiana sherds, including a fine bowl sherd with a possible ladder motif (ES-RB-5) of the Mehmeh phase and another with a possible dot motif (LS-RB-10) of the Farukh phase. Since all these sherds are small and battered, it seems likely that they were transported from nearby Musiyan (DL-20) in fill. There are two Late Uruk diagnostics, a heavy flared round rim jar (UU-RJ-3) and a jar shoulder with groove-and-oblique decoration (UU-O-3; Fig. IV.35 j). Since they are well-preserved and since there is no Late Uruk occupation at Musiyan, they most

likely represent an actual occupation. From the Early Dynastic period, there are a range of conical cup sherds and jar sherds, including the solid footed (ED-BC-1) cup base variant, a fine ledge-rim jar (ED-RJ-4) with polychrome motifs (cf. Wright 1981: Fig. 57 a), and jar shoulders with arc-and-ray polychrome motifs (ED-O-6; cf. Wright 1981: Fig. 58 e-i), all typical of the Early Dynastic I–II phase. The wide range of forms suggests actual occupation rather than use simply as a cemetery.

7. **Comment**: The platform area of 0.42 ha is ascribed to the Late Uruk phase and the Early Dynastic I–II phase. Since this Late Uruk site is only 110 meters from the contemporary occupation area at DL-61, it is possible that these are parts of a single larger Late Uruk site, but there is no evidence of this visible on the ground or on the available aerial photographs. See Chapter VI for a discussion of associated canal DL-115.

Figure IV.35. Uruk ceramics from DL-61 and DL-62

a. Open Beaded Rim Bowl with Thumb-impressed Strip (US-RB-7) (DL-61) Vegetal and medium sand inclusions, Body white (2.5Y 8/3), Diam ?

b. Open Beaded Rim Bowl (US-RB-6) (DL-61) Vegetal and calcite inclusions, Body light brown (7.5Y 6/4), Diam ca. 38 cm.

c. Incurved Beaded Rim Bowl with Hatched Strip (US-RB-12) (DL-61) Vegetal and calcite inclusions, Body white (5Y 8/2), Diam ca. 35 cm, Pale red (10R 6/4) slip (Wright 1981: Fig 41m).

d. Neckless Ledge Rim Jar (UU-RJ-2) (DL-61) Calcite and vegetal inclusions, Body pale brown (10YR 6/3), Diam 12 cm (cf. Johnson 1973: Pl. III).

e. Flared Neck Jar (US-RJ-7) (DL-61) Fine Sand Inclusions, Body reddish yellow (5YR 7/5), Diam 17 cm, Surface white (2.5Y 8/3) (cf. Wright 1981: Fig. 48e, but perhaps Susiana cf. Hole, Flannery and Neely 1969: Fig. 48u).

f. Jar Shoulder with Cross-hatch band (UU-O-5) (DL-61) Medium sand inclusions, Body white (2.5Y 8/2), (Wright 1981: Fig 55a, b).

g Jar Shoulder with Black-on-red Decoration (UU-O-8) and Nose Lug (UU-O-1), (DL-61) Fine sand and hematite inclusions, Body pink (5YR 7/4), Trace of red slip, (Wright 1981: Fig 57h).

h. Spout Probably from Carinated Bowl (cf. UU-RB-5) (DL-61) Fine Sand Inclusions, Body light brown (7.5YR 6/4), Red (10R 5/6) slip, Spout hole blocked with lime plaster.

i. Flat Twist Handle (UU-O-13) (DL-61) Fine Sand Inclusions, Body light gray (2.5Y 7/2).

j. Jar Shoulder with Groove-and-oblique Decoration (UU-O-3) (DL-62) Medium sand and vegetal inclusions, Body White (5Y 8/2), Neck Diam ca. 13. (Wright 1981: Fig. 55g).

k. Jar Shoulder with Black-on-red Decoration (UU-O-8) (DL-61) Fine Sand Inclusions, Body White (2.5Y 8/3), Diam ?, Possible red slip, Paint gray (10YR 5/1) (Wright 1981: Fig 57, cf. Fig 56 l).

l. Solid Footed Goblet Base (ED-BC-1) (DL-61) Trace of fine sand, Body very pale brown (10YR 8/3) (Wright 1981:45f, g).

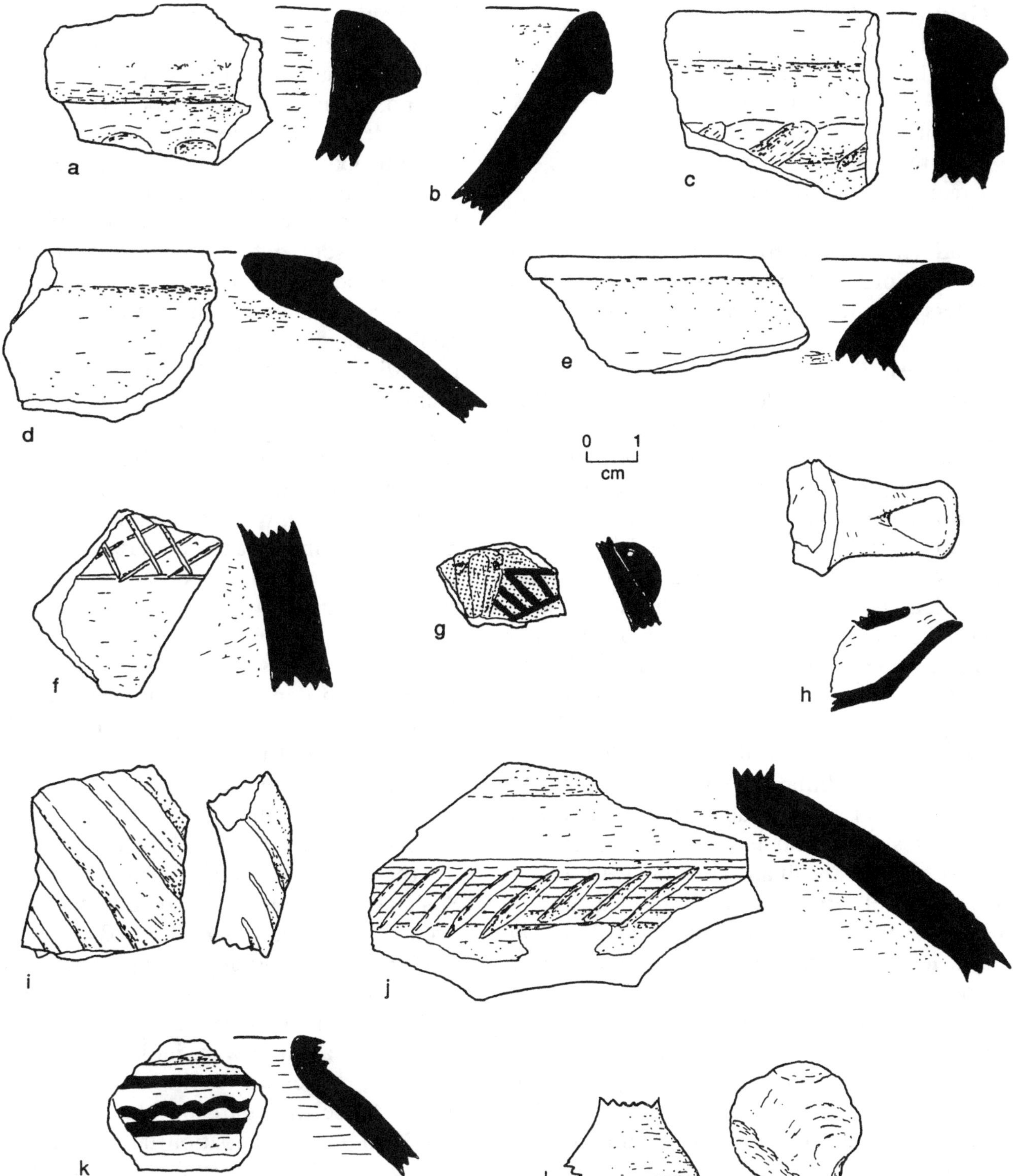

Figure IV.35. Uruk ceramics from DL-61 and DL-62

1a. **Number**: DL-71
1b. **Name**: Aliabad (Aly-Abad, Kolah)
2. **Grid**: 1719.6–1173.3
3. **Dimensions**:

Length:	80 m NE-SW
Width:	70 m NW-SE
Height:	3.5 m
Circumference:	250 m
Area:	0.50 ha

4. **Modern Environmental Context**: On the alluvial fan of the Dawairij River, about three kilometers west of the present river channel.

5. **Features**: This site consists of two well-defined architectural complexes representing different periods of occupation. The dimensions presented above, as well as the majority of the following descriptive data, focuses on the earlier of these two components.

Upon approaching the site one first sees the relatively well-preserved late wall that encloses the elliptical mound representing the earlier occupations of the site (Fig. IV.36). The eroded 158 by 152 meter outer wall is made of mud bricks and packed mud. It has four corner bastions, as well as brick towers on either side of an entryway in the southwestern wall. This wall probably dates to the Sasanian period. Within the enclosure's walls, the earlier mound is situated about ten meters from the northwest wall and is centrally located between the northeast wall and the southwest wall. It is irregularly elliptical in plan and measures 80 meters (NE-SW) by 70 meters (NW-SE). The summit, located at the northeastern extremity of the mound, rises to a height of 3.5 meters above the plain. While the mound's northern slope is quite steep, its other slopes are gentle.

Four excavation units were clearly visible in the northern portion of the mound. Although they do not exactly match the size and location of those shown on the map of Gautier and Lampre (1905: Fig. 99), they probably are the remnants of their work at this site. An eroded wall or linear mound of earth, from 0.75 to 2.0 meters high and 2 to 3 meters wide at the base, surrounds the main mound. To the northwest and northeast, this wall-like feature lies about three meters from the edge of the mound. To the southeast and southwest, the wall-like feature overlies the lower portions of the mound, separating it from the terraced area. This wall-like feature is neither mentioned nor illustrated by Gautier and Lampre. It is possible that it is debris from their excavations, or from some later, unrecorded, surface-stripping effort. It may also represent a feature built during the later Sasanian occupation of the site.

A comparison of our map of DL-71 with that published by Gautier and Lampre (1905: Fig. 99) immediately reveals certain differences. The most dramatic of these are the larger relative size and southward shifting of the mound vis-à-vis the surrounding rectangular wall in Gautier and Lampre's drawing. As no scale was included with the French site map, we may assume that their map is not to scale and that the features surrounding the mound were added to the map without adequate measurement.

6. **Phases**: Our sectorial survey of the site indicated a high density of earlier ceramics on and immediately surrounding the main mound. A small quantity of flaked stone was also noted. No ground stone items were seen. A carinated bowl rim with solid paint (ES-RB-12), probably of the late Khazineh or early Mehmeh phase, was found on the southeast slope of the mound. Later Susiana sherds which may be Bayat and/or Farukh occur. Many fine bowls (US-RB-3), open bowls (UU-RB-4–7) including examples with diagnostic thumb-impressed strips, neckless ledge rim jars (US-RJ-3), and high expanded band rim jars (US-RJ-10) of Sargarab ware indicate Early Uruk occupation, particularly earlier during the time span of the phase. Standard beveled rim bowls (US-RB-2) indicate occupation later in the Uruk period, while the carinated flat lip bowl (UU-RB-5) and various jars (UU-RJ-3,4,8) of Uruk ware are no later than the early part of the Middle Uruk phase. None of the highly distinctive Late Uruk

variants occur, even though the collection is large. However, we recovered many items characteristic of the Jemdet Nasr or Early Dynastic phases, for example various conical cup fragments, bowl and jar rims, painted jar shoulders, and raised strips on jars. The predominance of solid-footed conical cup fragments (UU-BC-1), the thin variant of the round lip jar (UU-RJ-2), and specific polychrome decorations (US-O-5) are of the Early Dynastic I–II phase. The French team excavated many typical Early Dynastic I–II "scarlet ware" jars in intrusive tombs (Gautier and Lampre 1905: Figs. 266, 283–286) along with dentate stamped gray ware (ibid.:287; cf. Wright 1981: Fig. 63 n) and many items of alabaster and metal. They also illustrate a jar with a typical Jemdet Nasr phase variant of polychrome shoulder decoration (Gautier and Lampre 1905:73–80, Fig. 282). However, all of these later ceramics could be tomb furnishings and items discarded after grave-side rituals. Although a few later, probably Sasanian, sherds were found on the main mound, the overwhelming majority were concentrated away from the main mound within and immediately outside of the rectangular enclosure walls. These will be discussed in a subsequent volume.

7. **Comment**: The Late Khazineh/Early Mehmeh occupation is arbitrarily assigned an area of 0.30 ha. The full area of the mound, i.e., 0.50 ha, is ascribed to the subsequent Early and Middle Uruk phase occupations. The small canal, a branch of canal DL-115B that is shown in Figure IV.36, probably dates to the Sasanian re-occupation of this site.

8. **References**: Gautier and Lampre 1905:73–80.

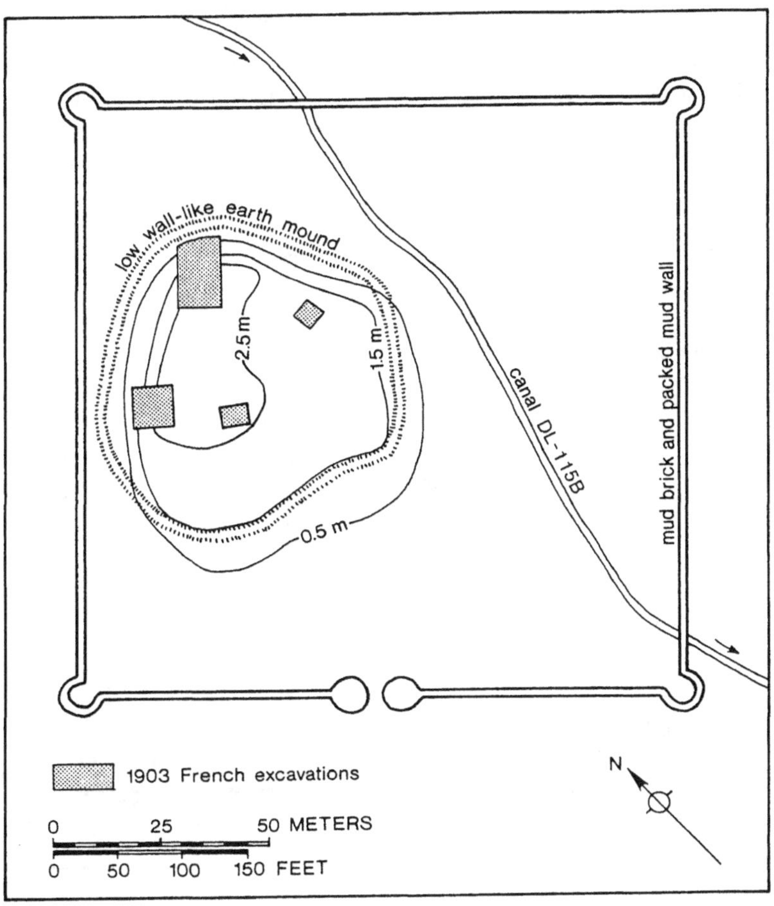

Figure IV.36. Map of Tepe Aliabad (DL-71)

1a. **Number**: DL-84 (DL-88X)
1b. **Name**:
2. **Grid**: 1727.7–1169.3
3. **Dimensions**:

Length:	60 m
Width:	55 m
Height:	3.5 m
Circumference:	180 m
Area:	0.26 ha

4. **Modern Environmental Context**: On the alluvial fan of the Dawairij River, just northeast of the present channel.

5. **Features**: DL-84 consists of one irregularly oval mound (Fig. IV.37). The north slope of the mound is relatively steep, while its south slope is less so, blending into the alluvial plain. The southernmost third of the mound, where the slope is gentlest, has been cultivated in recent times. It is in this cultivated area that the majority of the ceramics were found, although a few sherds were also recovered from midway up the mound on its northwest side.

6. **Phases**: The small collection of early items from this site contains the rim of a bowl with crossed lines on the exterior, and reserve pendant triangles on the interior (ES-RB-8; Fig. IV.30 f; cf. Hole 1977: Fig. 50 c, d; Hole, Flannery and Neely 1969: Fig. 57 n), probably of the Chogha Mami Transitional phase. There is also a plain oval basin rim of the straight-sided variant found in the Chogha Mami Transitional or Sabz phase assemblages (Hole 1977:134, Fig. 51 k, m; Hole, Flannery and Neely 1969:127–128, 136, Fig. 47 b-d, 49 a). A sherd from the shoulder of a strongly incurved bowl with negative wavy lines (ES-RB-15; Fig. IV.30 g; ibid.: Fig. 52 b), characteristic of the Khazineh phase, was also found. Other painted sherds (e.g. Fig. IV.30 h) cannot be ascribed. A celt poll, several blade segments, and what appears to be a chipped stone perforator were collected. The site was occupied at least during the Chogha Mami Transitional and Khazineh phases.

7. **Comment**: The full site area of 0.26 ha is ascribed to these two phases. See Chapter VI for a discussion of canal DL-317.

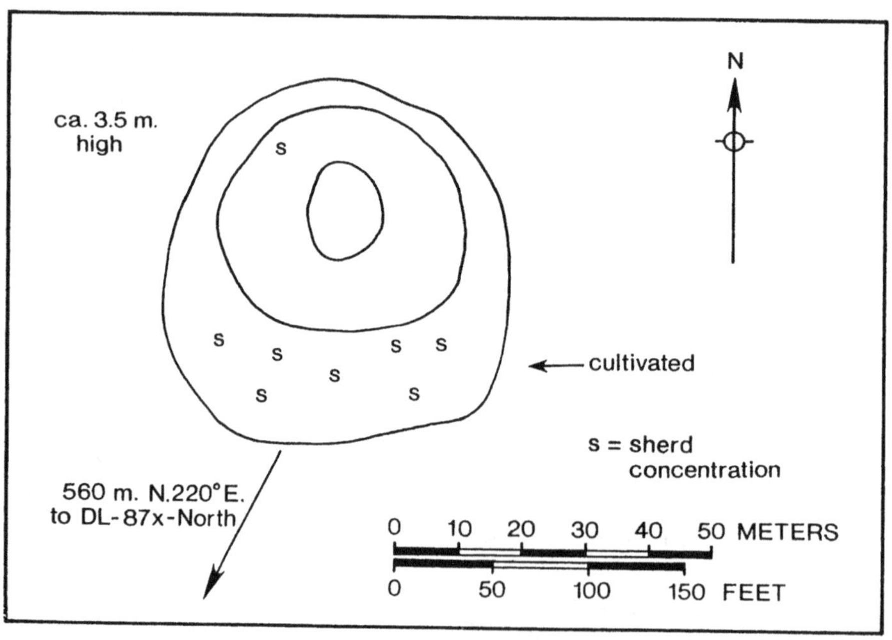

Figure IV.37. Map of DL-84

1a. **Number**: DL-85 (DL-87X; DK-11).
1b **Name**: Tepe Muradabad (Mourad-Abad)
2. **Grid**: 1727.7–1168.6
3. **Dimensions**:

Length:	175 m
Width:	95 m
Height:	8.25 m
Circumference:	425 m
Area:	1.44 ha

4. **Modern Environmental Context**: On the alluvial fan of the Dawairij River, just northeast of the present channel.

5. **Features**: Muradabad is an interesting bi-lobed site with three easily discernible mounds visible (Fig. IV.38). The site is presently surrounded by a small, functioning irrigation canal (a branch of a modern canal paralleling canal DL-94). The circumference of this canal has been given as the maximum circumference of the site. However, it seems likely that the site was originally somewhat larger. The mounds sit atop a large platform or low, relatively flat mound that is

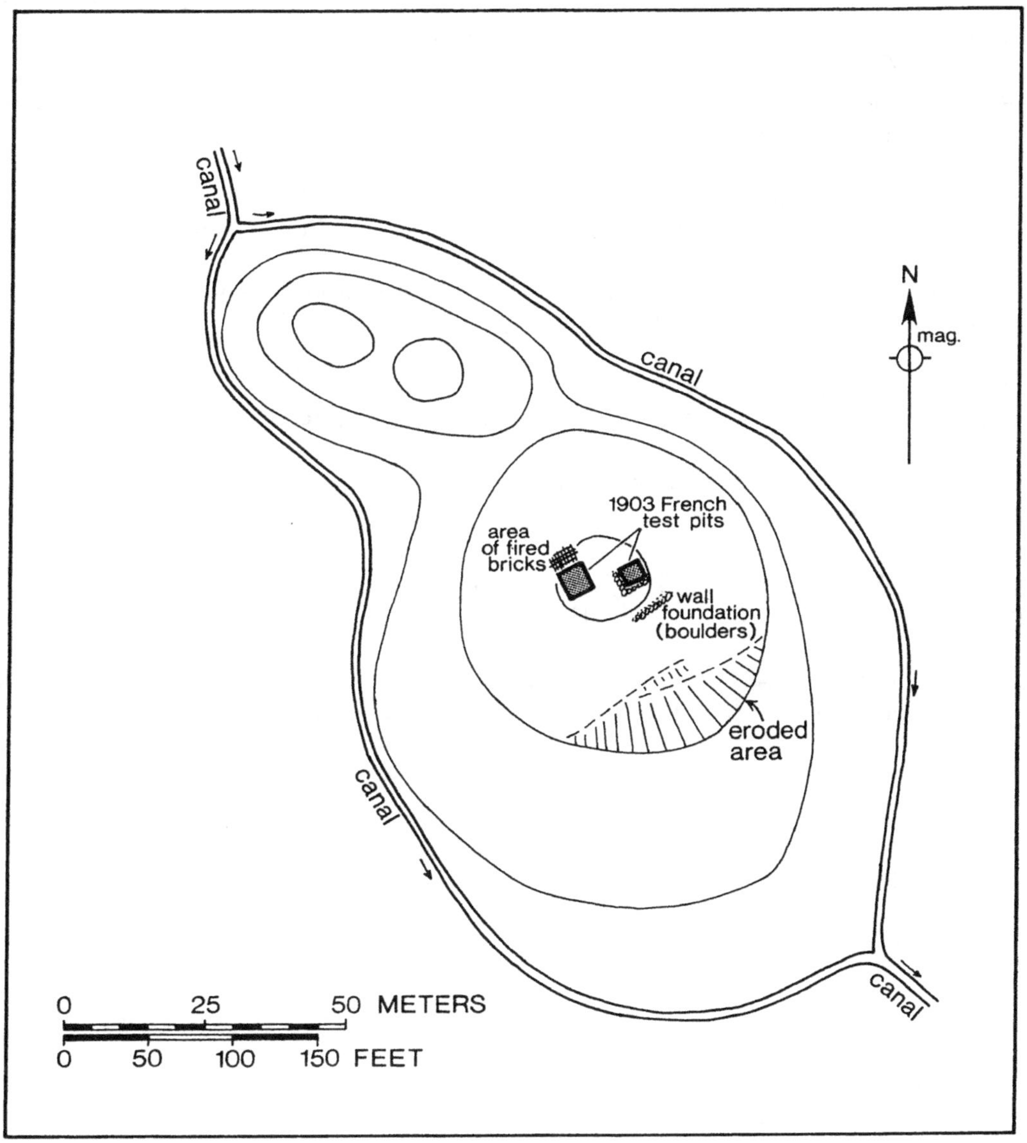

Figure IV.38. Map of Tepe Muradabad (DL-85)

Figure IV.39. Chogha Mami Transitional, Khazineh, and Mehmeh ceramics from the main mound of Tepe Muradabad (DL-85)

a. Small Bowl Rim with Exterior Grid and Interior Ticking (ES-RB-7) (South Terrace) Medium sand inclusions, Body grayish brown (2.5Y 5/2), Diam ca. 16 cm, Paint very dark gray (2.5Y 3/1), (Hole 1977: Fig 51a).

b. Bowl Sherd with Exterior Bands and Interior Pendant Triangle (South Terrace) Medium sand inclusions, Body white (2.5Y 8/2), Paint very dark gray (10YR 3/1) (cf. Hole 1977: Fig. 50).

c. Carinated Bowl Sherd with Interior Cross-hatch (ES-RB-11) (South Terrace) Fine sand inclusions, Body white (2.5Y 8/2), Paint very dark gray (2.5Y 3/1) (cf. Hole, Flannery, and Neely 1969: Figs. 56d, e, 57p).

d. Bowl Sherd with Right Triangle Motif (ES-RB-6) (Mound Summit) No visible inclusions, Body very pale brown (10YR 8/3), Body diam ca. 14 cm, Paint eroded (cf. Hole, Flannery, and Neely 1969: Fig. 62c).

e. Basin Rim with Triangles on Lip (ES-RB-18) (South Slope) Traces of medium sand, Body white (10YR 8/2), Diam ca. 40 cm, Paint dark gray (10YR 4/1) (cf. Hole, Flannery, and Neely 1969: Fig. 59a).

f. Small Bowl Rim with Interior Vertical Lines (Mound Summit) Traces of medium sand, Body pale yellow (5Y 8/3), Diam ca. 32 cm, Paint very dark gray (5Y 3/1)

g. Bowl Sherds with Exterior Ladder Motif (ES-RB-5) (Mound Summit) Medium sand inclusions, Body pale yellow (5Y 7/3), Diam warped, Paint dark gray (2.5Y 4/1) overfired kiln "waster" (cf. Hole, Flannery and Neely 1969: Fig. 62i).

h. Bowl Rim with Exterior Zig-zag motif (Mound Summit) No visible inclusions, Body very pale brown (10YR 8/4), Diam ca. 12 cm, Paint dark gray (N/4) (cf. Wright 1981: Fig. 22a).

i. Bowl Rim with Exterior Rectilinear Motif (South Terrace) Medium sand inclusions, Body white (5Y 8/3), Diam ca. 23 cm, Glossy paint very dark gray (2.5Y 3/1) (cf. Hole, Flannery, and Neely 1969: Fig. 55h).

j. Bowl Sherd with Zoomorphic Figures (Mound Summit) No visible inclusions, Body pale yellow (2.5Y 8/3), Paint dark gray (10YR 4/1) (cf. Hole, Flannery and Neely 1969: Fig. 62c).

k. Chariot Wheel Spindle Whorl Fragment (ES-O-2) (South Slope) No visible inclusions, Body white (5Y 8/2), Diam 4.5 cm, Paint very dark grayish brown (10YR 3/2) (cf. Hole, Flannery, and Neely 1969: Fig. 89).

l. Mehmeh Red-on-red Jar Sherd (ES-SJ-2) (Mound Summit) Inclusions not noted, Body pink (7.5YR 8/4), Exterior dusky red (10R 3/2) paint, Interior light red (2.5YR 6/6) slip, (cf. Hole, Flannery and Neely 1969: Fig. 65).

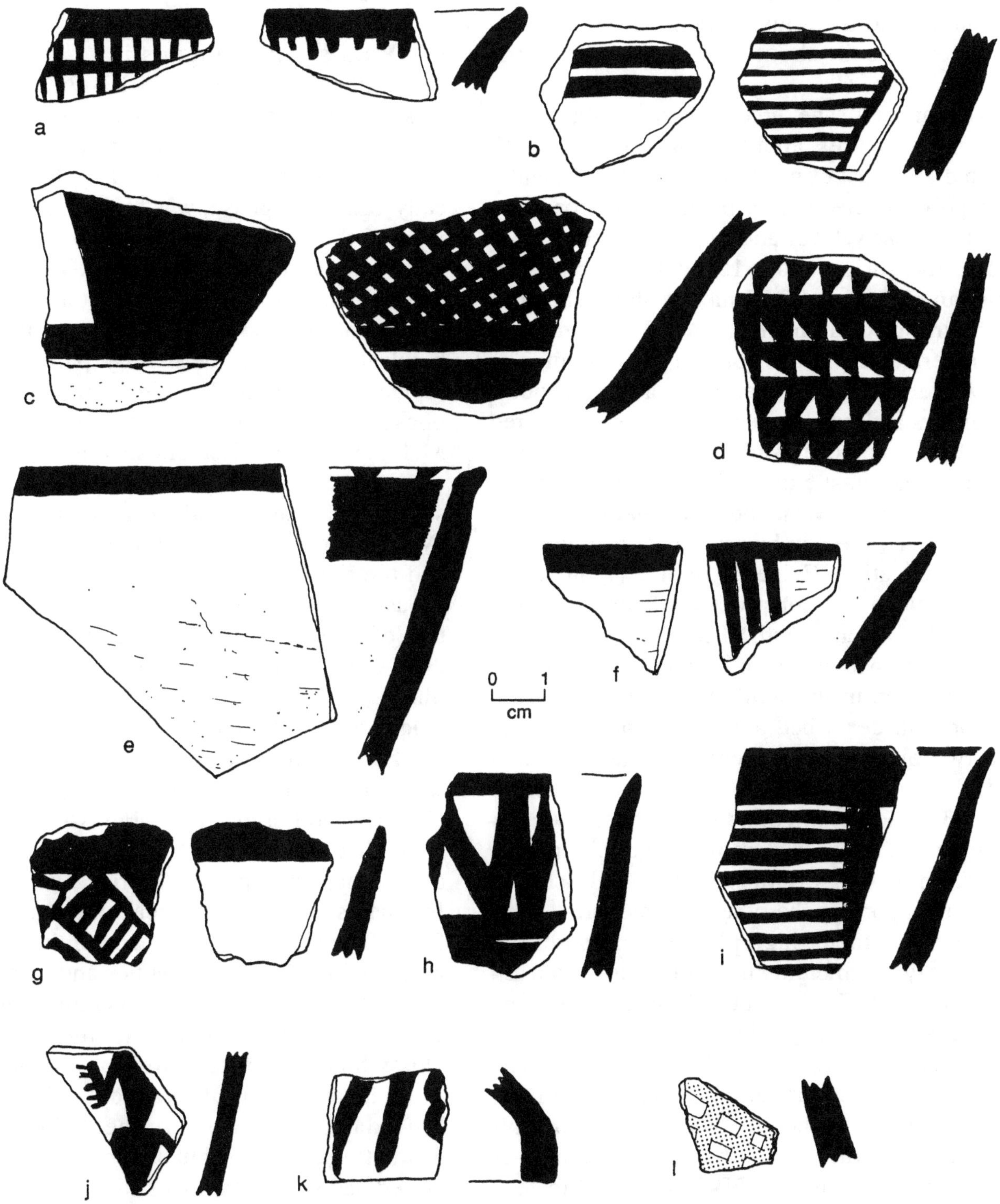

Figure IV.39. Chogha Mami Transitional, Khazineh, and Mehmeh ceramics from the main mound of Tepe Muradabad (DL-85)

generally of an irregular figure-eight shape in plan. The edges of this platform blend almost imperceptibly into the alluvial plain while its maximum elevation is about 4.5 meters above the plain.

The largest of the three mounds is elliptical in plan and measures about 63 meters in length (oriented 24° west of north) by 55 meters in width at the point where it rises from the platform. Its summit is nearly level and approximately square in plan, measuring about 15 by 15 meters. This level summit is about 8.25 meters above the alluvial plain surrounding the site. We found two quadrilateral excavations cut into the summit. The northwestern most excavation measured about 5 by 5 meters and what appears to be a wall of fired bricks forms the north wall of the excavation unit. The southeast-most excavation measured about 3 by 4 meters and its west and south walls have evidently defined the southwest corner of a boulder wall or foundation. Evidence of at least one other wall or foundation constructed of boulders was seen just below and south of the summit, about 5 meters southeast of and paralleling the boulder alignment seen in the south wall of the latter excavation unit described above. We presume that these two quadrilateral excavations are the tests briefly mentioned by Gautier and Lampre (1905:83). The main mound is separated by a depression or saddle, 5 meters wide and 0.25 meters deep, from the slightly raised, elliptically-shaped platform supporting the other two mounds at this site. This 0.50 meter high platform measures approximately 51 meters in length and about 24 meters in width. It is about 4.5 meters high, and the long axis of the platform is oriented 68 degrees west of north. A small mound, circular in plan and measuring about 12 meters in diameter and 0.50 meters in height, was situated on this platform a few meters southeast of its center. A slightly larger, 15 meters (NW-SE) by 10 meters, but lower (0.25 meters) elliptical mound was situated on the low platform a few meters northwest of the center of the platform. Its summit is 4.75 meters above plain level. A low saddle about 5 meters wide separates the circular mound from the elliptical mound.

6. **Phases**: A diagnostic Chogha Mami Transitional bowl rim (ES-RB-7; Fig. IV.39 a) was found on the south side of the main south mound. A carinated bowl with interior cross-hatched design (ES-RB-11; Fig. IV.39 c), typically Khazineh phase, was found on the south terrace of the south platform. Incurved bowl rims with wavy exterior motifs (ES-RB-15), also typically Khazineh, were found on the north mound. Hemispherical bowls (ES-RB-9) and carinated bowls (ES-RB-12) with fully painted interiors, typically of the late Khazineh and early Mehmeh phases, were found on all parts of the site. Mehmeh phase indicators such as Mehmeh Red-on-red (ES-SJ-2; Fig. IV.39 l) jar sherds, bowl sherds with exterior ladder motifs (ES-RB-5; Fig. IV.39 g; cf. Gautier and Lampre 1905: Fig. 216) and the right triangle motif (ES-RB-6; Fig. IV.39 d), as well as bowl or basin sherds with goat motifs (cf. Gautier and Lampre 1905: Figs. 212, 216, 208) were found only on the larger south mound. Sherds of fine bowls with step motifs (LS-RB-15), diagnostic of the later Farukh phase, occur only on the summit of the south mound. The French team retrieved a nearly complete example (Gautier and Lampre 1905: Fig. 151) and it is possible that these mounds represent some limited use, perhaps as a place of burial. Suse phase bowl fragments with large vertical chevron motifs (LS-BR-17) were found on all parts of the site. Branch motifs (LS-RB-19; cf. Gautier and Lampre 1905: Fig. 196) and grid motifs (Gautier and Lampre 1905: Fig. 152), some with the characteristic glossy Suse phase paint, were also found.

These distributional data indicate that Muradabad began in the Chogha Mami Transitional phase, but the remains are deeply buried and we cannot assess the size of the earliest occupation. By later Khazineh phase times the entire area of the site was occupied, but during the succeeding Mehmeh phase only the southern portion of the site shows evidence of use. There is no definite evidence of Bayat occupation, and Farukh phase use was limited. The entire site was once again occupied in Suse phase times.

7. **Comment**: We will not hazard a guess regarding the area covered by deeply buried Chogha Mami Transitional phase occupation. Given the above discussion, we can ascribe the full site area of 1.44 ha to the Khazineh occupation. Only 1.34 ha was covered during the Mehmeh phase, and there was only a trace of Farukh occupation. However, the full site area can be ascribed to the Suse phase occupation. See Chapter VI for a discussion of canals DL-94 and 317.

8. **References**: Gautier and Lampre 1905:83; Miroschedji 1981:173–175, Plate XX, 1.

1a. **Number**: DL-89 (DL-85X, DK-28)
1b. **Name**:
2. **Grid**: 1728.4–1167.0
3. **Dimensions**:

Length:	50 m (N-S)
Width:	30 m
Height:	1.8 m
Area:	0.10 ha

4. **Modern Environmental Context**: On the alluvial fan of the Dawairij River, just northeast of the present channel.

5. **Features**: The site consists of a moderate-sized mound with two distinct lobes at the north and south ends joined by a "saddle". Very few sherds were found on the mound or on the surrounding plain .

6. **Phases**: The small collection at Texas contains—in addition to several later, probably Parthian, sherds—a straw tempered Khazineh Red sherd and a coarse Susiana Plain sherd. These sherds suggest a relatively early Susiana assemblage. Miroschedji, however, reports later Susiana ceramics.

7. **Comment**: Measurements from Miroschedji 1981:173–175. See Chapter VI for a discussion of canal DL-317B.

8. **References**: Miroschedji 1981.

1a. **Number**: DL-90 (DL-84X, Miroschedji DK-27)
1b. **Name**:
2. **Grid**: 1728.6–1167.0
3. **Dimensions**:

Diameter:	30 m
Height:	2.0 m
Area:	0.07 ha

4. **Modern Environmental Context**: On the alluvial fan of the Dawairij River, just northeast of the present channel.

5. **Features**: A sherd scatter, with very few sherds.

6. **Phases**: Miroschedji reports later Susiana ceramics. The small sample at Texas contains a jar rim and three plain body sherds of Susiana ware. Also, there are a medium gray chert proximal blade segment and a blade core fragment.

7. **Comment**: All observations from Miroschedji 1981:173–175. See Chapter VI for a discussion of canal DL-317B.

8. **References**: Miroschedji 1981:173–175.

1a. **Number**: DL-91 (DL-83X, DK-26)
1b. **Name**:
2. **Grid**: 1729.0–1166.6
3. **Dimensions**:

Length:	50 m (NW-SE)
Width:	40 m (NE-SW)
Height:	4.5 m
Area:	0.14 ha

4. **Modern Environmental Context**: On the alluvial fan of the Dawairij River, immediately to the north of the present channel.

5. **Features**: This site consists of a single moderate-sized, steep-sided mound. The mound is elliptical in plan, with its longer axis oriented 40 degrees west of north. Evidences of what appear to be stone foundations or wall footings were found eroding from the sides of the mound. None were exposed sufficiently to provide data as to the size and shape of the structures they represent. A relatively small amount of ceramics as well as flaked stone artifacts were seen scattered over the mound and the adjacent surrounding ground surface. No ground stone materials were noted.

6. **Phases**: A small sample of later Susiana ceramics were found on this site. The Bayat Red bowl rim, Susiana bowl bases (LS-BB-1, 4), as well as Susiana bowl rims with bands (LS-RB-2–4) and horizontal curved lines (LS-RB-4) could occur in the Mehmeh, Bayat, or Farukh phases. However, fully painted shoulders of large jars (cf. LS-RJ-1) and the fine bowl rim with fully painted exterior (LS-RB-4) are typically Bayat, and so we ascribe this site to the Bayat phase.

7. **Comment**: Miroschedji gives the dimensions as 45 meters (East-West) by 20 meters and 2.5 meters high, probably because he did not include the adjacent scatter of ceramics. The height of the central area of the site suggests that it contains the remains of a mud-brick platform. We ascribe the full site area of 0.14 ha to the Bayat phase. See Chapter VI for a discussion of canal DL-317B.

8. **References**: Miroschedji 1981:173–175.

1a. **Number**: DL-104 (DL-74X)
1b. **Name**:
2. **Grid**: Southwest: 1717.0–1171.2;
Northeast: 1717.2–1172.2
3. **Dimensions**:
Length: West: 120 m (NW-SE);
East: 65 m (E-W).
Width: West 75 m (NE-SW);
East 60 m N-S).
Height: West: 3.25 m; East: 2.5 m.
Circumference: West: 335 m;
East: 200 m.
Circumference of entire site: 650 m.
Area: Total area of site: 3.36 ha

4. **Modern Environmental Context**: At the junction of the southern alluvial slopes of the plain and the alluvial fan of the Dawairij River, about seven kilometers southwest of the present Dawairij channel and six kilometers east of the present Mehmeh channel.

5. **Features**: This site consists of two well-defined relatively large mounds, distinctly separated by a low area, about 10 meters in width, and surrounded by a level, grass-free area. As indicated by the sherd and lithic scatter, the site evidently extends a short distance beyond the canal that surrounds the two mounds and the level exposed area. The smaller east mound had relatively few sherds and lithic artifacts present, while the larger west mound had great quantities of both. No stone or clay wall footings or other architectural features were visible.

6. **Phases**: The scarcity of Sargarab ware, and the absence of beveled rim bowls with tapered lips (US-RB-1) and many other distinctive bowl

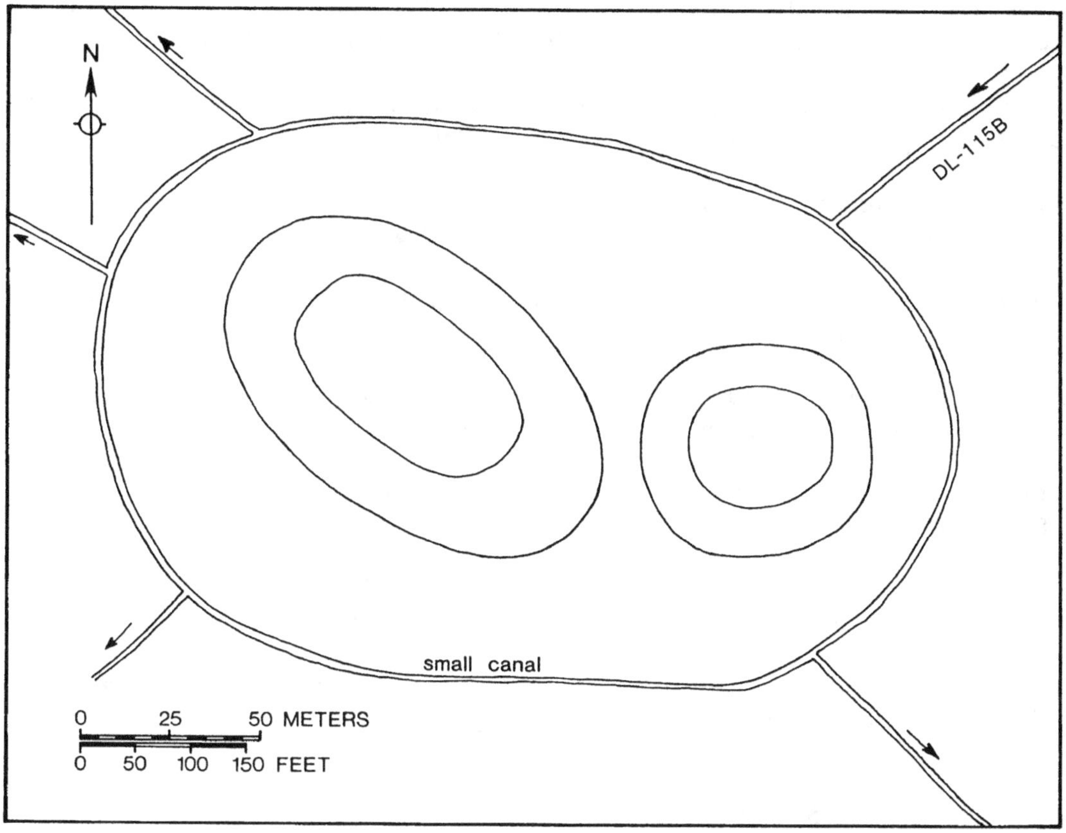

Figure IV.40. Map of DL-104

and jar rim variants indicate that the site was not occupied in the Early Uruk phase. While some Uruk ceramic types here, such as standard beveled rim bowls (US-RB-2), the low expanded band rim jar (UU-RJ-6; Fig. IV.41 e), the jar shoulder with cross-hatch incised band (UU-O-5; Fig. IV.41 g) which could have decorated such a jar, and the plain strap handle (UU-O-12; Fig. IV.41 j) could have been made in either the Middle or Late Uruk period, many others allow more specific ascription. Characteristic of the Middle Uruk phase are the Sargarab flared round lip jar (US-RJ -6; Fig. IV.41 c), the Uruk ware heavy jars with round lip (UU-RJ-3; Fig. IV.41 b) and flared expanded neck jars with grooved lips (UU-RJ-4) (particularly the red slipped example), the heavy expanded neck jar (UU-RJ-8; Fig. IV.41 d), and the jar shoulder fragment with red-on-black painted decoration (UU-O-8; Fig. IV.41 i). These Middle Uruk types were found scattered on both mounds. Characteristic of the Late Uruk phase are the band rim bottle (UU-RJ-11; Fig. IV.41 f), the droop spout (UU-O-11) which would have been attached to such a bottle, and the small jar shoulder with groove-and-oblique shoulder decoration (UU-O-3), all found on the larger western mound.

Quantities of Jemdet Nasr or Early Dynastic ceramics were found mostly on the larger western mound, but no painted sherds which would facilitate more precise datings were seen. There is nothing definitely of the Jemdet Nasr phase. The high proportion of solid footed cup fragments (ED-BC-1; Fig. IV.42 b, c) and the finer examples of ledge-rim jars (ED-RJ-4; Fig. IV.42 n) suggest an Early Dynastic I–II date. However, the heavier ledge-rim (ED-RJ-4; Fig. IV.42 o) and

Figure IV.41. Middle and Late Uruk ceramics from DL-104

a. Ledge Rim Jar with Punctates and Reserve Slip (UU-RJ-9) (Area 1) Medium sand inclusions, Body pale orange-yellow (10YR 8/3), Diam 14 cm, Surface yellowish gray (10YR 8/2) (cf. Johnson 1973: Pl. IV a).

b. Heavy Round Lip Jar (cf. UU-RJ-3) (Area 1) Medium sand inclusions, Body pale orange-yellow (2.5YR 7/4), Diam 17 cm, Surface yellowish gray (10YR 8/2) (cf. Wright 1981: Fig. 48i-j).

c. Flared Round Lip Jar (UU-RJ-6) (Area 5) Vegetal and calcite inclusions, Body orange (2.5YR 6/7), Diam 12 cm, Surface yellowish white (2.5Y 9/2), Red slip (10R 5/4). (cf. Wright 1981: Fig. 43k-l).

d. Heavy Expanded Rim Jar (UU-RJ-8) (Area 5) Coarse sand and chert pebble inclusions, Body light brown (7.5YR 6/ 4), Diam 21 cm, Surface pale yellow (2.5Y 8/3) (cf. Wright 1981: Fig. 50g-i).

e. Low Expanded Band Rim Jar (UU-RJ-6) (Area 5) Medium sand inclusions, Body yellowish pink (7/5YR 8/3), Diam ca. 28 cm, Surface olive brown (2.5Y 9/2) (cf. Wright 1981: Fig. 52a-g).

f. Band Rim Bottle (UU-RJ-11) (Area 5) Fine sand inclusions, Body pale yellow (2.5Y 8/3), Diam 5 cm, Surface pale yellow (2.5Y 8/3) (cf. Wright 1981: Fig. 54c).

g. Jar Shoulder with Double Cross Hatch Band (UU-O-5) and Nose Lug (UU-O-1) (Area 5) Fine sand inclusions, Body yellowish pink (5YR 7/4), Surface yellowish gray(10YR 8/2) (cf. Wright 1981: Fig. 55a-b).

h. Jar Shoulder with Groove-and-Oblique Incising (UU-O-3) (Area 5) Coarse sand and crushed calcite inclusions, Body yellowish pink (10R 7/4), Surface erode (cf. Wright 1981: Fig. 55f-g).

i. Jar Shoulder with Painted Black-on-Red design (UU-O-8) (Area 5) Fine sand inclusions, Body and Surface yellowish pink (5YR 7/5), Red slip (10R 5/6) (cf. Wright 1981: Fig. 57a).

j. Strap Handle (UU-O-12) (Area 5) Fine sand inclusions, Body yellowish gray (5Y 8/2), Surface grayish yellow (5Y 8/3) (cf. Wright 1981: Fig. 55j).

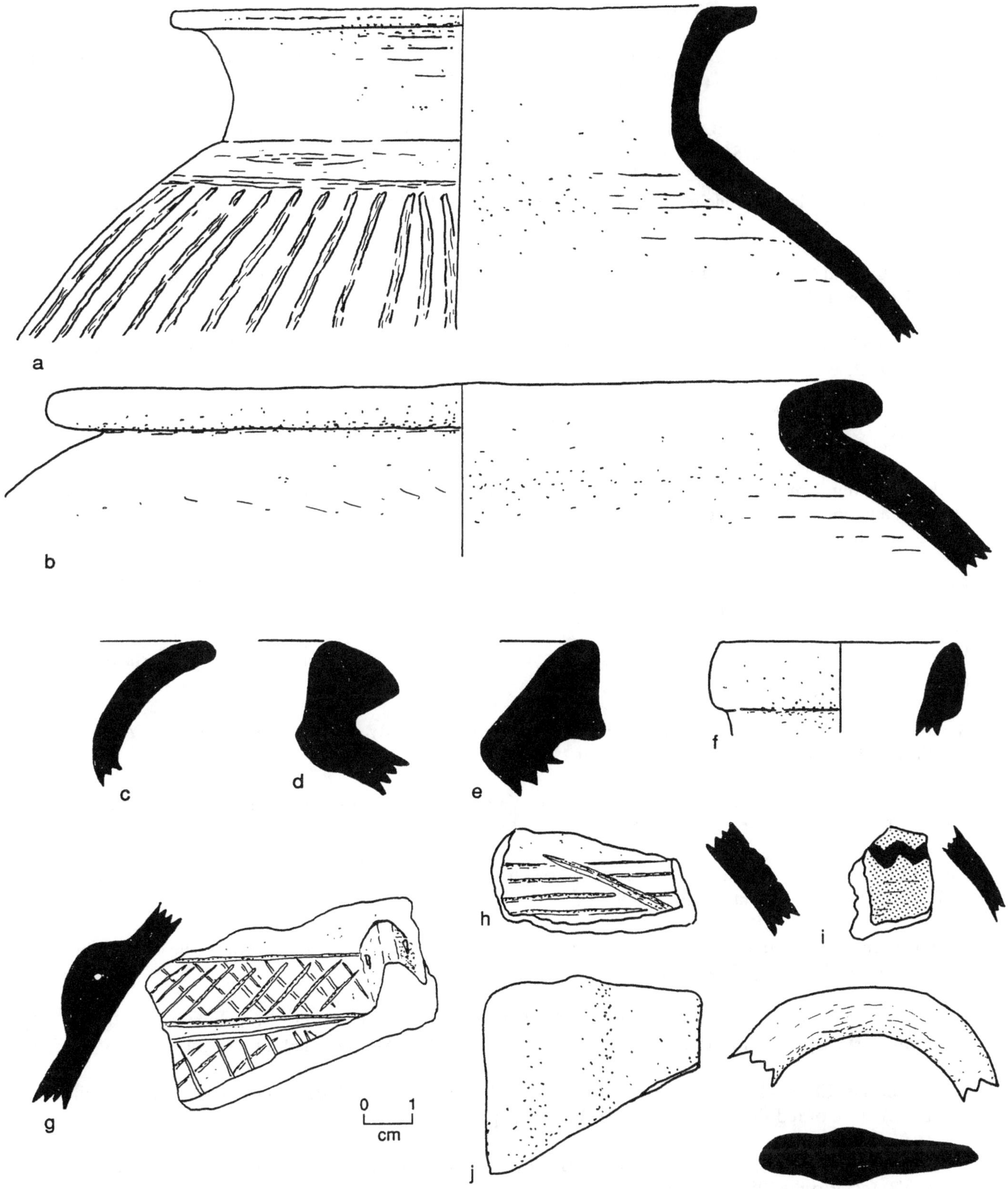

Figure IV.41. Middle and Late Uruk ceramics from DL-104

Figure IV.42. Jemdet Nasr and Early Dynastic ceramics from DL-104

a. Narrow Conical Cup Base (ED-BC-2) Fine sand inclusions, Body light yellowish brown (10YR 7/4), Base diam 3.1 cm, Surface light yellowish brown (7.5YR 7/4) (cf. Wright 1981: Fig. 45 d-e).

b. Solid-footed Cup Base (ED-BC-1) Fine sand inclusions, Body light yellowish brown (7.5YR 7/4), Base diam 2.2 cm, Surface pale yellow (2.5Y 8/3) (cf. Wright 1981: Fig. 45 f-g).

c. Same (ED-BC-1) Fine sand inclusions, Body yellowish white (2.5Y 9/2), Base diam 2.2 cm, Surface pale yellow (2.5Y 8/4) (cf. same).

d. Incurved Conical Cup Rim (ED-RC-1) Fine sand inclusions, Body pale yellow (2.5Y 7/3), Diam 14 cm, Surface light yellowish brown (10YR 7/3) (cf. Wright 1981: Fig. 49 l).

e. Conical Cup Rim (ED-RC-1) Fine sand inclusions, Body yellowish gray (10YR 8/2), Diam 8 cm, Surface pale yellow (2.5Y 8/3) (cf. Wright 1981: Fig. 45 h).

f. Round Lip Bowl (ED-RB-1) Fine sand inclusions, Body light yellowish brown (10YR 7/3), Diam 29 cm, Surface pale yellow (2.5 Y 8/3) (cf. Wright 1981: Fig. 46 d).

g. Rolled Lip Ring, No inclusions, Body yellowish gray (5Y 8/2), Diam 8.5 cm, Surface yellowish gray (5Y 7/2). Note chipping and horizontal abrasion on the lower lip; this item was found in an area of ceramic slag concentration (Wright 1969: Fig. 21d; Wright 1981: Fig. 76 n).

h. Beveled Lip Bowl (ED-RB-2) Fine sand inclusions, Body light yellowish brown (7.5YR 7/4), Diam 39 cm, Surface pale orange-yellow (10YR 8/3) (cf. Wright 1981: Fig. 47 i-j).

i. Same (ED-RB-2) Fine sand inclusions, Body light yellowish brown (7.5YR 7/4), Diam 42 cm, Surface yellowish gray (2.5Y 8/3) (cf. Wright 1981: Fig. 47 c, i, l).

j. Same (ED-RB-2) with Plain Strip (Type ??) Fine sand inclusions, Body light yellowish brown (7.5YR 7/4), Diam ca. 38 cm, Surface pale yellow (2.5Y 8/3) (cf. Wright 1981: Fig. 47 e).

k. Same (ED-RB-2) Medium sand inclusions, Body light reddish brown (2.5YR 6/5), Diam ca. 48 cm, Surface yellowish pink (5YR 6/4) (cf. Wright. 1981: Fig. 47 c, i, l).

l. Round Lip Jar (ED-RJ-1) Fine sand inclusions, Body light yellowish brown (10YR 7/3), Diam 13 cm, Surface yellowish white (7.5Y 9/1) (cf. Wright 1981: Fig. 49 a-f).

m. Lock Rim Jar. Fine sand inclusions, Body yellowish pink (5YR 7/4), Diam 15 cm, Surface pale orange-yellow (10YR 8/3) (cf. Wright 1981: Fig. 54 k).

n. Ledge Rim Jar (ED-RJ-4) with polychrome motif (ED-O-4), Fine sand inclusions, Body light brown (7.5YR 6/6), Diam ca 16 cm, Surface pale yellow (5Y 8/3), Grayish red slip (7.5R 4/3), Motif eroded (cf. Wright 1981: Fig. 54 d, 58 a).

o. Ledge Rim Jar (ED-RJ-4) Fine sand inclusions, Body yellowish gray (2.5Y 8/2), Diam 20 cm, Surface yellowish white (2.5Y 9/2), trace of red slip (cf. Wright 1981: Fig. 53 p-q).

p. Band Rim Jar (ED-RJ-5) Fine sand inclusions, Body yellowish white (7.5Y9/2), Diam 13 cm, Surface yellowish white (7.5Y 9/2) (cf. Wright 1981: Fig. 54 h-j).

q. Gray Ware Round Lip Jar (ED-RJ-7) Crushed limestone inclusions, Body light olive brown (2.5Y 5/2), Diam 19 cm, Surface brownish gray (7.5YR 5/1) (cf. Wright 1981: Fig. 66 f-i).

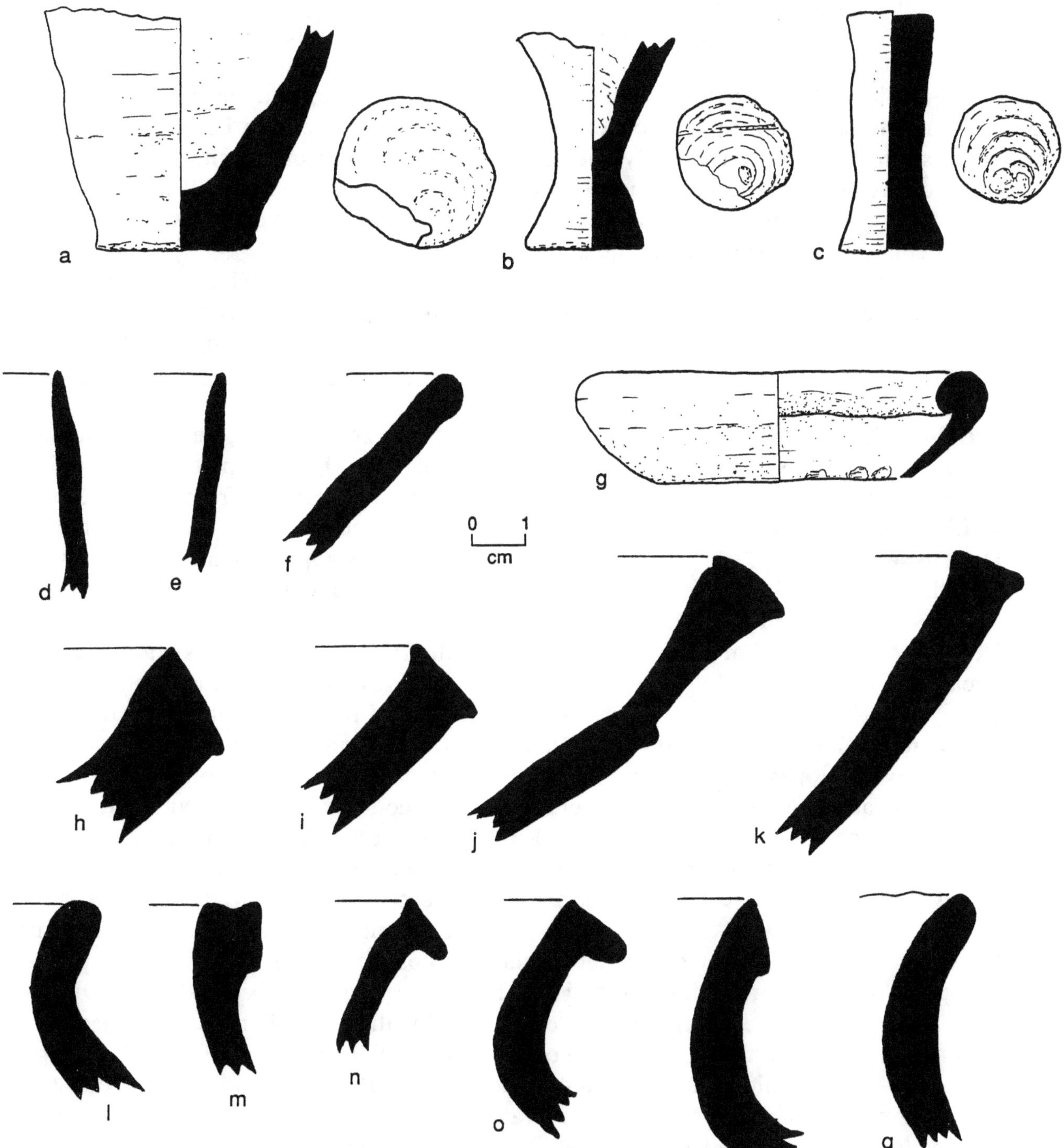

Figure IV.42. Jemdet Nasr and Early Dynastic ceramics from DL-104

round lip (ED-RJ-1; Fig. IV.42 l, q) jars suggest some Early Dynastic III occupation. A rolled rim ring (Fig. IV.42 g), probably a scraper used in pottery manufacture (Alden 1988; Wright 1981:154, Fig. 76 n), was found in a concentration of ceramic wasters.

Achaemenid, Seleuco-Parthian, and Sasanian ceramics, localized to the upper portion of the larger, western mound—particularly the many "wasters" of Achaemenid and Seleuco-Parthian ceramic types, as well as the "saggers," "stilts," and stone debitage from the northwest quadrant of the larger mound, that very probably indicate a craft area—will be discussed in a later volume.

7. **Comment**: This site was originally recorded in the field notes as two sites—DL-104 and DL-105. Since the two are adjacent and surrounded by a continuous artifact scatter we have conflated the two sites into one. We ascribe the 0.95 ha mounded portion of the site area to the Middle Uruk phase, and the 0.63 ha area of the west mound to the Late Uruk phase. The surrounding debris north of the site is primarily Early Dynastic, and we assign 2.0 ha to these phases. See Chapter VI for a discussion of canal DL-115B.

8. **References**: This may be the "Tepe Mohr" visited by the French team early in the 20th century (Gautier and Lampre 1905:81, Fig. 9).

1a. **Number**: DL-169 (DL-72X)
1b. **Name**: Sargarab ("Sargaru" in the local Luri dialect)
2. **Grid**: 1714.8–1192.0
3. **Dimensions**:

Length:	195 m
Width:	45 m
Height:	ca 1.0 m
Area:	0.66 ha

4. **Modern Environmental Context**: On the northern alluvial slopes of the plain near the mountain front, about 800 meters south-southwest of the present brackish Ab-i Garm spring DL-170. The Ab-i Garm stream DL-276A begins at this spring and flows southward just west of the site.

5. **Features**: Sargarab is located atop and on the upper slopes of a long, narrow ridge of land in the piedmont zone (Fig. IV.43). Access to the site was achieved by way of the northeast, upper end of the piedmont spur ridge, which was protected by a boulder wall with a narrow, stepped entryway flanked by large, unmodified stone slabs. The visible architecture of this site consists of a large number of boulder alignments that comprise terrace walls, wall foundations or footings, and other features. The foundations or footings of at least 80 rooms or structures, ranging in size from approximately 1.0 by 1.3 meters to 5 by 7 meters (with floor areas ranging from about 1.3 m^2 to 34.3 m^2), were recorded. The majority of these rooms or structures appear to have been constructed around at least four open, level courtyard areas.

The earlier rooms are located on the crest of the ridge. Terrace walls and some possible tower footings are clear to the west. The footings of additional rooms or structures, abutting these earlier were found on leveled terraces constructed along the side of the piedmont spur just below the edge of the summit to the south and east. In the intermittent drainages flanking the architecturally terraced site are traces of small check-dams. Remnants of small canals (DL-5) were found coursing along the sides of these same drainages. Those to the east of this site are probably contemporary with the occupation of DL-169. It is possible that an earlier outlet of the nearby hot spring (DL-170) may have flowed through this gully when the site was inhabited. Rain-fed agriculture might also have been possible.

A good deal of erosion has revealed the wall footings and other features at Sargarab, however, we estimate that cultural fill of perhaps one meter or more still underlies much of the site's present surface.

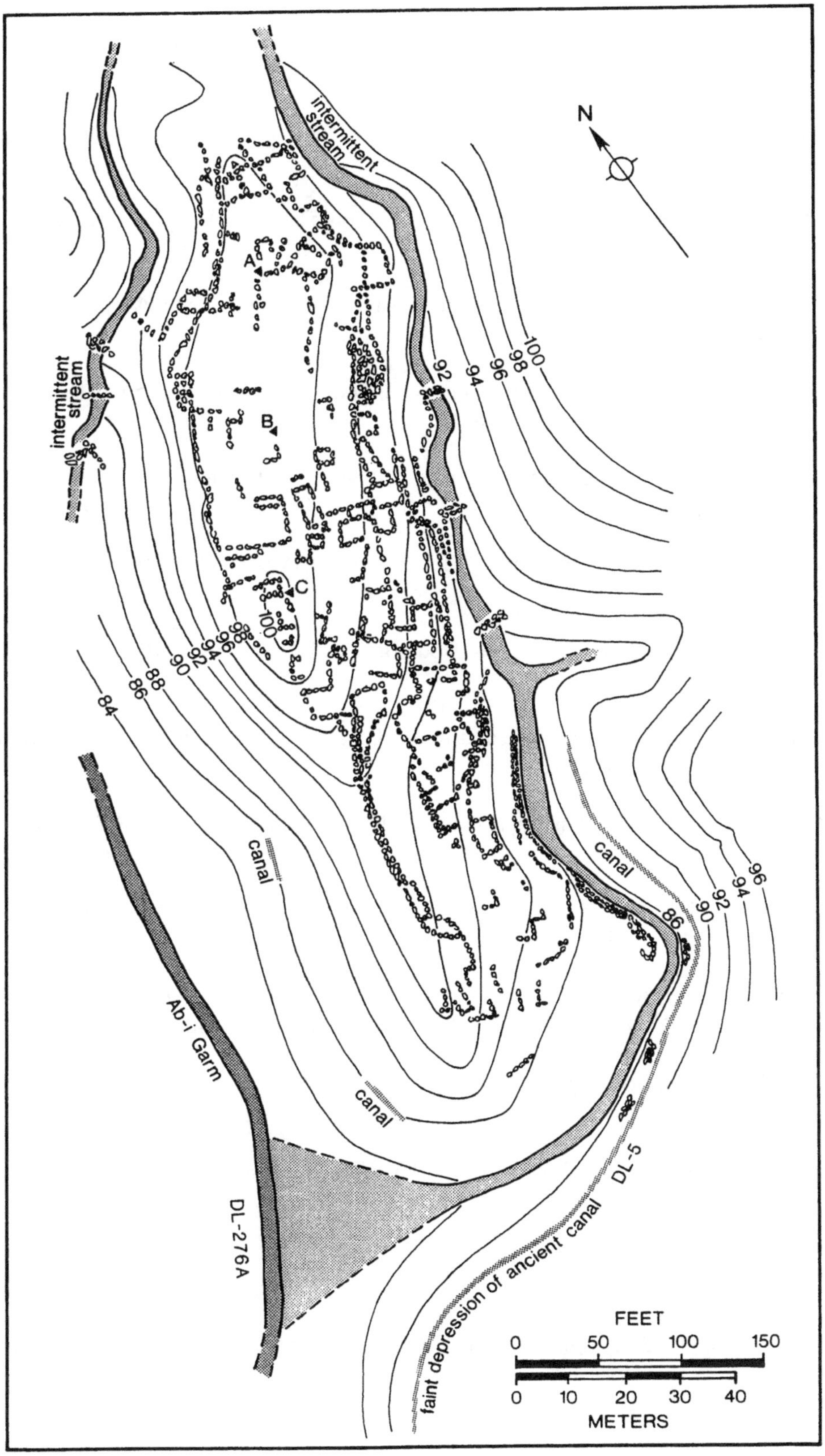

Figure IV.43. Map of Sargarab (DL-169)

Figure IV.44. Early Uruk bowl parts and varia from Sargarab (DL-169)

a. Fine Bowl (US-RB-3) (SW: 155) Vegetal and calcite inclusions, Body yellowish gray (7.5Y 8/2), Diam 18 cm, Surface white (7.5Y 9/1) (cf. Wright 1981: Fig. 43b-c).

b. Same (US-RB-3) (SW: 115) Inclusions same, Body light gray (10YR 8/1), Diam 21 cm, Surface light reddish brown (2.5YR 6/5) (cf. same).

c. Same (US-RB-3) (SW: 171) Vegetal inclusions, Body light brown (5YR 6/5), Diam 17 cm, Surface pale orange-yellow (10YR 8/3) (cf. Wright 1981: Fig. 40e).

d. Same (US-RB-3) (SW: 199) Vegetal and calcite inclusions, Body light yellowish brown (7.5YR 7/4), Diam 18 cm, Surface yellowish gray (5Y 8/1) (cf. same).

e. Same (US-RB-3) with Painted Bands (C:80) Same inclusions, Body light olive gray (5Y 6/1), Diam 18 cm, Surface yellowish gray (7.5Y 8/1), Paint grayish brown (5YR 4/2).

f. Fine Jar (US-RJ-1) (SW: 108) Same inclusions, Body pale yellow (5Y 8/2), Diam 13 cm, Surface yellowish gray (5Y 7/2 (cf. Wright 1981: Fig. 43a, f-j).

g. Same (US-RJ-1) (SW: 161) Same inclusions, Body yellowish white (5Y 9/1), Diam 19 cm, Surface yellowish gray (2.5Y 8/1). (cf. same).

h. Small Tray (US-RB-15) (SW: 185) Same inclusions, Body light yellowish brown (10YR 6/3), Diam ca. 35 cm, Surface yellowish gray (5Y 8/1).

i. Incurved Bowl, Round Lip, with Thumb Impressed Strip (cf. US-RB-9) (C:1) Same inclusions, Body light reddish brown (10YR 5/7), Diam ca. 24 cm, Surface badly eroded.

j. Round Lip Bowl (US-RB-4) (SW: 191) Same inclusions, Body brownish orange (2.5YR 5/8), Diam 20 cm, Surface yellowish gray (10YR 8/1).

k. Incurved Bowl with Flattened Lip (NE: 468) Same inclusions, Body pale yellow (5YR 5/5), Diam warped, Surface yellowish gray (5Y 8/2), Interior slip? yellowish brown (10YR 5/3).

l. Open Bowl with Beaded Rim (US-RB-6) (SW: 14) Same inclusions, Body light brown (5YR 5/5), Diam ca. 46 cm, Surface yellowish pink (7.5R 7/3) (Wright 1981: Fig. 41 l; Le Brun 1971: Fig. 40:1).

m. Same (SW: 192) Same inclusions, Body light reddish brown (2.5YR 5/3), Diam ?, Surface light reddish brown (10YR 5/3).

n. Same (SW: 135) Same inclusions, Body yellowish white (5Y 9/1), Diam ca. 40 cm, Surface yellowish pink (2.5Y 8/3).

o. Same (SW: 92) Same inclusions, Body yellowish pink (2.5YR 7/5), Diam 34 cm, Surface pale yellow (2.5Y 8/3).

p. Same (NE: 441) Same inclusions, Body yellowish gray (5Y 8/1), Diam ca. 25 cm, Surface pale yellow (2.5Y 8/4).

q. Same (NE: 440) Same inclusions, Body light brown (5YR 6/3), Diam ca. 35 cm, Surface yellowish gray (5Y 8/1). (Wright 1981: Fig. 41h).

Figure IV.44. Early Uruk Bowl parts and varia from Sargarab (DL-169)

Figure IV.45. Early Uruk bowl and jar parts from Sargarab (DL-169)

a. Open Basin with Beaded Rim (cf. US-RB-6) (NE: 438) Chopped grass and calcite inclusions, Body pinkish gray (10R 7/4), Diam ca. 50 cm, Surface yellowish gray (2.5Y 8/1).

b. Heavy Beaded Rim Bowl with Thumb Impressed Strip (US-RB-8) (NE: 399) Same inclusions, Body mottled light reddish brown (10R 6/4), Diam 48 cm, Surface yellowish gray (5Y 8/1).

c. Incurved Beaded Rim Bowl (US-RB-10) (NE: 448) Same inclusions, Body grayish yellow (5Y 7/3), Diam 40 cm, surface grayish yellow (5Y 7/3).

d. Heavy Incurved Beaded Rim Basin with Thumb Impressed Strip (US-RB-13) (SW: 124), Same inclusions, Body yellowish gray (7.5Y 8/2), Diam ca. 38 cm, Surface yellowish gray (7.5Y 8/2).

e. Ledge Rim Bowl (US-RB-6) (SW: 245) Same inclusions, Body dark orange-yellow (7.5YR 6/8), Diam ca. 50 cm, Surface eroded. (Wright 1981: Fig. 43d-e, l; Le Brun 1971: Fig. 40:1).

f. Same (UU-RB-6) (SW: 24) Fine sand and calcite traces, Body grayish reddish orange (2.5YR 6/6), Diam 37 cm, Surface light reddish brown (2.5YR 6.5). (cf. same).

g. Basin with Thumb Impressed Strip (cf. LS-RB-1) (SW: 141) Fine sand and vegetal inclusions, Body grayish yellow (2.5Y 8/3), Diam ca. 47 cm, Surface yellowish gray (10YR 8/2). (Stève and Gasche 1971: Pl. 34, 16–17; Johnson 1973: Plate II b, d).

h. Heavy Straight Neck Jar (US-RJ-5) (C:22) Chopped straw and calcite inclusions, Body yellowish gray (7.5Y 8/2), Diam ca. 24 cm, Surface grayish yellow (2.5Y 8/3).

i. Straight Neck Jar with Rounded Lip (US-RJ-4) (NE: 369) Same inclusions, Body moderate orange (2.5YR 6/7), Diam ca. 17 cm, Surface grayish reddish orange (10R 6/5).

j. Straight Neck Jar with Rounded Lip (US-RJ-4) (NE: 368) Same inclusions, Body light yellowish brown (7.5YR 7/5), Diam 16 cm, Surface grayish yellow (2.5Y 8/2).

k. Straight Neck Jar (US-RJ-4) with Oval Nose Lug (US-O-1) (NE: 381) Same inclusions, Body grayish reddish orange (2.5YR 6/5), Diam 13 cm, Surface light brown (5YR 6/3).

l. Neckless Ledge Rim Jar (US-RJ-2) (SW: 198) Coarse angular calcite inclusions, Body light yellowish brown (7.5YR 7/5), Diam 17 cm, Surface pale orangish yellow (10YR 8/3). (Johnson 1973: Pl. III l; Le Brun 1971: Fig. 40:6).

m. Same (C:37) Same inclusions, Body moderate orange (5YR 6/6), Diam ca. 25 cm, Surface eroded. (cf. same).

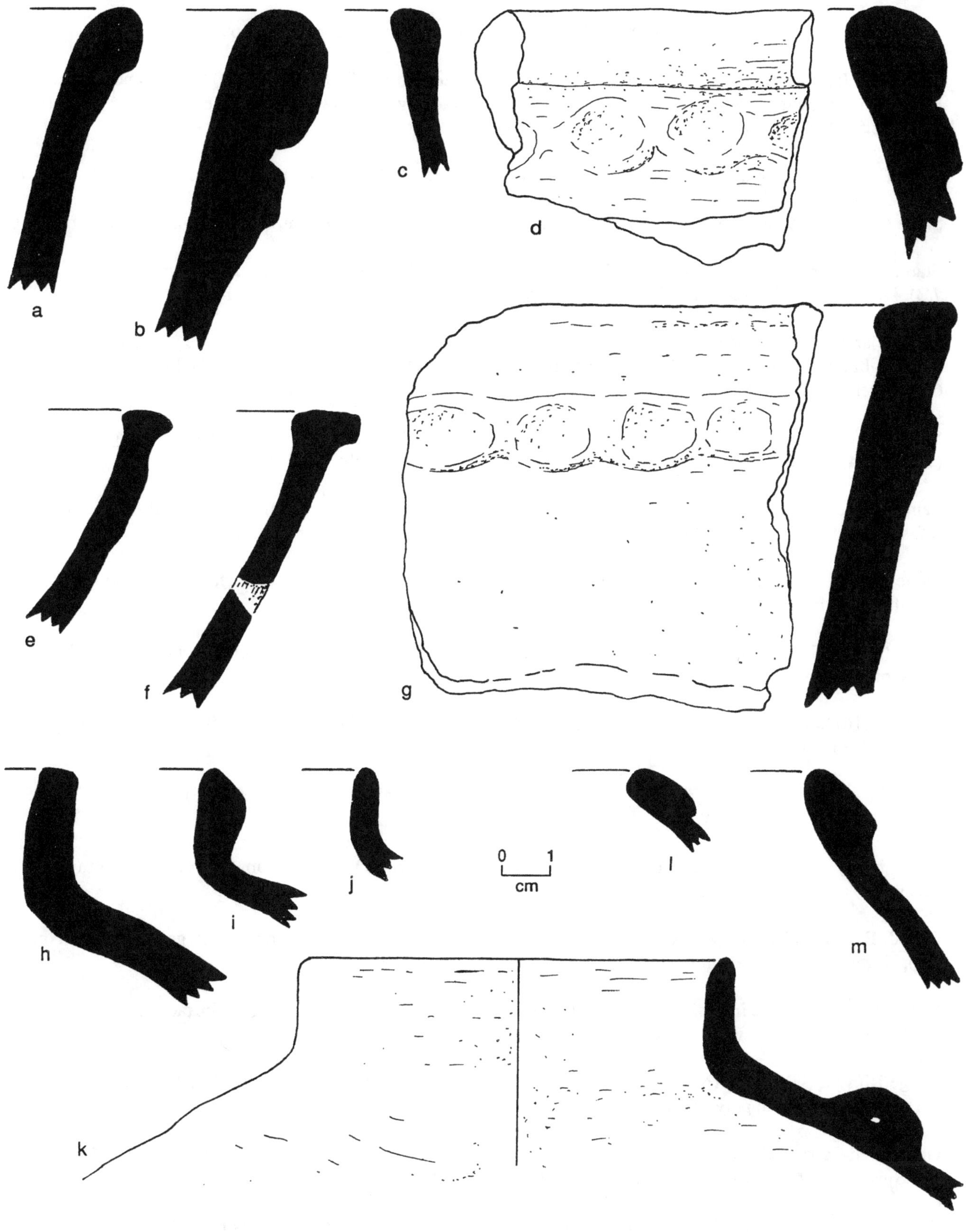

Figure IV.45. Early Uruk bowl and jar parts from Sargarab (DL-169)

Figure IV.46. Early Uruk jar parts from Sargarab (DL-169)

a. Low Neck Jar with Beaded Lip (US-RJ-3)with Black-on-Red Paint (US-O-3) (NE: 394) Calcite and vegetal inclusions, Body light yellowish brown (10YR 6/3), Diam 15 cm, Surface light yellowish brown, Red paint (2.5YR 5/4), Black bands (2.5YR 4/1) (Wright 1981: Fig. 57c).

b. Same (NE: 387) Same inclusions, Body light reddish brown (2.5YR 5/6), Diam 13 cm, Surface eroded.

c. Same (SW: 180) Same inclusions, Body reddish orange (10R 5/7), Diam 14 cm, Surface light reddish brown (10R 5/4).

d. Flared Neck Jar with Tapered Rounded Rim (US-RJ-6) (SW: 356) Same inclusions, Body light yellowish brown (10YR 7/3), Diam 14 cm, Surface variable light brown (primarily 7.5YR 6/3) (Wright 1981: Fig. 42d).

e. Small Flared Expanded Rim Jar (cf. US-RJ-6),with Black-on-Red Paint (US-O-3) (NE: 371) Trace of same inclusions, Body light reddish brown (2.5YR 6/5), Diam 14 cm, Surface yellowish pink (5YR 7/4), Light reddish brown slip (2.5YR 6/5), Black Bands (10YR 4/1).

f. Small Flared, Expanded Rim Jar with Rounded Lip (US-RJ-6) (SW: 219) Same inclusions, Body light yellowish brown (7.5YR 7/4), Diam 17 cm, Surface yellowish gray (2.5Y 8/2) (cf. Wright 1981: Fig. 44e-g)

g. Same (NE: 395) Same inclusions, Body light olive brown (2.5Y 5/2), Diam 13 cm, Surface yellowish gray (2.5Y 8/2). (cf. same and Le Brun 1971: Fig. 40:8).

h. Same (NE: 615) Same inclusions, Body yellowish pink (2.5YR 7/3), Diam 23 cm, Surface yellowish gray (5Y 8/1) (cf. Wright 1981: Fig. 44c-d).

i. Same (SW: 188) Same inclusions, Body light reddish brown (2.5YR 6/3), Diam 24 cm, Surface yellowish gray (5Y 8/1) (cf. same).

j. Same (C:16) Same inclusions, Body grayish reddish orange (2.5YR 6/5), Diam 17 cm, Surface yellowish gray (2.5Y 8/1) (Wright 1981: Fig. 42e).

k. Same, heavy variant (SW: 167) Same inclusions, Body grayish reddish orange (2.5YR 6/6), Diam ca. 35 cm, Surface eroded. (Wright 1981: Fig. 42c).

l. Same, heavy variant (NE: 382) Same inclusions, Body light brown (5YR 6/4), Diam 25 cm, Surface grayish yellow (2.5Y 8/2) (Wright 1981: Fig. 44f, g).

m. Flared, Expanded Rim Jar with Grooved Lip (US-RJ-9) (SW: 158) Same inclusions, Body grayish reddish orange (10R 5/6), Diam 28 cm, Surface grayish yellow (5Y 8/3) (Wright 1981: Fig. 44c).

n. Same (SW: 329) Same inclusions, Body dark grayish yellow (2.5Y 6/3), Diam 28 cm, Surface grayish yellow (2.5Y 7/3), Badly eroded overfired Black-on-Red Painted Decoration.

o. Ledge Rim Jar (UU-RJ-9) (NE: 366) Fine sand and trace of vegetal inclusions, Body grayish yellow (5Y 8/2),Diam 12 cm, Surface yellowish gray (2.5Y 8/1) (cf. Le Brun 1971: Fig. 40:7).

p. Out-turned Expanded Rim Jar (UU-RJ-7) (SW: 39) Fine sand and calcite inclusions, Body orange (2.5YR 6/7), Diam 14 cm, Surface light yellowish brown (7.5YR 7/4) (cf. Wright 1981: Figs. 43k, 44j).

q. Straight Spout (UU-O-9) (SW: 336) Fine sand inclusions, Body light yellowish brown (7.5YR 7/4), Surface pale orange yellow (10YR 8/3) (Wright 1981: Fig. 40b).

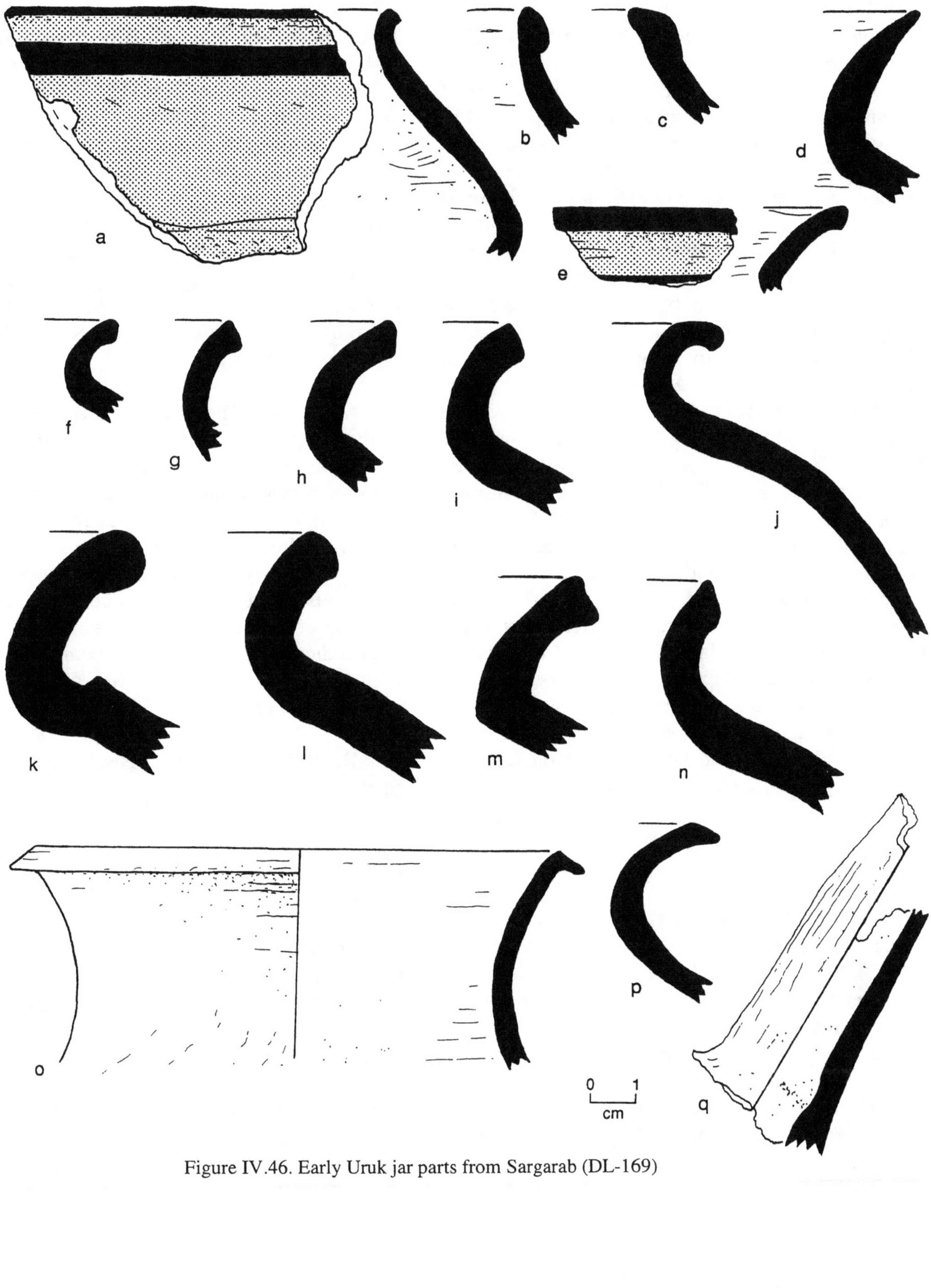

Figure IV.46. Early Uruk jar parts from Sargarab (DL-169)

6. **Phases**: A relatively dense scatter of sherds and flaked stone covered the site. The diagnostic ceramics indicate a rather brief occupation. Few differences were noted in the collections from the northeastern, central, or southwestern portions of the site, so these are reported as a group. Most of the ceramics have a mixture of chopped straw (perhaps dung) and crushed calcite inclusions, termed "Sargarab ware" after this site. Fine bowls (US-RB-3; Fig. IV.44 a-d) and fine jars (US-RJ-1; Fig. IV.44 f-g) are common. Among the larger bowls, open forms predominate (US-RB-4 to 8; Figs. IV.44 j-q; IV.45 a, b, e), but incurved forms (US-RB-9 to 13; Figs. IV.44 i; IV.45 c, d) occur. Thumb impressed strips (Figs. IV.44 i; IV.45 d) are the sole decoration. Among the jars are neckless ledge-rim variants (typically with few vegetal inclusions) (US-RJ-2; Fig. IV.45 l, m), low neck jars with beaded lips, several with black-on-red decoration (US-RJ-3; Fig. IV.46 a-c), and straight neck variants with round or flat lips (US-RJ-4–5; Fig. IV.45 h-k, m). Flared expanded neck variants with rounded, flattened, or grooved lips, some very large (US-RJ-6–10; Fig. IV.46 d-n) are present. These Sargarab Ware ceramics are thought to be earlier than the later Early Uruk assemblage from Farukhabad, Excavation B, Layers 35–36. In addition, there are also a few vessels of Uruk ware with sand inclusions. The rim of an open basin with thumb impressed strip decoration (cf. LS-RB-1; Fig. IV.45 g) is a type diagnostic of the Terminal Suse phase on the Susiana Plain (Wright, Neely, Johnson, and Speth 1975:137–139; Johnson 1973:59, Pl. II b). Also found were high ledge-rim jars (UU-RJ-9; Fig. IV.46 o) and a related out-turned jar rim (UU-RJ-7; Fig. IV.46 p). A straight spout (UU-O-9; Fig. IV.46 q) could have been on one of these jars. These items, all from the northeast area of the site, are earlier Uruk forms in Iraq and on the Susiana Plain. A ledge-rim bowl of Uruk ware (UU-RB-6; Fig. IV.45 f) cannot be ascribed to a specific phase. A rectangular, gable-shaped stamp seal with a representation of two dogs pursuing two caprids (Wright, Neely, Johnson, and Speth 1975:137, Fig. 4) was also found.

7. **Comment**: The basin with thumb-impressed strip suggests a date contemporary with the Terminal Suse phase (Johnson 1973:59–61, Wright, Neely, Johnson, and Speth 1975) for the beginning of occupation at DL-169. Other forms, however, should be taken to indicate occupation during the Early Uruk period. Although this 0.66 ha site is primarily of one cultural phase, the abutting of the architectural remains shown in the plan indicates that during the course of its occupation, it grew to the south. See Chapter VI for a discussion of channel DL-276A.

8. **References**: Wright, Neely, Johnson, and Speth 1975:134–137.

1a. **Number**: DL-222 (DL-11XA)
1b. **Name**:
2. **Grid**: 1704.2–1188.8
3. **Dimensions**:

Diameter:	80 m
Height:	1.0 m
Circumference:	250 m
Area:	0.50 ha

4. **Modern Environmental Context**: On the alluvial fan of the Mehmeh River, near its juncture with the northern alluvial slopes of the plain, about one kilometer northeast of the present Mehmeh channel.

5. **Features**: This site is situated on the open alluvial plain and consists of one low mound that is irregularly circular in shape. What appear to be the stone foundations or footings of five small house-size structures, such as those discovered at Tepe Ashrafabad (DL-29), were found eroding out of the sides of the mound in various locations. These alignments were only slightly exposed so no statements about the size or shape of these

structures can be made. The footings are constructed of unmodified cobbles and boulders that were dry-laid, though they may well have been set into a clay mortar indistinguishable from the alluvium around them. The construction techniques employed include both the double-faced walls, with their pebble-filled cores, and the "solid" single-faced walls.

6. **Phases**: The small series of ceramics from this site include a Mehmeh Red-on-red sherd, a painted basin rim (ES-RB-16) with interior pendant arcs, hemispherical bowl sherds, several with fully painted interiors (ES-RB-9) as well as one with small solid diamonds between rim bands (ES-RB-4), and a carinated bowl base with a motif of radiating lines (Hole, Flannery and Neely 1969: Fig. 56 b). These occur in both the later Khazineh and early Mehmeh phases. A stone celt (ibid.:189, 192–193) and circular stone socket for a door pivot (ibid.:196–198) were also found.

7. **Comment**: The full site area of 0.50 ha is assigned to the Khazineh and Mehmeh phases. See Chapter VI for a discussion of canal DL-13.

1a. **Number**: DL-240 (DL-35X)
1b. **Name**:
2. **Grid**: 1704.8–1187.0
3. **Dimensions**:

Length:	46 m (NE-SW)
Width:	15 m (NW-SE)
Height:	0.10 m
Circumference:	83 m
Area:	0.05 ha

4. **Modern Environmental Context**: On the alluvial fan of the Mehmeh River, near the northern slopes of the plain, about one kilometer northeast of the present Mehmeh channel.

5. **Features**: DL-240 consists of two small, low, gravel-covered mounds (Fig. IV.47). The larger mound is generally circular in plan, and is approximately 0.10 meters high. It is 9.2 meters in diameter, 29 meters in circumference, and 67 m^2 in area. The smaller mound is 19 meters southwest of the first. It is elliptical in plan with its long axis oriented 45° east of north. It is also approximately 0.10 meters high and is 11 meters (NE-SW) by 6 meters (NW-SE) with a circumference of 25 meters and an area of only 50 m^2. Neither stone foundations nor other direct evidence of architecture was found. However, a relatively high density of pebbles eroding out of the mounds and covering the surrounding area may indicate the former presence of pebble-cored walls, known from nearby Tepe Ashrafabad (DL-29) and Tepe Sabz (DL-31) (Hole, Flannery and Neely 1969:58–60), or pebble pavings or platforms.

6. **Phases**: The moderate numbers of sherds and flaked stone items were distributed evenly across the site, and extended as a very light scatter some forty meters further north. The few diagnostic early ceramics found were on or near the two low mounds. The small collection from this site contains large plain basin rims (LS-BN-1), as well as bowl body sherds with multiple bands (LS-RB-3) and a heavy vertical curved line motif (LS-RB-9). The last is found only in Bayat phase assemblages, and the other items are common in such assemblages. Many sherds dating to the later Sasanian-Early Islamic occupation of the site were on and around the mounds and lightly scattered to the north toward an area of boulder alignments that appear to have been agricultural terracing. These will be discussed in a subsequent volume.

7. **Comment**: The full site area of 0.05 ha is assigned to the Bayat phase. DL-240 could well be the result of the movement of the small community from nearby, slightly earlier DL-241. See Chapter VI for a discussion of the possible associations of this site with canals DL-13 and 246.

1a. **Number**: DL-241 (DL-20X)
1b. **Name**:
2. **Grid**: 1704.7–1187.0
3. **Dimensions**:

Length:	43 m (NNE-SSW)
Width:	37 m (NNW-SSE)
Height:	0.60 m
Area:	0.11 ha

4. **Modern Environmental Context**: On the alluvial fan of the Mehmeh River, near the juncture with the northern alluvial slopes of the plain, about one kilometer northeast of the present Mehmeh channel.

5. **Features**: This site consists of a single low mound, the lower edges of which blend almost imperceptibly into a very slight rise in the terrain. This slight rise may well represent a larger man-made feature, but it is presently not possible to determine its exact nature or origins.

The low mound is generally oval in plan with its longer axis oriented about 12 degrees east of north (Fig. IV.47). The orientation of the mound changes slightly in form and drastically in orientation about half way up the gentle slope. The form becomes elliptical and the long axis of the mound changes to about 84 degrees west of north.

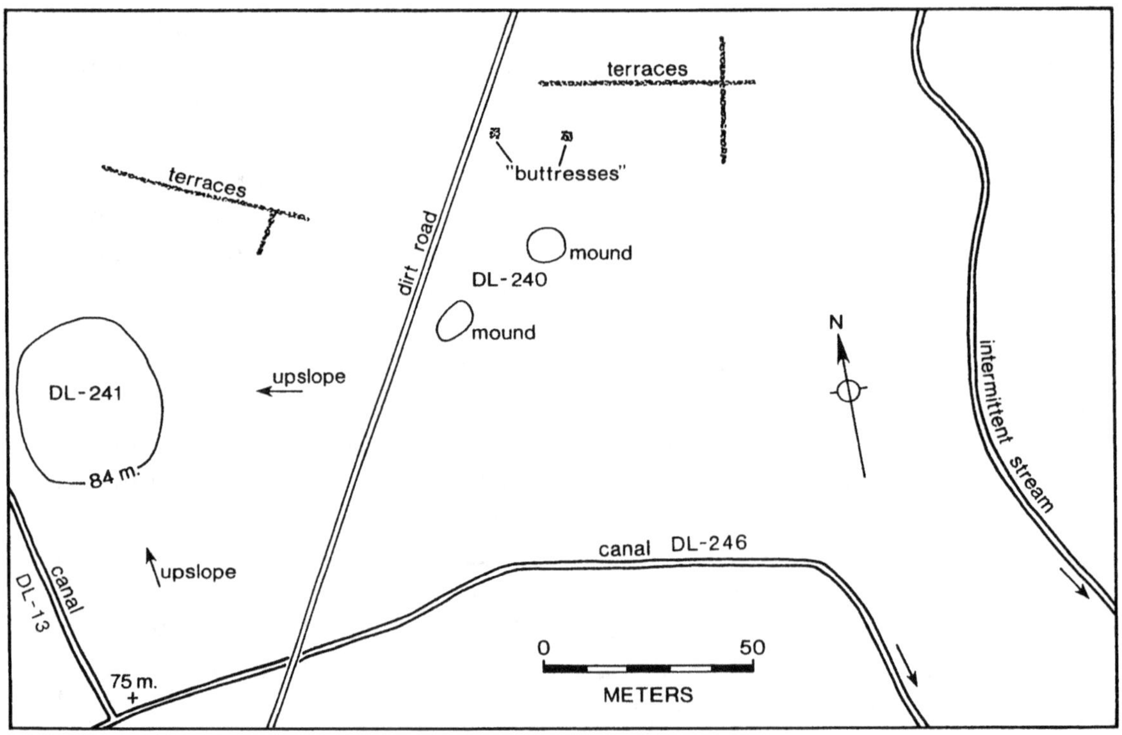

Figure IV.47. Map of DL-240 and DL-241

As with many of the sites on the Deh Luran Plain, DL-241 has two major periods of occupation. In this case, the earlier occupation is evidently the larger. Although building stone is visible on the surface of the site, most are attributable to the later occupation. Two relatively small areas with dense, predominantly early, artifact and stone concentrations may prove to be early constructions. These concentrations are located about 10 meters south of the mound (approximately 10 meters in diameter) and about 12 meters southeast of the mound (approximately 8 by 32 meters in maximum dimensions). Unfortunately, however, the stones were scattered and no alignments could be discerned.

6. **Phases**: There were moderate quantities of sherds and flaked stone artifacts covering the site. The densest concentration (20 to 40 artifacts per square meter) was found on the summit of the mound. The vast majority (about 95%) of these materials are attributable to the late occupation, and associated with a well-preserved stone house foundation. Late materials diminished, while the early artifact types increased, as one walked down the gentle slopes of the low mound. At its foot the earlier materials predominated. Even in the two artifact concentrations mentioned above, the ceramics in units with 20 artifacts per square meter areas were predominantly early.

The early ceramics include many Mehmeh Red-on-red (ES-SJ-2) sherds and fragments of Susiana ware hemispherical bowls with a ladder motif (ES-RB-5) and right triangle motifs (ES-RB-6), which are definitely of the Mehmeh phase. Also, there are sherds from carinated bowls, including a basal sherd (ES-BB-4) and rims with fully painted interiors (ES-RB-12) which could be either Khazineh or Mehmeh phase, and rims with interior cross-hatch (ES-RB-11), certainly of the Khazineh phase.

7. **Comment**: The full site area of 0.11 ha is assigned to the Khazineh and Mehmeh phases. See Chapter VI for a discussion of canal DL-13.

1a. **Number**: DL-247 (DL-78X)
1b. **Name**:
2. **Grid**: 1706.3–1186.4
3. **Dimensions**:

Length:	150 m (NW-SE)
Width:	90 m (SW-NE)
Height:	0.0 m
Circumference:	290 m
Area:	0.67 ha

4. **Modern Environmental Context**: On the alluvial fan of the Mehmeh River, near the edge of the saline depression, a kilometer and a half northeast of the present Mehmeh channel.

5. **Features**: This is a large sherd and lithic scatter with no discernible architecture or elevation present. The site is irregularly oval in plan and is located between two small intermittent erosional drainages that flow southward to join a larger intermittent drainage that passes about 20 meters south of DL-247 (Fig. IV.48). About 150 meters southeast of this site, two nearly horizontal caliche-like layers were found in the cut bank of the intermittent drainage. One of these layers was located at about 1.2 meters below the present surface of the alluvial plain, while the second was at about 2.0 meters below the ground surface. Lithic flakes resulting from human tool-making activities were found atop and imbedded in the upper few centimeters of the upper of these two layers. These artifacts may be scatter from site DL-247, and the caliche-like layer may represent the ground surface level when that site was occupied.

6. **Phases**: The ceramics collected are exclusively later variants of Susiana wares and Bayat Red ware. Indicative of the later Farukh phase are bowl fragments with step motifs (LS-RB-15; Fig. IV.49 d) and sigma motifs (LS-RB-14; Fig. IV.49 e). Indicative of the Suse phase are bowl fragments with branch motifs (LS-RB-19; Fig. IV.49 i, l), grid motifs (LS-RB-18; Fig. IV.49 n), large chevrons (LS-RB-17; Fig. IV.49 p), and vertical panels (LS-RB-16; Fig. IV.49 q). The brown painted bowl rim of a redware with vegetal inclusions (Fig. IV.49 f) is similar to Mehmeh Red-on-red bowls of the Mehmeh phase and earliest Bayat phase reported from Tepe Sabz (Hole, Flannery and Neely 1969:164 ; Fig. 66 c, d; Table 23) suggesting some earlier use of the site.

7. **Comment**: The full site area of 0.67 ha is assigned to both the Farukh and Suse phases. It is possible that this site was once supplied with water by a branch of canal DL-13 or DL-246. See Chapter VI.

8. **References**: Wright 1981:67, Fig. 32. However, only the Farukh phase ceramics on the site were recognized in that publication.

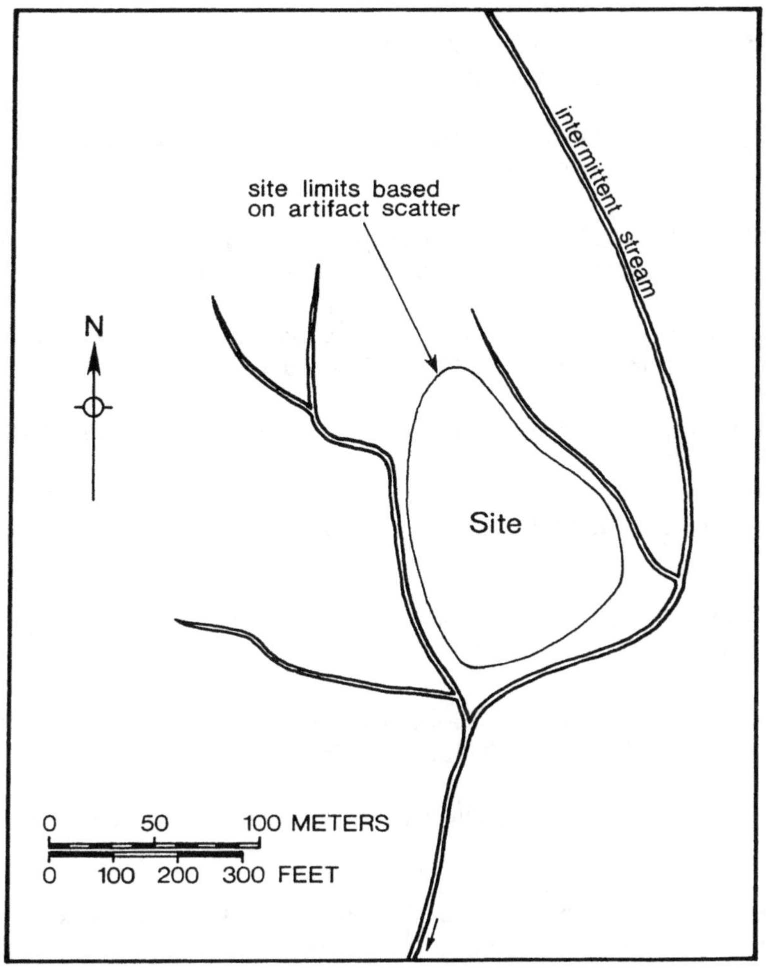

Figure IV.48. Map of DL-247

Figure IV.49. Farukh and Suse Phase ceramics from DL-247

a. Basin with Painted Band on Rim (LS-BN-2), Fine sand inclusions, Body pale yellowish green (7.5Y 9/2), Diam ca. 32 cm, Paint Olive-brown (2.5Y 4/4) (Hole, Flannery and Neely 1969: Fig. 60a-h; Wright 1981: Fig. 23g).

b. Bowl with Single Painted Band on Rim (LS-RB-2), Fine sand inclusions, Body light yellowish brown (10YR 7/4), Diam 22 cm, Paint eroded (Wright 1981: Fig. 15a- b).

c. Bowl with Multiple Painted Bands on Rim (LS-RB-3), Fine sand inclusions, Body yellowish gray (2.5Y 8/3), Diam 35 cm, Paint dark grayish yellow-brown (10YR 3/2) (cf. Wright 1981: Fig. 15c-h)

d. Bowl with Step Motif (LS-RB-15), Fine sand and trace of vegetal inclusions, Body yellowish gray (5Y 8/3), Diam 10 cm, Paint brown (7.5YR 4/4) (Wright 1981: Fig. 19a-f).

e. Bowl with Sigma Motif (LS-RB-14), No visible inclusions, Body grayish yellow (2.5Y 8/4), Diam 17 cm, Paint yellowish brown (10YR 5/4) (Dollfus 1971: Fig. 14:1;Wright 1981: Fig. 18a-c)

f. Redware Bowl with Painted Interior Cross-hatch, Vegetal inclusions, Body and slip orange (5YR 6/6), Diam ?, Paint reddish brown (10R 4/6) (cf. Hole, Flannery and Neely 1969: Fig. 66c).

g. Bowl with Unusual Painted Motif, No visible inclusions, Body grayish yellow (2.5Y 8/4), Diam ca. 18 cm, Paint Dark grayish yellow-brown (10YR 3/2).

h. Bowl with Unusual Painted Motif, No visible inclusions, Body yellowish gray (2.5Y 8/2), Diam ?, Paint Olive brown (2.5Y 4/2).

i. Bowl with Heavy Branch Motif (LS-RB-21), No visible inclusions, Body pale yellow (2.5Y 8/3), Diam 18 cm, Paint light olive brown (2.5Y 5/4).

j. Small Jar Shoulder with various motifs (cf. LS-RJ-4), Fine sand inclusions, Body grayish yellow (2.5Y 8/3), Neck diam ca. 11 cm, Paint Olive brown (2.5Y 4/4). (cf. Dollfus 1971: Fig. 16:5–22).

k. Bowl sherd with Small Triangles, No visible inclusions, Body yellowish gray (2.5Y 8/2), Diam ?, Paint dark yellowish brown (10YR 3/3).

l. Bowl sherd with Sigma (LS-RB-14) and Large Branch Motifs (LS-RB-19), Fine sand inclusions, Body yellowish gray (2.5Y 8/2), Body diam ca. 20 cm, Paint olive brown (2.5Y 4/3).

m. Bowl sherd with Triangles and Grid Motif (LS-RB-18), Fine sand inclusions, Body grayish yellow (2.5Y 8/3), Warped, Paint olive brown (2.5Y 4/3).

n. Bowl sherd with Grid (LS-RB-18), Fine sand inclusions, Body grayish yellow (5Y 8/3), Body diam 26 cm, Paint yellowish brown (10YR 4/4) (cf. Dollfus 1971: Fig. 12:14).

o. Bowl sherd with Opposed Triangle Motifs, Trace of vegetal inclusions, Body grayish yellow (5Y 8/3), Body diam 19 cm, Paint olive brown (2.5Y 4/2) (Dollfus 1971: Fig. 13:10).

p. Bowl sherd with Large Chevrons (LS-RB-17), No visible inclusions, Body grayish yellow (2.5Y 7/3), Body diam 17 cm, Paint dark yellowish brown (10YR 3/3) (Dollfus 1971: Fig. 14: 12).

q. Bowl sherd with Vertical Panels (LS-RB-16), No visible inclusions, Body grayish yellow (2.5Y 8/4), Body diam 17 cm, Paint olive brown (2.5Y 4/2) (Dollfus 1971: Fig. 13:1).

Figure IV.49. Farukh and Suse Phase ceramics from DL-247

1a. **Number**: DL-248 (DL-32X) and DL-249 (DL-33X)
1b. **Name**:
2. **Grid**: 1705.4–1186.1
3. **Dimensions**:

Length:	284 m (N-S)
Width:	100 m (E-W)
Height:	0.75 m
Circumference:	ca. 500 m
Area:	1.99 ha, of which 1.12 ha is a possible garden.

4. **Modern Environmental Context**: On the alluvial fan of the Mehmeh River, near the juncture with the northern alluvial slopes of the plain, about 750 meters northeast of the present Mehmeh channel.

5. **Features**: The features described below were divided into two distinct sites (DL-248 and DL 249) when first surveyed. When considering the data it seems more likely that the features and artifacts are associated and that the two loci can be considered a single site.

DL-248 is a large site situated on the long, narrow point of land that lies between a large intermittent drainage flowing from the alluvial slopes and one of its tributaries (Fig. IV.50). The site consists of four relatively small mounds and a large scatter of ceramics. The mounds are situated near the end of the point of land, with the sherd scatter extending upstream away from the mounds and the juncture of the two drainages. The three mounds closest to the end of the point are all irregularly elliptical in plan, are only ten centimeters high, and are covered with pebbles. The largest is 60 meters (E-W) by 20 meters (N-S), and 150 meters in circumference. The second is 35 meters (E-W) by 15 meters (N-S), and 100 meters in circumference. The smallest is 20 meters (E-W) by 15 meters (N-S) and 60 meters in circumference. About 25 meters north of the largest mound described, beyond an off-shoot drainage channel that is about three-to-five meters wide and may have been man-made, is a fourth small, irregularly elliptical mound. This mound measures 18 meters (NW-SE) by 12 meters (NE-SW) and is about 0.75 meters in height. Unlike its

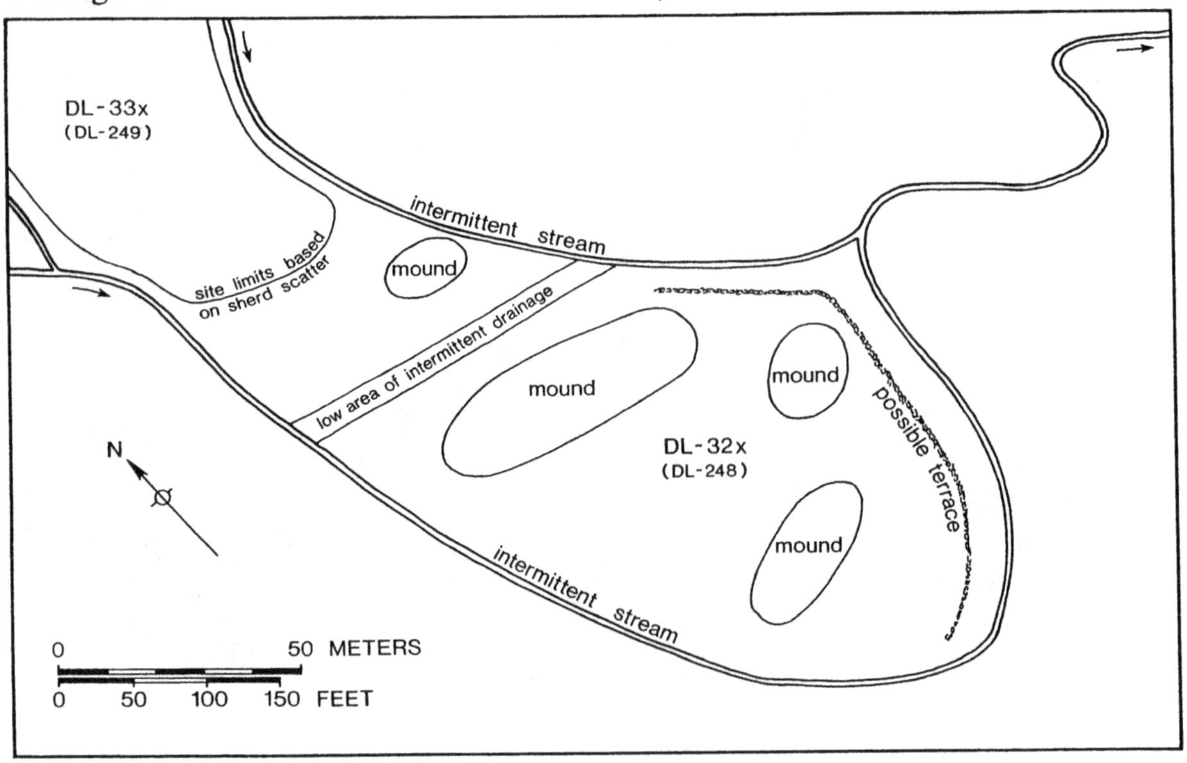

Figure IV.50. Map of DL-248

three neighbors to the south, the surface of this mound is clean silt, lacking a gravel covering. A few indistinct alignments of boulders that probably represent wall footings are being exposed by erosion on the mounds and surrounding surfaces of the site. In addition, a long, intermittently present, alignment of large cobbles and boulders, perhaps a terrace wall, outlines the eastern edge of the site just above the juncture of the two drainages.

A large sherd scatter, originally designated DL-249, begins about 15 meters north of the fourth mound described above, and covers an area about 170 meters (N-S) by 55 meters (E-W). No stone alignments or mounds were found in this area. Its location between two intermittent drainages suggests it may have been an agricultural field area.

6. **Phases**: DL-248 produced only later Susiana sherds not specific to phase, including a plain basin rim (LS-BN-1) and two bowl bases, one a ring base (LS-BB-4) and one a narrow base (LS-BB-2). DL-249 yielded another ring base, a wide bowl base (LS-BB-1), and the body sherd of a fine bowl with solid black exterior paint. These are known from Bayat phase layers at Tepe Sabz and Tepe Farukhabad (Wright 1981:58–59). This occurrence suggests a Bayat phase ascription, as was argued above for nearby site DL-240.

7. **Comment**: The occupied area of 0.87 ha is assigned to the Bayat phase. The northernmost mound may have been a mud brick platform. It is possible that this site was supplied with water from a branch of DL-13. See Chapter VI.

1a. **Number**: DL-262 (DL-19X)
1b. **Name**:
2. **Grid**: 1708.1–1184.4
3. **Dimensions**:
Length: West mound: 35 m (NW-SE);
East mound: 51 m (NW-SE)
Width: West mound: 28 m (NE-SW);
East mound: 27 m (NE-SW).
Height: West mound: 1.75 m;
East mound: 1.0 m.
Circumference: West mound 108 m;
East mound: 175 m.
Circumference of entire site: 650 m.
Area: Total area of site: 3.36 ha.

4. **Modern Environmental Context**: On the northern edge of the saline depression, near the edges of the Mehmeh River alluvium and the northern alluvial slopes of the plain, about three kilometers northeast of the present Mehmeh channel.

5. **Features**: Two well-defined mounds, joined by a low "saddle"-like terrace and surrounded by a level, grass-free area, comprise this site (Fig. IV.51). The total area of the site is fairly well defined by the extent of the artifact scatter and the distribution of rather indistinct, partially exposed stone wall footings. The long axis of the larger, eastern mound is oriented slightly more northward than that of the western mound. However, due to a good deal of disturbance caused by black-tent encampments, the northern portion of this mound is poorly defined. The two mounds are joined by a 5 meter long, 50 centimeter high (at lowest point) saddle-like terrace that blends smoothly upward into each mound and downward to the level area surrounding the mounds. The partially exposed stone wall footings noted above were seen throughout the site, eroding out of the mounds as well as on the surrounding level area. None of these footings were exposed sufficiently to determine room or structure size. However, it was possible to discern that some of these footings were faced with larger stones on both sides (see Hole, Flannery and Neely 1969: Fig. 17), while others had large stones only on one side, apparently the interior. At the eastern edge of the site are remnants of what appear to have been one or more terracing or retaining walls. These walls

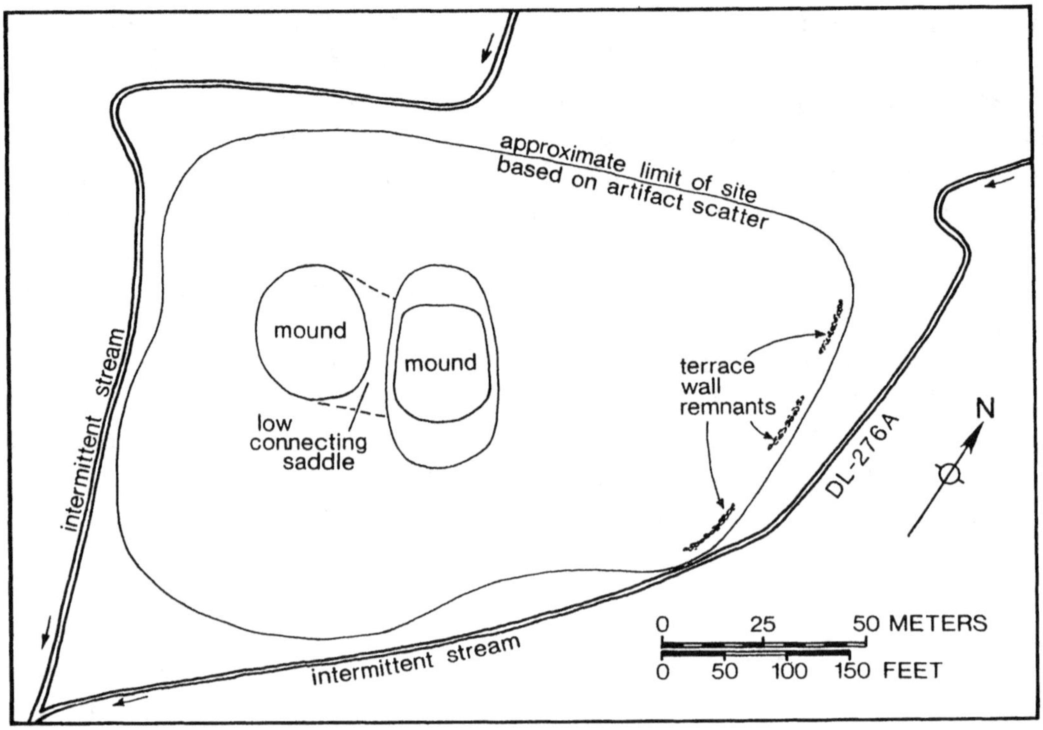

Figure IV.51. Map of DL-262

probably served to increase the size of the level area of the site toward the east, while preventing erosion by the intermittent channel DL-276A that lies a short distance away. Adjacent alluvial deposits, nearby relatively wide stream channels, and evidence of small canals, provide the means for both flood plain, "wash bottom", farming and irrigation agriculture.

6. **Phases**: The artifacts indicate a relatively small early occupation clustered along the southern and eastern flanks of the two mounds and extending out from the mounds onto the alluvium for several meters. Diagnostic early sherds were rare. A Bayat Red ware bowl sherd could be either Bayat, Farukh, or Suse phase. However, the shaved base (LS-BB-3) of a conical bowl is diagnostic only of the Farukh phase. The major mound occupation is evidently Sasanian and/or Early Islamic, and will be discussed in a subsequent volume.

7. **Comment**: An area of 0.20 ha is assigned to the Farukh phase. See Chapter VI for a discussion of channel DL-276A.

1a. **Number**: DL-286 (DL-79X)
1b. **Name**:
2. **Grid**: 1706.0–1180.1
3. **Dimensions**:
Length: Mound: 170 m;
Platform 323 m.
Width: Mound: 140 m;
Platform 90 m.
Height: Mound: 6.0 m;
Platform 1.5 m.
Circumference: Mound: 535 m;
Platform 506 m.
Area: Mound: 2.28 ha;
Platform 2.04 ha.

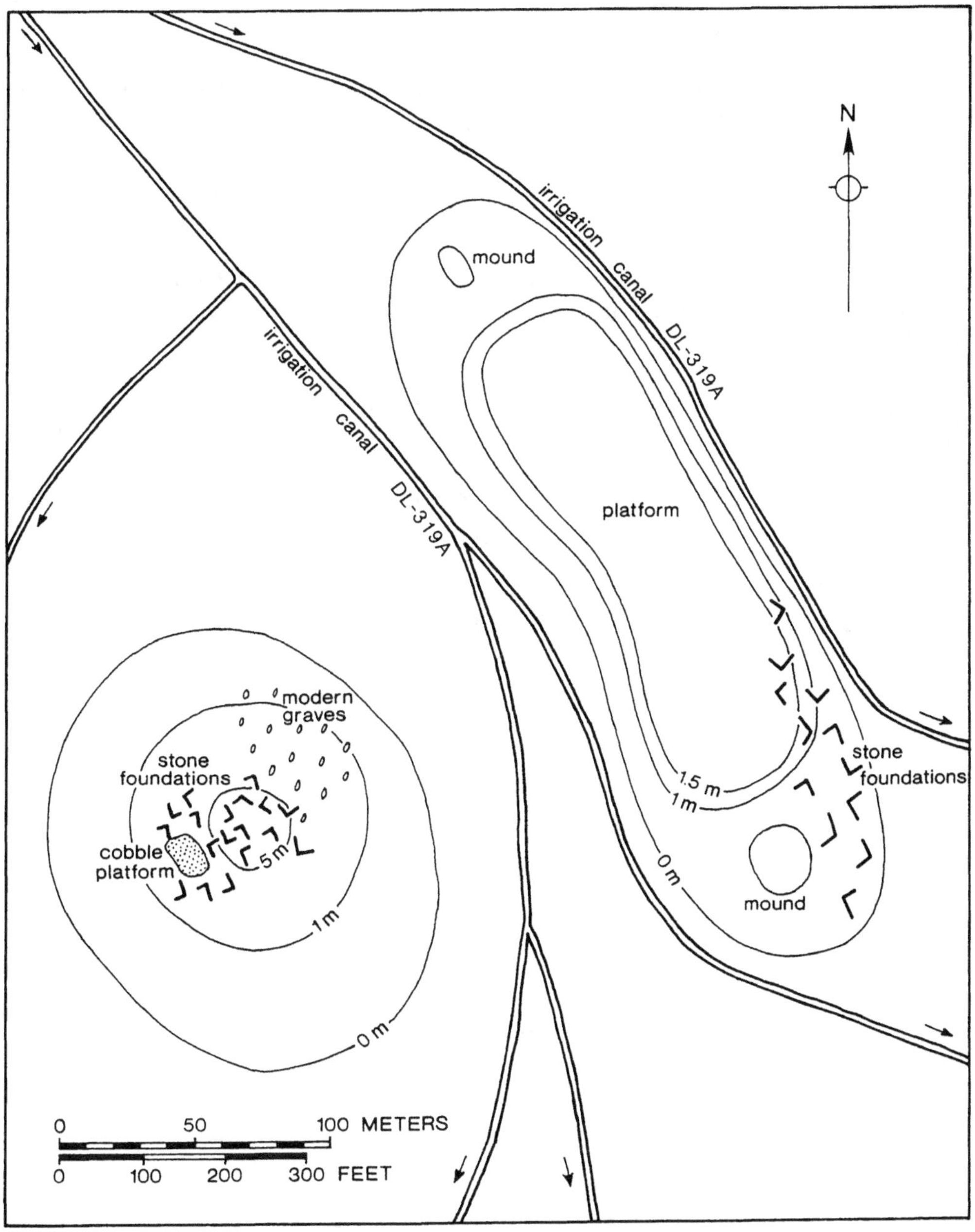

Figure IV.52. Map of DL-286

Figure IV.53. Chogha Mami Transitional, Sabz, and Khazineh Phase ceramics from the northeast mound of DL-286

a. "Sabz Pot" Rim with Vertical Line Motif (ES-RB-10), Fine sand inclusions, Body white (5Y 8/2), Diam ca. 14 cm, Surface white (2.5Y 8/2), Paint brown (7.5YR 5/2) (Hole, Flannery and Neely 1969: Fig. 50f).

b. Bowl Rim with Diamond Pattern (cf. ES-RB-15), Fine sand inclusions, Body white (2.5Y 8/2), Diam ca. 19 cm, Surface white (10YR 8/2), Paint dark reddish brown (5YR 3/2) (cf. Hole, Flannery and Neely 1969: Fig. 52a, e).

c. Bowl Rim with Interior Pendant Triangle (ES-RB-7), Fine sand inclusions, Body pale yellow (5Y 8/3), Diam warped, Surface white (2.5Y 8/2), Paint dark gray (2.5Y 4/1) (Hole 1977: Fig. 50c).

d. Sherd with Exterior Negative Zig-Zags, Fine sand inclusions, Body white (5Y 8/2), Diam 19 cm, Surface white (10YR 8/2), Paint dark gray (10YR 4/1) (Hole Flannery and Neely 1969: Fig. 52b).

e. Jar Shoulder and Neck with Pendant Triangles, Fine sand inclusions, Body pink (5YR 8/4), Neck Diam 11 cm, Surface white (5Y 8/2), Paint dark gray (10YR 4/1) (Hole, Flannery and Neely 1969: Fig. 58i, j).

f. Carinated Bowl Sherd with Interior Negative Zig-Zags, Fine sand inclusions, Body white (2.5Y 8/2), Surface white (2.5Y 8/2), Paint very dark grayish brown (10YR 3/2).

g. Carinated Bowl Sherd with Exterior Zig-Zag, Interior Cross-hatch Variant (ES-RB-11), Fine sand inclusions, Body white (2.5Y 8/2), Surface white (10YR 8/2), Paint dark brown (7.5YR 3/2) (Hole, Flannery and Neely 1969: Fig. 56a (exterior), 56d-e, 57p).

h. "Star Shaped" Spindle Whorl (ES-O-1), Fine sand inclusions, Weight 13.9 grams (Estimated 15.0 when complete) Body white (2.5Y 8/2), Surface pinkish white (7.5YR 8/2), Paint eroded (Hole, Flannery and Neely 1969: Fig. 88e).

i. Plain Basin Rim. Medium sand inclusions, Body pink (5YR 7/5), Diam 25 cm, Surface eroded (Hole, Flannery and Neely 1969: 48a-c).

j. Bowl Sherd with Exterior Heavy Horizontal Lines (ES-RB-14), Fine sand inclusions, Body white (5Y 8/2), Surface white (2.5Y 8/2), Paint very dark gray (10YR 8/3) (Hole, Flannery and Neely 1969: Figure 54b).

Figure IV.53. Chogha Mami Transitional, Sabz, and Khazineh Phase ceramics from the northeast mound of DL-286

Figure IV.54. Farukh Phase ceramics from the west mound of DL-286

a. Bowl Rims with Multiple Bands (LS-RB-2) Traces of fine sand, Body white (2.5Y 8/2), Diam 29 cm, Paint dark gray (10YR 4/1) (Wright 1981: Fig. 15b).

b. Bowl Rims with Multiple Bands (LS-RB-3) No visible inclusions, Body white (5Y 8/2), Diam 11 cm, Paint gray (10YR 5/1) (Wright 1981: Fig. 15g).

c. Bowl Sherd with Fine Dot Motifs (LS-RB-10) No visible inclusions, Body light gray (2.5Y 7/2), Body diam 12 cm, Paint gray (10YR 5/1) (cf. Wright 1981: Fig. 17).

d. Bowl Sherd with Exterior Cross Hatch (LB-RB-2) Fine sand inclusions, Body white (2.5Y 8/2), Body diam 22 cm, Paint dark gray (7.5YR 4/1).

e. Bowl Sherd with Horizontal Curved Lines (LS-RB-5) No visible inclusions, Body white (2.5Y 8/3), Diam ca. 27 cm, Paint dark gray (N/4) (Wright 1981: Fig. 16a-c).

f. Bowl Sherd with Cross Hatch Triangle (cf. LB-RB-2) Traces of fine sand, Body white (2.5Y 8/3), Diam ?, Paint dark gray (10YR 4/1) (Wright 1981: Fig. 20b)

g. Bowl Sherd with Vertical Lines (LB-RB-8) No visible inclusions, Body white (2.5Y 8/2), Body diam ca. 19 cm, Paint gray (10YR 5/1)

h. Bowl Sherd with Rectilinear Motif (LB-RB-16) Traces of fine sand, Body white (2.5Y 8/3), Body diam ca. 17 cm, Paint brown (10YR 5/3)

i. Perforator. Medium gray chert, probably heat-treated.

j. Stamp Seal

Figure IV.54. Farukh Phase ceramics from the west mound of DL-286

4. **Modern Environmental Context**: On the alluvial fan of the Mehmeh River, about 250 meters southwest of the present Mehmeh channel.

5. **Features**: Site DL-286 is comprised of one relatively large mound and two smaller mounds situated on a platform (Fig. IV.54). The larger isolated mound is a generally elliptical in shape, 170 meters in length (NW-SE) by 140 meters wide (NE-SW) and oriented 40° west of north. The top of this mound, 6.0 meters above the plain and nearly level, is about 30 meters in diameter. Evidences of a few stone foundations were seen eroding from this summit surface and from the slopes just below the summit. A short distance (about 1.5 to 2 meters) below the summit on the west side, additional foundations and a cobblestone platform were partially exposed by erosion. Stone foundations on this mound, as well as elsewhere on the site, were not well enough exposed to determine the sizes of the structures present, however, both single- and double-faced masonry construction appears to have been utilized. The northeastern slope of the mound has many modern graves. The linear depressions of irrigation canals (DL-319A) run from north to south, passing the main mound on its east and west sides. Sherds were common on the northeast slope, and many were of Khazineh Red ware, suggesting earlier occupation here, though no diagnostic ceramics were found. Sherds on the top and southwest slope of the mound were from the site's later occupation.

Across the canals, some 80 meters to the northeast and east, lies the second of the site's mounds. It is a long mound oriented 26° west of north, relatively narrow and low. The platform has a maximum height of about 1.5 meters. The surface of this platform is level except at the northern and southern extremities, where it slopes gently downward to blend into the alluvial plain. Atop each end of this low platform is situated a small mound of elliptical shape. The summit of the northernmost small mound is about 1 meter above the platform and 1.5 meters above the adjacent alluvium. It is 10 meters long (oriented 40° west of north) and 8 meters wide. The summit of the southern-most small mound is also about 1 meter above the platform and 1.5 meters above the alluvium. However, it is larger than its northern counterpart, measuring about 26 meters long (oriented 30° west of north) by 22 meters wide. The latter mound was measured at 70 meters in circumference, giving it a maximum area of approximately 0.04 hectares. Early ceramics and stone foundations were concentrated on the southeast end of this segment of the platform.

6. **Phases**: The northeastern mound yielded a range of early ceramics. There is a bowl rim with pendant interior triangles (ES-RB-7; Fig. IV.53 c) of the Chogha Mami Transitional phase. There is also the rim of a "Sabz Pot" (ES-RB-10; Fig. IV.53 a) of the Sabz phase. Small incurved bowl sherds with exterior cross-hatch motifs, a star-shaped spindle whorl (ES-O-1; Fig. IV.53 h), as well as a possible pedestal base sherd could be of either the Chogha Mami Transitional phase or the Sabz phase. Open bowls with closely spaced exterior bands (cf. ES-RB-1; Fig. IV.53 j) and carinated bowls with interior wavy elements (ES-RB-13) and interior cross-hatch variants (cf. ES-RB-11; Fig. IV.53 g) are diagnostic of the Khazineh phase, and probably date to relatively early in that phase. The other diagnostic bowl (Fig. IV.53 d, f) and jar (Fig. IV.53 e) sherds are in the range of variation of Chogha Mami, Sabz, and Khazineh ceramics.

The top and southwest slope of the southwestern mound yielded only later Susiana ceramics, though a concentration of Khazineh Red ware suggests earlier use. Bowl sherds with bands (LS-RB-2, 3; Fig. IV.54 a, b), horizontal curved lines (LS-RB-5; Fig. IV.54 e), fine dot motifs (LS-RB-10; Fig. IV.54 c), step motifs (LS-RB-15), cross-hatched diamond motifs (LS-RB-2; Fig. IV.54 d, f), and rectilinear motifs (LS-BR-14; Fig. IV.54 h), as well as large jar necks with painted bands

(LS-JR-3) indicate Farukh phase occupation. The other sherds all could be of the Farukh phase. On the top of the central eminence, we also found a chert perforator of a type common in Farukh phase layers at nearby Farukhabad (DL-32) (Fig. IV.54 i; Wright 1981: Fig. 25 b-d) and a rectangular stamp seal with three animal representations (Fig. IV.54 j), possibly a bull, a bear, and a goat. The modeling of detail on these animals resembles late IVth millennium seals, and it is possible this item was in an intrusive feature such as a grave.

7. **Comment**: We ascribe 1.0 ha, the approximate area of the southeastern end of the earlier platform, to the Chogha Mami, Sabz, and Khazineh phases. The site may well have been larger during some of these phases, but we cannot be certain. It is surprising that such a large and high mound as that forming the southwest part of DL-286, had certain evidence of occupation during only one phase. It is possible that the central eminence is an architectural construction, perhaps a mud brick platform, such as those recorded in Farukh phase layers at nearby Tepe Farukhabad (DL-32) (Wright 1981:19–29, Figs. 4, 6, 9 d). We ascribe to the Farukh phase an area of 0.40 ha. Whether the canal traces (DL-319A) noted adjacent to DL-286 date to the time of its early occupation will be discussed in Chapter VI.

8. **References**: Wright 1981:67. Fig. 3.

1a. **Number**: DL-290 (DL-80X)
1b. **Name**:
2. **Grid**: 1704.3–1182.8
3. **Dimensions**:

Diameter:	75 m
Height:	1.75 m
Circumference:	236 m
Area:	0.44 ha

4. **Modern Environmental Context**: On the alluvial fan of the Mehmeh River, about half a kilometer southwest of the present Mehmeh channel.

5. **Features**: This site is composed of a single moderate-sized mound located a short distance west of the much larger site DL-27 (Tenel Ramon). We recorded a relatively light scatter of ceramics with very few lithic tools present on the surface of the mound and extending irregularly out onto the alluvial plain for about 20 meters in all directions. Only a relatively few diagnostic early ceramics were found. The late ceramics (i.e. post 500 B.C.) which appear to be concentrated on the summit and western slope of the mound, will be discussed in a subsequent volume.

6. **Phases**: The later Susiana ceramics include a sherd from a high-necked jar with fully painted neck (LS-RJ-1), a very fine plain bowl sherd (LS-BR-1), as well as another bowl sherd with fully painted exterior and unusual interior oblique lines (cf. LS-RB-4). Except for the interior motif on the latter bowl sherd, these are most similar to Bayat phase ceramics. A celt blank and a celt of calcite (Hole, Flannery and Neely 1969:189, 192–193) were also found here.

7. **Comment**: The full site area of 0.44 ha is ascribed to the Bayat phase. See Chapter VI for a discussion of associated canals DL-319 and 320.

1a. **Number**: DL-292 (DL-81X)
1b. **Name**:
2. **Grid**: 1703.4–1184.0
3. **Dimensions**:

Length:	530 m (N-S)
Width:	300 m (E-W)
Height:	1.75 m (maximum), 1.25 m (average)
Area:	8.4 ha

4. **Modern Environmental Context**: On the alluvial fan of the Mehmeh River, almost one kilometer southwest of the present Mehmeh channel.

5. **Features**: This is a large site with ceramics similar to those of Sargarab (DL-169) on the northeast slopes of the plain (Wright, Neely, Johnson, and Speth 1975). DL-292 consists of a long, low, irregularly-shaped ridge-like mound with its long axis generally oriented in a N-S direction and its edges blending imperceptibly into the surrounding alluvial plain (Fig. IV.55). The site is composed of five low, generally elliptical mounds. These ranged in size from about 140 meters (NE-SW) by 90 meters (NW-SE) to 38 meters (NE-SW) by 20 meters (NW-SE). Lack of time prevented a thorough investigation of this site, however, we were able to observe rock alignments that appeared to be remnants of foundations. These alignments varied in size, and were of both single- and double-faced construction technique, though evidently constructed entirely of cobble-sized rocks. Remnants of a platform constructed of cobbles was seen eroding from the northern side of the northernmost mound. Relatively few sherds were found scattered across the site and no sherd concentrations were noted. However, temporally diagnostic sherds indicating only one brief period of occupation were found. In contrast, there was a dense scatter of flaked stone tools and debitage covering the entire site. An irrigation canal (DL-321) was noted in close proximity, and what appears to be a branch canal cuts from northeast to southwest through the southern portion of the site. These canals appear to be directly associated and contemporaneous with DL-292. It is likely that a large Early Uruk canal system was present.

6. **Phases**: This small collection is highly weathered, and the lack of beveled rim bowls (US-RB-1, 2), fine bowls (US-RB-3), fine jars (US-RJ-1), and various red-slipped variants could be a result of post-depositional processes. The surviving sherds are all of Sargarab ware. Incurved bowls (US-RB-10; Fig. IV.56 b, d-i) predominate, but open bowls (US-RB-6; Fig. IV.56 c) occur. The two are not clearly differentiated in this collection, as is the case in later Early Uruk layers at Farukhabad and in contrast to the earlier Terminal Suse phase or Early Uruk phase at the site of Sargarab (DL-169) itself. Unfortunately, we found none of the impressed or hatched strips which might support our chronological assessment of the bowls. Among the jars, the neckless ledge-rim jar (US-RJ-2; Fig. IV.56 j) and flared neck jars with round lip (US-RJ-6; Fig. IV.56 n, o) are relatively early in the Early Uruk phase. The heavy thickened round lip jars (US-RJ-8; Fig. IV.56 k, l) and flared expanded neck jars with grooved lip (US-RJ-9; Fig IV.56 p) are more likely to be later in the Early Uruk phase or even early in the Middle Uruk phase, as is the heavy basin with burnished red-slip (Fig. IV.56 a) which is well known from Farukhabad (Wright 1981:93, Fig. 42 j-o). The straight neck jar (US-RJ-4) and high expanded band rim jars (US-RJ-10; Fig. IV.56 q, r) could have been made from the beginning of the Early Uruk phase through the beginning of the Middle Uruk phase. The complete absence of Uruk ware in our DL-292 collection, however, argues against the possibility of a Middle Uruk occupation. Thus, the overall weight of ceramic evidence suggests occupation during the Early Uruk phase at this large site.

7. **Comment**: This large site probably has a complex developmental history. If it has survived recent events, it merits detailed study. The full

area of 8.4 ha is ascribed to the Early Uruk phase. See Chapter VI for a discussion of associated canal DL-321.

8. **References**: Wright, Neely, Johnson, and Speth 1975:137; Wright 1981:182, Fig. 78.).

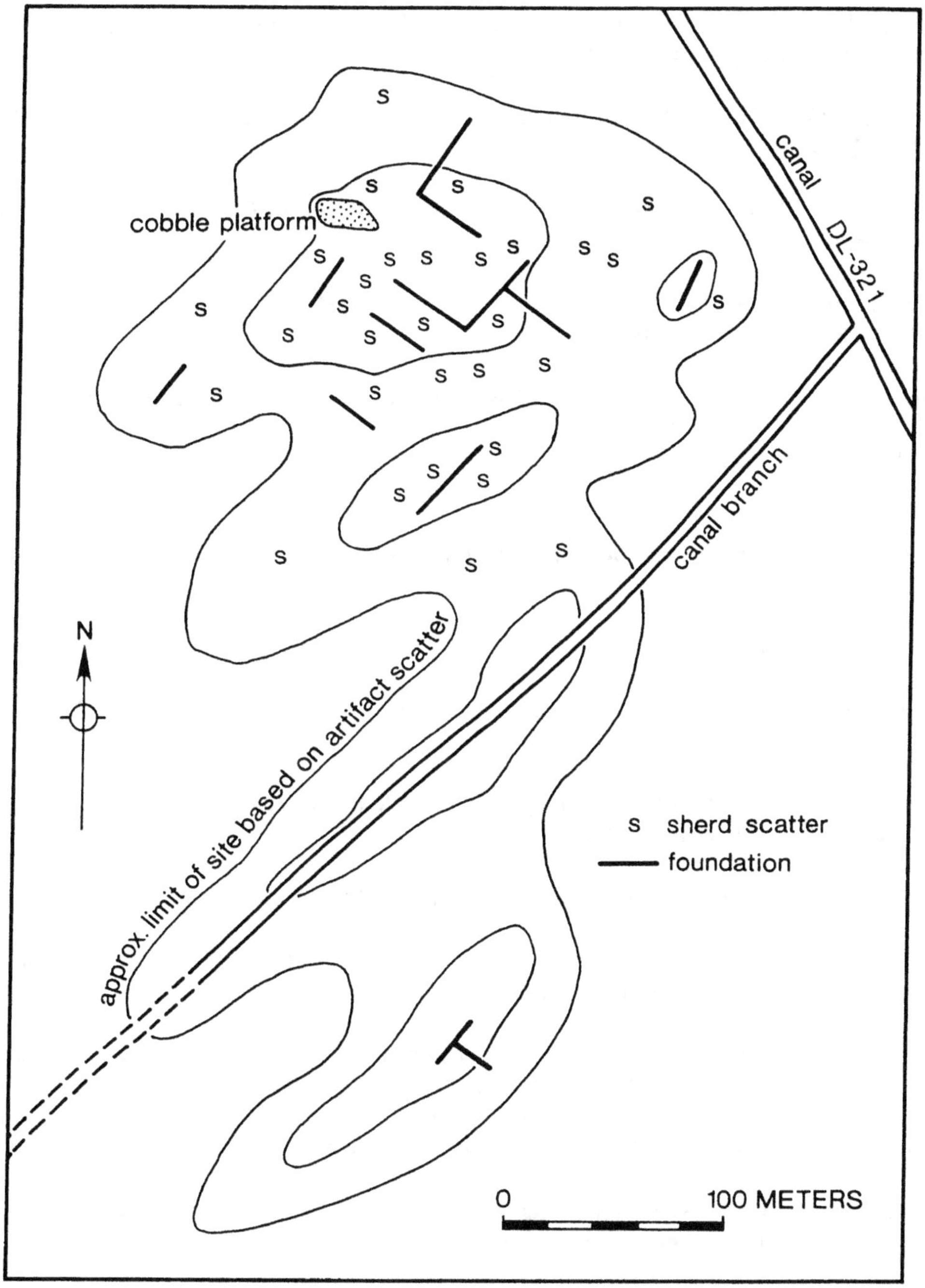

Figure IV.55. Map of DL-292

Figure IV.56. Early Uruk ceramics from DL-292

a. Thickened Rim Basin (17) Vegetal inclusions, Body light brown (7.5YR 5/4), Diam ?, Red slip (7.5R 5/6) (cf. Wright 1981: Fig. 42j-l).

b. Incurved Bowl with Beaded Rim (US-RB-10) (14) Vegetal and calcite inclusions, Body light yellowish brown (7.5YR 7/4), Diam 36 cm, Surface pale yellow (2.5Y 8/3) (cf. Wright 1981: Fig. 41g, i, k).

c. Open Bowl with Beaded Lip (US-RB-6) (24) Vegetal and calcite inclusions, Body yellowish pink (2.5YR 7/4), Diam 37 cm, Surface yellowish gray (2.5Y 8/2) (cf. same).

d. Heavy Incurved Basin (US-RB-13) (18) Same inclusions, Body pale yellow (5Y 8/3), Diam ca. 52 cm, Surface pale yellow (5Y 8/3) (cf. same).

e. Incurved Bowl with Beaded Lip (US-RB-10) (8) Same inclusions, Body yellowish pink (7.5YR 8/3), Diam ?, Surface yellowish gray 10YR 8/2) (cf. Wright 1981: Fig. 41 l, m).

f. Same (19) Same inclusions, Body yellowish pink (5YR 7/4), Diam 44 cm, Surface pale yellow (7.5Y 8/3) (cf. same).

g. Same (3) Vegetal inclusions, Body dark yellowish pink (2.5YR 6/6), Diam ?, Surface yellowish gray (2.5Y 8.2). (cf. same).

h. Same (28) Vegetal and calcite inclusions, Body yellowish pink (5YR 7/4), Diam 45 cm, Surface yellowish gray (2.5Y 8/2) (cf. Wright 1981: Fig. 41h).

i. Same (31) Same inclusions, Body orange (5YR 7/6), Diam 48 cm, Surface yellowish white (2.5Y 9/2) (cf. same).

j. Neckless Ledge Rim Jar (US-RJ-2) (5) Coarse calcite inclusions, Body grayish red-orange (2.5YR 5/7), Diam ca. 20 cm, Surface eroded (cf. Johnson 1973: Pl. III l).

k. Heavy Thickened Round Lip Jar (US-RJ-8) (25) Vegetal and calcite inclusions, Body pale yellow (5Y 8/3), Diam 18 cm, Surface pale yellow (5Y 8/3) (cf. Wright 1981: Fig. 42c, e).

l. Same (16) Same inclusions, Body pale yellow (5Y 8/3), Diam 25 cm, Surface same (cf. same).

m. Straight Neck, Round Lip Jar (US-RJ-4) (29) Vegetal inclusions, Body yellowish pink (5YR 7/6), Diam 9 cm, Surface yellowish gray (2.5Y 8/2) (cf. Wright 1981: Fig. 43o).

n. Flared Expanded Rim Jar with Round Lip (US-RJ-6) (26) Vegetal and calcite inclusions, Body pale yellow (5Y 8/3), Diam 10 cm, Surface grayish yellow (2.5Y 8/3) (cf. Wright 1981: Fig. 44c-i).

o. Same (7) Same inclusions, Body pale yellow (5Y 8/3), Diam 20 cm, Surface yellowish gray (5Y 8/2) (cf. same).

p. Flared Expanded Rim Jar with Grooved Lip (US-RJ-9) (13) Inclusions same, Body grayish red-orange (2.5YR 5/6), Diam 19 cm, Surface light yellowish brown (10YR 7/4) (cf. same).

q. High Expanded Band Rim Jar (US-RJ-10) (1) Calcite and vegetal inclusions, Body light yellowish brown (7.5YR 7/4), Diam 29 cm, Surface pale orange-yellow (10YR 8/3) (cf. Wright 1981: Fig. 44a, b).

r. Same, heavy (30) Same inclusions, Body grayish yellow (5Y 7/3), Diam 26 cm, Surface eroded.

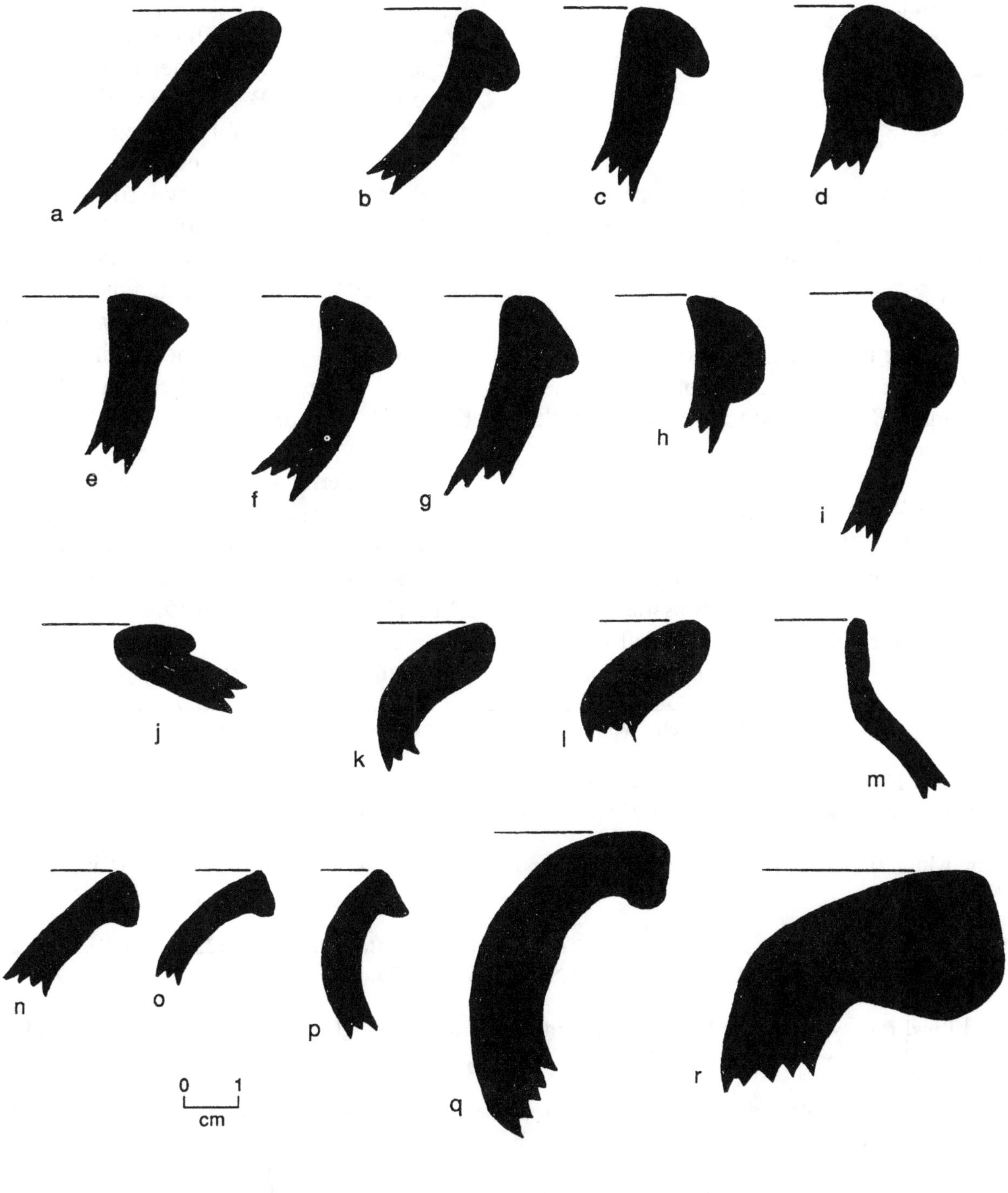

Figure IV.56. Early Uruk ceramics from DL-292

1a. **Number**: DL-312 (Miroschedji DK-14)
1b. **Name**: Tepe Jelise or Imamzadeh Ali Na'ir
2. **Grid**: 1742.5–1160.0
3. **Dimensions**:

Length:	275 m (NE-SW)
Width:	200 m
Height:	4.0 m
Area:	ca. 3.8 ha

4. **Modern Environmental Context**: On the alluvial fan of the Chikab (locally called "Chiku") River, just west of the present channel.

5. **Features**: The site consists of a single large, roughly triangular mound. Even though there was a cover of *Prosopis* bushes and pebbles, the sherd cover was dense. However, since we had intended to return, our collection is small.

6. **Phases**: The small collection made by Wright in 1968, and now at Yale, contains—in addition to several later, perhaps Sasanian, sherds—a carinated bowl rim with interior cross-hatch (Fig. IV.57 a), a similar rim with an unusual exterior motif (Fig. IV.57 b), a basin rim with painted bands and lip triangles (ES-RB-18; Fig. IV.57 c), and a bowl base with interior motifs (Fig. IV.57 d), all of which are similar to Khazineh or Mehmeh phase examples. Sherds with right triangle motifs (ES-RB-6; Fig. IV.57 e) and ladder motifs (ES-RB-6) are diagnostic of the Mehmeh phase, while a bowl sherd with a horizontal curved line (LS-RB-7; Fig. IV.57 f) and other embellishments is probably of the Mehmeh phase (cf. Hole, Flannery and Neely 1969: Fig. 61 i). The standard beveled rim bowl rim (US-RB-2; Fig. IV.57 g) is of the Middle or Late Uruk phase. Miroschedji (p. c.) notes an out-turned expanded jar rim (ES-RJ-7), a carinated beveled-lip bowl (UU-RB-5), and a jar shoulder with cross-hatched incision (UU-O-5), but no distinctive Late Uruk variants. We provisionally ascribe this site to the Khazineh, Mehmeh, and Middle Uruk phases.

7. **Comment**: The full area of 3.8 ha is assigned to the Khazineh and Mehmeh phases. The Uruk occupation was limited to the summit of the mound, about 2.0 ha. Site measurements are from Miroschedji 1981:173–175.

8. **References**: Miroschedji 1981.

Figure IV.57. Khazineh, Mehmeh, and Uruk ceramics from Tepe Jelise (DL-312)

a. Carinated Bowl Rim with Interior Crossed Lines, Traces of calcite and fine sand, Body very pale brown (10YR 7/3), Diam 34 cm, Paint weak red (10R 4/3) (cf. Hole, Flannery, and Neely 1969: Fig. 56b, f).

b. Bowl rim with Exterior Cross-hatched Motif, Fine sand inclusions, Body pale yellow (5Y 7/3), Diam ?, Paint very dark gray (2.5Y 3/1)

c. Small Basin with Triangles on Lip (ES-RB-18), Traces of fine sand, Body light gray (2.5Y 7/2), Diam ca. 25 cm, Paint very dark gray (10YR 3/1) (cf. Hole, Flannery and Neely 1969: Fig. 59a).

d. Rounded Bowl Base with Interior Motifs, Fine sand inclusions, Body light gray (5Y 7/2), Paint very dark gray (10YR 3/1) (cf. Hole, Flannery and Neely 1969: Fig. 57f).

e. Bowl Sherd with Right Triangle Motif (cf. ES-RB-6), Fine sand inclusions, Body pale olive (5Y 7/3), Paint dark gray (5YR 4/1)(cf. Hole, Flannery and Neely 1969: Fig. 62c).

f. Bowl Sherd with Horizontal Curved Lines (cf. LS-RB-7), No visible inclusions, Body white (5Y 8/2), Body diam ca. 31 cm, Eroded paint dark gray (10YR 4/1) (cf. Hole, Flannery, and Neely 1969: Figs. 61i; 62d, e).

g. Beveled Rim Bowl Rim (US-RB-2) Vegetal and fine sand inclusions, Body pale yellow (5Y 7/3), Diam ca. 24 cm.

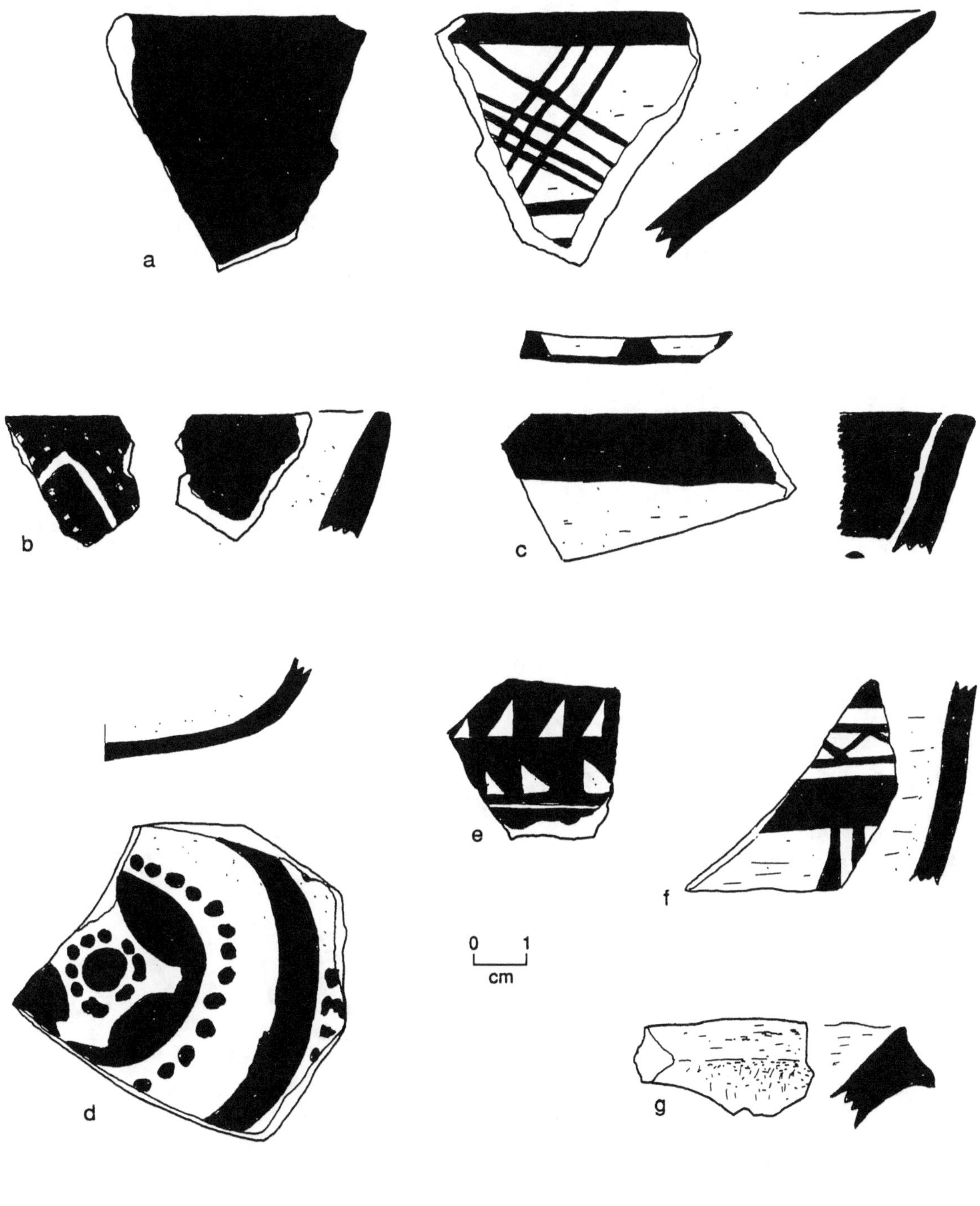

Figure IV.57. Khazineh, Mehmeh, and Uruk ceramics from Tepe Jelise (DL-312)

Chapter V

Early Settlement Patterns On The Deh Luran Plain

The excavations at Ali Kosh, Chagha Sefid, Tepe Sabz, Tepe Musiyan, and Tepe Farukhabad have resulted in the definition of a sequence of nineteen successive cultural phases dating between sometime in the VIIIth millennium B.C. and the middle of the IInd millennium B.C. These excavations provide us with evidence of changing economic and social life in some of the Deh Luran communities. However, complementary evidence of changes in regional population and organization can come only from archaeological survey.

The Paleolithic Foragers

During the immense span of the Pleistocene, human groups must have passed through the Deh Luran Plain, gathering and hunting many of the same resources that attracted the first villagers of the early Holocene. However, in only a few areas did intensive survey coverage reach the valley margins where sites of these early periods might have been exposed by erosion. The only Paleolithic site actually recorded is in the southwestern portion of the valley on the slopes of the Jebel Hamrin at 'Ain Girzan. Today, this is the only truly fresh water source on the entire plain, the rivers and the Ab-i Garb or Sargarab spring being charged with salts and other minerals. In very arid periods during the Pleistocene it may have been the only water source in the region. Eroding from surficial silts in a small basin around the spring mouth, we found 97 stone tools, including flakes, blades, and blade cores (Dzodin 1980). This assemblage is most similar to the Late Baradostian industries of the nearby Zagros mountain valleys (Hole and Flannery 1968).

Table V.1: Chogha Mami Transitional Phase Settlement

Site Number	Name	Area (ha)	Type
20	Musiyan	?	b
21	Ali Kosh	0.40	a
23	Chagha Sefid	0.42	b
25	—	0.05	c
28	Khazineh	?	c
32	Farukhabad	?	d
84	—	0.26	d
85	Muradabad	?	d
286NE	—	ca 1.00	c

[a. preceding occupation; b. preceding and succeeding occupation; c. succeeding occupation; d. neither preceding nor succeeding occupation]

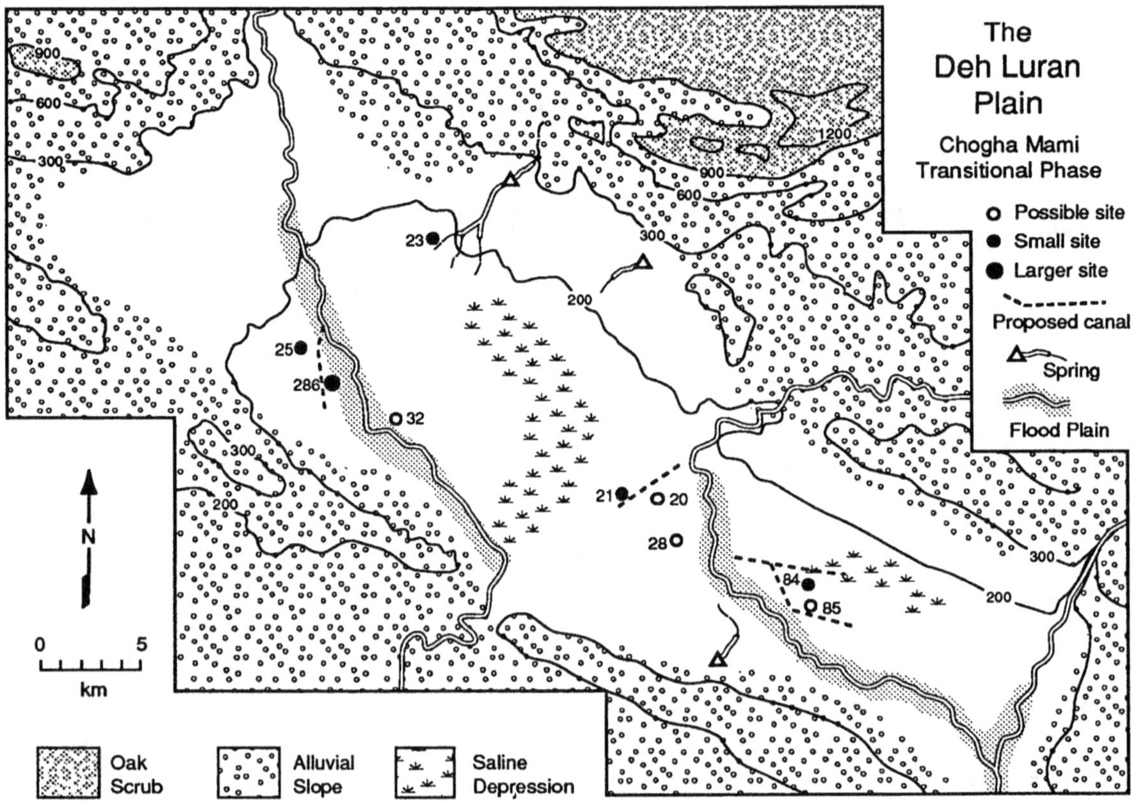

Figure V.1. Settlements of the Chogha Mami Transitional Phase

The Early Phases

The excavations at Ali Kosh and Chagha Sefid have documented the gradual development of agricultural villages occupied through much of the year (Hole 1987). During the Bus Mordeh phase, around 7500 B.C., occupation is known only at the seasonally occupied settlement of goat herders and foragers on the edge of the then freshwater marsh at Ali Kosh (DL-21) (Hole, Flannery and Neely 1969). In the succeeding Ali Kosh and Muhammed Jaffar phases, settlement also occurred on the northeastern piedmont at Chagha Sefid (DL-23) (Hole 1977). The dry farming of wheat and barley as well as the herding of sheep and goats prospered, and substantial one- to two- room mud slab houses, perhaps nuclear family homes, were constructed. A variety of crafts were pursued and exchange brought exotic commodities such as obsidian from Anatolia and turquoise from Central Asia. The mortuary evidence indicates that some individuals achieved honored status in their lifetimes, but there is no indication of hereditary positions of authority. These patterns continue in the subsequent Sefid and Surkh phases. Because the ceramics of the early village phases do not survive on the surfaces of sites, our best indicator of occupation during these phases is the occurrence of symmetrical microlithic chert cores, termed "bullet cores." These cores were found on the west slope of Chagha Sefid and the east side of Ali Kosh. They have also been found on the southeastern extremity of Musiyan (DL-20). At least by the Surkh phase, the last phase in which such cores were commonly made, settlement had begun at what would be the main center of the Deh Luran Plain.

The durable and distinctive Chogha Mami Transitional ceramics have been recognized on nine sites. Of these occurrences (Figure V.1), four are isolated sherds on larger, later sites, and it is not possible to make even an informed guess about their size. The remaining five all have some later occupation, and may have been even smaller in this early phase than we estimate. They appear to range in size from 0.05 up to about 1.00 ha (Table V.1). The largest site, DL 286 NE, is difficult to assess, as noted in the previous chapter. It may have been even larger. The clearest feature of the settlement pattern for this phase (Figure V.1) is the occurrence of sites in four areas, all probably at the lower edges of early Holocene alluvial fans. The three areas with small clusters of sites are adjacent to the alluvial fans of the Mehmeh and Dawairij rivers, where fields could be watered with natural flooding and expanded as well as improved upon through the construction of simple water-management features or canals. The one isolated site not part of a cluster is Chagha Sefid (DL-23), which is in a similar location where the waters of the spring-fed Ab-i Garm spread out onto the more level area of the plain. During this phase, there is no architectural or mortuary evidence of social hierarchy either from the excavated sites in Deh Luran or from contemporary sites elsewhere in southwestern Iran or southern Iraq. What is indicated for Chogha Mami Transitional layers at Chagha Sefid, and well documented from both Chogha Mami on the Mandali Plain about 210 km to the northwest (Oates 1969) and Djaffarabad on the Susiana Plain about 100 km to the southeast (Dollfus 1971, 1978) is the use of large multiroom residences, indicating that large extended families were involved in the earliest irrigation cultivation (see Chapter VI).

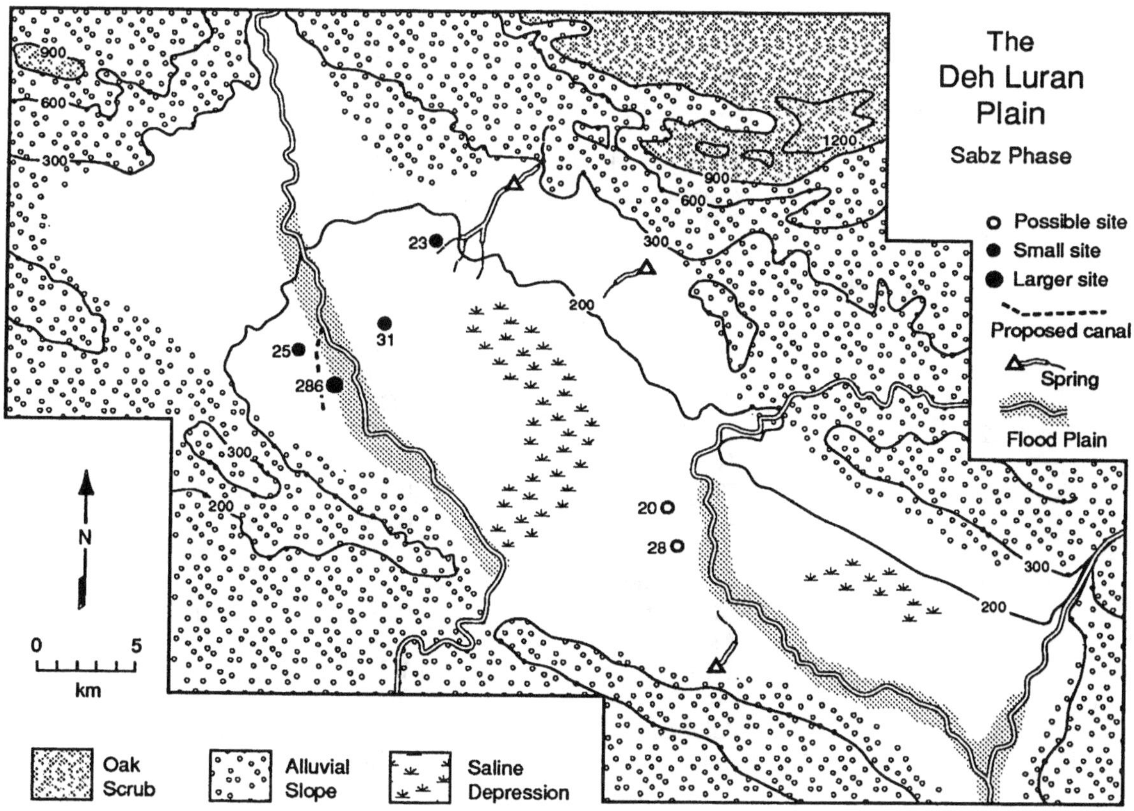

Figure V.2. Settlements of the Sabz Phase

Table V.2: Sabz Phase Settlement

Site Number	Name	Area (ha)	Type
20	Musiyan	?	b
23	Chagha Sefid	0.33	b
25	—	0.05	b
28	Khazineh	?	b
31	Sabz	ca 0.50	c
286NE	—	ca 1.00	b

Definite Sabz phase ceramics have been found on only six sites. All but one (Tepe Sabz itself, DL-31) had previous Chogha Mami Transitional phase occupation. As was the case in the preceding phase, these sites are small and occur in alluvial fan areas where waters from natural floods could be directed through the construction of simple water-control features, and small canals could be used (Table V.2; Figure V.2). Supporting this probability are Helbaek's observation that carbonized seeds from Sabz phase layers at Tepe Sabz indicate that crops such as barley, lentils, and flax were irrigated (Hole, Flannery and Neely 1969: 412–424). Faunal remains indicate that domestic cows supplemented the herds of sheep and goats (Hole, Flannery and Neely 1969: 265). However, most of the Sabz phase sites are in the western part of the plain in areas close to the Mehmeh River, and it is possible that for some reason Sabz phase communities were not occupying the eastern part of the Deh Luran Plain.

Table V.3: Khazineh Phase Settlement

Site Number	Name	Area (ha)	Type
Possible Centers			
20	Musiyan	ca 2.00	b
32	Farukhabad	ca 1.50	c
85	Muradabad	1.44	c
312	Jelise	?	c
Smaller Settlements			
11	Garmasi	0.28	d
14	—	1.15	d
15	—	0.25	c
19	Chakali	0.26	d
21	Ali Kosh	0.15	c
22	Tepe Sefid	0.15	c
23	Chagha Sefid	0.31	b
25	—	0.05	b
26	—	0.05	c
27	Tenel Ramon	ca 0.50	c
28	Khazineh	0.52	b
29	Ashrafabad	0.54	c
31	Sabz	ca 1.00	b
33	—	0.78	d
71	Aliabad	0.30	c
84	—	0.26	d
222	—	0.50	c
241	—	0.11	c
286NE	—	ca 1.00	a

The Khazineh Phase

The distinctive ceramics of this phase have been recognized at 23 sites on the Deh Luran Plain. These cover at least 13.1 hectares. Although we can distinguish early and late Khazineh assemblages from the excavation at Tepe Sabz, this distinction can be made only for some of the larger surface samples, and so we report the Khazineh sites as an aggregate (Table V.3; Figure V.3), even though it is unlikely that the sites are all contemporary. The dense cluster of Khazineh settlements on the western plain reaches high up the fan of the Mehmeh, probably suggesting the use of somewhat larger, but still relatively small, irrigation canals several kilometers in length. The largest precisely measured Khazineh site is Tepe Muradabad (DL-85) on the eastern plain. Its 1.44 ha area is divided into two discrete sections (Fig. IV.38). Three other sites—Tepe Jelise (DL-312) on the eastern end of the plain, Tepe Musiyan (DL-20) in the center, and Tepe Farukhabad (DL-32) on the western end of the plain—may be as large or larger, but in each case later occupation has obscured the Khazineh site. Muradabad and Musiyan have nearby hamlet sites ranging from 0.15 to 0.30 ha in size, and it seems likely that the larger sites dominated these smaller neighbors. However, the limited evidence of settlement dominance provides the only suggestion of social hierarchy on the Deh Luran Plain during this phase. There is no mortuary evidence from this period, and the architectural traces from Tepe Sabz are not informative about social differences.

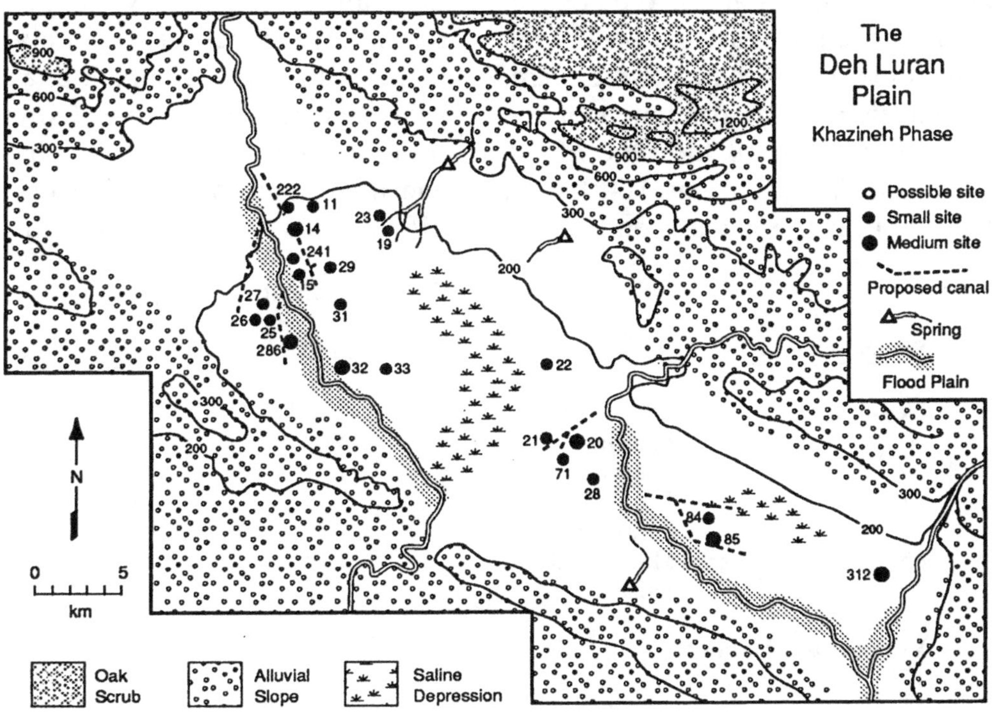

Figure V.3. Settlements of the Khazineh Phase

The Mehmeh Phase

We were able to recognize definite Mehmeh phase ceramics on 18 sites covering at least 13.1 ha (Table V.4; Figure V.4). Architectural fragments are known from excavations at Musiyan (DL-20) and Tepe Sabz (DL 31), and plans of buildings have been recorded from Tepe Ashrafabad (DL-29) (Hole, Flannery and Neely 1969:73). The houses appear to be spaced 6 to 10 m apart, and evidently have two to four rooms with platforms for sleeping or storage. The density we suggest for Ashrafabad, about 102 people per hectare, is very close to the density of 100 per hectare proposed by Hole, Flannery and Neely (1969) based on Naroll's (1962) method. Since the Mehmeh phase was relatively short and most of the recorded sites were probably occupied at the same time at about 5600 B.C. (4800 b.c.), one can calculate a total population of about 1300 people on the Deh Luran Plain. The settlement distribution is similar to that of the preceding phase, and the same patterns of small scale canal irrigation and herding continued. Several of the Mehmeh sites are quite large. Centrally located Musiyan has Mehmeh phase ceramics throughout its southern and central part, and architecture has been observed in locations 120 meters apart. We suggest that Musiyan had reached at least 4.0 ha in area and had emerged as the major center of the plain, which it would continue to be for much of the succeeding three millennia until the time of the Sukkalmahhu Elamite kings, about 1600 B.C. Tepe Jelise (DL-312) on the eastern end of the plain may have been almost as large, but other centers were smaller. Tepe Sabz (DL-31) is estimated to have grown to about 1.51 ha, Tepe Muradabad (DL-85) appears to have shrunk to 1.34 ha, and Tepe Farukhabad (DL-32) perhaps maintained the size, about 1.5 ha, proposed for the preceding phase. Musiyan was ringed by smaller hamlets and villages, and Farukhabad and Sabz were located so that the villages and hamlets of the western plain could not have communicated with Musiyan except by way of these larger settlements. This suggests that in times of relative centralization, there was a three-level settlement hierarchy on the Deh Luran Plain. It is important to keep in mind that in times of conflict, centralization would break down, and the discrete settlement clusters in the western and central part of the plain were probably independent. There is little other evidence of social complexity from the plain. All known Mehmeh phase architecture appears to represent houses of similar size and composition. No Mehmeh burials have been excavated and there is no other evidence of socioeconomic differences between social units or sites.

Table V.4: Mehmeh Phase Settlement

Site Number	Name	Area (ha)	Type
Centers			
20	Musiyan	ca 4.00	b
29	Ashrafabad	1.27	b
31	Sabz	1.51	b
32	Farukhabad	ca 1.50	b
85	Muradabad	1.34	a
312	Jelise	?	a
Villages and Hamlets			
15	—	0.67	a
21	Ali Kosh	0.15	a
22	Tepe Sefid	0.10	a
23	Chagha Sefid	0.31	b
25	—	0.05	a
26	—	0.05	a
27	Tenel Ramon	ca 0.50	b
28	Khazineh	0.52	a
43	—	0.26	c
71	Aliabad	0.30	b
222	—	0.50	a
241	—	0.11	a

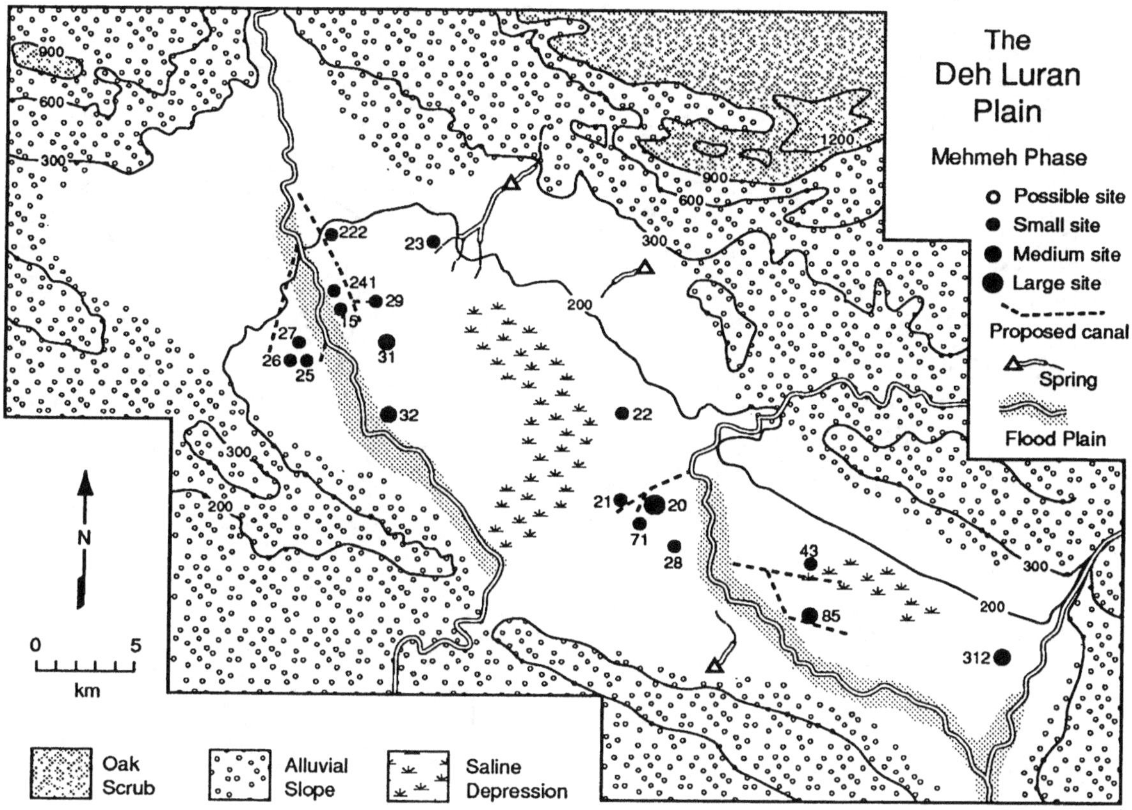

Figure V.4. Settlements of the Mehmeh Phase

Table V.5: Bayat Phase Settlement

Site Number	Name	Area (ha)	Type	Platform?
Centers				
20	Musiyan	ca 4.00	b	—
29	Ashrafabad	1.29	b	yes
31	Sabz	1.51	a	—
32	Farukhabad	ca 2.00	b	yes
Villages and Hamlets				
23	Chagha Sefid	0.26	b	—
27	Tenel Ramon	ca 1.00	b	—
43	—	0.26	a	—
71	Aliabad	?	b	—
91	—	0.14	d	yes
240	—	0.05	d	—
248/9	—	0.87	d	yes
290	—	0.44	d	—

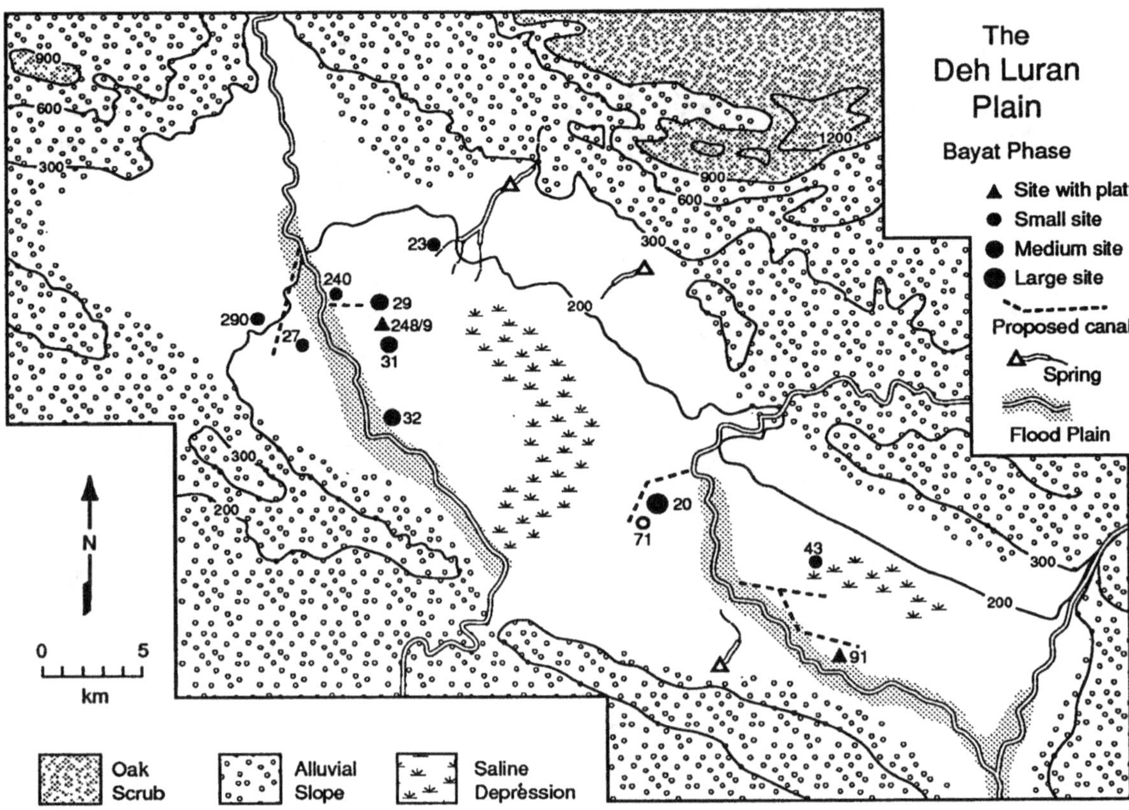

Figure V.5. Settlements of the Bayat Phase

The Bayat Phase

Ceramics of this phase were found on 12 sites, estimated to cover more than 11.8 ha (Table V.5; Fig. V.5). We emphasize, however, that most Bayat ceramic types continue into the subsequent Farukh phase, and few variants are characteristic only of this phase, so some Bayat phase sites may not have been recognized. Indeed, sites classified as Bayat phase (cf. Wright 1981: Fig. 31) with less strict criteria (for example DL-22 and DL-222) are not included in the present list. Architectural elements and stratified deposits have been excavated at Sabz (DL-31) and Farukhabad (DL-32). If we use the same density factors to estimate the population of the plain, the population would have been at least 1100 people. Site location and the evidence of plants and animals indicate that small-scale irrigation and herding continued as before. Musiyan was still the largest center of the plain, though it lacked nearby dependent hamlets or villages. Farukhabad and Sabz continued as small centers. The residential architecture on both these sites is relatively elaborate, which may indicate that the small excavations in the highest points of these mounds have cut into areas occupied by social groups of higher status. Unfortunately, we do not have evidence of modest housing of the Bayat phase. Two small sites, DL-248/249 on the west and DL-91 near abandoned Tepe Muradabad on the east, have higher mounds of clean mud brick debris, which may be the remnants of platforms of mud brick, supporting or associated with the houses of prominent social groups. In sum, there is not only settlement size evidence, but some indications in architecture and settlement morphology that social differences existed during Bayat times.

The Farukh Phase

Ceramics of this phase were found on 12 sites, estimated to cover more than 16.5 ha (Table V.6, Fig. V.6). Thus there seem to be more sites covering a greater area than in the previous phase, but as noted above, this could be an artifact of the lesser visibility of sites of the previous phase. Given the population density suggested for earlier phases, the population of the Deh Luran Plain during the Farukh phase would have been about 1700 people. However, architectural evidence from Farukhabad (DL-32) suggests a dense packing of housing in this small center, and some housing may have had two stories. If housing was denser at centers, approaching the densities recorded by F. G. L. Gremliza for the Susiana Plain in the mid-20th century (Gremliza 1962), the population in the centers could have reached as high as 200 per hectare, and one could calculate population approaching 3200 people for the plain. The settlement distributions as well as the faunal (Redding in Wright 1981) and floral (Miller in Wright 1981) evidence from Farukhabad indicate that small scale canal irrigation, predominantly of wheat, herding of sheep, goats and cows; and hunting of gazelle and onager continued on the Mehmeh alluvial fan. However, most small settlements in the central area around the large center of Musiyan were abandoned as Musiyan grew even larger, and almost all settlement on the eastern end of the plain was abandoned. Parts of the eastern area may have been prone to salinization. However, salinization would be unlikely in the Musiyan area, so the nucleation in this area must be due either to the attractions of life in the center or threats to smaller communities in the east. Settlement hierarchy is well developed with the largest centrally located settlement of Musiyan (DL-20) covering about 9.0 hectares, the secondary centers of Farukhabad (DL-32) and Garmasi (DL-11) covering about 1.5 to 2.5 hectares, and 9 other settlements covering a hectare or less. This evidence of settlement hierarchy is confirmed by the evidence of residential groups of differing status at Farukhabad. Elaborate houses whose occupants controlled large storage structures, consumed more beverages and more meat, with preferential access to certain wild animals, as well as to exotic chipped stone raw material, in contrast with modest houses in other parts of the site (Wright 1981:65–66). The rebuilding of the elaborate houses on the same spot generation after generation suggests that important social position was hereditary.

Table V.6: Farukh Phase Settlement

Site Number	Name	Area (ha)	Type	Platform?
Centers				
11	Garmasi	1.54	d	—
20	Musiyan	ca 9.00	b	—
32	Farukhabad	ca 2.50	a	yes
Villages and Hamlets				
15	—	0.67	d	—
23	Chagha Sefid	0.12	a	—
27	Tenel Ramon	ca 1.00	a	yes
29	Ashrafabad	0.40	a	—
71	Aliabad	?	a	—
85	Muradabad	trace	c	yes
247	—	0.67	c	—
262	—	0.20	d	yes
286SW	—	0.40	d	yes

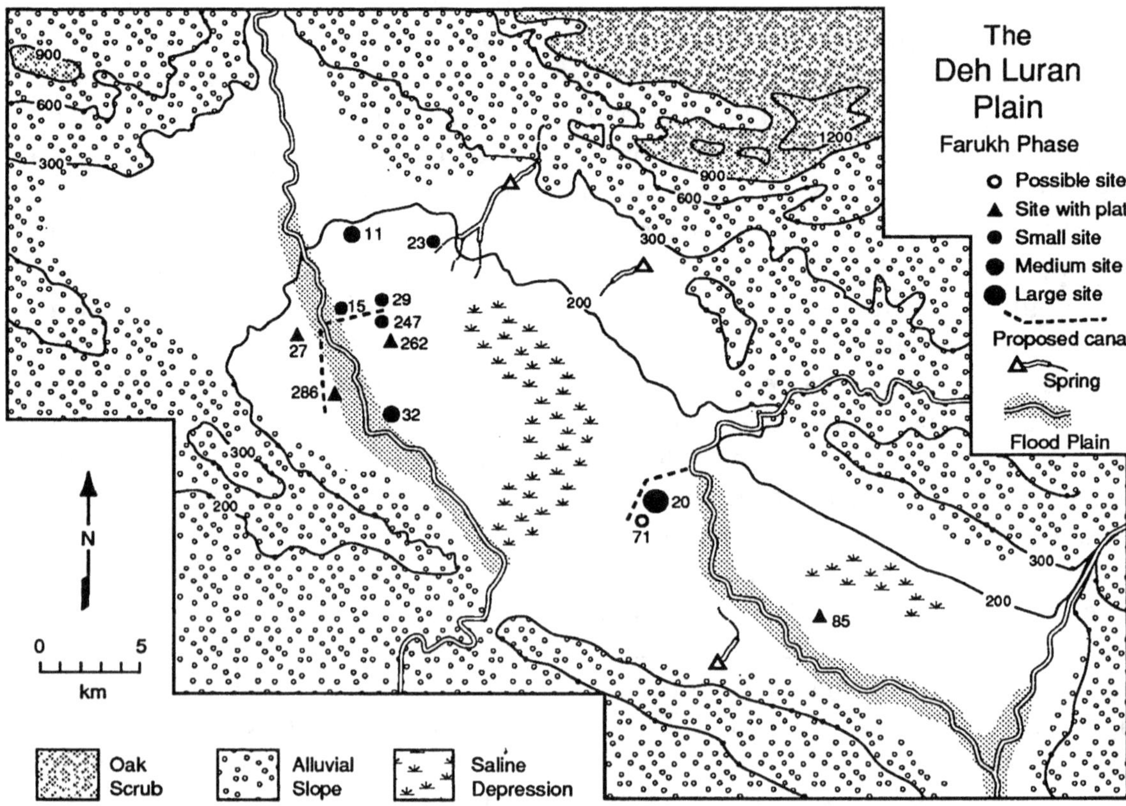

Figure V.6. Settlements of the Farukh Phase

The Suse Phase

Ceramics of this phase definitely occurred on only three sites, estimated to cover a total of 7.11 ha (Table V.7; Fig. V.7). We have no excavated Suse phase samples from the plain, but the evidence of the settlement pattern alone provides striking evidence of disruption and decline. The Mehmeh alluvium, is largely abandoned for the first time in millennia. Only two large sites, the somewhat diminished center at Musiyan (DL-20) and the smaller center at Muradabad (DL-85), survive. The one site to the west, DL-247, is a surface scatter of ceramics, lacking the elevation built up by decaying mud architecture, and may be a transhumant camp rather than a village. It is reasonable to suppose that a threat or actual attack from the west forced the abandonment of much of the plain.

Table V.7: Suse Phase Settlement

Site Number	Name	Area (ha)	Type
Centers			
20	Musiyan	ca 5.00	a
Villages and Hamlets			
85	Muradabad	1.44	a
247	—	0.67	a

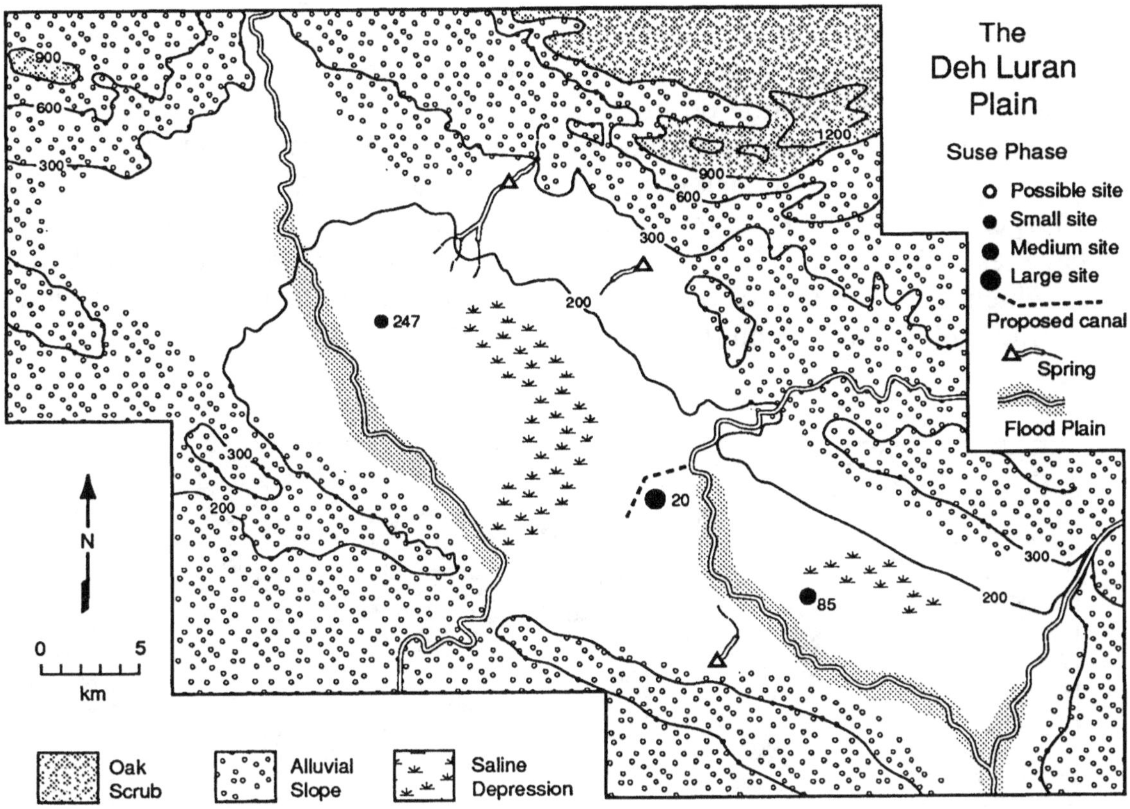

Figure V.7. Settlements of the Suse Phase

The Early Uruk Phase

This phase sees the re-colonization of the Mehmeh alluvium, though the eastern plain remains little occupied (Table V.8; Fig. V.8). We have recorded 11 sites covering 16.9 hectares. Most of these sites, covering a total of 14.0 hectares, have indications of occupation earlier in this period. Those with indications of occupation later in the period include most of the larger sites, and cover 11.5 hectares. Stone footings at several sites permit us to estimate a population density of 115 people per hectare, indicating at least 1500 people on the plain during the earlier part of the phase and at least 1300 during the later part of the phase. As during the later Susiana phases, these sites are concentrated around the easily irrigated areas of the Mehmeh and Ab-i Garm alluvium, and traces of possibly stone-lined canals are associated with the large unnamed site (DL-292) west of the Mehmeh and at Sargarab (DL-169) beside the Ab-i Garm. Unfortunately, we do not have any floral remains from this period. However, the evidence of the faunal remains indicates that the herding patterns of Susiana times continued, though hunting increased in importance (Redding in Wright 1981:259). The settlement size hierarchy of the Early Uruk phase seems similar to that of the Farukh phase, with a single larger center of 8.4 hectares, two possible smaller centers of 1.5 to 2.3 hectares, and a number of smaller settlements of a hectare or less. However, the spatial pattern is notably different because the larger center is on the western margin of the plain. Additional survey farther west might have revealed a few more small sites, but the position of the center in the settlement distribution as a whole would not be greatly affected. It is tempting to argue that the location of this larger settlement guards the western approaches to the plain, but the site is diffuse, and there is no evidence of defenses which might corroborate such an argument. The available architectural and artifactual evidence from the Early Uruk sites contributes little further information about social organization during this phase. While we have some evidence of modest house plans from smaller sites, we lack coherent plans of the larger sites where emergent social units might have resided.

The sites which lack evidence of occupation later in this period include the one on the alluvial slopes (DL-169) and those toward the eastern end of the plain (DL 43, 61 and 71). All are small, but some have large sherd collections, so the lack of evidence is unlikely to be simply an artifact of inadequate samples. An abandonment of smaller sites and a general contraction of the settlement distribution is likely to be a consequence of unsettled conditions surrounding the rise of complex polities during the Early Uruk Period in Sumer to the southwest and on the Susiana Plain to the southeast.

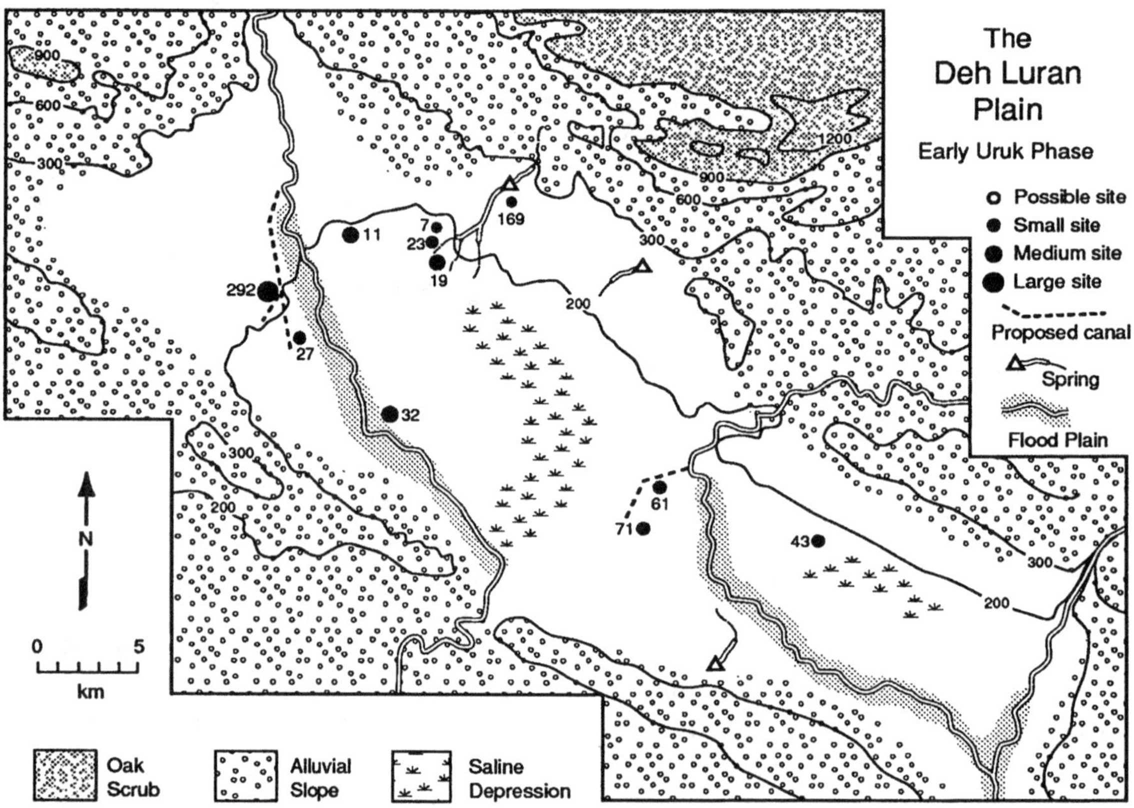

Figure V.8. Settlements of the Early Uruk Phase

Table V.8: Early Uruk Settlement

Site Number	Name	Area (ha)	Type	Subphases?
Centers				
11	Garmasi	1.54	d	E
19	Chakali	2.31	c	E, L
292	—	8.40	d	E, L
Villages and Hamlets				
7	Gendarmary	0.24	d	E, L?
23	Chagha Sefid	0.31	c	E, L
27	Tenel Ramon	ca 1.00	d	?
32	Farukhabad	ca 1.00	c	L
43	—	0.26	d	?
61	—	0.68	c	?
71	Aliabad	ca 0.50	c	E
169	Sargarab	0.66	d	E

[E: Earlier; L: Later; L?: Possibly Later; ?: Subphases Uncertain]

The Middle Uruk Phase

Ceramics of this phase were found on 7 sites, estimated to cover a total of 7.5 ha (Table V.9; Fig. V.9). Even if the large site on the eastern approach to the plain, Tepe Jelise (DL-312), is of this phase, the total settled area would only be about 9.5 hectares. Thus, there seem to have been fewer sites covering a lesser area than in the previous phase. Given the population density suggested by the architecture of the Early Uruk phase, the population of the Deh Luran Plain during the Middle Uruk phase would have been about 1100 people. Three of these sites are some what larger (DL-19, 32 and 312) covering two to three hectares, but there is no single larger center. Four are small sites covering less than a hectare. The sites are scattered very widely on the plain, all but one (DL-104) are in river fan areas where small scale canal irrigation would be possible. DL-104 would require a longer canal (see Chapter VI). The scatter of relatively small settlements suggests there was little threat of conflict. That this scattered settlement distribution may relate to changing strategies of food production is suggested by the excavated samples from Middle Uruk Farukhabad. In comparison with Farukh phase samples, cows become rare, and goats increase in proportion to sheep (Redding in Wright 1981:258–260). Also, the proportion of barley exceeds that of wheat for the first time (Miller in Wright 1981:228). These changes could relate to local increases in aridity, since goats and barley are more tolerant of water deficits. However, an increasing focus on goats could also relate to fiber production, increase of which is indicated by increases in spindle whorls (Wright 1981:153–154) and in possible loom weights (Wright 1981:147–148, 270-271). There are also indications of increased preparation of local chert for exchange (Wright 1981:267). On the other hand, import of marine shell appears to increase (Wright 1981:274–275), and local pottery styles are increasingly supplemented by those widespread in the Uruk world. The presence of a spherical bulla with stamp and cylinder seal impressions (Wright 1981:156) indicates the receipt or storage of messages by someone at Farukhabad. Unfortunately, the excavations at Farukhabad revealed only fragmentary Middle Uruk domestic structures and we can infer little about the sociopolitical organization which coordinated the decentralized settlement network and the prospering exchange relations of the Middle Uruk Phase.

Table V.9: Middle Uruk Settlement

Site Number	Name	Area (ha)	Type
Centers			
19	Chakali	ca 2.59	b
32	Farukhabad	ca 2.50	b
312	Jelise	ca 2.00	c
Villages and Hamlets			
23	Chagha Sefid	0.17	b
61	—	0.68	b
71	Aliabad	ca 0.50	a
104	—	ca 0.95	c

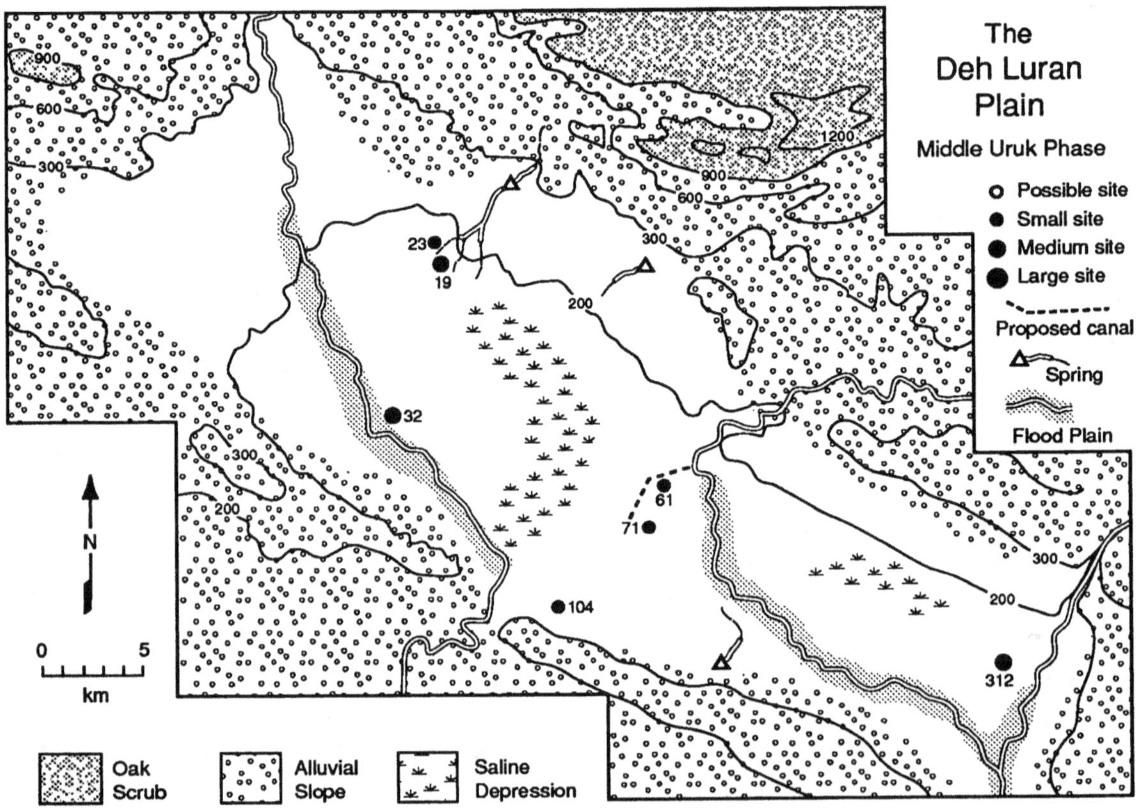

Figure V.9. Settlements of the Middle Uruk Phase

The Late Uruk Phase

Restudy of the Deh Luran ceramics has increased the number of known Late Uruk sites, and altered our understanding of this period on the Deh Luran Plain (cf. Wright 1981:185–188). Ceramics of this phase were found on 7 sites, estimated to cover a total of 4.8 ha (Table V.10; Fig. V.10). Thus, though there were the same number of sites, they covered a lesser area than those of the previous phase. Given the population density suggested by the architecture of the Early Uruk Phase, the population of the Deh Luran Plain during the Late Uruk phase would have been about 500 people. At first glance, Farukhabad (DL-32), the largest settlement at 3.0 hectares, appears to dominate surrounding smaller settlements on the western and central plain, with the possible settlement at Jelise far away to the East. However, the situation may have been more complicated. Two small sites in the center of the plain—DL-61 and 62—are about 110 meters apart, and the ground around them is obscured by later debris. It is possible that there was a single larger Late Uruk settlement here. If so, the plain would have had a center and a larger population than we have estimated with presently available evidence. Certainly, when future field visits are feasible, this possibility should be checked.

Whatever is learned from such re-study, the extant evidence from the excavations at Farukhabad indicates several economic and political changes during the Late Uruk phase. First, while goats become the predominant domestic animal and barley remains the predominant cultivated grain, there is little evidence for local textile

Table V.10: Late Uruk Settlement

Site Number	Name	Area (ha)	Type
Centers			
32	Farukhabad	ca 2.50	b
Villages and Hamlets			
19	Chakali	trace	a
23	Chagha Sefid	0.09	a
43	—	trace	d
61	—	0.68	a
62	—	0.42	d
104	—	0.63	a

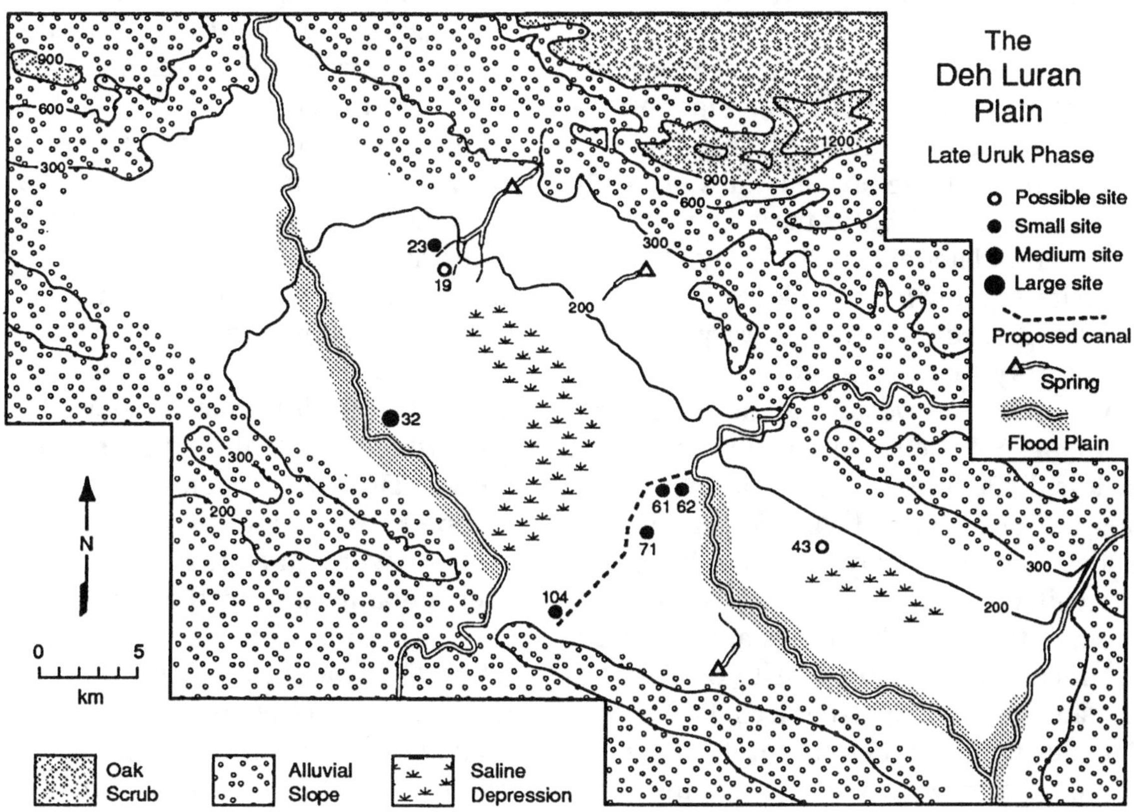

Figure V.10. Settlements of the Late Uruk Phase

production. Second, there is evidence not only for increased chert export, but also for increased local production and export of bitumen (Wright 1981:267–270). The evidence of the processing of flint and bitumen is concentrated near non-domestic structures in one excavated area, in contrast to low densities around modest domestic structures in other areas. Third, there is little evidence of import, but ceramics made in the local tradition become rare, and vessels indistinguishable from Late Uruk ceramics in the areas of Warka and Susa predominate (Wright 1981:186–188). The presence of sealings at Farukhabad may indicate the local presence of administrators concerned with the storage of goods. In sum, the evidence indicates that Farukhabad came under the dominance of another center, and that primary materials were exported for finishing elsewhere with little recompense.

The Jemdet Nasr and Early Dynastic I–II Phases

These phases see greatly increased occupation on the plain (Tables V.11–12; Figs. V.11–12). We have recorded 10 sites covering about 32 hectares. In addition, there are four sites probably used only as cemeteries. All of these have indications of occupation later during the Early Dynastic I–II phase, but very few have evidence of occupation during the preceding Jemdet Nasr phase. We are confident only that Farukhabad (DL-32) and Baulah (DL-24) on the western plain, covering a total of about 5.1 hectares, were occupied. However, it is difficult to recognize a few Jemdet Nasr items in dense Early Dynastic scatter, and some Jemdet Nasr sites may not have been recognized. Architectural densities at Farukhabad are high, and some two-story buildings are indicated. With an estimated population density of 200 people per hectare we can suggest at least 900 people on the plain during the earlier part of this time and about 6500 during the later part of this time. Such an increase could probably not have been accomplished by the Deh Luranis themselves and would require immigration onto the plain. During the Early Dynastic I–II phase, a marked settlement hierarchy is evident. Musiyan, the large center, covered 15 hectares. The major cemeteries cluster around this center. There were two definite smaller centers of about three to four hectares on the western plain (DL-24 and DL-32) , and it is possible that the easterly site which would become paramount in the next period (DL-41) was also a small center. Subsidiary to these centers are smaller settlements of 2.0 ha or less. The evidence from the excavations at Farukhabad indicates that the food production patterns of the Late Uruk phase continue. Goats remain the predominant domestic animal and barley remains the predominant cultivated grain. There is once again evidence for local textile production, while local chert and bitumen production for export appear to have diminished. On the other hand, import of exotic chert, marine shell, and other exotic materials increases. Clearly, this was a period of local growth and prosperity. More elaborate domestic units on the summit of Farukhabad have evidence of the processing of bitumen and chert for export and greater access to exotic foods and materials, while modest domestic structures both on the summit of the mound and at its base have little evidence of such activities. It is also interesting to note that as the unit in one excavated area becomes poorer, that in the other becomes richer, suggesting competition between groups (Wright 1981: 189–192). Unfortunately, there is no evidence directly informative about the political system which controlled the plain during these phases. However, given the large population and complex settlement hierarchy, and the fact that states were arising throughout Greater Mesopotamia during the early IIIrd millennium B.C., it seems likely that by Early Dynastic I–II times Musiyan was the center of a small state integrating the villages of the plain, and perhaps nomadic peoples of the foothills (Vanden Berghe 1968, 1970). The rarity of small sites suggests some insecurity, but there is no direct evidence of conflict.

Table V.11: Jemdet Nasr Settlement

Site Number	Name	Area (ha)	Type
18	Sabz East	?	c
20	Musiyan	?	c
24	Baulah	2.09	c
32	Farukhabad	ca 3.00	b

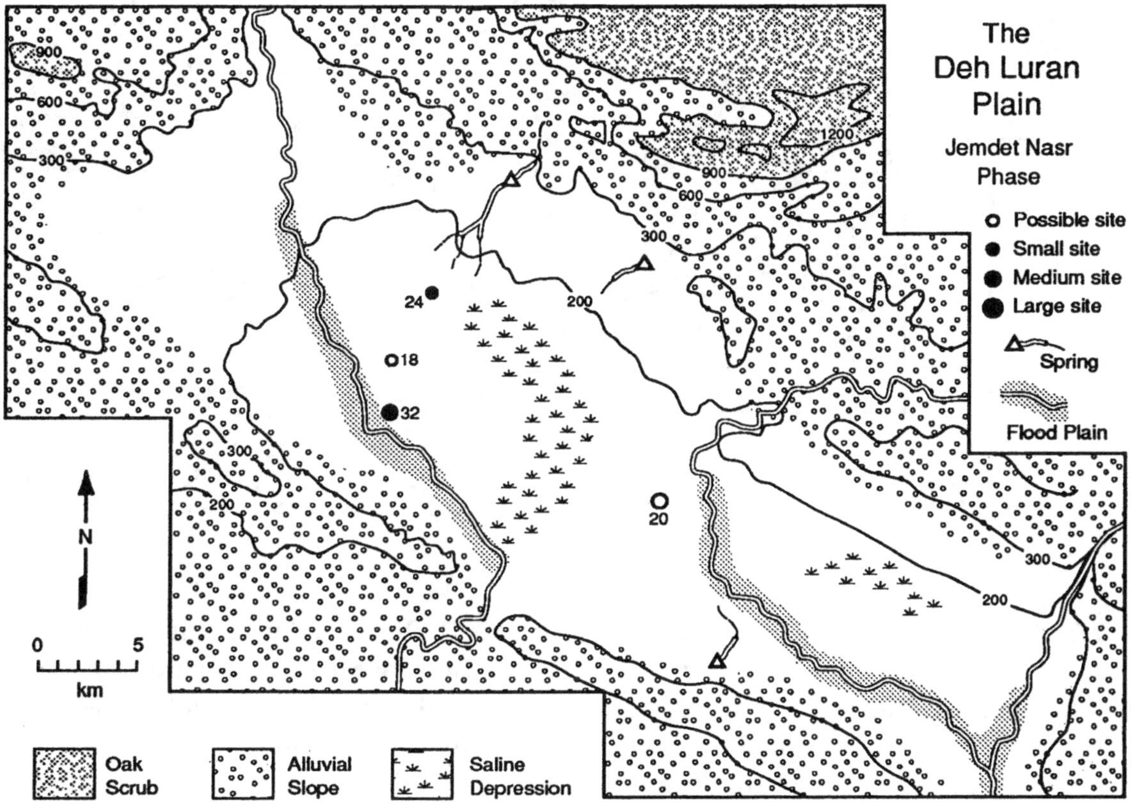

Figure V.11. Settlements of the Jemdet Nasr Phase

Table V.12: Early Dynastic I–II Settlement

Site Number	Name	Area (ha)	Type
Centers			
18	Sabz East	3.10	a
20	Musiyan	ca 15.00	b
24	Baulah	4.18	b
32	Farukhabad	ca 3.00	b
Villages and Hamlets			
27	Tenel Ramon	ca 2.00	d
34	Garan	ca 1.50	c
41	—	?	c
54	Tepe Soza	ca 1.00	c
62	—	0.42	d
104	—	ca 2.00	c

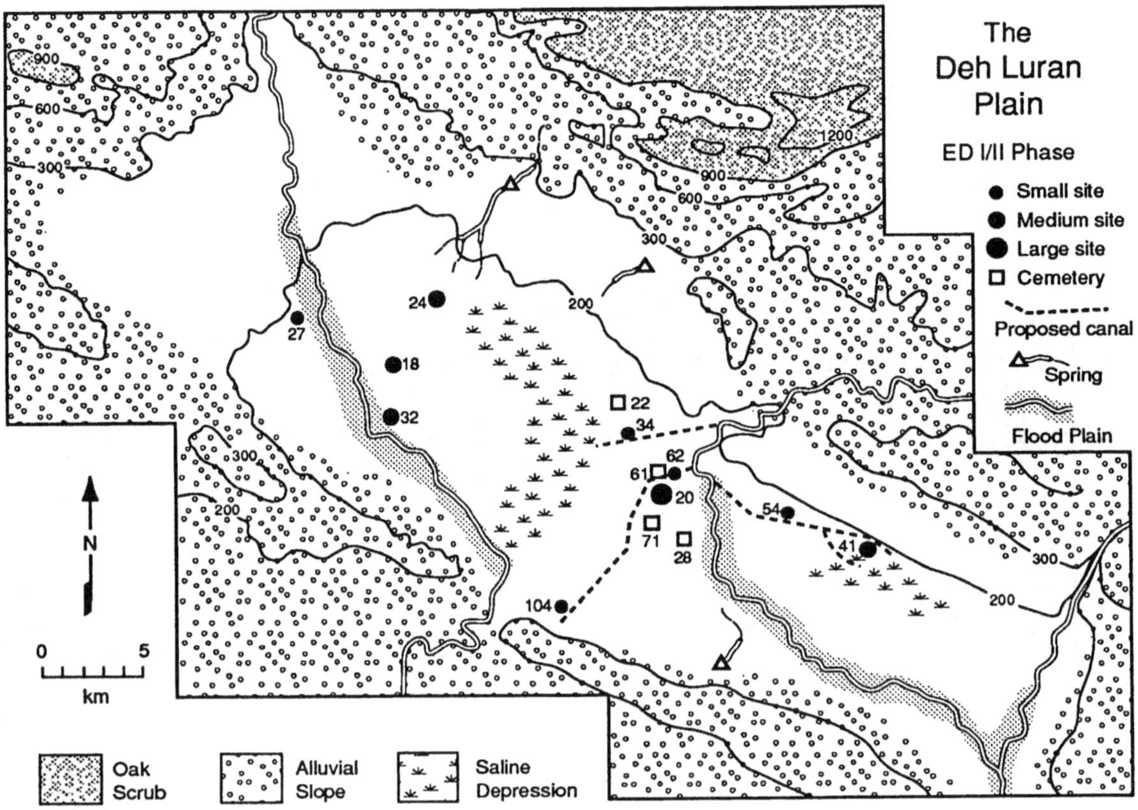

Figure V.12. Settlements of the Early Dynastic I–II Phase

The Early Dynastic III Phase

The discovery by Pierre de Miroschedji of another large walled site of this phase has altered our understanding of this time on the Deh Luran Plain (cf. Wright 1981:192–194). Ceramics of this phase were found on 7 sites, estimated to cover a total of 46.9 ha (Table V.13; Fig. V.13). If this is so, and given the population density suggested by the architecture of the Early Dynastic I–II phase, the population of the Deh Luran Plain during the Early Dynastic III phase would have been about 9,400 people. However, the sudden construction of a short-lived mid-IIIrd millennium center east of the Dawairij (DL-41), just about the time that Farukhabad (DL-32) and other sites were abandoned and Musiyan may have become smaller, may indicate population displacement within the plain. If so, perhaps about 25 hectares of settlement would have been occupied at one time, and the population of the plain would have been about 5000. Since this was a time of widespread warfare in Southwest Asia, such a proposition seems reasonable, but its evaluation will require further study of these sites.

Unfortunately, layers of this period at Farukhabad were eroded and disturbed, and we have limited excavation evidence only for the beginning of this period. We do know that occupation, with differential involvements in crafts and exchange, continues in the contrasting elaborate and modest buildings. We also know that the byproducts of export of bitumen and import of copper and lapis lazuli are more common in these Farukhabad layers than in earlier ones. Excavation at better preserved sites, if it is possible, with development of more precise chronologies and sampling of fortifications and buildings, will be needed if Deh Luran is to contribute to our understanding of this period of state conflict and the rise of empires.

Table V.13: Early Dynastic III Settlement.

Site Number	Name	Area (ha)
Centers		
20	Musiyan	ca 15.00
24	Baulah	4.18
41	—	ca 20.00
54	Tepe Soza	ca 3.22
Villages and Hamlets		
32	Farukhabad	ca 1.00
34	Garan	ca 1.50
104	—	ca 2.00

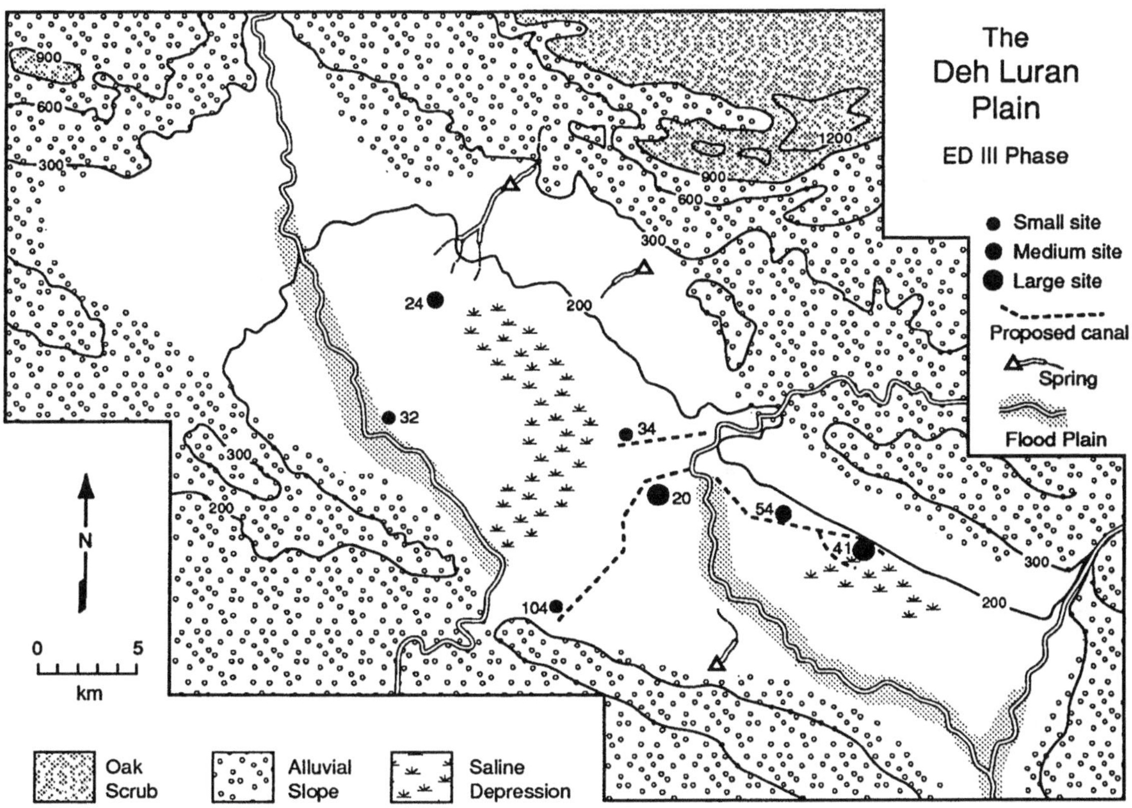

Figure V.13. Settlements of the Early Dynastic III Phase

Chapter VI

Irrigation and Population on the Deh Luran Plain: 5400–2600 B.C.

The preceding chapter presented a summary of the survey evidence for the earlier cultural phases of the Deh Luran Plain in the way that such studies are usually presented. For each phase, we discussed agriculture in terms of general associations between sites and land forms, and population in terms of numbers of sites and total occupied area. In this chapter we discuss the problems of the development of irrigation systems and the changes in population as framed in our original research design, and as discussed in the introduction to this monograph. If, in our effort to develop a more processual perspective on these variables and their relationships, we have pushed well beyond the limits of prudence, we hope at the least that we have raised challenges for future investigators.

Changing Water Management and Irrigation during the Early Phases of Occupation on the Deh Luran Plain

Introduction

Even with intensive survey of most of the Deh Luran Plain, we are still unable to conclusively point to the remains of specific, tangible features and systems of water management and irrigation or to conclusively state that they were built during the phases of occupation addressed in this volume.

Our best evidence for the earliest use of water management technology is that represented by indirect data in the form of macrobotanical remains. In this regard, we have two sets of evidence from excavations at two different sites on the Deh Luran Plain.

The first set of evidence was discovered by Hans Helbaek (Hole, Flannery, and Neely 1969: 405–11, 415–24) during his analysis of the macrobotanical remains recovered by Neely in excavations at Tepe Sabz (Hole, Flannery, and Neely 1969: 50–64).

Helbaek studied in detail the macrobotanical remains recovered from cultural deposits of the Sabz phase of about 5200 to 5000 B.C. (^{14}C 4600 b.c. to 4400 b.c.; see Hole 1987: Table 2) at Tepe Sabz (DL-31). In his considered opinion, these remains represented several plants (flax, lentil, 6-row hulled barley, hexaploid free-threshing wheat, bread wheat, etc.) that had been grown by means of irrigation agriculture. Helbaek writes:

> If the present-day traces of irrigation systems around Tepe Sabz must be regarded as unrelated to the foundation of the village, what, then, is the evidence upon which the postulate is based, that the founders employed this novel technique?
>
> We need not, in fact, look beyond the plant table to find proof of significant changes in crop choice, indisputably pointing at an intensification of human mastery of growth conditions, an advance that can only be as-

> cribed to control of water supply. (Helbaek in Hole, Flannery, and Neely 1969: 416).

Helbaek continues and reinforces the above statement with the following narrative regarding the Deh Luran Plain and the macro-botanical materials recovered from the earliest levels of Tepe Sabz:

> Without controlled irrigation it is not possible to make up for failing precipitation during the winter—a misfortune that may hit these low, arid tracts as often as every four to six years. Nor is it feasible to extend the period of humid soil conditions into the hot late spring. Both these unfortunate situations can be counteracted artificially if water is at hand, and if their technical skill enables the farmers to distribute it according to the best interests of the various crop species.
>
> That is what the Sabz people knew.... This knowledge is reflected in their cultivated plants, species which were either not grown in Deh Luran previous to their arrival, or which had appeared sporadically and disappeared again for lack of propitious growth conditions. (Helbaek in Hole, Flannery, and Neely 1969: 417).

The second body of evidence was recovered by Frank Hole during his excavations at the site of Chagha Sefid (DL-23) in 1968 and 1969 (Hole 1977). Hole's findings in specific levels at Chagha Sefid, analyzed by Jane Renfrew, included nearly the same corpus of irrigated plants found by Helbaek at Tepe Sabz, but in an earlier context. Furthermore, analysis of samples of plant remains as late as those of the Early Dynastic of the early IIIrd millennium B.C. (Miller in Wright 1981: 227–32) indicate that many of the elements of this suite of irrigated plants continued to be important. Finally, analysis of the rodent remains from Deh Luran sites indicates that lush, permanently wet fields existed in the area into the early IIIrd millennium B.C. (Redding in Wright 1981: 252–60). Thus multiple lines of evidence indicate the existence of irrigation agriculture from about 5400 B.C. until after 2600 B.C. However, these forms of evidence imply little about the scale and organization of irrigation systems.

Apart from these ethnobotanical and ethnozoological studies, our evidence for possible features dating to these early phases of occupation are based solely on the juxtaposition and association of some of the archaeological sites we have described in Chapter IV of this monograph, with the now faint slight depressions of canal channels and what currently appear to be relatively small intermittent drainages. This approach to the identification and dating of irrigation channels parallels that successfully used by Adams (1962) on the Susiana Plain.

The Origin of Water Management and Irrigation Technology on the Deh Luran Plain

Currently there appear to be two alternative possibilities as to the origin of water management and irrigation technology on the Deh Luran Plain. Evidence of cultural disjunction in his excavations at Chagha Sefid led Hole (1977:12) to argue that both the domestic plants and the irrigation technology needed to grow them were introduced to the Plain, perhaps by an actual migration of peoples from a nearby area in what is now eastern Iraq. In this area, the same complex of irrigated crops (Helbaek 1972) and actual traces of canals (Oates 1969) are attested earlier than they are known from the Deh Luran Plain.

Alternatively, it is possible that irrigation technology developed on the Plain itself. If so, the topography, hydrology, and soils found on the Plain (Kirkby 1977) lead us to envision the precursors of the earliest form of water management and irrigation as natural seasonal phenomena of water course overflow and floodplain inundation. The rich alluvial soils in locations inundated by the waters from seasonal natural sources (rainfall, snowmelt, etc.) would retain the moisture necessary to germinate and foster the growth of planted crops. Such events could, naturally, be both advantageous and detrimental to agricultural pursuits. On one hand they would provide the necessary moisture for crop growth and renew the nutrients in the soils or add new soils, while on the other hand they could wash out the planted crops or bury them with layers of alluvium.

Building upon such natural phenomena and conditions, it would seem a logical next step for the agriculturalists to envision their control of such water-supplying events through the excavation of small channels or ditches leading from water sources to their fields. The preceding scenario generally parallels the argument of Adams (1962, 1965: 40–1) for other nearby parts of the Middle East. Thus, whether irrigation technology was brought to the Deh Luran Plain or developed there *in situ*, this model fits the extant natural conditions present on the Plain and elsewhere in the Middle East and can serve as a guide to our research, generating implications to be tested in the field.

Regardless of its origin, when was this technology first utilized on the Deh Luran Plain? Based on his study of the macrobotanical remains from Tepe Sabz and elsewhere throughout the Middle East, Helbaek suggested that this manipulation of the water resources may have taken place perhaps some 800 years before the earliest cultural deposits exposed at Tepe Sabz.

> Accepting the estimated dates for the Anatolian, Mesopotamian, and Deh Luran settlements here discussed, it seems justifiable to suggest that controlled irrigation was initiated in many places about or not long after 6000 B.C. (Helbaek in Hole, Flannery, and Neely 1969: 424. N.B.: This radiocarbon date is not calibrated).

Hole's excavations at Chagha Sefid provided a more precise and restricted time span for the introduction of the hybridized plants and the knowledge of irrigation technology. The macrofloral materials recovered from deposits of the Chogha Mami Transitional phase of about 5400 to 5200 B.C. (^{14}C 4800 b.c. to 4600 b.c.; see Hole 1987: Tables 2–3; calibrated with CALIB 3.0, Stuiver and Pearson 1993) levels at Chagha Sefid indicate that these plants and the knowledge of this technology made their appearance on the Deh Luran Plain sometime prior to 5400 B.C.

With the above in mind, let us now turn to the data from our 1968–69 survey of the Deh Luran Plain to see what evidence was recovered concerning water management technology during the early phases of occupation. The relationships of the sites to the drainages we propose below may seem tenuous, but considering the data at hand, our interpretations seem to be warranted, at least as starting points for future work. It is indisputable that the occupants of these sites required a domestic water supply, as well as water for irrigation purposes, and the specific watercourse we have associated with certain sites would be the closest potential sources.

The Data from the 1968–69 Deh Luran Plain Survey

The data from the 1968–69 Deh Luran Plain survey will be presented below in the following manner.

Three primary water resources have been identified as very probably having been modified by water management and irrigation technology during the early phases of village life on the Deh Luran Plain. These are: the Ab-i Garm spring, the Mehmeh River, and the Dawairij River (see Appendix Map 1B). The following presentation of data will be organized to consider these water resources in the order just given. For each of the three water resources, specific drainages or canals that may pertain to the early phases will be described as they occur from north to south on the

Plain. With the discussion of each specific drainage or canal, the early phase sites that were found to be in close association will be considered in chronological order. Finally, in a concluding section, we will summarize and discuss the findings of the survey relevant to the development of water management and irrigation technology on the Deh Luran Plain.

In order to refine this analysis, and to reduce the element of chance co-occurrence, a drainage or canal will be considered as having been utilized during a specific phase of occupation only if two (2) or more sites with components dating to that same phase of occupation are found in close association. This requirement of at least two sites in association is also concordant with the assumption that some form of cooperative arrangement between small communities located along a drainage or canal was needed to construct and maintain even a small system (see Adams 1965: 40–1; Fernea 1959: 139–48, 1970: 157–62).

The minimum number of people implied by the sizes of the sites should at least be sufficient to plan, construct, and maintain an irrigation system of a certain size and length. Periods of evident non-use and rejuvenation seen in the following data are therefore considered to be directly related to a complex interplay of environmental conditions and the size and density of the population or labor force present and available. One exception may be when a previously existing natural drainage is used with only slight modification. In such a case, many of the requirements for the planning and construction, and to some degree the maintenance, of a more formal canal system may not be necessary because the drainage was already extant and the sites were apparently founded nearby to take advantage of an already existing situation.

In several instances (see the discussions pertaining to sites DL-34 and DL-292, below) we have not followed the requirement that at least two sites of a phase be in close association in order to ascribe a channel to that phase. In both cases noted above, the single site present is so large, as to, in our opinion, indicate the presence of a work force adequate to construct and maintain the associated irrigation system. In these cases we have taken the position that the irrigation system dates to the phase(s) of occupation indicated by the single associated site.

The channels that we have identified as canals dating to the early phases of occupation on the Deh Luran Plain vary in their depth (from about 0.01 to 0.50 meters), width (from about 0.6 to 2.0 meters), and general appearance. Some are relatively well defined channels; an easily discernible, broadly U-shaped, smooth-sided depression, with a low spoil bank to either of its sides and a nearly straight trajectory. Others are much more difficult to perceive; with some represented by little more than an alignment of somewhat denser or greener vegetation cover. In yet other instances, we were only able to discern the continuation of a specific canal, or identify the presence of a canal not recognizable on the ground, by carefully scanning aerial photographs. In some cases, we feel that the "natural" appearance of some of the channels identified as canals results from lack of use and maintenance for long periods of time. Some have subsequently become natural drainages or have been "captured" by nearby natural drainages and incorporated into the natural drainage system. Furthermore, we consider it probable that drainages or canals that were once in use for irrigation purposes and then abandoned were frequently brought back into use after relatively long periods of disuse.

Unlike most of the canals described in this chapter, one of the channels evidently associated with the sites of the early phases discussed in Chapter IV of this work is not clearly definable as a canal, *per se*. Upon first observation, this channel, the effluent of the Ab-i Garm (DL-276; see below and Appendix Map 1B) has the aspect of a natural drainage. It is larger than the hand-excavated channels (ranging up to about 2.5 meters in depth and 7.5 meters in width). Its channel courses in a relatively sinuous manner across the contours of the Plain, and it has an often irregular cross-section. In fact, this channel very probably was a natural drainage that was modified by the excavation of small offtake ditches to divert waters to habitation sites for domestic use and to fields for irrigation.

The Ab-i Garm Spring Resource

The Ab-i Garm spring drainage begins at the Ab-i Garm spring (DL-170) in the piedmont or alluvial slope zone of the north-central portion of the Plain, approximately four km northeast of the present community of Deh Luran (see Appendix Map 1B). In its course southwestward to Deh Luran this drainage is entrenched deeply into piedmont alluvial sediments and it is joined by many natural side channels. Just north of Deh Luran the stream floodplain broadens to form the head of a delta, and the drainage course bifurcates.

Drainage DL-276A: This feature, the longer of the two branches, courses westward as it passes to the north of Deh Luran. West of the community it again turns south-southwestward. Its course maintains a southwesterly direction for about 7.75 km, where it joins another drainage with a south-southeastward flow. In this course it cuts through the broad alluvial fan produced by this drainage over several millennia. The drainage then continues in a south-southeasterly direction for about 8.2 km where it flows into the Mehmeh River at a point about 2.5 km southeast of Tepe Farukhabad (DL-32).

There are seven (7) sites with early occupations in close proximity (i.e., 300 meters or closer) to the course of DL-276A, the northerly branch of this drainage. From north to south, these sites are: DL-169, 7, 23, 262, 31, 18, and 33.

Drainage DL-276B: This, the second, shorter, of the two branches of the Ab-i Garm, continues southwestward passing through Deh Luran. Beyond the modern town, it continues to DL-19, where it turns to the north and then west of the site. At this point, it is quite close to the northerly branch of the Ab-i Garm drainage, and at various times in the past the two could have joined here. The present drainage, however, takes a more southerly route passing just east of DL-24 and continuing southward to join a large drainage that passes just east of that site.

There are only two (2) sites associated with DL-276B, the southerly branch of the Ab-i Garm drainage. From north-to-south, these are: DL-19 and DL-24.

We propose that, at various times, all nine (9) of the sites mentioned above could have been related to a single water management and irrigation system. This proposition is based on the fact that all these sites are associated with two branches of the same water source, the Ab-i Garm spring, because they are in relatively close juxtaposition to one another on the rich soils of the Ab-i Garm alluvial delta, and because they comprise a reasonable complex of co-occurring settlements during several of the early phases dealt with in this volume.

As may be noted from the data in Chapters IV and V, these sites do not all have occupations that date to the same phases or periods. Considering this, we may envision the waters from this modified natural drainage to have been used by seven (7) "sets" of two or more sites occupied in sequence through time.

(1) The earliest minimal number of sites to co-occur, forming the first "set" on this system, were sites DL-23 and 31 on the west drainage (DL-276A), both occupied during the Sabz phase.

(2) Sites DL-23 and 31 were joined by sites DL-19 and 33 during the Khazineh phase. Both the west (DL-276A) and east (DL-276B) drainages would have been in use during this phase.

(3) Sites DL-23 and 31 on the west drainage continue their occupations during the Mehmeh and Bayat phases.

(4) Site DL-23 continues in the subsequent Farukh phase, and DL-262, also on the west branch, is occupied.

(5) Site DL-23 continues, and sites DL-169, 7, and 19 are founded, during the Early Uruk

phase. Both branches of the Ab-i Garm system are in use.

(6) Sites DL-19 and 23 continue to be occupied during the Middle and Late Uruk phases.

(7) The final use of the Ab-i Garm drainage as a domestic water source and for irrigation during the early phases of occupation on the Plain was apparently during the Jemdet Nasr and Early Dynastic I–II phases, when DL-18 and 24 were inhabited.

The major site of Farukhabad (DL-32) has a long occupation and is in relatively close proximity to canal DL-276A. Its relative size strongly suggests it was an important site on the Plain, one which could not have flourished without water management during the early phases of occupation on the Deh Luran Plain. Though DL-32 is located some 1.3 km from canal DL-276A and we were unable to discern any interconnecting canals, it seems possible that there was some relationship between this site and the canal system under discussion. The only other possibilities are canals DL-267 and/or part of DL-269, which offtake from the eastern bank of the Mehmeh about 7.0 and 5.5 km above Farukhabad, respectively. Their traces, however, have been obscured over much of their courses by the lateral erosion of the Mehmeh River. Assuming a connection to canal DL-276A, this would place DL-23 (Chagha Sefid) and DL-32 (Farukhabad) near each end of canal DL-276A as early as the Chogha Mami Transitional phase. DL-32 could then have been associated with the western drainage of this system almost continuously though the Early Dynastic III phase.

One further observation must be made relative to one of the sites discussed above, Sargarab (DL-169). The nature and location of this site leads us to believe that Sargarab was a defensive site that controlled the Ab-i Garm spring. Although it is currently located nearly one kilometer south of the spring (see Appendix Map 1B), it is conceivable that the spring was located closer to the site during the Early Uruk phase. It is possible that there has been headward erosion and a northward migration of the spring mouth.

The Mehmeh River Resource

There are at least four (4) different canals, occurring singly or in groups, that appear to branch off of the Mehmeh River and which have sites in close proximity that date to the early phases being considered. These will be discussed from north to south as they appear along the river (see Appendix Maps 1B and 1D).

<u>Canal DL-13 and DL-246</u>: On the east side of the river, a long, relatively straight channel that appears to be a constructed canal passes, from north to south, about 200 meters west of site DL-222, immediately east of site DL-14, west of site DL-241, and about 80 m east of site DL-15 (see Appendix Maps 1B, D). A short distance south of DL-15 this feature can no longer be seen on the ground or on the available aerial photographs. The source of this canal is undoubtedly the Mehmeh River, and its point of juncture with the river appears to be about 5.5 km north-northwest of DL-14 at a pronounced, easterly oriented cut-bank bend in the river.

As noted above, DL-14, 15, 222, and 241 are the four sites that appear to have been associated with this probable canal. These four sites form two (2) site sets.

(1) Sites DL-14, 15, 222, and 241 were occupied during the Khazineh phase, and form the first site set.

(2) Of the above sites, only DL-15, 222, and 241 appear to sustain their occupations into the Mehmeh phase to comprise the second set of sites.

It is also possible that site DL-29 (Tepe Ashrafabad) was associated with canal DL-13. Although it is a little over a kilometer east of that canal, it may have been linked to DL-13 by means of the canal (DL-246) that was found to pass immediately north of Tepe Ashrafabad (see Appendix Maps 1B, D). The relationship between canals DL-13 and 246 was not clear, and both were evidently used in more recent phases of occupation on the Plain. If Tepe Ashrafabad (DL-29) was associated with DL-13, this would mean that five associated sites were occupied during the Khazineh phase, and four were populated during the Mehmeh phase.

During the Bayat and Farukh phases, there is no evidence that canal DL-13 was in use, and it is possible that canal DL-246 was fed directly from the Mehmeh. Along this shorter canal, there are two possible later site sets.

(1) Two sites (DL-29 and 240) were occupied during the Bayat phase.

(2) Two sites (DL-15 and 29) were also occupied during the Farukh phase.

Canal DL-321: On the west side of the Mehmeh River, site DL-292 has a relatively large canal (DL-321) a short distance from and paralleling its eastern edge (see Appendix Maps 1B, D). A smaller canal branches from this larger canal and courses toward the southwest through the southern portion of the site (Figure IV.55). The large canal appears to have its offtake some 5.0 airline km to the north where a well-defined canal system is seen to diverge from a westerly-oriented meander of the Mehmeh River, and can be traced 2.0 km southwards, beyond DL-292. Parts of this canal may be stone-lined.

As noted in Chapters IV and V, the occupation of DL-292 has been dated to the Early Uruk phase by the ceramic assemblage found on its surface.

Site DL-292 has been included in this listing of sites in spite of the fact that it appears to have no known contemporaneous counterpart in association with canal DL-321. We wish to consider it a valid case for inclusion for two reasons. First, circumstances allowed us to carefully survey only about one quarter of the course of this canal, and it is possible that there were other Early Uruk sites along it. Second, because of its large size (ca. 8.4 ha) relative to the other four contemporaneous sites (ca. 3.52 ha total [DL-169: 0.66 ha; DL-23: 0.31 ha; DL-7: 0.24 ha; DL-19: 2.31 ha]) located on the east side of the Mehmeh River, its occupants could have excavated and maintained the associated canal system (DL-321) without depending on cooperation from the inhabitants of other sites.

Canal DL-320: On the west side of the river, sites DL-25, 26, 27, and 290 all seem to have been serviced by a canal system that is clearly visible on the ground surface and on aerial photos (see Appendix Maps 1B, D). This canal can be seen to branch off of the Mehmeh River some 3.5 airline km to the north-northwest of the above mentioned cluster of sites. This canal could easily have watered fields lying between its offtake and the sites, supplied water for domestic use by the inhabitants of these sites, and then sustained the fields lying south of the sites where it disappears from sight.

At least three (3) site sets are represented by these four sites in relation to one another.

(1) The earliest set is represented by the continued occupation of DL-25, as well as the founding of sites DL-26 and DL-27, in the Khazineh phase.

(2) The second set is formed by the continued occupation of sites DL-25, 26, and 27 in the Mehmeh phase.

(3) The third set sees the continued habitation of DL-27 and the founding of site DL-290 during the Bayat phase.

Canal DL-319: On the west side of the river, certainly associated with site DL-286 and probably associated with sites DL-25, 26, and 27, is another clearly visible canal. The offtake from the Mehmeh River is located less than 500 meters east-southeast of DL-27 (see Appendix Map 1B). This canal courses south-southwest and then changes its course toward the south-southeast. About 2.5 km from its offtake point, this canal is joined by another canal coursing southeast. This latter canal has a clearly visible origin from a seasonal wash marked on the map as the "Shakar Ab". There are two possible interpretations of the function of this latter canal. Either occasional storm flow in the Shakar Ab was captured and fed into the DL-319 system, or at certain times during the middle Holocene, before the Mehmeh became deeply entrenched in its present course, the Mehmeh itself flowed in what is now a dry wash. In any event, after the juncture of the two canals, they course together as one for about another 500 meters to site DL-286. It is not clear if the canal extends south of DL-286, but it is likely that it did. Site DL-286 is located about 2.0 airline km north-northwest of where the Shakar Ab joins with the Mehmeh River.

The surface assemblages of ceramics collected from sites 25, 26, 27, and 286 indicate that these four sites form four (4) "sets" of sites occupied during the same phases.

(1) DL-25 and 286 comprise the first set of sites, having occupations from the Chogha Mami Transitional phase through the Sabz phase.

(2) Sites DL-25, 27, and 286, with occupations during the subsequent Khazineh phase, form the second site set.

(3) The Mehmeh phase components of occupation were found at Sites DL-25, 26 and 27. These sites are close to the presumed offtake, and the canal may have been maintained for only a portion of its length.

(4) The final set of sites is composed of Sites DL-27 and 286, occupied during the Farukh phase.

The Dawairij River Resource

There are two (2) different canals and one (1) qanat and canal branching off of the Dawairij River which have sites dated to the early phases of occupation in close proximity. These will be discussed from north to south as they appear along the river.

Qanat and Canal DL-121: On the west side of the Dawairij River, there are remnants of several *qanat* systems—tunnels excavated and maintained from a line of wells (discussed below)—that branch off of the cut-bank side of a large westerly-oriented meander of the river located near the juncture of the alluvial slope with the older alluvial plain (see Figure 1.2 and Appendix Map 1B). Two of these qanat systems course southwestward for nearly 2 km where they break to the ground-surface as two canals and continue in a southwesterly direction to pass Tepe Garan (DL-34), one to the north and one to the south. About 2.0 km west of DL-34, these two canals join to form a single canal that continues southwestward. This canal continues for about another 2.0 km, where it again divides into two clearly visible canal channels. These two channels are easily traceable, lying about 250 meters apart and generally paralleling one another, for about another 2.5 km, where our aerial photo coverage of this portion of the Deh Luran Plain ends.

The early occupation of DL-34 (approximately 1.5 ha in area) that may be associated with this qanat and canal system has been assigned to the Early Dynastic I–III phases.

As in the case of site DL-292 and canal DL-321 noted above, we have included site DL-121 in this listing of canals in spite of the fact that there are no sites contemporaneous with DL-34 adjacent to canal DL-121. Although the case for inclusion is not as strong as that of canal DL-321, we wish to consider it a case because it has several neighbors on an adjacent canal system (DL-115), and is part of a relatively large Early Dynastic settlement nexus located in the central portion of the Deh Luran Plain. Though it is relatively small, we suggest that the occupants of DL-34 depended on cooperation with the inhabitants of the other contemporary sites in the general vicinity to excavate and maintain the associated canal system (DL-121).

The fact that this water management system (DL-121) has its offtake in the form of a qanat rather than a canal raises interesting issues. If DL-34 is not associated with this system, then either its conventional canal source has been completely obliterated or it had no domestic water source. If the association of DL-34 with this qanat and canal system during the Early Dynastic I–III phases (ca. 3000 to 2350 B.C.) is correct, this is the earliest use of qanat technology on the Deh Luran Plain, and perhaps the earliest evidences of qanat technology yet found in the Middle East. Clarification of this issue will be a priority for future regional research in the Deh Luran area.

Canals DL-115 and 114: On the west side of the river, canal DL-115 begins immediately south of qanat and canal system DL-121 described above (see Appendix Map 1B). It generally parallels

DL-121, and an intervening later alignment of qanat well shafts, DL-122, and passes around the next large meander of the river to the south. It is possible that the original offtake of DL-115 was from this lower meander, but as the Dawairij cut its bed down, the offtake had to be moved upstream. Just after it passes around the river meander, the canal branches, sending another channel (DL-114) toward the south.

Canal DL-115, however, continues its course southwestward, passing north of Tepe Musiyan (DL-20). Just before Musiyan, a small branch passes southward, between sites DL-61 and 62, probably providing water to Musiyan itself. The westernmost branch of canal DL-115A courses west-southwestward to pass just south of Tepe Ali Kosh (DL-21), continuing until our aerial photo coverage ends. Soon after passing Tepe Musiyan, DL-115A branches again, sending another channel (DL-115B) southwestward past DL-71 and to eventually pass just east of site DL-104, more than 10 km south of the southernmost possible offtake. Linear marks beyond DL-104 were not surveyed, and may be traces of roads rather than canals.

As noted above, canal DL-114 begins some 2.5 km southwest of the offtake of DL-115 at the Dawairij River. Due to the eroded nature of the cutbank it was not possible to determine for certain, but it appears that DL-114 may also have had its own offtake near its branching from DL-115A at the cut-bank side of the next major westerly-oriented meander in the river. Most of the system of canals termed DL-114 is associated with later settlements.

Only one early settlement, Tepe Khazineh (DL-28) may have been watered by a branch of DL-114. As with other isolated small sites, we cannot make a strong argument regarding its water source.

The main part of this canal system (DL-115) appears to be associated with six (6) sites of the phases of occupation covered in this study. These sites are: DL-20, 21, 61, 62, 71, and 104. These sites may be grouped into eight (8) sets of sites representing occupations beginning in the Chogha Mami Transitional phase, after a possible hiatus in the Sabz phase, continuing through the Farukh phase. There is another possible hiatus during the Suse phase, and then further occupation from the Early Uruk phase through the Early Dynastic III phase. Although this study terminates with the Early Dynastic III phase, these canals continued to be used throughout later times. Parts of this system are still in use. It is thus, the longest-lived canal system on the Deh Luran Plain. The site sets we have identified are:

(1) Sites DL-20 and 21 are the first sites for which we can propose an association with canal system DL-115. Ceramics collected from the surfaces of these sites indicate that they had occupations during the Chogha Mami Transitional phase.

(2) Sites DL-20, 21, and 71 were occupied during the Khazineh and Mehmeh phases, indicating that canal DL-115B was in use.

(3) Occupations at sites DL-20 and 71 indicate continued use during the Bayat and Farukh phases. Since Musiyan was the largest center on the plain during the Suse phase, partial maintenance must have continued, but we have no evidence.

(4) Though Musiyan was abandoned during the Early Uruk phase, there was occupation at sites DL-61 and 71, so canal DL-115B was probably in use.

(5) The occupations at sites DL-61 and 71 are joined by that at DL-104 during the Middle Uruk phase indicating the lengthening of canal DL-115B.

(6) DL-61, 62, and 104 represent the Late Uruk phase.

(7) Sites DL-20, 61, 62, 71, and 104 were all found to have ceramics made during the Early Dynastic I–II phases. However, because these phases may be represented only by intrusive burials at sites DL-61, and 71 (see Figure V.12); it seems more probable that sites DL-20, 62, and 104 should comprise this set of sites.

(8) The final site set associated with canal DL-115B is that of the Early Dynastic III phase, comprised of two sites, DL-20 and 104.

Canals DL-116 and Canal and Qanats DL-317: To the east of the Dawairij River, there are two groupings of canals, perhaps forming a single system, correctly located to supply water to the sites in this area of the Deh Luran Plain dating to the phases considered by this study.

The rather segmented evidence of the northernmost grouping of canals is located in a unusual place in relation to the river; they are mostly seen to be in the area of the fill-bank of a westerly-oriented meander (see Appendix Map 1B). These canal segments, designated as a group as canal system DL-116 by our survey, are very difficult to interpret. Their points of origin and their continuations toward the southeast are unclear. Their segmentation and lack of clarity are due to apparent shifts in the course of the river as well as heavy alluviation. It seems reasonable to assume that the river has shifted its course enough in this location to erase the significant portions of the canals that would indicate that their offtakes were, in fact, in the cut-bank of the next easterly-oriented meander to the north. It is possible that these traces represent canal offtakes for the DL-317 system at one point in its history.

The southernmost group of water management features, designated as DL-317, has least one canal and two qanat offtakes from the cut-bank of a moderate-sized easterly-oriented meander of the river. This meander is located immediately south of the fill-bank having most of the canal segments (DL-116) discussed above.

The canal of DL-317 is clearly visible for about 1.5 km, and then can no longer be seen on the ground or the aerial photos. However, if one extends this canal southeastwardly for a distance of about 1.0 kilometer it would join with a canal that is clearly visible. About 500 meters south of the offtake of the canal just described is the offtake of the first of the two qanats in this group of features.

The offtake of the second qanat is about 300 meters south of that of the first qanat. These two qanats merge at a point about 750 meters from the river. They then disappear from view on the aerial photos. At a distance of about 1.0 kilometer southeast of where the qanat is no longer visible, one can again see an alignment of qanat well holes.

These well holes continue south-southeast for approximately 500 meters, before they disappear from view again. A canal is visible on the aerial photos in alignment with and about 250 meters from where the qanat well holes terminate. While the interrupted channels of the canal and the two qanats all appear to lead to the canals designated as DL-317A and 317C, it was not possible to determine the sequence and chronology of their use. However, assuming that the Dawairij was cutting downward and upward into its alluvial fan (Kirkby 1977), we can propose that the earliest canal offtake was the one farthest downstream, perhaps where segment DL-317A approaches a bend on the river northeast of site DL-59 (see Appendix Map 1B). The next offtake would be that of canal DL-317, and the latest actual canal offtakes may have been those of the segment grouped under the designation DL-116. When the Dawairij cut too deeply to extend offtakes upstream, canal builders were forced to construct qanats to replace the canal offtakes. Fortunately, these could be placed much farther downstream near the former canal DL-317 offtake. This proposed sequence can only be evaluated and precisely dated with further field studies.

The canal to the southeast of the various canal and qanat offtakes bifurcates almost immediately. Based on the dating of the sites in association, it appears that the more southerly branch, designated as DL-317A was the original canal. It courses southward for about 2.2 km and then trends southeastwards for another 1.5 km, where it bifurcates into canals DL-317A and 317B. DL-317A continues toward the southeast, passing about 400 meters north of site DL-84 and 700 meters north of site DL-85, to disappear from view on the ground and from the aerial photos. DL-317B takes a more south-southeasterly route for about 1.1 km where it bifurcates again. The more northerly of the two channels, which we have designated as DL-94, passes approximately 100 meters south of site DL-85 and some 600 meters south of site DL-84. It too courses to the southeast where it eventually is lost from view. We have continued to use the designation DL-317B for the more southerly branch of the bifurcation. DL-317B is difficult to see on the ground and on the aerial photos, but there is enough evidence visible to consider its presence as probable. It passes between, and less than 100 meters from, sites DL-89 and 90, then proceeds southeasterly, to pass less than 100 meters north of site DL-91, and eventually is completely lost from view, more than 8.0 km from its likely offtake.

The more northerly of the canals resulting from the bifurcation of canal DL-317 noted at the beginning of the previous paragraph, has been labeled DL-317C. This part of the system must take its water from the more northerly canal or qanat offtakes of DL-317 or DL-116. This canal can be seen to flow toward the southeast to pass about 400 meters south of site DL-54, approximately 400 meters north of site DL-43, and only 250 meters north of site DL-41. It may be seen to extend further toward the southeast, and then disappear from view. Near the end of its visible course, a ditch branches off to the south toward the small recently occupied village of Patak Paín. Canal DL-317D is seen to branch south-southeasterly from canal DL-317C a short distance east of site DL-43. It passes around the southwest corner of site DL-41, perhaps just outside its western wall, and continues for about another 1.0 km, before disappearing from view about 12 km from its likely offtake.

There is one more branching of canal DL-317C visible. This branch occurs about 900 meters southeast of the point where DL-317C branches from DL-317A. This branch has been designated as canal DL-83. It courses in an east-southeasterly direction and can be seen to pass about 350 meters south of DL-54, approximately 900 meters north of DL-43, about 1.1 km north of DL-41, and continues. It would appear that this canal is relatively late and was built to service nearby later sites in the vicinity.

The DL-317 canal system just described evidently serviced the area of sites DL-41, 43, 54, 84, 85, and 91. These six (6) sites may be grouped into five (5) sets of sites that were occupied in sequence through time as follows:

(1) Sites DL-84 and 85 were first occupied during the Chogha Mami Transitional phase, thus these two sites comprise the first set. These could have been watered by the earliest phases of canals DL-317A and 317B.

(2) After a hiatus during the Sabz phase, sites DL-84 and 85 were reoccupied during the Khazineh phase.

(3) In the subsequent Mehmeh phase, the set is comprised of sites DL-43 and 85. The same two canals would have watered these sites.

(4) The fourth set of sites in this grouping consists of DL-43 and DL-91, both of which were occupied during the Bayat phase. These could also have been watered by canals DL-317A and 317B.

(5) The final site set pertains to the Early Dynastic I–III phases, and is represented by sites DL-41 and 54, when canals DL-317C and 317D must have been in use.

The above narrative descriptions of the canal systems and associated sites has been summarized and put into a format more easily used for comparative studies in tables in the following section.

Summary and Discussion

In reviewing the preceding data we can make a number of observations. However, it must be remembered that these data are derived from survey coverage and must be considered as relatively incomplete. One further warning must be made relative to the data at hand. The channels recognized herein as canals are the end-product of several phases of construction and/or modification, and most certainly have been affected by the hand of man and the elements since they ceased functioning. The following observations, must be tested through additional intensive, problem-oriented, survey and excavation when the situation permits.

As noted above, three perennial water sources (the Ab-i Garm spring, the Mehmeh River, and the Dawairij River) were probably modified with various water management technologies to supply the domestic and irrigation needs of the Deh Luran Plain's occupants during the early phases covered in this volume. Although the use of irrigation technology has been determined, it is also known that irrigated agriculture was augmented by dry-farmed agriculture, the herding of domesticated animals, as well as by hunting, fishing, and the gathering of wild plant resources. These six interrelated strategies of subsistence acquisition have been verified by excavated macrofloral and macrofaunal evidence representing the Plain's earliest phases of settled life and later (see Hole 1977; Hole, Flannery, and Neely 1969; Miller and Redding in Wright 1981).

The non-irrigated, dry-farming agricultural strategy very probably was carried out in various locations on the Plain by using several different water management techniques. Seasonally cropped fields located in natural drainages would have been very likely. The drainage channels could easily have been modified to improve crop production through the use of channel bottom weir terraces (Doolittle 1988: 48–50), diversion dams/weirs, and check dams (Neely 1974b: Fig. 3.3, 28–30; In Press). Linear contour borders and terraces (Neely 1974b: 28–30; In press) located on the channel banks and the alluvial slopes at the northern extreme of the Plain could also have been used to expand the area of cultivable land. Unfortunately these features are often washed away or covered by alluvium when they are no longer used and maintained. The difficulty in finding water management features is frequently only surpassed by the difficulty one has in assigning dates to their origin and use. Such features recorded by our survey, for which dates of use could be assigned, were found to belong to periods subsequent to the early phases of occupation on the Plain. In spite of this, the likely use of these and similar features should be kept in mind during further investigations of broad-spectrum subsistence strategies. The discovery of such features that could be securely dated to the Chogha Mami Transitional phase or earlier would provide invaluable information regarding the origins of water management technology on the Plain. Such features dated to subsequent early phases of occupation would flesh out the details of the development of the technology.

We were not able to identify offtakes and canals branching from the natural drainage channel of the Ab-i Garm spring. Such features may have been severely affected by erosional and alluviational processes, but it is possible that the inhabitants of the nearby sites took water for domestic uses by dipping it directly from this channel and that irrigation waters were diverted into fields adjacent to the drainage in a flooding process by constructing simple weirs of stone and/or vegetation. Should this have been the case, the Ab-i Garm channel may represent the earliest form of irrigation technology on the Plain. In contrast to the natural appearance of the Ab-i Garm channel, the canals branching from the Mehmeh and Dawairij Rivers all have a more formalized, prepared aspect, indicating that they were purposefully excavated channels.

Information gathered from the intensive survey, and excavations at three of the sites, on the Deh Luran Plain indicates that irrigation technology was introduced to the occupants of the Plain during the Chogha Mami Transitional phase (ca. 5400 to 5200 B.C.). It is evident that this technology was rapidly disseminated and adopted throughout the Plain. This is clearly attested to by two observations. First, the apparent association of all nine of the sites identified as having a Chogha Mami Transitional phase component (see Tables V.1, VI.1, VI.2) with a drainage or a canal. Second, the wide-spread distribution of these sites and their associated water management features across the Plain, to utilize all three of the Plain's perennial water sources, within a relative short period of time.

Once irrigation technology had been introduced and accepted on the Deh Luran Plain, it evidently attained a major role as part of the general subsistence technology throughout the subsequent phases of occupation. Of the forty-one (41) Deh Luran Plain sites recorded as having at least one well-dated component of the early phases of occupation considered in this volume, thirty-seven (37), or 90%, of the sites can be identified as probably being associated with water management features. Table VI.1, below, illustrates that during the thirteen (13) phases represented by sites discussed herein, seven phases (54%) had all representative sites associated with such features; while in each of four phases (31%), only one site was not found associated with these features; and in each of two phases (15%), two sites were not found associated with water management technology.

Table VI.1: Sites and Water Sources of the Early Phases

This Table presents a summary of specific information gleaned from the forty-one (41) well-dated archaeological sites discussed in Chapters IV and V. The Table presents: the total estimated site area for all sites, the mean site area (calculated only on those sites for which an area estimate has been made), the total number of sites, and the total number of sites associated with water sources, for each of the early phases dealt with in this manuscript. The plus (+) indicates that sites were present for which we were unable to provide an area estimate.

Phase	Total Site Area (ha)	Average Site Area (ha)	Number of Sites	Number of Sites Associated with Water Sources
CMT	2.13+	0.43	9	9
Sabz	1.88+	0.47	6	6
Khazineh	13.10+	0.60	23	21
Mehmeh	13.14+	0.77	18	17
Bayat	11.82+	1.08	12	11
Farukh	16.50+	1.65	12	10
Suse	7.11	2.37	3	2
Early Uruk	16.90	1.54	11	10
Middle Uruk	9.39	1.34	7	7
Late Uruk	6.82+	1.14	8	8
Jemdet Nasr	5.09+	2.55	4	4
Early Dynastic I–II	32.20+	3.58	10	10
Early Dynastic III	46.90+	6.70	7	7

What of the four sites (DL-11, 22, 247, and 248) that were not associated with a particular water management feature? Some of them may have been dry-farming or herding sites. Due to the locations of sites DL-11, 247, and 248 (see Appendix Maps 1B, D), it is entirely feasible that ditches that are no longer visible once branched from canal DL-13 to service these sites. Site DL-22, however, is most likely to have been a dry-farming or herding site because we found no evidence of contemporaneous canals or other water management features anywhere in its vicinity. Obviously, the reason for the apparent lack of association of these sites with canals begs attention during any future fieldwork on the Deh Luran Plain.

Setting these four sites aside, thirty three (33) sites were found in association with eight (8) water channels—interpreted as one drainage and seven canals—that evidently transported water for domestic and irrigation purposes. The Ab-i Garm drainage, which arguably served as a type of canal, was about 27.5 km in length and had nine (9) associated sites. Table VI-2 presents the data by period for the twenty four (24) sites closely associated with the seven possible formal canals. Of the seven possible canal systems within the purview of this study, the minimum length of the shortest (DL-286) was approximately 2.4 km, while the minimum length of the longest branch (DL-317D) was about 12.0 km long. The total length of later visible traces of the longest single system (DL-317) was more than 37 km. The total length of all of the channels discussed above was approximately 114 km, while the mean total length of a canal system was about 12.7 km. Because of the sustained use, and probable modification, of these canals over several occupational phases, it was difficult to discern differences in actual canal length during each of the periods of use. We have attempted to estimate the minimum length of some of the better-defined canals in Table VI.2. Certainly, it is the case that, because of the distance of some of the associated habitation sites from the primary water resource (i.e., the Mehmeh and Dawairij Rivers), the lengths of the canals excavated during the earliest phases (i.e., the Chogha Mami Transitional, Sabz, and Khazineh phases) were substantial.

Table VI.2: Proposed Formal Canals on the Deh Luran Plain

The distribution, by phase, of the identified formal canals and the dated components of the twenty four (24) sites found in association with these water management systems is presented in this table. These data are accompanied by estimates of the area of occupation of each site for each of the phases as well as the total and mean occupation area for each phase based on the estimates presented in Chapters IV and V. We have also included the minimum length of each of these formal canals for each of its phases of use, as indicated by site locations and traces on aerial photos. It should be pointed out that we have included sites DL-29, 34, and 292 (see our comments, above, on the relevance of these sites) in this and in the subsequent tables.

(A) Chogha Mami Transitional phase:

Canal DL-319 : DL-25 (0.05 ha), 286 (1.00 ha).

Two (2) components, totaling 1.05 ha (mean = 0.53 ha), Minimal Length: **4.3 km.**

Canal DL-115A: DL-20 (no area estimate), 21 (0.40 ha).

Two (2) components, totaling over 0.40 ha, Minimal Length: **6.0 km.**

Canal DL-317A, B: DL-84 (0.26 ha), 85 (no area estimate).

Two (2) components, totaling over 0.26 ha, Minimal Length: **5.0 km.**

(B) Sabz phase:

Canal DL-319 : DL-25 (0.05 ha), 286 (1.00 ha).

Two (2) components, totaling 1.05 ha (mean = 0.53 ha), Minimal Length: **4.3 km.**

(C) Khazineh phase:

Canal DL-13: DL-14 (1.15 ha), DL-15 (0.25 ha), DL-29 (0.54 ha), DL-222 (0.50 ha), DL-241 (0.11 ha).

Five (5) components, with a total area of 2.55 ha (mean = 0.51 ha), Minimal Length: **7.4 km.**

Canal DL-320: DL-25 (0.05 ha), DL-26 (0.05 ha), DL-27 (0.50 ha).

Three (3) components, with a total of 0.60 ha (mean = 0.20 ha), Minimal Length: **4.6 km.**

Canal DL-319 : DL-25 (0.05 ha), DL-26 (0.05 ha), 27 (0.50 ha), DL-286 (1.00 ha).

Four (4) components, totaling 1.60 ha (mean = 0.40 ha), Minimal Length: **4.5 km.**

Canal DL-115: DL-20 (2.00 ha), DL-21 (0.15 ha), DL-71 (0.30 ha).

Three (3) components, totaling 2.45 ha (mean = 0.81 ha), Minimal Length: **6.5 km.**

Canal DL-317A, B: DL-84 (0.26 ha), 85 (1.44 ha).

Two (2) components, totaling 1.70 ha. (mean = 0.85 ha), Minimal Length: **5.0 km.**

(D) Mehmeh phase:

Canal DL-13: DL-15 (0.67 ha), DL-29 (1.27 ha), DL-222 (0.50 ha), DL-241(0.11 ha).
Four (4) components, with a total area of 2.55 ha, (mean = 0.64 ha). Minimal Length: **7.4 km**.

Canal DL-320: DL-25 (0.05 ha), DL-26 (0.05 ha), DL-27 (0.50 ha).
Three (3) components, with a total of 0.60 ha (mean = 0.20 ha), Minimal Length: **4.6 km**.

Canal DL-319: DL-26 (0.05 ha), DL-27 (0.50 ha).
Two (2) components, totaling 0.55 ha (mean = 0.28 ha), Minimal Length: uncertain.

Canal DL-115A, B: DL-20 (4.00 ha), DL-21 (0.15 ha), DL-71 (0.30 ha).
Three (3) components, totaling 4.45 ha (mean = 1.48 ha), Minimal Length: **6.5 km**.

Canal DL-317A, B: DL-43 (0.26 ha), DL-85 (1.34 ha).
Two (2) components, totaling 1.60 ha. (mean = 0.80 ha), Minimal Length: **5.0 km**.

(E) Bayat phase:

Canal DL-246 DL-29 (1.29 ha), DL-240 (0.05 ha).
Two (2) components, with a total area of 1.34 ha, (mean = 0.67 ha), Minimal Length: **2.4 km**.

Canal DL-320: DL-27 (1.0 ha), DL-290 (0.44 ha).
Two (2) components, with a total of 1.44 ha (mean = 0.72 ha), Minimal Length: **5.0 km**.

Canal DL-115B: DL-20 (4.00 ha), DL-71 (no area estimate),
Two (2) components, totaling over 4.00 ha, Minimal Length: **6.5 km**.

Canal DL-317A, B: DL-43 (0.26 ha), DL-91 (0.14 ha).
Two (2) components, totaling 0.40 ha (mean = 0.20 ha), Minimal Length: **5.0 km**.

(F) Farukh phase:

Canal DL-246 DL-15 (0.67 ha), DL-29 (0.40 ha).
Two (2) components, with a total area of 1.07 ha, (mean = 0.54 ha), Minimal Length: **2.4 km**.

Canal DL-319: DL-27 (1.00 ha), DL-286 (0.40 ha).
Two (2) components, totaling 1.4 ha (mean = 0.70 ha), Minimal Length: **4.5 km**.

Canal DL-115B: DL-20 (9.00 ha), DL-71 (no estimate of area).
Two (2) components, totaling over 9.00 ha, Minimal Length: **6.5 km**.

(G) Suse phase:

Canal DL-115: DL-20 (9.00 ha),
One (1) component, totaling over 9.00 ha, Minimal Length: **uncertain.**

(H) Early Uruk phase:

Canal DL-321: DL-292 (8.4 ha).
Minimal Length: **8.5 km**.

Canal DL-115B: DL-61 (0.68 ha), DL-71 (0.50).
Two (2) components, totaling 1.18 ha (mean = 0.59 ha), Minimal Length: **6.5 km**.

(I) Middle Uruk phase:

Canal DL-115B: DL-61 (0.68 ha), DL-71 (0.50 ha), DL-104 (0.95 ha).
Three (3) components, totaling 2.13 ha (mean = 0.71 ha), Minimal Length: **10.2 km**.

(J) Late Uruk phase:

Canal DL-115B: DL-61 (0.68 ha), DL-62 (0.42 ha), DL-104 (0.63 ha).

Three (3) components, totaling 1.73 ha (mean = 0.58 ha), Minimal Length: **10.2 km**.

(L) Early Dynastic I–II phases:

Qanat and Canal DL-121 : DL-34 (1.5 ha).

Minimal Length: **6.5 km**.

Canal DL-115B: DL-20 (15.00 ha), DL-62 (0.42 ha), DL-104 (2.00 ha).

Three (3) components, totaling 17.42 ha (mean = 5.81 ha), Minimal Length: **10.2 km**.

Canal DL-317C, D: DL-41 (no area estimate), DL-54 (1.00 ha).

Two (2) components, totaling over 1.00 ha, Minimal Length: **12.0 km**.

(M) Early Dynastic III phase:

Qanat and Canal DL-121: DL-34 (1.5 ha).

Minimal Length: **6.5 km**.

Canal DL-115B: DL-20 (15.00 ha), DL-104 (2.00 ha).

Two (2) components, totaling 17.00 ha (mean = 8.50 ha), Minimal Length: **10.2 km**.

Canal DL-317C, D: DL-41 (20.00 ha), DL-54 (3.22 ha).

Two (2) components, totaling 23.22 ha (mean = 11.61 ha), Minimal Length: **12.0 km**.

Examination of this table shows that for the earliest Chogha Mami Transitional phase, the minimal length of measurable canal is rather short, ranging from 4.3 to 6.0 km. Because the few Sabz phase sites are isolated, little can be said about the scale of canals during this phase. However, in the succeeding Khazineh and Mehmeh phases, somewhat longer canals were dug, and the minimal length of measurable canal ranges from 4.5 to 7.4 km. During the Bayat and Farukh phases, the minimal length of measurable canal ranges from 2.4 to 6.5 km. No Suse phase canal is measurable.

To obtain some appreciation of the time and labor that was invested in the construction of the canals attributable to the early phases of occupation on the Plain, and because figures on the amount of earth that can be excavated under primitive conditions are difficult to obtain, we have turned to labor estimates derived from the American Southwest. Interviews conducted early in this century with elderly Pima Indians in Arizona (Southworth 1931) indicate that, in the sand and gravel of the Salt River Valley, a canal builder could move approximately 1.6 cubic meters of canal fill a day. It must be noted that these data relate to situation in which the excavation of irrigation canals was still conducted by hand labor with a minimum use of metal tools or other modern equipment. Taking canal DL-320 as an example, we find the following. This canal, which was one of the shortest of the Deh Luran canals recorded in the time frame being considered in this monograph, was traced for a distance of 4.3 km (4,300 m) and was approximately 1.5 meters in width. Assuming a constant depth of 1.5 meters, a parabolic cross-section for the canal, and a similar soil to that of the Salt River Valley in Arizona, this canal would have required the expenditure of about 4,030 person-days of labor. Using this figure, a labor force of 100 workers could have excavated this canal in about 40 days. Of course we recognize several problems: the 1.5 meter canal depth is an estimate, the parabolic cross-section is an assumption, the canal depth would not have been constant for its entire length, and the Deh Luran alluvium is not identical to that of the Salt River Valley in Arizona. Conceding all of these problems involved with the calculations presented above, one can still obtain a general idea of the amount of labor and time it would take to excavate these features. In reality, although it was a significant effort, it was not as awesome a task as one might initially think, especially if it was spread over several years as the local population prospered and grew.

In the Early Uruk phase, newly constructed canal DL-321, providing water to the one larger town on the plain, DL-292, was at least 8.5 km long. In Middle and Late Uruk times, canal DL-115B feeding the Musiyan area on the central plain was lengthened to 10.2 km. Nothing is known about Jemdet Nasr water control features. In Early Dynastic times, a new canal (DL-317D) was opened east of the Dawairij, watering the south-eastern plain. This reaches at least 12.0 km in length, bringing water to the large newly-established town of DL-41. Fernea (1959, 1970) reports that in nearby Iraq during the early 20th century, traditional canals greater than 10 km in length were beyond the scale easily maintained under the aegis of kin group leaders. It seems likely that centralized management was required to maintain the larger canals on the Plain during the Early Dynastic phases, if not before. The minimal length of measurable canals during the Early Dynastic phases ranges from 6.5 to 12.0 km.

We can obtain an appreciation of the time and labor that was invested in the construction of the IIIrd millennium canals by making calculation similar to that made for the smaller, earlier canals. A canal of 12.0 km in length would have required approximately 11,250 person/days simply to move the dirt, assuming rates of work similar to those reported by Pima canal builders. Using this figure, a labor force of 100 workers could have excavated this canal in about 112 days. As discussed in the next section, however, the large towns of the IIIrd millennium were capable of fielding far more than 100 workers for such projects.

In comparing the early canal systems branching from the Mehmeh River with those taking waters from the Dawairij River, it is notable that the former are characterized by a relatively large number of short canal systems whereas the latter have but a few systems of greater length. The reasons for this variation are not certain. It could be a result of geographical conditions such as the distribution of available arable land or relatively greater amounts of downcutting of the Mehmeh River channel. It could also result from variation in the socio-political and economic organization of the two sides of the Plain, with the northwestern part of the plain being characterized by a series of more autonomous communities and the center and south-eastern parts characterized by a higher degree of political and economic integration. These are issues for future study.

It is interesting to consider the apparent lack of use of the perennial water sources on the Plain during particular cultural phases. The Ab-i Garm drainage apparently lacks Suse phase occupation. Also, we could identify neither a Suse phase occupation, nor any occupation after the Early Uruk phase, associated with the canals of the Mehmeh River source. However, as noted above, it is possible that DL-247, which has a Suse phase component, may have been associated with a now-obscured canal from the Mehmeh River, and Farukhabad (DL-32) which has Uruk and later components, may have taken its water from the Mehmeh. For the Dawairij River water source, the relatively large Suse phase occupations we have recognized at Tepe Musiyan (DL-20) and at DL-85 certainly required water sources. Similarly for the Jemdet Nasr phase, it is interesting to note that no site is definitely associated with a formal canal. We must consider the possibility that water control systems were not maintained after the end of the Late Uruk phase. In cases of phases with relatively few components, however, it is possible that the assumption requiring at least two sites of a phase on a canal in order to date it to that phase prevents recognition of actual associations.

The issue of the use of *qanats* merits discussion. We have argued above for the association and contemporaneity of qanat and canal system DL-121 with the Early Dynastic I–II and III occupations of site DL-34. There are also associations between the canal DL-115 and qanat DL-122 and between the qanat and canal segments of DL-317, but there are sites of so many phases associated with these systems, that we cannot date the use of qanats in them.

It is notable that the particular use of qanat technology in DL-121 is unlike later traditional qanat systems. In this possible IIIrd millennium example, the tunnel appears to have taken water directly from the Dawairij River, rather than from a subterranean aquifer (Cressy 1958, 1960: 149–55; English 1968; Sajjadi 1982). Perhaps the most logical possible explanation of this apparently precocious use of labor-intensive tunnels is that such tunnels would serve to offset the effects of the downcutting of the river channels on the plain, and the corresponding drop in the water table. Kirkby (1977) dates this downcutting in part to the to the IIIrd millennium, correlating with this first possible use of qanat technology. However, testing the implications of this hypothesis will require more geomorphological field studies.

As will be discussed in subsequent volumes, later qanats in the Deh Luran Plain usually do not have evidence of a direct connection with a river. Rather they begin close to a river and run generally parallel to it before changing their courses toward habitation sites and fields. It seems likely that such qanat systems obtained water from the nearby river that was filtered through deep alluvium. It is possible that, at the same time, other underground aquifers were simultaneously tapped by such systems. Such filtration could have had been helpful in alleviating two common problems in canal systems. (1) One of the greatest threats to the effective functioning of any canal system is the accumulation of silt in the canal offtake, especially during floods (Adams 1962, 1965). The use of a qanat would reduce the amount of silt in the water and reduce the amount of maintenance needed. (2) Another problem evidently faced by Deh Luran farmers was salt accumulation in irrigated fields (Helbaek in Hole Flannery and Neely 1969: 422; Woosley and Hole 1978: 66). Both the Mehmeh and the Dawairij rivers carry relatively large amounts of mineral salts, in both solution and suspension. The percolation of river waters through meters of alluvium before they reached the qanat tunnel would certainly filter out suspended grains of gypsum (calcium sulphate) and similar suspended material. It might even provide an opportunity for dissolved salts to be deposited as caliche layers through evaporation at the top of the aqueous zone, thus reducing the amount of dissolved salts. Such hypothetical effects, which may be fortuitous rather than intended consequences, merit investigation by hydrologists.

It is obvious from the preceding that much more investigation of Deh Luran water management systems is warranted if we are to not only understand how such systems operated and why they were constructed as they were, but also to help those who might plan such systems in the future.

Changing Population Patterns during the Early Phases of Occupation on the Deh Luran Plain

[with contributions by Robert E. Dewar]

In the recent settlements studied in the Near East (Kramer 1980) and elsewhere (Naroll 1962) population seems closely correlated with room and feature density, site size, and other variables. However, the estimation of past population sizes using settlement pattern evidence is not straightforward. Even when one has confidence that most archaeological sites have been adequately located and dated, population estimates such as those proposed in Chapter V—using architectural densities, site sizes, and site numbers—provide maximal limits at best. A major problem is that within the time span during which a cultural phase existed, settlements were founded, grew, declined, and were abandoned or moved to other locations. How can we estimate the number of settlements, and therefore the number of people, existing at one point in time? The problem has been noted by a number of archaeologists (Ammerman 1981, Tolstoy 1975, Weiss 1977), but even in those rare cases where individual rooms could be dated to the year (Dean 1969) estimation was difficult. Gradually, however, ways of extracting settlement parameters from archaeological data and modeling settlement life histories to derive simultaneous estimates of site population have been developed (Dewar 1991, Plog 1973, Plog and Hantman 1990, Schacht 1984).

As an aid to working out settlement dynamics we have used a probabilistic model of site abandonment and creation (Dewar 1991:617–19) In this approach, the *abandonment rate* is estimated from the number of sites occupied at the beginning of a phase, but not continuing in the subsequent phase, plus the number of sites founded but abandoned during the phase in question, divided by the span of the phase in years. The *establishment rate* is estimated from the number of sites founded during a phase, divided by the span of the phase. A simple iterative model applies these rates to the number of sites assumed to have been occupied at the beginning of the phase, as indicated by the presence of occupation both in this phase an the one preceding it. For each year and for each site, a random number between 0 and 1.0 is chosen. If the first number is less than the abandonment rate, the site is eliminated. If the second random number is less than the rate of establishment, a new site is begun. The number of sites remaining at the end of each year is counted. The average number of sites for all the years in a single simulation can be calculated. These iterations are repeated 1000 times, and a grand mean and standard deviation can be calculated.

The overall results are presented in Table VI.3. All sites with recorded occupations between 5600 and 2500 B.C. are included, with the exception of DL-89 and 90, which could not be precisely dated, and DL-312, which was isolated from the more intensively surveyed areas. For each phase, the table begins by giving its estimated span of years, adapted from Hole (1987). Then follows the number of sites occupied in the preceding phase and the one in question (a), the number with occupation in both the preceding and succeeding phases (b), the number which begin in this phase and continue in the succeeding phase (c), and the number that are occupied during the phase in question, but not during the preceding or succeeding ones (d). Next, we give the rates of establishment and abandonment calculated from these counts and the span of the phase. Then the simulated mean number of occupations at any point and the standard deviation

Table VI.3: Settlement Dynamics on the Deh Luran Plain

Phase	Phase Span	a	b	c	d	Establishment Rate	Abandonment Rate	Mean Simultaneous Occupation	S.D.	Mean Occupation Span
CMT	200	1	2	3	3	.030	.020	3.97	1.72	199
Sabz	150	0	5	1	0	.007	.000	5.50	0.56	—
Khazineh	300	1	5	11	5	.053	.020	11.51	2.75	553
Mehmeh	200	9	7	1	0	.005	.045	11.98	1.82	266
Bayat	200	2	6	0	4	.020	.030	7.19	1.79	240
Farukh	300	5	1	2	4	.020	.030	4.74	2.01	158
Suse	200	3	0	0	0	.000	.015	1.66	0.73	111
Early Uruk	300	0	0	5	6	.036	.020	3.40	1.80	170
Middle Uruk	250	1	4	1	0	.004	.004	5.02	0.82	1256
Late Uruk	200	4	1	0	2	.010	.030	3.19	1.37	106
Jemdet Nasr	150	0	1	3	0	.020	.000	2.50	1.00	—
ED I–II	300	1	3	4	2	.020	.010	5.41	1.72	541

of this mean are given. Finally, the estimated average life span of a site, which is the inverse of the mean rate of abandonment per village per year, is calculated whenever an abandonment rate can be calculated. This does not estimate actual site longevities, since the phases are short and conditions change constantly from phase to phase. Rather this indicates the longevity sites would have if the conditions of the given phase continued for a long time, which is a useful indicator of settlement stability.

The Chogha Mami Transitional and Sabz Phases

Analyses of the settlement data for these phases are suspect because the land surfaces on which they occur have been deeply buried by later alluvium. Also, since the low-fired ceramics which characterize phases preceding the Chogha Mami Transitional Phase do not last long on the surfaces of site, we may not recognize these earlier occupations, and misjudge the number of newly established Chogha Mami Transitional sites. In this and subsequent sections, we first present the sites organized in terms of the complete corpus of channels discussed above, seeking local patterns of stability and instability, then we consider the estimates of the number of sites simultaneously occupied, and implications for settled area and population.

Table VI.4: Chogha Mami Transitional Phase Settlement Trajectories

Sites	Occupational Pattern	Site Area
Drainage DL-276		
23	b	0.42
Canal DL-319		
25	c	0.05
286	c	1.00
Canal DL-114–115		
21	a	0.40
20	b	—
28	c	—
Canal DL-317		
84	d	0.26
85	d	—
Unascribed		
32	d	—

The only continuing stable occupation is Chagha Sefid (DL-23) on the spring-fed Ab-i Garm drainage, and perhaps Tepe Musiyan (DL-20) on the west bank of the Dawairij. The sites established on the west bank of the Mehmeh on a relatively small canal (DL-319) will continue into the next phase. On the central alluvium on the west bank of the Dawairij, one earlier site is abandoned, and another site commences a long occupational history, suggesting a shift from one field area to another. Finally, the effort to settle an area on the east bank of the Dawairij watered by a small canal (DL-317) seems to have been short-lived. With all the suggestions of movement from site to site, and even to different parts of the plain, it is no surprise that the site stability index of 199 and the mean estimate of 3.97 simultaneously occupied sites are low. Multiplying this by a mean site size of 0.53 ha, suggests only 2.1 simultaneously occupied hectares during this phase.

In the succeeding Sabz Phase, the dynamics appear to have been quite different, and the seeming reduction in settlement one might infer from simple site counts proves illusory.

Table VI.5 : Sabz Phase Settlement Trajectories

Sites	Occupational Pattern	Site Area
Drainage DL-276		
23	b	0.33
Canal DL-319		
25	b	0.05
286	b	1.00
Canal DL-114–115		
20	b	—
28	b	—
Unascribed		
31	c	0.50

Occupation continued adjacent to the drainage (DL-276) in the spring-fed area, along the canal (DL-319) off the west bank of the Mehmeh, and along the canals (DL-114 and 115) off the west bank of the Dawairij. Only the eponymous site of Tepe Sabz (DL-31) on the alluvium of the east bank of the Mehmeh (but likely to have drawn water from the Ab-i Garm source, as discussed above) is newly founded. Note, however, that the Sabz Phase layers at this site are deeply buried, and might not have been recognized without excavation. It is possible that other sites of this phase are hidden below the thick sediments and occupation deposits of the later prehistoric phases. Given the known sites, however, the stability of settlement results in an increased mean estimate of 5.50 simultaneously occupied settlements. Multiplying this by mean site size, also 0.53 ha, suggests about 2.92 occupied hectares. We do not know enough about architectural density in the settlements of these two early phases to make precise estimates of settled population, but it is clear that the human population during the early phases of the irrigation economy was relatively low and grew slowly at best. In reality, of course, there were probably many climatic reverses, alternations in the small canal systems, and changes in population in the centuries during which these cultural phases flourished.

The Khazineh Phase

The Khazineh phase is the earliest for which the durability and distinctiveness of the ceramics gives confidence that we can recognize most components and for which we can make population estimates.

Table VI.6: Khazineh Phase Settlement Trajectories

Sites	Occupational Pattern	Site Area
Drainage DL-276		
19	d	0.26
23	b	0.31
31	b	1.00
33	d	0.78
Canal DL-13		
14	d	1.15
15	c	0.25
29	c	0.54
222	c	0.50
241	c	1.00
Canal DL-319–320		
25	b	0.05
26	c	0.05
27	c	0.50
286	a	1.00
Canal DL-114–115		
20	b	2.00
21	c	0.15
28	b	0.52
71	c	0.30
Canal DL-317		
84	d	0.26
85	c	1.44
Unascribed		
11	d	0.28
22	c	0.15
32	c	1.50

During this relatively long phase, there was proliferation of settlement along the spring-fed Ab-i Garm drainage and the canals off the west bank of the Dawairij (DL-114 and 115), both long-occupied areas. There was movement of settlement toward the head of the old canal (DL-319) on the west bank of the Mehmeh, and digging of a new canal (DL-320) to service these sites. Much new settlement springs up along a major new canal (DL-13) on the east bank of the Mehmeh. The apparently abandoned canal (DL-317) on the east bank of the Dawairij was refurbished, and the sites of the Chogha Mami Transitional Phase were reoccupied. The stability of settlement results in an increased mean estimate of 11.51 simultaneously occupied settlements. Three of these would be larger settlements occupied throughout the phase, with a total area of 4.94 ha. Multiplying the remaining 8.51 sites by the mean size of the remaining observed sites of 0.43 ha yields 3.66 ha. Adding together areas of the large sites and small sites gives total of about 8.60 occupied hectares. Assuming architectural densities similar to those of the succeeding Mehmeh Phase, the mean settled population at one point in time during this phase would have been about 875 people.

The Mehmeh Phase

This appears to be a period of continued growth and settlement coalescence.

Table VI.7: Mehmeh Phase Settlement Trajectories

Sites	Occupational Pattern	Site Area
Drainage DL-276		
23	b	0.31
31	b	1.51
Canal DL-13		
15	a	0.67
29	b	1.27
222	a	0.50
241	a	0.11
Canal DL-319–320		
25	a	0.05
26	a	0.05
27	b	0.50
Canal DL-114–115		
20	b	4.00
21	a	0.15
28	a	0.52
71	b	0.30
Canal DL-317		
43	c	0.26
85	a	1.34
Unascribed		
22	a	0.10
32	b	1.50

During the Mehmeh Phase, along the Ab-i Garm drainage, the Mehmeh canals, along the canals in the central plain off the west bank of the Dawairij, and in the various parts of the plain where we cannot demonstrate the use of the canals, smaller settlements were everywhere abandoned. However, larger settlements continued and even grew substantially. In spite of the reduced stability of settlement there is an increase to a mean estimate of 11.98 simultaneously occupied settlements. Three of these larger settlements with a total area of

7.00 ha were occupied throughout the phase. Multiplying the remaining 8.98 sites by the mean size of the remaining observed sites of 0.41 ha, yields 3.68 ha. Adding together the large site and small site areas gives a total of about 10.68 occupied hectares. As discussed in Chapter V, architectural densities of the Mehmeh Phase indicate a population density of about 102 people per hectare. If so, the mean settled population at one point in time during this phase would have been about 1090 people.

The Bayat Phase

The demographic patterns of the preceding phase continue. The far southeastern end of the plain is abandoned during this phase.

Table VI.8: Bayat Phase Settlement Trajectories

Sites	Occupational Pattern	Site Area
Drainage DL-276		
23	b	0.26
31	a	1.51
Canal DL-246		
29	b	1.29
240	d	0.05
248/9	d	0.87
Canal DL-319–320		
27	b	1.00
290	d	0.44
Canal DL-115		
20	b	4.00
71	b	—
Canal DL-317		
43	a	0.26
91	d	0.14
Unascribed		
32	b	2.00

While some sites, primarily those of larger settlements, continue to be occupied and to grow in most areas of the plain other than the far southeast, many small sites and at least one larger site, Tepe Sabz (DL-31), appear to have been abandoned. There is a slight reduction in the stability of settlement and a decrease to a mean estimate of 7.19 simultaneously occupied settlements. Three of these would be larger settlements occupied throughout the phase, with a total area of 7.51 ha. Multiplying the remaining 4.19 sites by the mean size of the remaining observed sites of 0.54 ha, yields 2.26 ha. Adding together the areas of larger and smaller sites gives total of about 9.77 occupied hectares. Assuming the architectural densities of Bayat Phase were similar to those of the preceding phase, this occupied area would indicate a mean settled population at one point in time during this phase would have been about 1000 people. If, however, centers had begun to manifest the higher population densities that are indicated for the succeeding Farukh Phase, then the total population would have been higher. If centers approached 150 people per hectare, then the settled population of the centers would have reached about 1130 people. Assuming that the smaller settlements continued to have densities of about 100 people per hectare, then the simultaneous mean of total settled population of the plain would have approached about 1350 people. Given the instability of settlement, these mean estimates must obscure many local fluctuations in response to environmental and political changes.

The Farukh Phase

The pattern of nucleation in the centers, the decline in numbers and importance of smaller settlements, and increased settlement instability continues in this phase. By the end of the phase, most settlements have been abandoned.

Table VI.9: Farukh Phase Settlement Trajectories

Sites	Occupational Pattern	Site Area
Drainage DL-276		
23	a	0.12
Canal DL-246		
15	d	0.67
29	a	0.40
Canal DL-319		
27	a	1.00
286	d	0.40
Canal DL-115		
20	b	9.00
71	a	—
Canal DL-317		
85	c	—
Unascribed		
11	d	1.54
32	a	2.50

Only Musiyan (DL-20) and the smaller centers of the Mehmeh alluvium continue to grow, and the latter are nonetheless abandoned by the end of this phase, as are all the smaller settlements watered by the canal (DL-246) off the east bank of the Mehmeh. The old canal (DL-319) on the west bank of the Mehmeh was refurbished, and earlier settlements briefly re-established, but this renovation was also abandoned by the end of the phase. There is only an ephemeral trace of settlement around Musiyan, most of the waters of the canal (DL-115) taking off from the west bank of the Dawairij probably being used to sustain the people of this large center. Finally, there are traces of re-use of the former small center (DL-85) in the southeast end of the plain, and this may indicate that the old canal system (DL-317) taking water from the east bank of the Dawairij, which will be important in the succeeding phase, was restored before the end of the Farukh phase. There is a slight reduction in the stability of settlement and a decrease to a mean estimate of 4.74 simultaneously occupied settlements. One of these is the larger center of Musiyan near the center of the plain, occupied throughout the phase, with a total area of 9.00 ha. At least one smaller center of about 1.50 ha appears to have been occupied at any one time on the Mehmeh alluvium in the northwest end of the plain. Since, as discussed in Chapter V, the Farukhabad excavation suggests denser housing in centers, approaching 200 people per hectare, the approximately 10.50 ha covered by centers at any one point in time, indicates a population of about 2100 people. Multiplying the remaining 2.74 sites by the mean size of the remaining observed sites of 0.49 ha, yields 1.34 ha. Assuming that these continued to have a population density close to those of sites in earlier times, the mean population would have been about 140 people. Adding together the areas of larger and smaller sites gives a total of about 11.84 occupied hectares. Adding together the estimated mean simultaneous populations implied by these occupied areas would indicate a mean settled population at one point in time during this phase would have been about 2240 people. Unquestionably such approximate mean estimates masks an overall decline from the beginning to end of the relatively long Farukh phase, as well as much interesting variation in settlement configuration, but the general implication of a few large and densely occupied centers in the northwest and central parts of the plain, fits well with the evidence of high densities, conflict, and the establishment of new centers such as Suse during this time on the larger Susiana Plain to the east (Wright and Johnson 1975:273; Wright 1981a:70).

The Suse Phase

This final cultural phase of the Susiana tradition on the Deh Luran Plain sees continued general decline and complete abandonment. There is, however, a brief recovery of settlement in the southeast part of the plain during this phase.

Table VI.10: Suse Phase Settlement Trajectories

Sites	Occupational Pattern	Site Area
Canal DL-13		
247	a	0.67
Canal DL-115		
20	a	5.00
Canal DL-317		
85	a	1.44

The remaining settlements comprise the small center occupying the north end of Musiyan (DL-20), a reoccupied settlement (DL-85) in the southeast area which must have been sustained by a refurbished earlier canal (DL-317), and a possible transhumant camp on the northwestern plain (DL-247), perhaps taking advantage of the growth of plants in abandoned fields and on the middens of abandoned Bayat and Farukh phase villages. The location of such settlements as survived in the center and southeast parts of the plain, together with the close affinity of the ceramics and other artifacts with those of the Susiana, suggest that the Deh Luran Plain is closely related to the Susiana Plain at this time. As one would expect with few unstable settlements, the simulation yields a low mean estimate of only 1.66 simultaneously occupied settlements, which multiplied by the mean settlement size suggests a mean simultaneously occupied area of 5.30 ha. However, with so few sites in a situation of settlement collapse, these figures can only be suggestive, and in the absence of any local architectural data whatsoever, we will not make a population estimate.

The Early Uruk Phase

While no Suse phase site is inhabited by an Early Uruk settlement, most Early Uruk sites were previously used by earlier communities of the Susiana tradition, and reoccupation must have involved restoring earlier canal systems.

Table VI.11: Early Uruk Phase Settlement Trajectories

Sites	Occupational Pattern	Site Area
Drainage DL-276		
7	d	0.24
19	c	2.31
23	c	0.31
169	d	0.66
Canal DL-319–320		
27	d	1.00
Canal DL-321		
292	d	8.40
Canal DL-115		
61	c	0.68
71	c	0.50
Canal DL-317		
43	d	0.26
Unascribed		
11	d	1.54
32	c	1.00

The drainages (DL-276) fed by the Ab-i Garm spring are used by four new communities. The sites at locations never previously utilized (DL-7 and 169) were abandoned before the beginning of the Middle Uruk phase. It is possible that their populations became part of the one large and growing community (DL-19) in this area.

The long-lived system (DL-115) which took water from the west bank of the Dawairij to sustain the major Susiana center at Musiyan (DL-20) is maintained, but Musiyan remains empty, and two small nearby sites (DL-61 and 71) are reoccupied. Also, there was yet another short-lived effort to refurbish to the old canal (DL-317) taking off from the east bank of the Dawairij, but the only settlement reoccupied in this area (DL-43) was very small. A major new canal (DL-321), cut from the west bank of the Mehmeh, watered the Early Uruk center (DL-292) in that area, and a previously occupied small site (DL-27) on canal DL-320 was briefly resettled. However, both of these sites were abandoned before the beginning of the Middle

Uruk phase. This raises a problem with the estimation of population. Since no sites are stable, we must use the aggregate mean area for all sites to estimate total settlement area, and these site areas have a skewed, non-normal distribution. The simulation of the Early Uruk settlement dynamics indicates high instability for all sites, with a mean estimate of 3.40 simultaneously occupied settlements. Multiplied by the mean size of settlement of 1.54 ha, this suggests a mean simultaneously occupied area of 5.24 ha. Given the 115 people per hectare indicated by architectural evidence, as discussed in Chapter V, this indicates a mean simultaneous population of about 600 people, much lower than the estimate produced with the conventional approach of Chapter V.

The Middle Uruk Phase

This is a time of modest but very stable settlement.

Table VI.12: Middle Uruk Phase Settlement Trajectories

Sites	Occupational Pattern	Site Area
Drainage DL-276		
19	b	2.59
23	b	0.17
Canal DL-115		
61	b	0.68
71	a	0.50
104	c	0.95
Unascribed		
32	b	2.50

Settlement continues to flourish on the Ab-i Garm drainage (DL-276) though most population is nucleated in one larger settlement (DL-19) close to the optimal area for fields. Sometime during this phase on the lengthened canal (DL-115) taking water from the west bank of the Dawairij, an earlier settlement (DL-71) is abandoned and a new settlement (DL-104) is added, suggesting movement from one to the other. The modest center of this settlement distribution is Farukhabad (DL-32), whose water source is unknown. Overall, there is a remarkable stability of settlement and an increase to a mean estimate of 5.02 simultaneously occupied settlements. Four of these, with a total area of 5.94 ha, are occupied throughout the phase. Multiplying the remaining 1.02 sites by the mean size of the remaining observed sites of 0.72 ha, yields 0.73 ha. Adding together the areas of the permanent and impermanent sites gives total of about 6.67 simultaneously occupied hectares. Assuming the same population density used for the Early Uruk estimates, this indicates a mean simultaneous population of about 770 people, notably greater than the Early Uruk estimate, even though there are fewer sites.

The Late Uruk Phase

During this phase, the Deh Luran Plain once again enters a period of instability and population decline.

Table VI.13: Late Uruk Phase Settlement Trajectories

Sites	Occupational Pattern	Site Area
Drainage DL-276		
19	a	—
23	a	0.09
Canal DL-115		
61	a	0.68
62	d	0.42
104	a	0.63
Canal DL-317		
43	d	—
Unascribed		
32	b	2.50

The basic canal patterns of the Middle Uruk phase continue into the Late Uruk phase, but most settlements are abandoned during the course of this phase. Only the small center of Farukhabad (DL-

32) continues. There is a decline in stability of settlement and a decrease to an estimated mean of 3.19 simultaneously occupied settlements. Only Farukhabad, with 2.5 ha, is occupied throughout the phase. Multiplying the remaining 2.19 sites by the mean size of the remaining observed sites of 0.46 ha, yields 1.01 ha. Adding together the areas of larger and smaller sites gives total of about 3.51 simultaneously occupied hectares. Assuming the same population density used for the Early Uruk, estimates would indicate a population of about 405 people. This density, however, may not be applicable, since the excavations at Farukhabad indicate much variation in architecture, and there is no clear figure for estimating population density. In addition, this is a period of decline with few sites, and under such circumstances estimating the mean simultaneous occupations is particularly difficult.

The Jemdet Nasr Phase

This relatively short phase is poorly documented, both because the characteristic ceramics are difficult to recognize, and because the refuse distributions of this phase are masked by those of flourishing later Early Dynastic communities.

Table VI.14: Jemdet Nasr Phase Settlement Trajectories

Sites	Occupational Pattern	Site Area
Drainage DL-276		
18	c	—
24	c	2.09
Canal DL-115		
20	c	—
Unascribed		
32	b	3.00

There is a decrease to an estimated mean of 2.50 simultaneously occupied settlements. Since we lack settlement area estimates for half of the settlements of the phase, an estimate of simultaneously occupied area is particularly dubious, but it is unlikely to have been less than 5.0 ha. The architectural evidence from Farukhabad indicates dense housing and some two-story residences, so a population density approaching 200 people per hectare is possible. Assuming 150 people per hectare would yield a mean simultaneous estimate of about 750 people.

The Early Dynastic I–II Phase

This relatively long and stable period was one of impressive growth on the plain.

Table VI.15: Early Dynastic I–II Phase Settlement Trajectories

Sites	Occupational Pattern	Site Area
Drainage DL-276		
18	a	3.10
24	b	4.18
Canal DL-320		
27	d	2.00
Canal DL-121		
34	c	1.50
Canal DL-115		
20	b	15.00
62	d	0.42
104	c	2.00
Canal DL-317		
41	c	—
54	c	1.00
Unascribed		
32	b	3.00

The main center of the Plain is once again Musiyan (DL-20). Musiyan, its suburbs and the reoccupied small settlement (DL-104) to the south must have been watered by a restoration of the old canal (DL-115) lengthened in Uruk times. There are also indications that a new canal-qanat link (DL-121) was cut from the west bank of the Dawairij to provide water to a new settlement (DL-34) north of Musiyan. The Ab-i Garm water source

(DL-276) is certainly being used by one small center, Baulah (DL-24). While this also may have contributed to the sustenance of a distant large village (DL-18), and thus to the nearby small center of Farukhabad (DL-32), the water sources of these two settlements may have been the Mehmeh. The restoration of one of the canals (DL-320) off the west bank of the Mehmeh to water a reoccupied small settlement (DL-27) did not long survive. However, a restructuring of the old system (DL-317) on the east bank of the Dawairij, creating a long canal which could carry water to higher land surfaces and new settlements (DL-41 and 54) in the southeast end of the plain, was a project which flourished in the succeeding Early Dynastic III period. Overall, with the increase in stability of settlement, there is an increase to a mean estimate of 5.41 simultaneously occupied settlements. Three of these—the larger center of Musiyan (DL-20) near the center of the plain, and two small centers, Baulah (DL-24) and Farukhabad (DL-32)—with a total area of about 22.18 ha, were occupied throughout the phase. Since, as discussed in Chapter V, the Farukhabad excavation indicates dense housing, we assume a density of 200 people per hectare. If so, these continuously occupied centers would have had a population of about 4400 people. Multiplying the remaining 2.41 sites by the mean size of the remaining observed sites of 1.60 ha, yields 3.86 ha. Assuming that these continued to have had a population density of about 150 people per hectare, lower than that of the centers, yields a mean simultaneous population of about 580 people. Adding together the areas of larger and smaller sites gives a total of 26.04 occupied hectares. Adding together the estimated populations implied by these occupied areas would indicate a mean settled population at one point in time during this phase would have been almost 5000 people. We cannot yet make similar estimates for the ED III phase, because we wish to reassess the ceramics of all ED III and subsequent Awan phase sites. We reserve detailed treatment of the Early Dynastic III population for a later volume.

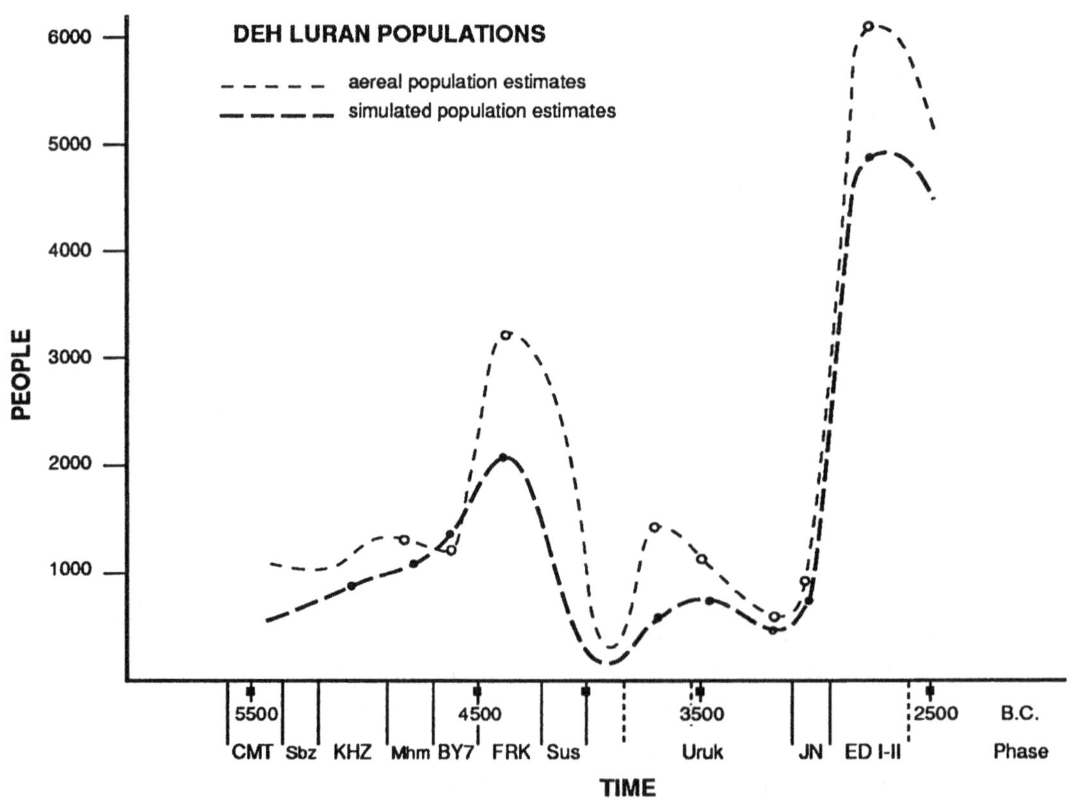

Figure VI.1. Population changes on the Deh Luran Plain

Table VI.16: Population and Irrigation of the Deh Luran Plain

In the following table, the areal population estimates are those based on the static calculations used in Chapter V. The simulated population estimates are those given in the above discussion, based on discussion of the data in Table VI.3. The population estimate for the largest center is simply its area multiplied by the density figure believed appropriate. The number of centers simultaneously occupied follows from the above discussions. The mean population of smaller settlements is based the mean size of the measured "village and hamlet" sites, presented in Tables V.1 to V.13, multiplied by the density figure believed appropriate. The number of smaller settlements simultaneously occupied is based on Table VI.3, less the number of simultaneously occupied centers. The longest minimum canal length is given in Table VI.2. Finally, the number of canals in simultaneous use during a phase includes those canals with either permanently occupied sites (b), or sites occupied in both the beginning (a) and end (c) of the phase. If there is one canal with only limited occupation, this is not counted. If there are two such canals, one more canal is added to the number in simultaneous use.

			Centers		Small Settlements		Canals	
Phase	Areal Population Estimate	Simulated Population Estimate	Population Estimate	Number	Mean Population	Number	Maximum of Minimum Length	Number
CMT	—	—	—	0	53	4.0	6.0	2
Sabz	—	—	—	0	53	5.5	5.5	2
Khazineh	—	875	200	3	45	7.5	7.4	3
Mehmeh	1300	1090	400	3	30	9.5	7.4	4
Bayat	1100	1350	400	3	45	4.2	6.5	3
Farukh	3200	2240	1350	2	50	2.7	6.5	3
Suse	—	—	750	1	—	—	—	1
Early Uruk	1400	600	970	1	65	2.4	8.5	2
Middle Uruk	1100	770	245	1	65	1.9	10.2	1
Late Uruk	500	405	245	1	50	2.7	10.2	1
Jemdet Nasr	900	750	450	1	—	—	—	1
ED I–II	6500	5000	3000	3	210	2.4	12.0	3

Summary and Discussion

A number of interesting observations may be made by considering Table VI.16 and Figures VI.1 and VI.2, which presents syntheses of the arguments put forward in Chapter VI. Comparing the conventional static and simulated dynamic population estimates in the table and in the Figure VI.1, it is clear that, as one expects, the estimations simulated with the dynamic model are less, particularly for longer periods. This has the effect of displacing inferred population peaks, and even eliminating an inferred population fluctuation during the Susiana phases. Clearly much depends on the actual length of phases, and this should provide motivation to seek more precise absolute dates.

In general, one may see from Table VI.16 that, in spite of the perturbations in the overall population of the plain and of the population nucleated in the major centers, the general trend is for the mean population size of smaller settlements to increase through time. This suggests that the internal organization of the basic social unit is changing through time. Precise definition of these changes, however, would require detailed work on village architecture and mortuary contexts.

The tabulated data indicate four successive dynamic patterns of organizational change.

—*First*, during the Chogha Mami Transitional and Sabz Phases (ca. 5400–5000 B.C.) populations are relatively small and grew slowly at best. We do not make quantitative estimates of the number of people because we may not have discovered all of the surviving larger sites and we know little about housing density during these phases. A few small canal systems are in use.

—*Second*, during the Khazineh to the middle of the Farukh phases, (ca. 5000 to 4300 B.C.) there is a steady increase in the population of the plain as a whole. Initially this results from an increase in the number of settlements, but after the Mehmeh phase, the number of small settlements diminishes, and growth results from expansion of the larger settlements. During this time the length of canals and the number of canal systems shows a slight general increase, then declines. The observed declines, however, can be an artifact of fewer sites, since our assumptions require that usually two sites must be present on a canal in order for it to be datable and measurable.

From late in the Farukh through the Suse phase (ca. 4300 - 4000 B.C.), all settlements decrease in size, and the plain appears to have been abandoned during the early portion of the Early Uruk phase, locally termed the Terminal Suse phase (See Chapter III).

—*Third*, during the Uruk phases on the Deh Luran Plain (ca. 3850 - 3100 B.C.) there was an increase in population, beginning with resettlement by a small population which changed occupied sites frequently, and developing into a relatively stable set of settlements with a larger but still small population. Relatively few, but increasingly larger, canal systems are attested.

During the Late Uruk phase, however, most settlements are abandoned, and most canal systems probably cease to be used.

—*Fourth*, during the Jemdet Nasr and Early Dynastic I–II phases, ca. 3100 - 2600 B.C., there is a rapid increase in the population of the plain as a whole and of the largest center. Immigration seems likely. There are more than twice as many people on the plain as during the previous Farukh Phase apogee. Canal systems are rebuilt and lengthened, but there is no indication that the total or mean length of the canal systems doubled. This implies more intensive cultivation of irrigated fields, or the use of other subsistence sources, or the import of food, as is discussed below.

What are the implications of our analyses for the relationship between changes in human population and in canal systems? The evidence from those canals for which we have evidence of occupation from the beginning of a phase until its end are present in Figure VI.2. Each point on this scatter plot represents the canal length (See Table VI.2) and the mean simultaneous population along that canal (calculated as the population of permanent sites, plus half those of the sites occupied for only part of the phase), for the phases during which the canal was used from the beginning to the end of the phase. Canal DL-246 is represented by two points because the precise date of the reduction of the size of DL-29 is not known. The solid point presumes DL-29 remained at its maximum size for some time after the change from the longer DL-13 canal system to the shorter DL-246 canal system, while the open point presumes that DL-29 became smaller about the time the canal system diminished. DL-114–115 is also represented by two points: the solid point representing the mean of all populations inferred from this long-lived canal, and the open point representing only the population inferred for the Sabz phase, before the canal became the locus of the major center on the plain. The implications of the difference between the points for DL-114–115 will be discussed below. If the open points represent correct assessments, then it can be seen that there is a close relation between the length of the main portions of the canals (the small branches of early canals, rarely observable on the surface, are not included in this measure) and the estimated number of people living along them, with about 17 people for each kilometer of canal. Whether this relationship results from the optimal number of adults needed to maintain canals, or from the number of people that can gain a secure livelihood from

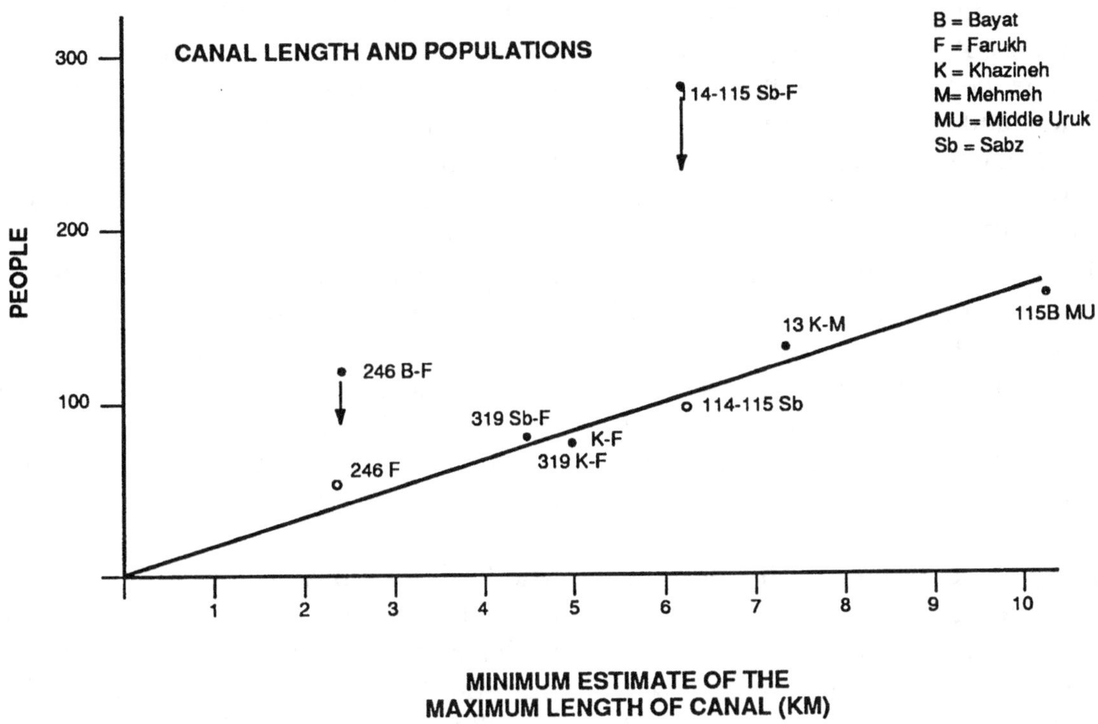

Figure VI.2. Local population and canal length

a certain amount of irrigated land, or from some combination of factors, we do not know. This relationship seems to hold up to at least the Middle Uruk phase. Unfortunately, after the Middle Uruk phase, none of the formal canal systems associated with smaller village-sized settlements are in continuous use throughout a phase, and measurements would be even more dubious than those recorded on Figure VI.2. Whatever the explanation of this relationship, it implies that the various periods of population growth we have inferred did not compel local intensification of irrigation agriculture.

How then did the people who lived in the major settlement of the plain, Musiyan (DL-20), during its two major periods of expansion find enough to eat? For each of these two periods. there are three possibilities: local intensification of agriculture, exploitation of other agricultural resources on the plain, and the import of food from other areas.

—During the earlier Vth millennium B.C. we estimate that Musiyan expanded to about 1350 inhabitants, at least 1200 more than were living elsewhere on the plain along canals of the size estimated for DL-114–115 at this time. There is one suggestion of local agricultural intensification at Musiyan: a Mehmeh phase sample from Musiyan had an occurrence of lentils, a protein-rich domestic legume which is often an irrigated summer crop. This is the only major occurrence of lentils recorded in an archaeobotanical sample from the Deh Luran Plain (Helbaek in Hole, Flannery and Neely 1969: 391, 411). Evidence suggesting exploitation of other agricultural resources also helps to account for the anomalous size of Musiyan during the early Vth Millennium B.C. On the east bank of the Dawairij, southeast of Musiyan, the number of local inhabitants estimated per kilometer of local canal DL-317, drops from 8 people during the Mehmeh phase to 4 during the Bayat phase to the merest trace during the Farukh phase. Even if small, poorly dated sites DL-89 and 90 could be added into the calculations, these extraordinarily low estimates would not greatly change. It seems likely that the people who maintained these canals, farmed these fields, and consumed their harvests, came from the large settlement at Musiyan. Increase in extensive rain-fed agriculture is also a possibility during the Vth millennium, since there are some indications for increased rainfall in Mesopotamia during this period (Woosley and Hole 1978:67; Larsen 1983:142–186). There is no evidence of the import of food during the early Vth millennium, even though many samples from several different sites have been studied. Indeed, there is not much evidence of any import or export. It is possible, however, that a combination of local intensification and exploitation of fields in other parts of the plain would suffice to feed the population of Musiyan, without recourse to imports.

—During the earlier IIIrd millennium B.C, we estimate that Musiyan expanded to about 3000 inhabitants, 2800 more people than we estimate to have lived along canal DL-115 during Middle Uruk times. There are no Early Dynastic archaeobotanical samples from Musiyan, but we do have indirect evidence of local agricultural intensification. The occurrence of the charcoal of poplar wood in ED I–II samples from Farukhabad suggests year-round irrigation in some parts of the plain, and therefore some degree of summer irrigation (Miller in Wright 1981: 231, 430). The frequency of a large variety gerbil *Tatera indica* at this time also indicates permanently lush areas (Redding in Wright 1981:253, Redding 1978). The placement of DL-34 in an area that is difficult to irrigate, and the possible use of a labor intensive tunnel system to bring water to this site (and perhaps to others in the area), both indicate investments of labor greater than simple canal construction near river levees. Indeed, as we noted above, such tunnel systems would supply a steadier supply of fresher water, facilitating summer irrigation. As in the Vth millennium B.C., we also have evidence that Musiyan exploited the agriculture potential of the east bank of the Dawairij, southeast of Musiyan. Canal system DL-317 was rebuilt and lengthened during Early Dynastic I–II times, but the number of local inhabitants estimated per kilometer of local canal is only five. It seems likely that many of the people who maintained these canals, farmed these fields, and consumed their harvests, came from the large settlement at Musiyan. Increase in extensive rain-fed agriculture is also a possibility during the early IIIrd millennium, since there are indications for increased rainfall in areas near Mesopotamia during this period (Larsen 1983:142–186). Finally, it is also notable that this is a period of increased local and long range exchange (Wright 1981:262–79), that the presence of domestic donkeys as early as the Middle Uruk phase (Payne 1988:99–100) would facilitate the transport of bulky foodstuffs, and that we have direct evidence of the import of dried fish from the Gulf or the lower Tigris to Farukhabad (Redding in Wright 1981: 235–36). As before, we do not know if a combination of local intensification, exploitation of fields in other parts of the plain, and import of food would suffice to feed the population of Musiyan, but this is a possibility.

We hope that this final chapter of our study of settlement in the foothills of southwestern Iran during the VIth to IIIrd millennia B.C. has shown the reader that it is possible to evaluate ideas about the dynamic interrelations between changing human population and alternative agricultural strategies, even with the data of archaeological survey. If we have focused on population and subsistence, and mentioned briefly if at all, such issues as conflict, exchange, social organization, political control, this is not intended to deprecate the importance of these other processes. There is much more archaeological research that could be done on the Deh Luran Plain, and we hope this contribution will be of use to the future archaeologists who will be privileged to return there.

References Cited

Adams, Robert McC.
1962 Agriculture and Urban Life in Early Southwestern Iran. *Science* 136:109–122.
1965 *Land Behind Baghdad*. Chicago: University of Chicago Press.

Adams, Robert McC. and Hans J. Nissen
1972 *The Uruk Countryside*. Chicago: University of Chicago Press.

Alden, John R.
1988 Ceramic Ring Scrapers: An Uruk Period Pottery Production Tool. *Paléorient* 14/1: 143–150.

Alizadeh, Abbas
1992 *Prehistoric Settlement Patterns and Cultures in Susiana, Southwestern Iran.* Technical Reports of the Museum of Anthropology, University of Michigan no. 24. Ann Arbor.

Ammerman, A. J.
1981 Surveys and Archaeological Research. *Annual Review of Anthropology* 10:63–88.

Caldwell, J.
1968 Ghazir, Tell-i. *Reallexikon der Assyriologie* 3:348–355.

Canal, Denis
1978 Travaux à la terrasse haute de l'Acropole de Suse. *Cahiers de la Délégation Archéologique Française en Iran* 9:11–55.

Carter, Elizabeth
1971 *Elam in the Second Millennium B.C.: The Archaeological Evidence.* Doctoral dissertation in Near Eastern Studies, University of Chicago.
1978 Suse 'Ville Royale.' *Paléorient* 4:197–211.

Cook, S. F. and Heizer, Robert F.
1968 Relationships among Houses, Settlement Areas, and Populations in Aboriginal California. In *Settlement Archaeology*, ed. K. C. Chang, pp. 79–116. Palo Alto, CA: National Press Books.

Cressey, George B.
1958 Qanats, Kariz, and Foggara. *Geographical Review* 48:17–44.
1960 *Crossroads: Land and Life in Southwest Asia*. Chicago: J. B. Lippincott.

Dean, Jeffery S.
1969 Chronological Analysis of Tsegi Phase Sites in Northeastern Arizona. *Papers of the Laboratory of Tree-Ring Research* no. 3. Tucson.

Dewar, Robert E.
1991 Incorporating Variation in Occupation Span into Settlement-Pattern Analysis. *American Antiquity* 56(4):604–620.

Dollfus, Geneviève
1971 Les fouilles à Djaffarabad de 1969 à 1971. *Cahiers de la Délégation Archéologique Française en Iran* 1:17–162.
1978 Djaffarabad, Djowi, Bendebal: Contribution à l'étude de la Susiane au Ve millénaire et au début du IVe millénaire. *Paléorient* 4:141–167.

Doolittle, William E.
1988 Prehispanic Occupance in the Valley of Sonora, Mexico: Archaeological Confirmation of Early Spanish Reports. *Anthropological Papers of the University of Arizona* no. 48. Tucson.

Dzodin, Joel S.
1980 *An Analysis of Ecological Conditions Affecting Prehistoric Subsistence at Tepe Ali Kosh and Ain Girzan, Iran* . Thesis submitted for a Master of Arts in Anthropology, Wayne State University, Detroit.

English, Paul W.
1968 The Origin and Spread of Qanats in the Old World. *Proceedings of the American Philosophical Society* 112(3):170–181.

Fernea, Robert A.
1959 *Irrigation and Social Organization Among the El Shabana: A Group of Tribal Cultivators in Southern Iraq*. Unpublished Doctoral dissertation in Anthropology, University of Chicago.
1970 *Shaykh and Effendi: Changing Patterns of Authority Among the El Shabana of Southern Iraq*. Cambridge: Harvard University Press.

Flannery, Kent V.
1969 Origins and Ecological Effects of Early Domestication in Iran and the Near East. In *The Domestication and Exploitation of Plants and Animals,* ed. P.J. Ucko and G.W. Dimbleby, pp. 73–100. Chicago: Aldine-Atherton.

Gautier, J.-E. and G. Lampre
1905 Fouilles de Moussian. *Mémoires de la Délégation en Perse* VIII:59–148, ed. Jacques de Morgan. Paris: Ernest Leroux.

Gremliza, F.G.L.
1962 *Ecology and Endemic Diseases in the Dez Irrigation Project*. A report to the Khuzistan Water and Power Authority and the Plan Organization of Iran. New York: Development and Resources Corporation.

Helbaek, Hans
1972 Samarran Irrigation Agriculture at Choga Mami in Iraq. *Iraq* 34:35–48.

Hole, Frank
1962 Archaeological Survey and Excavation in Iran, 1961. *Science* 137: 524–26.
1966 Investigating the Origins of Mesopotamian Civilization. *Science* 153:605–611.
1977 *Studies in the Archaeological History of the Deh Luran Plain: The Excavation of Chagha Sefid*. Memoirs of the Museum of Anthropology, University of Michigan no. 9. Ann Arbor.
1978 Pastoral Nomadism in Western Iran. in *Explorations in Ethnoarchaeology*, ed. R. A. Gould, pp. 127–167. Albuquerque: University of New Mexico Press.

Hole, Frank, editor
1969 *Preliminary Reports of the Rice University Project in Iran 1968–1969*. Houston: Rice University, Department of Anthropology. (Mimeograph).
1987 *The Archaeology of Western Iran. Settlement and Society from Prehistory to the Islamic Conquest*. Washington: Smithsonian Institution Press.

Hole, Frank and K.V. Flannery
1962 Excavations at Ali Kosh, Iran, 1961. *Iranica Antiqua* 2:97–148.
1968 The Prehistory of Southwestern Iran: A Preliminary Report. *Proceedings of the Prehistoric Society* 33:147–206.

Hole, Frank, K.V. Flannery, and James A. Neely
1969 *Prehistory and Human Ecology of the Deh Luran Plain*. Memoirs of the Museum of Anthropology, University of Michigan no. 1. Ann Arbor.

Johnson, Gregory A.
1973 *Local Exchange and Early State Development in Southwestern Iran.* Anthropological Papers of the Museum of Anthropology, University of Michigan no. 51, Ann Arbor.

Kirkby, Michael
1977 Land and Water Resources of the Deh Luran and Khuzistan Plains. In *Studies in the Archaeological History of the Deh Luran Plain: The Excavation of Chagha Sefid,* by F. Hole, pp. 251–288. Memoirs of the Museum of Anthropology, University of Michigan no. 9. Ann Arbor.

Kramer, Carol
1980 Estimating Prehistoric Populations: An Ethnoarchaeological Approach. In *L'Archéologie de l'Iraq du début de l'époque Néolithique à 333 avant notre ère* [Colloques Internationaux du Centre National de la Recherche Scientifique no. 580], ed. M.-T. Barrelet, pp. 315–334. Paris: Editions du Centre National de la Recherche Scientifique.

Larsen, Curtis E.
1983 *Life and Land Use on the Bahrain Islands*. Chicago: University of Chicago Press.

LeBlanc, Stephen A.
1971 An Addition to Naroll's Suggested Floor Area and Settlement Population Relationship. *American Antiquity* 36:210–211.

Le Breton, Louis
1947 Note sur la céramique peinte aux environs de Suse et à Suse. *Mémoires de la Mission Archéologique en Iran* 30:120–219.
1957 The Early Periods at Susa, Mesopotamian Relations. *Iraq* 19(2):79–124.

Le Brun, Alain
1971 Recherches stratigraphiques à l'Acropole de Suse, 1969–1971. *Cahiers de la Délégation Archéologique Française en Iran* 1:163–216.

Lorimer, D. L. R.
1908 A Report on the Pusht-i Kuh. [Unpublished account of Luristan in the possession of the authors].

Miroschedji, Pierre de
1981 Prospections archéologiques au Khuzistan en 1977. *Cahiers de la Délégation Archéologique Française en Iran* 12:169–192.

Naroll, Raoul
1962 Floor Area and Settlement Population. *American Antiquity* 27:587–589.

Neely, James A.
1974a *The Prehistoric Lunt and Stove Canyon Sites, Point of Pines, Arizona*. Doctoral Dissertation in Anthropology, University of Arizona, Tucson. Ann Arbor: University Microfilms.
1974b Sassanian and Early Islamic Water-Control and Irrigation Systems on the Deh Luran Plain, Iran. In *Irrigation's Impact on Society,* ed. Theodore E. Downing and McGuire Gibson, pp 21–42. Anthropological Papers of the University of Arizona no. 25. Tucson.
In press Mogollon/Western Pueblo Soil and Water Control Systems of the Reserve Phase: New Data from West-Central New Mexico. In *Proceedings of the New Mexico Archaeological Council Agricultural Symposium* (tentative title), ed. H. W. Toll. Albuquerque: Publications of the New Mexico Archaeological Council.

Neely, James A. and Alan P. Olson
1977 *Archaeological Reconnaissance of Monument Valley in Northeastern Arizona.* Museum of Northern Arizona, Research Paper Series, RS 3. Flagstaff.

Oates, Joan
1969 Chogha Mami, 1967–68: A Preliminary Report. *Iraq* 31:115–152.

Payne, Sebastian
1988 Animal Bones from Tell Rubeidheh. In *Tell Rubeidheh: An Uruk Village in the Jebel Hamrin*, ed. R. G. Killick, pp. 98–135. Warminster GB: Aris and Phillips.

Plog, Fred T.
1973 Diachronic Anthropology in *Research and Theory in Current Archaeology*, ed. C. L. Redman, pp. 181–98. New York: John Wiley.

Plog, Steven and J. L. Hantman
1990 Chronology Construction and the Study of Prehistoric Culture Change. *Journal of Field Archaeology* 17:439–456.

Redding, Richard W.
1978 Rodents and the Archaeological Paleoenvironment: Considerations, Problems and the Future. In *Approaches to Faunal Analysis in the Middle East*, ed. R. H. Meadow and M. A. Zeder, pp. 63–68. Cambridge, MA: Peabody Museum of Archaeology and Ethnology.

Sajjadi, Seyyed Mansour Seyyed
1982 *Qanat/Kariz: storia, tecnica construttiva ed evoluzione.* Teheran: Instituto Italiano di Cultura.

Schacht, Robert M.
1984 The Contemporaneity Problem. *American Antiquity* 49(4):678–695.

Southworth, C. H.
1931 Gila River Survey Report, Vol. 1, Supplemental Exhibits. Manuscript on file at the Pueblo Grande Museum, Phoenix, Arizona.

Stève, M.-J. and Hermann Gasche
1971 L'Acropole de Suse. *Mémoires de la Délégation Archéologique en Iran* 46. Paris: Geuthner.

Stuiver, Minze and G. W. Pearson
1993 High-Precision Bidecadal Calibration of the Radiocarbon Time Scale: AD 1950 to 500 B.C. and 2500 to 6000 B.C. *Radiocarbon* 35:1–23.

Tolstoy, Paul
1975 Settlement and Population Trends in the Basin of Mexico (Ixtapaluca and Zacatenco phases). *Journal of Field Archaeology* 2:97–104.

Vanden Berghe, Louis
1968 La nécropole de Bani Surmah. *Archéologia* 24:53–63.
1970 La nécropole de Kalleh Nissar. *Archéologia* 32:64–73.

Weiss, Harvey
1977 Periodization, Population and Early State Formation in Khuzistan. In *Mountains and Lowlands: Essays in the Archaeology of Greater Mesopotamia* , ed. L. D. Levine and T. C. Young Jr., pp. 347–369. Malibu, CA: Undena.

Woodbury, Richard B. and James A. Neely
1972 Water Control Systems of the Tehuacan Valley. In *The Prehistory of the Tehuacan Valley*, Vol. 4: *Chronology and Irrigation,* ed. Frederick Johnson, pp 81–153. Austin: University of Texas Press.

Woosley, Anne and Frank Hole
1978 Pollen Evidence of Subsistence and Environment in Ancient Iran. *Paléorient* 4:59–70.

Wright, Henry T.
1969 *The Administration of Rural Production in an Early Mesopotamian Town*. Anthropological Papers of the Museum of Anthropology, University of Michigan no. 38. Ann Arbor.
1981 *An Early Town on the Deh Luran Plain: Excavations at Tepe Farukhabad.* Memoirs of the Museum of Anthropology, University of Michigan no 13. Ann Arbor.
1981a The Southern Margins of Sumer. In *Heartland of Cities,* by Robert McC. Adams, pp. 295–345. Chicago: University of Chicago Press.

Wright, Henry T. and Gregory A. Johnson
1975 Population, Exchange and Early State Formation in Southwestern Iran. *American Anthropologist* 77:267–289.

Wright, Henry T., James A. Neely, Gregory A. Johnson, and John Speth
1975 Early Fourth Millennium Developments in Southwestern Iran. *Iran* 13:129–141.

Young, T. Cuyler Jr.
1969 *Excavations at Godin Tepe: First Progress Report*. Royal Ontario Museum Art and Archaeology Occasional Paper 17.

Appendix A:

Counts of Artifacts in Survey Collections

Table A1: Earlier Susiana Ceramics of the Deh Luran Plain

			DL-11	DL-15	DL-20: Musiyan 1	2	3	4	DL-22
Ceramics									
ES-SJ-1	Khazineh Red Jar Parts		1	5	-	1	2	1	-
ES-SJ-2	Mehmeh Red-on-red Jar Parts	(Mm)	-	2	-	-	3	-	-
Susiana Buff Ware									
Bowl Bases									
ES-BB-1	Medium Flat Bases		-	-	-	-	-	-	-
ES-BB-2	Wide Early Ring Bases		-	1	-	-	-	-	-
ES-BB-3	Fine Early Ring Bases		-	1	-	-	-	-	-
ES-BB-4	Carinated Basal Sherds	(Kh +)	-	-	-			-	-
Hemispherical Bowl Parts									
ES-RB-1	Exterior Bands		1	-	-	-	-	-	1
ES-RB-2	Exterior Chevrons/Obliques		2	1	-	-	-	-	-
ES-RB-3	Exterior Vertical Triangles		-	-	-	1	-	1	-
ES-RB-4	Exterior Diamonds		1 F?	1	-	-	-	1	-
ES-RB-5	Exterior Ladder Motif	(Mm ±)	-	2	-	-	-	-	-
ES-RB-6	Exterior Right Triangle Field	(Mm)	-	2	-	-	-	1	1
	Other Exterior Motifs		-	-		-			-
ES-RB-7, 8	Interior Pendant Triangles	(CMT)	-	-	-	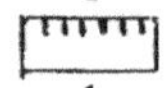	-	-	-
ES-RB-9	Interior Fully Painted		-	-	-	1	-	-	-
	Other Interior Motifs		2	-	-	-	-	-	-
Carinated Bowl Parts									
ES-RB-10	"Sabz Pot"	(Sb)	-	-	1	-	-	-	-
ES-RB-11	Interior Cross-Hatch	(Kh)	1	-	-	-	1	-	-
ES-RB-12	Interior Fully Painted	(Kh+)	2		1	-	-	-	-
ES-RB-13	Interior Wavy Elements	(Kh)	-	-	-	-	1	-	1
ES-RB-14	Interior Multiple Bands	(Kh+)	-	-	-	1	-	-	1
	Other Interior Motifs		-		-	-	-	-	-
Incurved Bowl Parts									
ES-RB-15	Exterior Zigzag Motifs		-	-	-	-	-	-	1
	Other Exterior Motifs		-	-	-	-	-	-	-
Large Basin Parts									
ES-RB-17	Flat Lips with Bands Only		-	-	-	2	1	-	-
ES-RB-18	Flat Lips with Triangles	(Kh-Mm)	1	-	-	-	-	-	-
ES-RB-19	Flat Lips with Goats	(Mm)	-	-	-	2	-	1	-
ES-RB 16	Other Basin Rims		-	-	-	-	-	-	-
Jar Parts									
ES-RJ-1	Cylindrical Necks		-	-	-	-	-	-	-
ES-RJ-2	Interior Ledge Necks		-	-	-	-	-	-	-
	Other Jar Necks		-	-	-	1 min	-	-	-
ES-SJ-3	Jar Shoulders, Painted Bands		-	-	-	-	-	-	-
	Jar Shoulders, Other Motifs		-	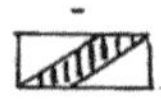	-		-	-	-
ES-B-1	Large Flat Bases		-	3	-	-	-	-	-
Other Susiana Ware Items									
ES-O-1, 2, 3	Spindle Whorls		-	-	-	-	-	-	-
ES-O-4	Other Items		-	-	-	-	-	-	-
Non-Ceramic Items									
ES-O-5	Hoes		-	-	-	-	-	-	-
ES-O-6	Celts		-	-	-	-	-	-	-

DL-27	DL-28	DL-29	DL-43	DL-61	DL-84	Muradabad DL-85	DL-222	DL-241	DL-286	Jelise DL-312
1	3	3	-	-	-	11	2	13	-	-
-	-	6	-	-	-	2	1	4	-	-
		2								
-	2 (1 pt)	5 (3 pt)	-	-	-	-	-	-	-	-
-	-	4 (3 pt)	1 pt	1 pt	-	-	-	-	-	-
-	-	2 pt	-	-	-	-	-	-	-	-
-		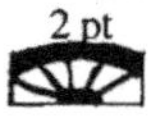	-	-	-	-			-	-
-	1	9	-	-	-	4	-	2	1	-
-	-	2	-	-	-	-	-	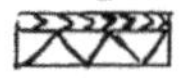	-	-
-	-	2	-	-	-	-	-	-	-	-
-	-	7	-	-	-	1	-	-	-	-
2	-	8*	1?	-	-	1	-	1	-	-
-	1*	1*	-	1	-	1	-	2	-	-
-		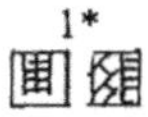	-	-				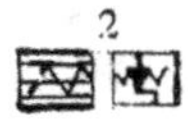		-
-		-	-	-			-	-		-
-		1	-	-	-	6	5	-	-	-
-	-	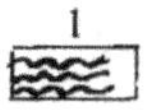	-		-		-	-	-	-
-	1	-	-	-	-	1	-	-		-
3	-	-	-	-	-	8	-	3	1*	-
-	-	6	-	-	-	-	-	7	1	-
1	2**	2	-	-	-	-	-	-	-	-
1	3	-	-	-	-	-	-	-	-	-
-		-	-	-	-	-	-	-		-
-		-	-	-			-	-	-	-
-	-	-	-	-	1	-	-	-		-
										-
-	1	2	1		-	1		-	-	-
-	2*	3*	-	-	-	2	-	-	-	1
-	3	2*	-	-	-	-	-	-	-	-
-		-	-	-	Cm, Sb	-	-	-	1 pl.*	-
-	-	-	-	-	-	-	-	-	-	-
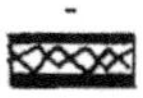	-	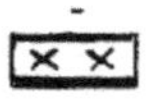		-	-		-		-	-
-		-	-	-	-	-	-	-	-	-
-	-	6	-	1	-	8	-	-	-	-
		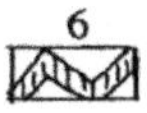	-	-	-		-	11	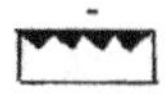	-
1	-	2	-	-	-	3	-	4	2 (pt)	-
1	-	2 cht*	-	-	-	1	-	-	1 str.*	-
ped.bs	-	1 mlr.	-	-	-	-	-	1 mlr.	7 ped.bs	-
1	1	4	-	-	-	-	-	1	-	-
1	-	1	-	-	1	1	-	3	-	-

Table A2: Bayat, Farukh, and Suse Phase Ceramics from the Deh Luran Plain

		←				BAYAT	
		DL-290	DL-91	DL-240	DL-23/2-3	DL-43	DL-29
	<u>Bayat Red Ware</u>						
	Bowls	-	1	-	3	-	2
	Other	-	-	-	1(bs)	4	10(2bs)
	<u>Susiana Black-on-buff</u>						
	Bowl Bases						
LS-BB-1	Wide Base	-	1	-	-	3	-
LS-BB-2	Narrow Base	-	-	-	2	2	-
LS-BB-3	Shaved Base	-	-	-	-	-	-
LS-BB-4	Ring Base	-	1	-	8	1	4
	Bowl Rims and Bodies						
LS-RB-1	Plain, Fine	1	-	-	8	-	5
LS-RB-2	Single Band	-	4	-	2	4	-
LS-RB-3	Multiple Bands	-	1	1	4	3	4
LS-RB-4	Solid Black Exterior	1	1	-	7	-	1
LS-RB-5	Horizontal Curved Line	-	1	-	5	1	11
LS-RB-6	Multiple Curved Lines	-	-	-	2	-	-
LS-RB-7	Horizontal Chevron	-	-	-	1	-	1
LS-RB-8	Vertical Lines	-	-	-	7	-	2
LS-RB-9	Vertical Curved Lines	-	-	1 (lg)	19 (lg)	2 (1 lg)	4 (1 lg)
LS-RB-10	Fine Dots	-	-	-	-	-	-
LS-RB-11	Solid Diamonds	-	-	-	-	-	-
LS-RB-12	Cross-Hatch Diamonds	-	-	-	7	2	2
LS-RB-13	Oblique Hatch Diamonds	-	-	-	-	-	-
LS-RB-14	Sigma Motifs	-	-	-	1	-	-
LS-RB-15	Step Motifs	-	-	-	-	-	-
LS-RB-16	Rectilinear Motifs	-	-	-	-	-	-
LS-RB-17	Large Vertical Chevron	-	-	-	-	-	-
LS-RB-18	Grids	-	-	-	-	-	-
LS-RB-19	Heavy Branch Motif						
	RB-Jar Rims						
LS-RJ-1	Solid Painted Necks	1	-	-	7	4	-
LS-RJ-2	Unpainted Necks	-	-	-	1	-	-
LS-RJ-3	Painted Bands	-	-	-	1	-	-
LS-RJ-4	Low Neck Jars	-	-	-	-	-	-
	Large Basin Rims						
LS-BN-1	Plain	-	-	1?	3	-	3
LS-BN-2	Painted	-	-	-	2	-	1
LS-BJ-1	Large Flat Bases	-	-	-	-	-	-
	Other	-	-	-	-	-	-

SUSE

FARUKH

DL-15	DL-23/1	DL-27	DL-11	DL-61	DL-286	DL-85	DL-247	
2	-	2	-	-	-	-	1	
2 (1bs)	-	2	-	-	4	-	5	bs: base
-	-	3	1	-	-	4	1	
4	-	5	1	-	3	2	-	
-	-	3	-	-	-	-	-	
3	1	4	5	-	1	-	1	
-	2	3	1	-	-	9	4	
-	1	4	-	1	3	5	6	
2	1	12	1	-	11	4	8	
-	-	1	-	-	-	2	-	
1	4	2	-	-	1	8	-	
-	-	-	4	-	-	-	-	
1	-	-	-	-	-	-	-	
2	1	2	-	-	1	4	1	
-	1	1	1?	-	-	-	-	lg: large curves
1?	2 (1c)	3 (2r)	1 (c)	1 (c)	1	-	-	r: with rectangles c: with curves
1?	-	-	-	-	1?	1	-	
4	-	4	-	1	1	2	-	
2	-	3	1	-	-	-	-	
1	-	-	-	-	-	-	3	
-	-	-	-	-	1	2	2	
-	-	4	-	-	2	-	1	
-	-	-	-	-	1	3	1	
-	-	-	-	-	-	-	5	
-	-	-	-	-	-	-	2	
-	-	3	3	-	1	-	-	
2	-	-	1	-	-	1	1	
2	-	2	1	1	1	-	1	
-	-	-	-	-	-	-	-	
-	-	-	1	-	-	3	-	
-	-	-	-	-	-	1	1	
-	-	-	-	-	-	-	-	
-	-	-	-	-	-	1 branch motif 1 birds	2 branch motifs	

Table A3: Bayat, Farukh, and Suse Phase Ceramics from Tepe Musiyan

		Area 1	Area 2		Area 3			Area 4		Area 5		Area 6E		Area 6W	
			1-2	3-4	1	2	3	1	2-3	1	2	2	1,3,4	1-3	4,5
	<u>Bayat Red Ware</u>														
	Bowls	5	1	5	1	5	-	4	3	2	-	2	-	1	7*
	Other	-	-	-	-	-	-	-	-	-	-	-	-	-	-
	<u>Susiana Buff Ware</u>														
	Bowl Bases														
LS-BB-1	Wide Base	4	5	-	-	-	5	3	1	5	1	7	2	5	4
LS-BB-2	Narrow Base	-	-	-	-	-	-	-	-	-	-	-	-	-	-
LS-BB-3	Shaved Base	-	-	1	-	-	1	-	-	-	-	1	-	-	-
LS-BB-4	Ring Base	5	-	1	-	-	4	5	3	1	2	5	1	1	4
	Bowl Rims and Bodies														
LS-RB-1	Plain, Very Fine	-	-	-	1	-	1	7	-	-	-	-	-	-	1
LS-RB-2	Single Band	2	4	-	3	-	19	18	5	1	2	10	1	12	5
LS-RB-3	Multiple Bands	17	1	-	4	-	10	-	-	8	4	14	15	21	20
LS-RB-4	Solid Black Exterior	-	-	-	-	-	-	-	-	-	-	-	-	–	-
LS-RB-5	Horizontal Curved Line	-	1	1	2	-	2	-	1	-	-	2	-	-	1
LS-RB-6	Multiple Curved Lines	-	-	-	-	-	-	-	-	-	-	-	-	3*	-
LS-RB-7	Horizontal Chevron	-	-	-	-	-	1	-	-	-	-	-	-	-	-
LS-RB-8	Vertical Lines	2	-	-	1	1	5	1	-	2	1	3	-	-	3
LS-RB-9	Vertical Curved Lines	6(1lg)	-	1	1(lg)	2(1lg)	4(3lg)	-	1(lg)	-	1	2	-	-	-
LS-RB-10	Fine Dots	1?	3	-	1	-	3(1r)	4(2r)	4	2	1	2(1r)	5(1r,1c)	2	1
LS-RB-11	Solid Diamonds	-	-	-	1	-	1	1	1	-	-	-	-	-	1
LS-RB-12	Cross-Hatch Diamonds	4	4	1	-	1	1	10	4	7	-	6	2	6	2
LS-RB-14	Sigma Motifs	2	2	1	1	-	1	1	-	1	-	-	-	1	3
LS-RB-15	Step Motifs	2	1	-	-	-	-	1	1	1	-	7	-	4	1
LS-RB-17	Large Vertical Chevron	1	-	-	-	-	-	1	-	-	-	1	-	-	-
LS-RB-18	Grids	1	-	-	-	-	-	1	-	-	-	1	-	1	7*
LS-RB-19	Slash Motifs	-	-	-	-	-	-	-	2	1	-	1	2	-	-
LS-RB-20	Concentric Circles	-	1	-	-	-	1	-	-	1	-	-	-	-	1
	Other Motifs	-	-	-	-	-	-	-	-	1 'x' 1br	-	1bv*	-	-	2x* 2bd*
	Jar Rims														
LS-RJ-1	Solid Painted Necks	-	-	1	4	-	9	4	-	3	-	4	1	4	-
LS-RJ-2	Unpainted Necks	-	1	-	-	-	-	-	-	-	-	-	-	4	3*
LS-RJ-3	Painted Bands	-	1	1	1	2	2	1	2	1	-	3	1	-	-
LS-RJ-4	Low Neck Jars	-	-	1	-	-	1	1	1	-	-	-	-	-	2*
	Large Basin Rims														
LS-BN-1	Plain	-	1	2	-	-	-	-	-	-	1	-	1	-	2*
LS-BN-2	Painted	-	1	-	1	-	5	2	-	-	1	2*	1	2	-
LS-B-1	Large Flat Base														
	Other	2	2	-	-	-	-	-	-	-	1 clou	3 clou	-	-	-

Table A4: Uruk Ceramics from the Deh Luran Plain (I)

EARLY URUK

		DL-7	Garmasi DL-11	Chakali DL-19	Sefid DL-23	Tenel Ramon DL-27	DL-43	DL-61	Kolah DL-71	DL-104	Sargarab DL-169	DL-292
	Straw-Tempered Ware											
ST-RB-1	Tapered Rim Beveled-Rim Bowl (Proto-BRB)	-	-	9	1	-	-	-	-	-	-	-
ST-RB-2	Standard Beveled Rim Bowl	-	6	10	6	-	4	7	2	41	-	-
ST-RB-3	Tray	-	-	1	-	-	-	-	-	-	4	-
	Sargarab Ware											
US-RB-3	Fine Bowl	1	16	-	2	-	-	-	-	-	32 (1 pt)	-
US-RJ-1	Fine Jar	-	1	4 (1 pt)	1	-	-	-	1	-	4	-
US-RB-4	Open Bowl, Round Lip	-	1 (rd)	-	-	-	-	-	-	-	6	-
US-RB-5	Open Bowl, Flat Lip	-	-	-	-	-	-	-	-	-	5	-
US-RB-6	Open Bowl, Beaded Rim	1	21	-	-	-	5	1	10 (1 rd)	-	95	6
US-RB-7	Open Bowl, Beaded Rim Impressed Strip	-	-	-	1	1	-	1	-	-	3	-
US-RB-8	Heavy Open Bowl, Beaded Rim	-	1 (i.s.)	-	-	-	-	-	-	-	14	-
US-RB-9	Incurved Bowl, Round Lip	1	-	-	1	-	-	-	-	-	3	-
US-RB-10	Incurved Bowl, Beaded Rim	6	8	-	1	-	-	-	2	-	3	12
US-RB-11	Incurved Bowl, Beaded Rim, Impressed Strip	-	3	7	1	-	-	-	-	-	3	-
US-RB-12	Incurved Bowl, Beaded Rim, Hatched Strip	-	1	-	-	-	-	1 (rd)	-	-	-	-
US-RB-13	Heavy Incurved Bowl, Beaded Rim	-	1 (i.s.)	-	-	-	-	-	2	-	1	1
US-RB-14	Open Basin, Flat Lip	-	-	-	-	-	-	-	-	-	2	-
US-RB-15	Small Tray	-	-	-	-	-	-	-	-	-	7	-
US-RJ-2	Neckless Ledge Rim Jar	3	4	-	2 (i.s.)	-	1 (i.s.)	1	-	-	2	1
US-RJ-3	Low Neck Beaded Rim Jar	-	-	-	-	-	-	-	-	-	8 (2 b-r)	-
US-RJ-4	Straight Neck, Round Lip, Jar	-	-	-	-	-	1	-	-	-	5	1
US-RJ-5	Straight Neck, Flat Lip, Jar	-	1	-	-	-	-	-	-	-	1	-
US-RJ-6	Flared Neck, Round Lip, Jar	-	10 (1 rd)	-	2 (i.g.)	-	1 (i.g.)	-	-	-	25 (1 pt, 2 b-r)	2
US-RJ-7	Flared Neck, Round Lip, Jar, Large	1	-	-	-	-	1	-	-	-	1	2
US-RJ-8	Heavy Flared, Thickened Round Lip Jar	1 (rd)	1 (rd)	-	-	-	-	1 (rd)	-	-	1	2
US-RJ-9	Flared Expanded Neck, Grooved Lip, Jar	-	6 (1 rd)	-	1	1	-	-	2	-	5 (1 b-r)	2
US-RJ-10	High, Expanded Neck, Band Rim Jar	-	2	3	-	1	1	-	-	-	-	2
US-O-1	Oval Nose Lug	-	-	1	1	-	-	1	-	-	6	-
US-O-10	Cross Hatch Shoulder Decoration	-	-	-	1	-	-	-	-	-	-	-
US-O-3	Painted Red-on-Black Shoulder	-	1	-	-	-	-	-	-	-	-	-
US-O-4	Impressed Strip on Shoulder	-	-	-	-	-	-	-	-	-	-	-
US-O-5	Straight Spout	-	-	1	-	-	-	-	-	-	-	1
US-O-6	Strainer	-	1	-	-	-	-	-	-	-	9	-

Table A5: Uruk Ceramics from the Deh Luran Plain (II)

LATE URUK

MIDDLE URUK

Code	Type	Sargarab DL-169	DL-292	Garmasi DL-11	DL-7	Kolah DL-71	Tenel Ramon DL-27	Chakali DL-19	DL-43	DL-61	DL-104	Sefid DL-23
Uruk Ware												
UU-RB-1	Conical Cups	-	-	-	-	-	-	1	-	-	-	-
UU-RB-3	Open, Flat Lip Bowls, Impressed Strip	-	-	1	-	-	-	1	-	-	1	-
UU-RB-4	Incurved, Round Lip Bowls, Hatched Strip	-	-	-	-	-	-	-	-	-	-	4
UU-RB-5	Carinated Flat Lip Bowls	-	-	1	-	-	-	-	-	1	-	-
UU-RB-6	Open Ledge Rim Bowl	1	-	-	-	-	-	-	-	-	-	-
UU-RJ-1	Straight Neck, Round Lip Jar	-	-	-	-	-	-	1	-	2	-	6
UU-RJ-2	Straight Neck, Flat Lip Jar	-	-	-	-	-	-	-	-	1	-	1
UU-RJ-3	Flared Neck, Round Lip Jar	-	-	-	-	-	-	1	-	2	3 (1 rd)	2
UU-RJ-4	Flared Neck, Grooved Lip Jar	-	-	-	-	-	-	3	-	-	-	-
UU-RJ-5	High, Expanded Neck, Band Rim Jar	-	-	-	-	-	-	-	-	1	-	-
UU-RJ-6	Low Expanded Neck, Band Rim Jar	-	-	-	-	-	-	1	-	1	2	5
UU-RJ-7	Out-Turned, Expanded Neck Jar	-	-	-	-	-	-	-	-	1	-	1
UU-RJ-8	Heavy Expanded Neck Jar	-	-	-	-	-	-	-	-	-	2	1
UU-RJ-9	Ledge Rim Jar	5	-	-	-	-	-	-	-	-	2 (1 rs)	-
UU-RJ-10	Ledge Rim Bottle	-	-	-	-	-	-	-	-	-	-	1
UU-RJ-11	Band Rim Bottle	-	-	-	-	-	-	-	-	-	1	1
UU-O-1	Triangular Nose Lug	-	-	-	-	-	-	-	-	1	1	1
UU-O-2	Grooved Incised Shoulder	-	-	-	-	-	-	-	-	-	-	5
UU-O-3	Groove, Oblique Incised Shoulder	-	-	-	-	-	-	-	-	1	1	3
UU-O-4	Reserve Slip Shoulder	-	-	-	-	-	-	-	-	1	-	-
UU-O-5	Cross-Hatch Band-Incised Shoulder	-	-	-	-	-	-	-	-	1	2	3
UU-O-6	Cross-Hatch Triangle-Incised Shoulder	-	-	-	-	-	-	1	-	-	-	3
UU-O-7	Rocker Stamp Shoulder	-	-	-	-	-	-	1	-	1	-	-
UU-O-8	Red-on-Black Painted Shoulder	-	-	-	-	-	-	-	-	3	1	-
UU-O-9	Straight Spout	1	-	-	-	-	-	1	-	-	-	-
UU-O-10	Conical Spout	-	-	-	-	-	-	3	-	-	-	-
UU-O-11	Droop Spout	-	-	-	-	-	-	2	1	2	1	8
UU-O-12	Strap Handle	-	-	-	-	-	-	-	-	1	1	3
UU-O-13	Flat Twist Handle	-	-	-	-	-	-	-	-	1	1	1
UU-O-14	Full Twist Handle	-	-	-	-	-	-	-	-	-	-	3
Other Items												
	Clay Sickle Fragments	-	-	9	-	-	-	-	3	-	1	1
	Cones	-	-	-	-	-	-	1	-	-	-	-

Table A6: Jemdet Nasr and Early Dynastic Ceramics from the Deh Luran Plain

JN/ED I: DL-104 · ED II–III: DL-61

		Kolah DL-71	DL-62	DL-104	DL-22	DL-43	DL-61	Baulah DL-24	Sabz East DL-18	DL-54
Uruk Ware										
ED-RC-1	Conical Cup	1	6	7	-	3	-	-	10	2
ED-RC-2	Incurved Conical Cup	-	-	4	-	-	-	-	2	-
ED-BC-1	Solid Footed Cup Fragment	4	3	56	-	1	3	2	11	1
ED-BC-2	Narrow Cup Base	-	2	7	-	4	-	-	2	-
ED-BC-3	Wide Cup Base	-	1	-	-	1	1	1	3	1
ED-RB-1	Round Lip Bowl	1	-	6	-	1	-	-	1	-
ED-RB-2	Beveled Lip Bowl	-	-	20	-	-	1	-	3	1
ED-RB-3	Ledge Rim Bowl	2	-	18	-	-	-	-	1	2
ED-RB-4	Carinated Bowl	-	-	-	-	-	-	-	-	2
ED-RJ-1	Round Lip Jar	-	1	3	-	-	3	6	19	2
ED-RJ-2	Thin Round Lip Jar	-	-	1	-	1	-	-	9	-
ED-RJ-3	Flared Expanded Jar	1	1	4	-	-	-	2	10	-
ED-RJ-4	Ledge Rim Jar	3	1 poly	8	-	-	1	1	13	2
ED-RJ-5	Band Rim Jar	5	-	9	-	-	-	1	10	2
ED-RJ-6	Small Carinated Pot	-	-	-	-	-	-	-	-	2
ED-O-3	Monochrome Lines	-	-	-	-	-	-	-	2	-
ED-O-4	Polychrome Lines	-	-	-	-	-	-	-	17	-
ED-O-5	Polychrome Motif	2	1 	-	1	-	-	4 2	4  1	2
ED-O-1	Plain Strip	4	-	2	-	1	-	-	41	-
ED-O-2	Hatched Strip	2	-	1	-	-	-	-	58	1
ED-B-2	Flat Base	1	-	-	-	-	-	-	4	-
ED-B-3	Turned Ring Base	1 lg	-	1	-	-	-	-	20 (6 lg)	-
ED-B-4	High Turned Ring Base	-	-	-	-	-	-	-	1	-
ED-B-5	Pinched Ring Base	-	-	1	-	-	-	-	16	-
ED-B-6	Fine Small Ring Base	-	-	-	-	-	-	-	-	1
	Other	res. slip	groove/ oblique					cone		1
Gray Ware									1	
	Jar Rim	-	-	1 lg	-	-	-	-	1	2
	Body Sherd	-	-	-	-	5 lg	1 sh	-	-	-

Table A7: Jemdet Nasr and Early Dynastic Ceramics from Tepe Musiyan

		Area 1	Area 2		Area 3			Area 4		Area 5		Area 6	Area 6	Area 6
			1-2	3-4	1	2	3	1	2-3	1	2-3	W	C	E
Uruk Ware														
ED-RC-1	Conical Cup Rim	8	1	2	1	5	-	-	-	-	1	-	8	-
ED-RC-2	Incurved Conical Cup	-	-	-	-	-	-	-	-	-	-	-	1	-
ED-BC-1	Solid Foot Cup Fragment	10	4	6	1	2	4	5	2	4	17	6	14	6
ED-BC-2	Narrow Cup Base	1	2	-	1	1	6	-	-	3	3	-	-	-
ED-BC-3	Wide Cup Base	8	-	1	6	13	6	-	-	2	2	-	1	-
ED-RB-1	Round Lip Bowl	2	-	-	-	1	-	-	-	-	-	-	4 (1 pt)	-
ED-RB-2	Beveled Lip Bowl	2	1	1	1	4	-	1	-	-	-	-	1	-
ED-RB-3	Ledge Rim Bowl	-	1	2	3	3	-	-	-	-	-	1	1	-
ED-RB-4	Carinated Bowl	-	-	1	-	-	-	-	-	-	-	-	-	-
ED-RJ-1	Round Lip Jar	3	1	5	2	1	-	-	-	1	3	-	-	1
ED-RJ-2	Thin Round Lip Jar	1	-	2	-	-	-	-	-	1	-	-	-	-
ED-RJ-3	Flared Expanded Jar	3	-	2 (pt)	-	1	-	2	-	-	3 (1 pt)	-	2 (1 pt)	1
ED-RJ-4	Ledge Rim Jar	8 (1 pt)	5	1	5	3	2 (1 pt)	-	1 (pt)	1	3	-	2 (1 pt)	2 (1 pt)
ED-RJ-5	Band Rim Jar	2	2	1	1 (lk)	1	-	1 (pt)	-	1	1	-	-	2
ED-RJ-6	Small Carinated Pot	-	1	-	-	-	-	-	-	-	-	-	-	-
ED-O-1	Plain Raised Strip	9	4 (3i)	2 (pt)	-	1 (pt)	-	1	1	1	-	4	13 (2 pt)	4 (3 pt)
ED-O-2	Hatched Strip	16	2	-	7	2	3	-	-	-	-	2	20 (1 pt)	6 (1 pt)
ED-O-3	Monochrome Lines	-	-	-	-	-	-	-	-	-	-	-	1	-
ED-O-4	Polychrome Lines	-	-	2	-	-	1	-	-	1	-	-	-	-
ED-O-5	Monochrome Motif	-	-	-	1	-	3	1	2 1	-	-	-	2	-
ED-O-6	Polychrome Motif	1	2	-	-	-	-	1	-	1	-	1	2 2	2
ED-O-7	Conical Spout	2	-	1	-	3	-	-	-	-	-	-	1	1
ED-O-8	Lug	-	1	-	-	-	-	-	-	-	-	-	-	1 (pt)
ED-O-9	Fenestrated Stand	-	-	-	-	-	-	-	-	-	-	1	-	1
ED-B-1	Round Thrown Base	-	-	-	-	-	-	-	-	-	-	-	-	-
ED-B-2	Flat Base	10	1	1	-	-	-	-	-	-	-	-	-	-
ED-B-3	Turned Ring Base	5 (1 pt)	2 (1 pt)	-	-	-	-	-	-	1	-	-	1 (pt)	1 (pt)
ED-B-4	High Turned Ring Base	2	1	2	5	3	6 (1 pt)	-	-	2	-	-	-	-
ED-B-5	Pinched Ring Base	4	1	1	-	-	2	-	-	2	2	-	-	-
ED-B-6	Fine X Ring Base	-	-	1	-	-	-	-	1 (pt)	-	-	-	-	-
Gray Ware														
ED JR 1	Jar Rim	2	1	2 (1 sh)	-	-	-	-	1	-	-	-	2	1
	Body Sherd	-	1	-	-	1	-	1	-	1	-	-	1	-

Appendix B:

Archaeological Base Maps

Appendix Map 1A
Regional Setting of the Deh Lurān Plain

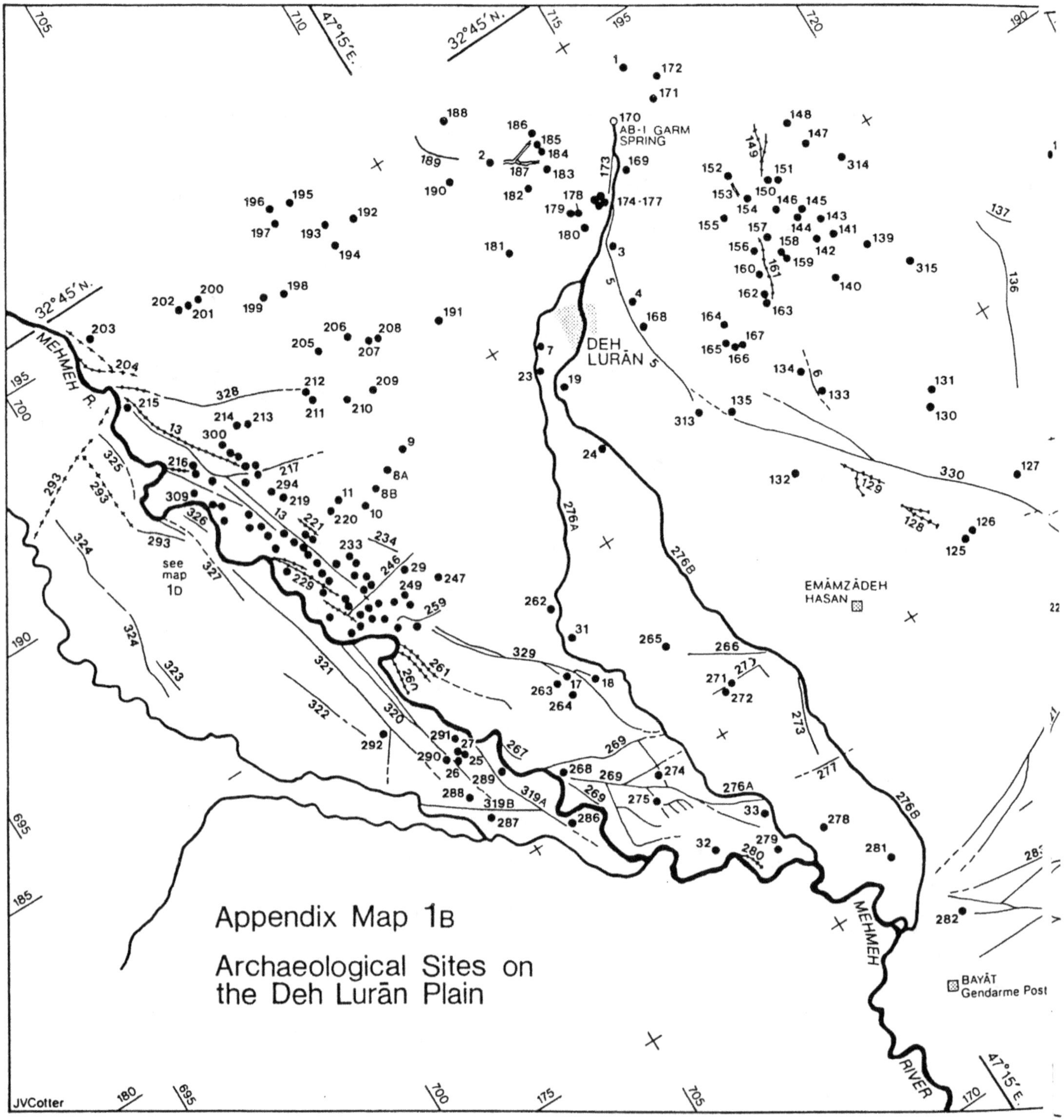

Appendix Map 1B

Archaeological Sites on the Deh Lurān Plain

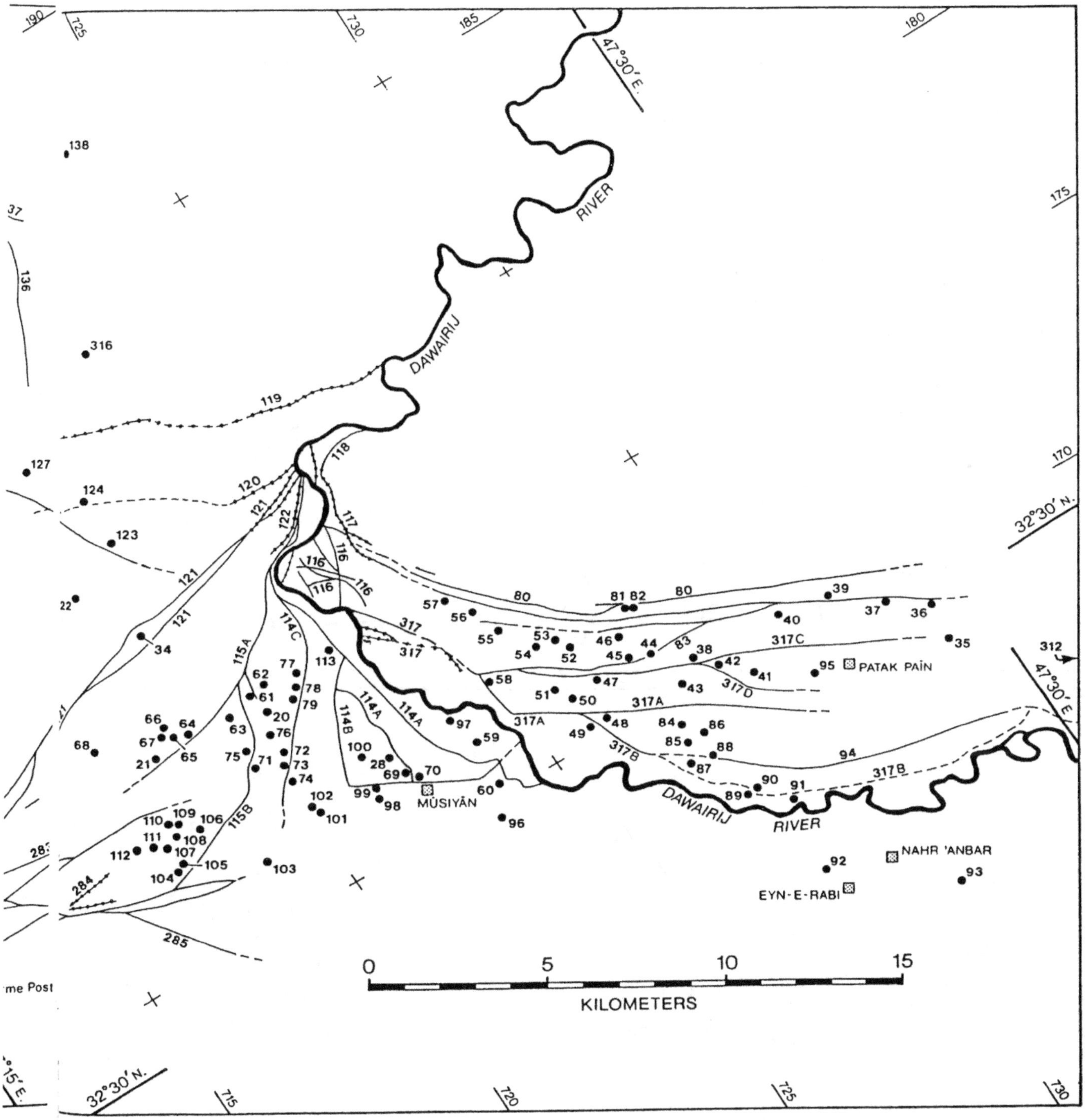
DAWAIRIJ RIVER
47°30′ E.
32°30′ N.
PATAK PAIN
MŪSIYĀN
NAHR 'ANBAR
EYN-E-RABI
0 5 10 15
KILOMETERS
me Post

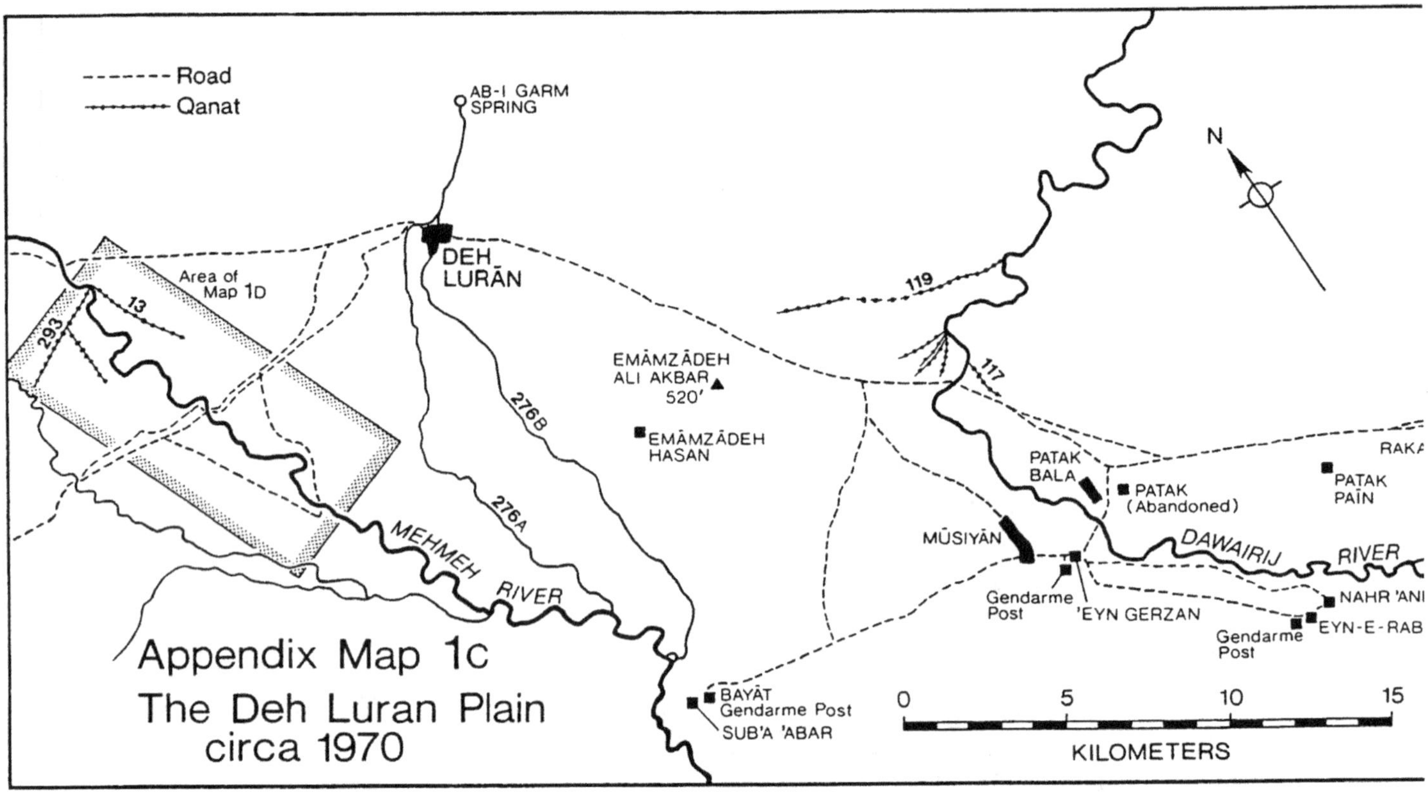

Appendix Map 1c
The Deh Luran Plain
circa 1970

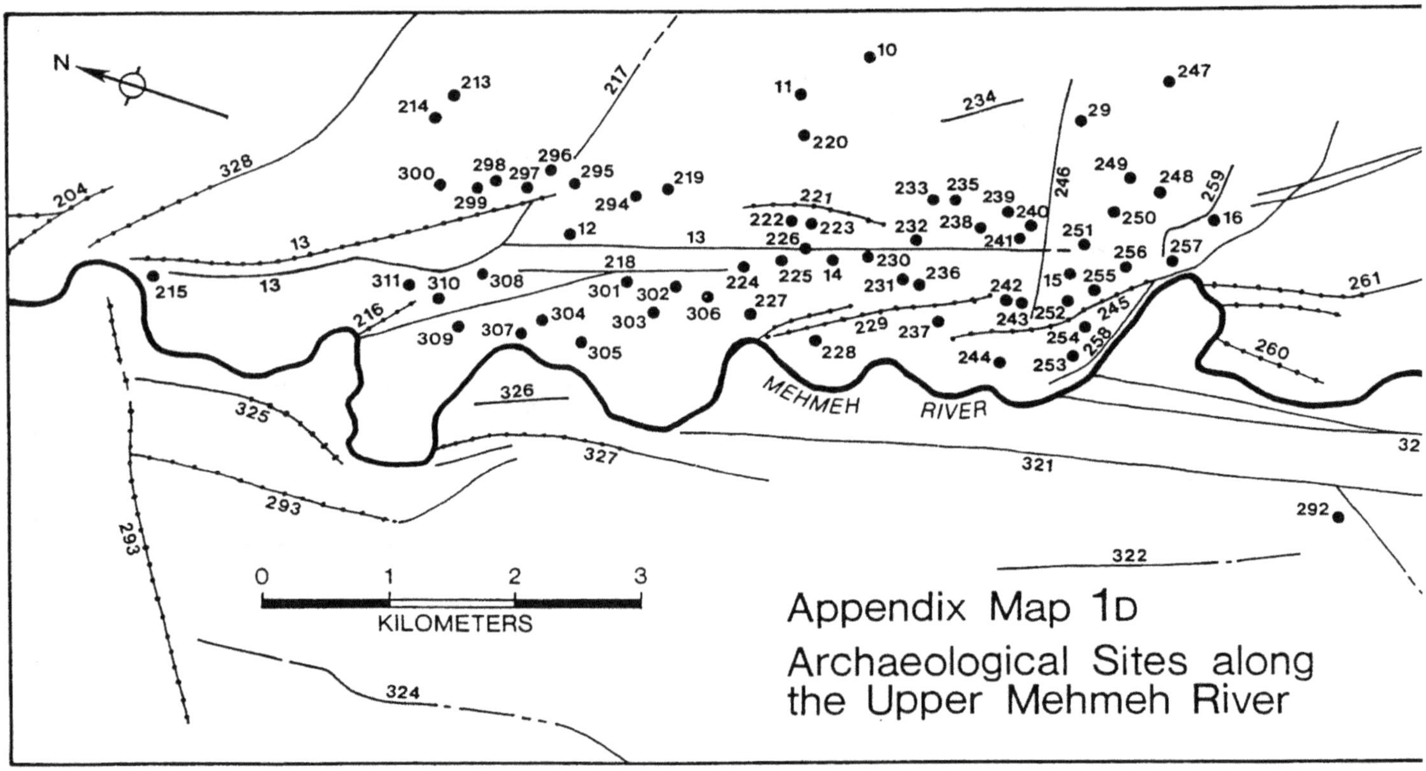

Appendix Map 1D
Archaeological Sites along
the Upper Mehmeh River

www.ingramcontent.com/pod-product-compliance
Lightning Source LLC
LaVergne TN
LVHW080303260826
846302LV00007B/22
9780915703364